D1196342

A History of Retirement

A History of Retirement

The Meaning and Function of
An American Institution, 1885–1978

WILLIAM GRAEBNER

New Haven and London, Yale University Press

Designed by Sally Harris
and set in Times Roman type.
Printed in the United States of America by Halliday Lithograph, West Hanover, Mass.

Acknowledgment is made to the Butler Library, Columbia University, for permission to
quote from the Marion B. Folsom Oral History Memoir, © by the Trustees of Columbia
University in the City of New York, 1977.

Library of Congress Cataloging in Publication Data

Graebner, William.
  A History of Retirement

  Bibliography: p.
  Includes index.
  1. Retirement—United States. I. Title.
HQ1064.U5G67   305.2'6   79–28849
ISBN 0–300–02356–1

10   9   8   7   6   5   4   3   2   1

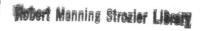

To my parents,
Elmer Graebner
and
Dorothy Zilisch Graebner

Contents

Preface

This book is intended to be something less, and something more, than a summary of the history of retirement in America. I have not attempted to describe or summarize retirement legislation in any systematic way, nor have I written much about how people have lived while retired. Whole subjects, some of more than marginal significance in the history of retirement, remain to be treated by other historians. Rather than attempt comprehensive coverage, I have allowed the content of the book to be shaped, within limits, by the availability of manuscript and printed materials capable of sustaining intensive analysis and rich description. At the same time, I have sought to ensure that these units of analysis and description reflect major events, stages, or thinking in the history of retirement and to place each component in the context of the history of American capitalism.

I have many debts. A two-year absence from the classroom was made possible by a year's fellowship from the American Council of Learned Societies and by the State University of New York, which provided leave, sabbatical, and a summer grant. Essential to the project were the resources of historical societies, libraries, and other institutions, including the National Archives, the Oral History Research Office and the Rare Book and Manuscript Library at Columbia University, the Western Reserve Historical Society Library, the Georgetown University Library, the Eleutherian Mills Historical Library, the Labor-Management Documentation Center at Cornell University, the Franklin Delano Roosevelt Library, the Buffalo Public Library, the Civil Service Commission Library, the Manuscript Division of the Library of Congress, the Chicago Historical Society, the National Association of Retired Federal Employees, and the Social Welfare History Archives at the University of Minnesota. Their staffs were invariably efficient and flexible. I am especially grateful to M. Fransiszyn, manuscripts and reference librarian at the Osler Library of the History of Medicine, McGill University, for assistance with bibliography relative to Sir William Osler's 1905 valedictory. The Library of Congress remains a superb environment for study and research. Mary Notaro, a woman of exceptional skill and enterprise, typed the manuscript.

I have benefited from the advice of several scholars. David Van Tassel and an anonymous referee for the *History of Education Quarterly* helped me improve the material on public-school teachers. Robert K. Webb sharpened my focus on the Carnegie pension system. Steve Welch read the chapter on the 1970s from the perspective of a labor economist. Brian Gratton examined my discussion of age discrimination with great care and insight. David Hackett Fischer and Thomas R. Cole read the entire manuscript. With his unerring sense of what makes a good book, Fischer confirmed my impressions of the manuscript's strengths and weaknesses; the final product, if not the book he himself would write, is better for his contribution. I had no reason to expect a reading as interesting, as revealing, and as full of effort as that which Tom Cole rendered; his assistance can only be described as invaluable.

Small as it is, my family continues to provide whatever it is that I need to carry on as a scholar. My wife, Dianne Bennett, helps when I need it most—with those frustrating, boring, but essential tasks like checking footnotes. She also read the manuscript for style, form, and substance. Most important, her willingness to rearrange her professional life allowed me to live for two years within commuting distance of Washington, D.C. My son Ben, who is now almost eight years old, learned to play by himself while Daddy wrote and to be ready with the soccer ball when the working day ended.

W. G.

Buffalo, New York
June 25, 1979

PART ONE CORPORATE CAPITALISM AND THE EMERGENCE OF RETIREMENT

1 Historical and Analytical Settings

William Osler was reluctant to leave Johns Hopkins, even to return to British soil as Regius Professor of Medicine at Oxford. His sixteen years in Baltimore as physician-in-chief of the university's new hospital had been triumphant ones, full of rewards commensurate with his growing stature as teacher, medical scholar, administrator, and man of letters. On February 22, 1905, Osler delivered a valedictory address, which he titled "The Fixed Period," after a novel by Anthony Trollope. Grateful for his contributions to the medical school and aware of Osler's reputation as a public speaker, the audience was large and receptive.[1]

A serious and ingenuous man, Osler took this opportunity to instruct, drawing a series of analogies between his own physical state and the human body on the one hand, and the health of the teaching and medical professions on the other. Although Osler's career was to last another fourteen years, the address had a retrospective quality, as Osler, extrapolating from his own history, discussed the universals of hard work, flagging energies, and the need for increased leisure. But his departure was more than the product of his own physical demands. "It may be asked in the first place," he continued, "whether metabolism is sufficiently active in the professoriate body, is there change enough? Would not the loss of a professor bring stimulating benefits to a university? . . . It is strange of how slight value is the unit in the great system." A mobile professo-

---

1. A. W. Franklin, ed., *Selected Writings of Sir William Osler: 12 July 1849 to 29 December 1919*, with an Introduction by G. L. Keynes (New York, 1951), pp. xvii–xviii; William Welch, "William Osler: 1849–1919," *Survey*, 10 January 1920, reprint in Osler clippings, MS C90, file 9, National Library of Medicine, Bethesda, Md.

Born in Ontario in 1849, Osler received his general education in Toronto and his medical education from the University of Toronto and McGill University. He spent the decade after 1874 teaching medicine at McGill and the next five years in the Chair of Clinical Medicine at the University of Pennsylvania. He came to Johns Hopkins in 1889. By 1900 he was, with William H. Welch and S. Weir Mitchell, among the best known of American physicians.

riate, he argued, was essential. "Change is the very marrow of [a professor's] existence—a new set of students every year, a new set of assistants, a new set of associates every few years to replace those called off to other fields; in any active department there is no constancy, no stability in the human surroundings."[2]

Had Osler chosen to diffuse the valedictory at this point, he would have emerged relatively unscathed, having aroused, one would imagine, no small measure of anxiety on the part of the older members of the faculty, but avoiding public vilification. This was not Osler's way. Instead, the lecture (for that, indeed, was what it had become) moved from the general to the concrete and from problem to solution, as Osler delivered the lines that were to have a considerable impact on his reputation and were to be associated with the eminent physican long after his death:

> I am going to be very bold and touch upon another question of some delicacy, but of infinite importance in university life: one that has not been settled in this country. I refer to a fixed period for the teacher, either of time of service or of age. . . . It is a very serious matter in our young universities to have all of the professors growing old at the same time. In some places only an epidemic, a time limit, or an age limit can save the situation. I have two fixed ideas well known to my friends, harmless obsessions with which I sometimes bore them, but which have a direct bearing on this important problem. The first is the comparative uselessness of men above forty years of age. This may seem shocking, and yet read aright the world's history bears out the statement. Take the sum of human achievement in action, in science, in art, in literature—subtract the work of the men above forty, and while we should miss great treasures, even priceless treasures, we would practically be where we are to-day. It is difficult to name a great and far-reaching conquest of the mind which has not been given to the world by a man on whose back the sun was still shining. The effective, moving, vitalizing work of the world is done between the ages of twenty-five and forty—these fifteen golden years of plenty, the anabolic or constructive period, in which there is always a balance in the mental bank and the credit is still good. In the science and art of medicine young or comparatively young men have made every advance of the first rank. . . .
>
> My second fixed idea is the uselessness of men above sixty years of age, and the incalculable benefit it would be in commercial, political and in professional life if, as a matter of course, men stopped work at this age. . . . In that charming novel, *The Fixed Period*, Anthony Trollope dis-

2. Sir William Osler, "The Fixed Period," in *Aequanimitas: With Other Addresses to Medical Students, Nurses and Practitioners of Medicine* (Philadelphia, 1910), pp. 391–411.

cusses the practical advantages in modern life of a return to this ancient usage, and the plot hinges upon the admirable scheme of a college into which at sixty men retired for a year of contemplation before a peaceful departure by chloroform. That incalculable benefits might follow such a scheme is apparent to any one who, like myself, is nearing the limit, and who has made a careful study of the calamities which may befall men during the seventh and eighth decades. Still more when he contemplates the many evils which they perpetuate unconsciously, and with impunity.[3]

One could, in short, tolerate the participation of the middle-aged, who were only uncreative. The aged, however, were positively dangerous; they must be retired.

The press, drawn to the event by Osler's fame and searching for something to entertain its readers (railroad rebates, the trusts, and the Russo-Japanese War had been in the news for some time), correctly perceived that the public would be most interested in Osler's forceful visions of aging.[4] The chloroform remark was not, as those who have examined the reaction to the speech have generally claimed, the focus of the public critique of Osler. Here and there, a newspaper took the remark about chloroform seriously, but most people—workers, businessmen, doctors, professionals—were affected less by Osler's hyperbole than by his very threatening view of the contributions and prospects of the old and the middle-aged. Senator Chauncey De Pew, interviewed by the *Baltimore American*, provided numerous examples of successful older people and, as if to deny any personal tendency to physical decline, furnished hour-by-hour details of his own strenuous schedule of speeches and travel.[5] Almost every newspaper with an interest in the story carried at least one essay extolling the historical achievements of men over forty: Franklin, Hawthorne, Webster, Lincoln, Gladstone, Disraeli, Jay Cooke, and Lew Wallace.[6] Striking a more hostile tone, the *Washington Times* wrote: "Dr. Osler declares that men are old at 40 and worthless at 60. There must be an age at which a man is an ass. What is the Doctor's age, anyhow?"[7]

There were the inevitable disagreements about just how old a man could be and remain productive. Speaking before alumni in Chicago, James R. Angell, president of the University of Michigan, insisted that men over sixty were not

3. Ibid.

4. Harvey Cushing, *The Life of Sir William Osler*, 2 vols. (Oxford, 1925), 1: 664; Wilder Penfield, "Psuedo-Sensility: Osler's Dictum Reconsidered," *Perspectives in Biology and Medicine* 4 (Summer 1961): 438; *Harper's Weekly*, 11 March 1905, p. 347.

5. *Baltimore American*, 24 February 1905, p. 13.

6. *Washington Evening Star*, 25 February 1905, pt. 1, p. 4; *Denver Republican*, as reported in *Washington Post*, 27 February 1905, p. 6.

7. Quoted in *Baltimore Sun*, 25 February 1905, p. 8.

useless. "I would like to extend the time of a man's life instead of shortening it. The experiment of killing off old men has been tried in Africa for centuries, and I would suggest to the distinguished physician that civilization has not advanced very rapidly there."[8] Older men could remain vital and productive in the decades after forty, claimed the *New York Evening Mail*, "if they did not in youth apply to their nerves the 'hot and rebellious liquors' of over-effort, of over-strenuousness, of too much 'hustle'. . . . We have each our capital of energy. Dr. Osler seems to advise the prodigal expenditure of it in early life, and there he is unwise."[9]

Osler's suggestion of retiring those over sixty provoked considerable comment, most of it negative. Before retirement could be carried out on a mass basis, said the *Brooklyn Eagle*, a major redistribution of wealth would be necessary. Otherwise, no one could afford it.[10] At *Harper's Weekly*, editor George Harvey thought Osler's notions of the productivity of those between twenty-five and forty "scandalous" but found some logic in retirement. The end of life, said Harvey, could be a "pleasure-time" in which adequate preparation would be followed by a variety of frivolous and irresponsible, but ultimately satisfying, activities. Resistance to such a concept, Harvey contended, was deeply ingrained in the national character. "We are like Rollo: our play is work, and it continues to be work in the case of most of us just as long as our work is marketable."[11]

In many accounts of the event, and even in Harvey Cushing's fine biography of Osler, there is a tendency to turn the entire incident, the speech and the response, into an event of no intrinsic importance. Douglas Southall Freeman, then editor of a Richmond, Virginia daily, wrote after Osler's death of the speech "which sensation-lovers warped into a demand for euthanasia."[12] Cushing assumes that the controversy was the product of a major misunderstanding. Lacking any real appreciation for Osler's style, humor, and commitment to human values, the public took these "innocent paragraphs said half in jest" as "the heartless view of a cold scientist who would condemn man as a productive machine."[13]

8. *New York Times*, 25 February 1905, p. 5. See also *Baltimore Sun*, 23 February 1905, p. 4, editorial.

9. Quoted in *Baltimore Sun*, 25 February 1905, p. 8.

10. Ibid.

11. *Harper's Weekly*, 11 March 1905, p. 347. Cf. David Riesman, *Individualism Reconsidered: And Other Essays* (Glencoe, Ill., 1954), p. 212.

12. Quoted in "Dr. Osler's Refutation of Himself," *Literary Digest*, 17 January 1920, p. 46.

13. Cushing, *Life*, 1: 669. See also Erwin F. Smith, "Some Thoughts on Old Age," *Journal of the Washington Academy of Sciences* 14 (4 June 1924): 232; W. W. Francis, "Osler and the Reporters,"; reprinted from *Canadian Medical Association Journal* 61 (1949): 68–69, copy in MS C146, Na-

Osler's defenders have focused on the chloroform remark, as if, by demonstrating the absurdity of a literal interpretation, they might cut the ground from beneath the critics and restore the personal and professional Osler to high repute. But in minimizing the broader implications of the event, these well-meaning authorities have, in fact, denied Osler a consistent history and ignored the critical ingredients of the professional medical experience in the late nineteenth century that molded Osler's thought and culminated in the Johns Hopkins valedictory.

Osler was defending an ideology of personal growth and professional progress to which he had been deeply committed for well over a decade. His ideas emerged naturally from his professional life. In 1892 he had publicly proclaimed the insidious nature of the aging process and its consequences for a medical faculty. The problem, as he saw it, was not so much a loss of judgment or memory, since these powers often remained unaffected through the fifth and sixth decades of life. "The change," he said, "is seen in a weakened receptivity and in an inability to adapt oneself to an altered intellectual environment. It is this loss of mental elasticity which makes men over forty so slow to receive new truths."[14] The only way the older physician could survive, he told the New York Academy of Physicians in 1897, is to "walk with the 'boys,'" to "travel with the men who are doing the work of the world, the men between the ages of twenty-five and forty."[15] Osler's willingness to risk censure for these ideas was demonstrated at the 1895 Baltimore meeting of the American Medical Association, when Osler, amid protest, openly affirmed the incompetence and demanded the resignation of the association's aging secretary, W. B. Atkinson. "You may hiss if you will," Osler announced from atop a chair, "but I unhesitatingly say that no more important step in advance will be taken by this association than when it changes its secretary."[16]

Here was the Osler his contemporaries refused to acknowledge fully: rationally and aggressively in search of efficiency and productivity, fearful lest old age interfere with medicine's intellectual and organizational progress, even, as many charged, "cold-blooded."[17] To Osler, medical progress was part of a proto-Darwinian contest in which those with "an instinct for truth, with a capacity to

---

tional Library of Medicine; William Bennett Bean, ed., and Robert Bennett Bean, collector, *Sir William Osler: Aphorisms from His Bedside Teachings and Writings* (New York, 1950), p. 146n; Penfield, "Psuedo-Sensility," pp. 438–39.

14. From "Teacher and Student," in Osler, ed., *Aequanimitas*, pp. 32–33. This address was delivered at the University of Minnesota in 1892.

15. From "Internal Medicine as a Vocation," in Osler, *Aequanimitas*, p. 151.

16. Quoted in Cushing, *Life*, 1: 415.

17. See William White, "Re-echoes of Sir William Osler's 'The Fixed Period,'" *Bulletin of the Institute of the History of Medicine* 5 (December 1937): 938; Cushing, *Life*, 1: 669.

pass beyond the routine of [the] day, and with a vision for the whole where others had seen but in part" struggled for supremacy against "opposition of men who could not—not who would not—see the truth."[18] He could conceive of opposition to change only in terms of the persistence of outmoded ideas and values, and he could locate it only in the individual, in the resistance of age. As he addressed his Baltimore audience on that February day in 1905, Osler had every reason to be confident that his remarks would be well received, for his colleagues shared both his conception of progress and his faith in its importance. This was only natural, for in some measure each had participated in what historian Donald Fleming has suggested may have been "the most audacious enterprise of the nineteenth century . . . the effort to organize a creative tradition in science; to make systematic the emergence of intellects hostile to system, routine, and tradition."[19] It was for this creative tradition that Osler had once more broached the issues of aging and retirement.

Put in these terms, the address seems perfectly harmless. Who but a few hoary physicians, isolated, easily identifiable, and notorious for their provincial defense of the old medicine, could possibly take offense? Why would the ordinary American be interested in what would seem, on the face of it, largely an internal conflict of the medical profession? The answer, of course, is that Osler's address touched a central nerve in American culture.

In the early weeks of 1905, when Osler was preparing his address, Andrew Carnegie, himself recently retired, was considering endowing a foundation to retire college teachers. He would read of Osler's address, and within months the Carnegie Foundation for the Advancement of Teaching would be a reality.[20] Later in the year, Admiral George Dewey warned that the nation would "assuredly meet with disaster in a naval war unless younger men are given command of the ships of our navy," and in Chicago, employees went forward with plans for an anti-age-limit league to counter age discrimination in private employment—a problem at least two decades old but recently intensified by a competitive economy, the eight-hour day, scientific management, and some new ideas about the importance of staffing with youth.[21] At E. I. Du Pont de Nemours and Co. in Wilmington, Delaware, an elderly employee with fourteen years' experience fought to prevent his separation. "His despair is so great," wrote a

---

18. William Osler, *The Growth of Truth: As Illustrated in the Discovery of the Circulation of the Blood*, Being the Harveian Oration Delivered at the Royal College of Physicians, London, 18 October 1906 (London, 1906), pp. 6, 8, 9.

19. Donald Fleming, *William H. Welch and the Rise of American Medicine* (Boston, 1954), p. 32.

20. "Dr. Osler's Refutation," p. 49.

21. *New York Times*, 23 October 1905, p. 8, editorial; ibid., 20 October 1905, p. 8.

friend, "I feel that he is not himself and does not think that life now is worth the living."[22] A Springfield, Ohio typographer analyzed the recently acquired youthful tenor of local printing establishments and found its origins, and that of the recent interest in pensions, in the new Mergenthaler typesetting machines. Because of this "intense productivity," he argued, "no longer can the mechanic in the printing craft—nor in any other, for that matter—look forward to a long career in his chosen vocation. Twenty-five to thirty years can safely be placed as the limit. So far as the mechanic is concerned, Osler's theory is a fact."[23] One would expect the skills of the printer to have held up better than those of the typesetter against the challenge of technology, and perhaps they did. But in the printing trades Osler's address induced a familiar litany of defense. It was one thing to bring youth into the business, another to put the forty-year-old printer, in his prime and full of knowledge of a variety of shop operations, on the shelf. "Printers, at least," wrote one of their number, "do not go into a state of innocuous desuetude at forty, and . . . chloroforming is not necessary even at sixty."[24]

Osler's remarks must have been no less relevant to hundreds of thousands of local, state, and national public employees, some seeking to resist retirement and others to achieve it. Postal clerks, bureaucrats, public-school teachers, police and firemen, librarians, and others sought to work out some accommodation with the advocates of efficiency. The alternative was the heady scene played out on March 1, 1907, in a mailbag repair department in Washington, D. C. where forty-one employees, nearly all of them old and a good many of them widows of Civil War veterans, without warning received yellow slips notifying them of their dismissal. This money-saving action was taken in spite of evidence that there was sufficient work for all shop employees. The separations were a bitter experience for the many workers who had grown old and dependent in the service of their government. One man said he deserved better treatment from the government for which he had fought; some unwritten compact had been violated. A woman became so distraught that police were summoned to remove her from the building.[25]

This, then, was the environment in which Osler lectured. As the spokesman for efficiency and progress, he threatened those in every class and every line of work whose continued employment was, or seemed to be, a source of inefficiency. Those who would benefit from the new order (twenty young victors in

22. John Bunting to Alfred I. Du Pont, 31 January 1904, E. I. Du Pont de Nemours and Co. Papers, series II, part 2, box 806, file "Personnel, 1903–1904," Eleutherian Mills Historical Library, Greenville, Wilmington, Delaware.
23. Letter, C. W. Rich, *Typographical Journal* 31 (October 1907): 387.
24. John C. Hill, "On the Dead Bank at Forty?" *Inland Printer* 35 (May 1905): 203–04.
25. *Washington Evening Star*, 1 March 1907, p. 1.

the civil service examination, seeking work repairing mailbags) would see Osler as the harbinger of an age of opportunity. Still others, by their own estimate past the age of productive and enjoyable labor, would take from Osler an implicit vision of retirement as a form of leisure, earned in the world of work but separate from it. In 1905 this idea was at odds with both the level of opportunity in the society and prevailing notions of work. The *Saturday Review* counseled resistance: "Men shrink from voluntarily committing themselves to an act which simulates the forced inactivity of death."[26] Thirty-five years later, with work increasingly scarce, especially for the old and middle-aged, and pensions, public and private, more readily available, this conception of retirement would fuse with social security and become a dominant ideology.

A society so intensely concerned with progress must also be vigilant against sources of decay. At this time, the perceived menaces to progress were, first, trusts and monopolies, which threatened to destroy opportunity and competition, the critical ingredients of capitalism, and second, the new immigration, which would, many feared, corrupt the racial fiber and vitiate national strength and purpose.[27] Osler brought to the surface a third source of cultural anxiety, the specter of an aging population, mired in its own demography. Sociologists would focus on this idea some forty years later and, in the process, create the profession of social gerontology.[28] In 1905 a consciousness of aging as a matter for social concern was just beginning to emerge; the Bureau of the Census announced in a substantial 1904 report on aging that relative to other countries, the United States had "an unusually large proportion of its population in the group of productive ages." Yet the meaning of this report lay not in its positive conclusions, but in its perception and definition of the problem. The problem was aging, the definition along the lines of productivity.[29] In each case, Osler only confirmed the values and fears of the larger culture.

RETIREMENT AND THE EVOLUTION OF AMERICAN CAPITALISM

On the eve of the American Civil War, the issues raised in Osler's valedictory were unknown to most Americans. In 1860, only state judges, and not in

26. "Life and Rest," *Saturday Review of Politics, Literature, Science, and Art*, 24 January 1903, p. 101.

27. "Mediocrity and Greatness," *Baltimore Evening News*, 17 March 1902, editorial, reprinted in Fabian Franklin, *People and Problems: A Collection of Addresses and Editorials* (New York, 1908), pp. 236–39.

28. Alfred Sauvy, "Social and Economic Consequences of the Ageing of Western European Populations," *Population Studies* 2 (June 1948): 115–24.

29. U.S., Department of Commerce and Labor, Bureau of the Census, "A Discussion of Age Statistics," by Allyn A. Young, *Bulletin* 13 (Washington, D.C., 1904), p. 28.

all states, were forced to retire because of advancing age. The first edition of Noah Webster's *American Dictionary*, published in 1828, lists the word *retirement* but does not suggest any peculiar applicability to the elderly.[30] Unencumbered by laws and regulations requiring they cease work, older people apparently labored until they chose to stop.

We also know that older people were not abused in print as they would be later in the century. According to historian Andrew Achenbaum, the nation's older people were valued for their insight into the sources of longevity, for their wisdom in the enormous task of creating a new world order in the United States, for the moral guidance they could bring to youth, for their knowledge of farming, and for their performance of domestic duties.[31]

Given this confluence—the absence of formal retirement, the veneration of the aged—one might conclude that rigid retirement regulations did not exist because older people were still perceived as entirely functional; no one thought of mandatory retirement, because no one thought of the aged as anything but just as productive as younger people. However, the categories of "usefulness" developed by Achenbaum conceal a peculiar softness; the aged were, it seems, valued for little more than their knowledge, advice, and guidance. They *did* very little. In fact, they shared with the sentimental, functionless females of the period the role of stabilizers in an era of rapid change.[32] Rather than participate in the central missions and concerns of the society—expansion, commercialization, urbanization—they functioned to counteract and balance, to warn the young, for example, "against the temptations and allurements of the world."[33] Therefore, it may be more accurate to say that mandatory retirement did not exist *even though* the aged were conceived in peculiarly limited terms that had little to do with the culture's main tasks. Older people may not have been conceived as equal, but they were not forcibly removed from the workplace.

This absence of mandatory retirement has several explanations. In some sense, forced retirement was simply inappropriate to nineteenth-century institutions. Most businesses were not yet large enough to rationalize. The few dozen employees in a sawmill or shoe factory were not enough to share easily the financial burdens of forced retirement on a pension. The close, personal relations of employer and employee in such enterprises perhaps made retirement without the pension (firing the older worker) uncomfortable and infrequent. As late as 1890, most older workers were engaged in farming, where we would not

30. W. Andrew Achenbaum, *Old Age in the New Land: The American Experience Since 1790* (Baltimore, 1978), pp. 20–22.
31. Ibid., chap. 1.
32. Ann Douglas, *The Feminization of American Culture* (New York, 1977), pp. 10–13, chap. 2.
33. Quoted in Achenbaum, *Old Age in the New Land*, p. 17.

expect mandatory retirement to arise.[34] Moreover, because the nation's population was still young, there was no demonstrable need even to make the argument that older, inefficient workers ought to be retired.

Let us examine another hypothesis: mandatory retirement did not exist because older workers were retiring voluntarily. This hypothesis assumes that even in the antebellum economy, there were pools of labor sufficiently large to invite the development of systems of mandatory retirement had the device seemed necessary. At least the textile industries and the railroads would qualify.[35] Had smaller firms (ironworks, for example) experienced problems with older workers, insurance companies would surely have moved in to pool risk and to create a labor force large enough to grade according to age with some statistical precision.[36]

Perhaps antebellum society did not produce such arrangements in part because some older workers were leaving the labor market before they became inefficient or superannuated. In 1840, about 70 percent of white males over sixty-five were gainfully employed; fifty years later, when industrialization had changed the face of the economy, that percentage was roughly the same. Massachusetts, a state that industrialized between 1840 and 1890, experienced a similar phenomenon: older workers continued working and retired in roughly the same percentages in the later period as in the earlier.[37] Thus, some 30 percent of white males over sixty-five were *not* in the labor market—some because they were physically incapable of working, some because they had been fired from jobs and had been unable to find new work, and some, presumably, because they were voluntarily retired.

The existence of such a voluntarily retired residual cannot be proven from the census, but neither can it be disproven, and that leaves us with the evidence of veneration and usefulness. This literature reveals that even in the early nineteenth century, Webster's first edition notwithstanding, Americans did have a concept of retirement that was applied in a special way to the elderly. The literature is as much proscriptive as descriptive; it defines a series of attitudes and behaviors and establishes expectations of conduct considered appropriate for older white males. Older people give advice, preserve the past, and demonstrate wisdom. They carry on such functions in part because they are otherwise limited. When, in 1812, Dr. Benjamin Rush described the preservation of the

34. Ibid., p. 72.

35. Herman E. Krooss and Charles Gilbert, *American Business History* (Englewood Cliffs, N.J., 1972), pp. 94–97, 124–28.

36. See Harold C. Livesay, "Marketing Patterns in the Antebellum American Iron Industry," *Business History Review* 45 (Autumn 1971): 269–95.

37. Achenbaum, *Old Age in the New Land*, pp. 69, 72.

"moral faculties" into old age, he did so within the context of the "decay of the intellectual faculties."[38] Twenty-two years after Judge Jeremiah Smith left the bench, a writer in the *North American Review* praised his withdrawal into the family circle and questioned "whether he was ever more useful to his fellow-men than in this genial autumn of his days."[39] This is nothing less than an ideology of retirement, a thinly veiled precursor of the sociologists' concept of disengagement, developed after 1955.

The history of retirement reflects the changing methodologies of American capitalism in the nineteenth and twentieth centuries. Voluntary retirement, carried out through proscriptive literature, was appropriate to small-scale, precorporate business units typical of entrepreneurial capitalism in antebellum America. There was no large, concentrated working class on which to apply mandatory retirement. Committed to the free market as a regulator of economic activity, Americans were committed, at the same time, to voluntary retirement as an application of the marketplace of ideas. Voluntary retirement was analogous to laissez faire capitalism. Rationality would emerge without coercion.

By 1885, capitalism had changed. The corporation was now the dominant mode of economic organization. A large, industrial, and bureaucratic working class had been separated from the home and removed to the factory and the office. Railroads had effectively nationalized the American market and created both intense competition and the desire to eliminate it. Organized systems of mandatory retirement now seemed possible (because the working class was organized into more manageable units) as well as more necessary. For leaders in business, labor, and the professions, retirement became a panacea for the ills that beset their particular fields. For business, retirement meant reduced unemployment, lower rates of turnover, a younger, more efficient, and more conservative work force; for labor, it was in part a way of transferring work from one generation to another in industries with a surplus of workers; for many religious denominations, it promised the recruitment of a young clergy capable of invigorating a moribund church; for educators like Osler, it held out hopes of developing university settings fully as committed to efficiency as their counterparts in industry.

In these circumstances, the tools of the early nineteenth century failed. The problem of age relations was too important to leave to the vagaries of the literary marketplace. Although ideas about the aged became increasingly negative between 1865 and 1900, corporations could no longer rely on them to achieve the

38. Ibid., p. 16.
39. Ibid., p. 23.

desired number of retirements or to reduce the age level of the work force. Therefore, at the same time as corporations were institutionalizing relationships to restrict competition—pools, trusts, and mergers—these efforts to rationalize economic relations were paralleled by attempts to rationalize, to make predictable, age relations in the workplace. Corporations began to restrict the hiring of older workers and to create mandatory retirement policies and programs. In many industries, these measures were also the product of competitive relations, intensified by the spread of the shorter workday after 1885.

The proscriptive techniques of the early nineteenth century proved inadequate, in part because older workers were digging in and holding on to the workplace; they were refusing to retire in acceptable numbers. Rates of employment remained as high in the industrial economy of 1890 as they had in the agrarian economy of 1840. Retirement to the family farm was one thing; retirement to a New York City tenement another. In the urban-industrial economy of 1900, workers without savings and without community ties to reduce the anxiety of retirement clung to their positions. Corporate and government bureaucracies became holding institutions—informal retirement mechanisms—for thousands of older workers.[40] The persistence of this holding function at the height of competitive capitalism is telling evidence that the economy contained significant precapitalist elements—in this case, an arrangement that inhibited the company or organization from becoming the fully rational agent of profit its owners or managers intended. The historic conflict between economic individualism and community, present in the American experience since the Puritans settled Massachusetts Bay, was still being worked out.[41] It was the function of retirement to allow employers to feel at ease with policies that eliminated older workers, secure in the knowledge that the retired would have some minimal competence on which to survive.

By 1900 the American economy had entered the era of state capitalism, in which the power of government was brought to bear on problems too intractable for the cooperative solutions of private enterprise. From the pools and trusts of the nineteenth century, capitalists now turned to the regulatory agencies of the twentieth: the Bureau of Corporations, the Federal Trade Commission, the Federal Reserve.[42] This expanding government bureaucracy brought the matter of superannuation into the consciousness of efficiency experts; before 1929, civil

40. This may also have been the case in the years before the Civil War. See ibid., 19–20.

41. See Bernard Bailyn's description of the Robert Keayne case, in *New England Merchants in the Seventeenth Century* (New York, 1964), pp. 41–44.

42. Gabriel Kolko, *The Triumph of Conservatism: A Reinterpretation of American History, 1900–1916* (Chicago, 1967).

service workers in six northeastern states and the federal government were subject to the retirement provisions of new pension laws.[43] The burdens of old-age assistance, once handled by local jurisdictions and private charity, were in part transferred to the states in the late 1920s and early 1930s and to the federal government under the Social Security Act of 1935. Federal railroad retirement legislation of the 1930s shifted retirement decisions from the private process of collective bargaining to national politics; the Social Security Act did the same for millions of private-sector employees. The Railroad Retirement Act was "sick" industry legislation, designed to apply the resources of the national government to chronic but predepression unemployment problems in a particular industry. The old-age insurance provisions of social security applied similar reasoning to the wider problems of an entire nation mired in a long-term depression and troubled by unemployment that many thought endemic. Coincident with the rise of state capitalism, business became less concerned with immediate profit and more interested in long-term stability, particularly in employer-employee relations. Some firms found that stable and conservative older workers best met these new needs and beat a retreat from the Progressive period orthodoxy of retirement as an ideal instrument of social and economic efficiency.

Capitalism experienced several other major changes in the twentieth century, each reflected in the history of retirement. First, consumption replaced production as the most important solution to the nation's economic problems. After the severe depression of the 1890s, it seemed to many businessmen that the productive capacities of the economy had outstripped existing markets. From this perception flowed many of the imperialist ventures of the Progressive Era, as well as a new emphasis on advertising, marketing, and consumerism to reach and develop virgin domestic markets.[44] During the Great Depression, the nation's older people experienced this transition from production to consumption, for they were now expected to retire (to cease to produce) and to spend their newly acquired retirement benefits (to consume). By the 1960s, retirement itself was an identifiable commodity, sold to consumers, old and young, like any other product.

Second, after 1885, Americans came increasingly to think of unemployment as a problem different from poverty and for which the state had some responsibility. Carroll Wright, head of the Massachusetts Bureau of Labor Statistics, in 1878 made the first attempt to count the unemployed. His 1887 report

---

43. Achenbaum, *Old Age in the New Land*, p. 121.
44. On the change from a producer to a consumer economy, see Stuart Ewen, *Captains of Consciousness: Advertising and the Social Roots of the Consumer Culture* (New York, 1976).

apparently contains the first mention of the word *unemployment*, not generally used until the severe depression of the mid-1890s.[45] The idea of a permanent and potentially dangerous residual of unemployed in some sense made age discrimination possible. It allowed employers, scientific managers, economists, and physicians to emphasize the benefits of employing superior workmen and the liabilities of keeping inefficient ones, instead of seeking to utilize all workers in a tight labor market. The shorter work life (retirement) was used to reduce unemployment in particular industries as early as the 1890s and became a part of national policy with the railroad retirement and social security legislation of the 1930s.

Third, after 1950, the American economy experienced a gradual, relative, but undeniable decline in its international competitive position. Germany, Japan, and Russia emerged as major challengers to American hegemony by 1955. Nationalist movements in Latin America, Africa, Southeast Asia, and the Middle East reduced American ability to penetrate foreign markets and to exploit the abundant raw materials of the third world. The Vietnam War and the Arab oil boycott of 1973 vividly demonstrated the difficulties facing the United States in the new postwar world.[46] American capitalists sought to redress these difficulties through innovative approaches to world markets (symbolized by Richard Nixon's trip to China in 1971), by producing abroad with cheaper foreign labor, and by making the economy more efficient. It is this last solution which has relevance for retirement. Reversing the historic relationship between retirement and efficiency, the Retirement Act of 1978 sought to induce increased efficiency by severely restricting the incidence of mandatory retirement in the federal government and the private sector. Employers were to be forced out of sloppy, bureaucratic modes of decision making which treated all workers of a given age as equally productive or unproductive. A return to merit-based personnel decisions would presumably bring increased efficiency while relieving the growing financial burdens on our public and private retirement systems.

A century after retirement became an important instrument of social and economic policy, we are preparing for its disappearance, again in a context established by the needs of capital and with the acquiescence of most Americans. We expected too much from retirement. We believed retirement would rejuvenate and stabilize the teaching profession, the churches, and the factories; spare us the distress of an aging bureaucracy; allow the payment of lower salaries;

45. John A. Garraty, *Unemployment in History: Economic Thought and Public Policy* (New York, 1978), pp. 108–09, 121.
46. Jeff Frieden, "The Trilateral Commission: Economics and Politics in the 1970s," *Monthly Review* 29 (December 1977): 1–18.

distribute work in declining industries and in an economy that, in many, sometimes lengthy periods over the last century, has failed to employ all who wanted to work. In our current difficulties, we assume that by reversing the process and dismantling the edifice of retirement, we can reinvigorate an economy that has lost its fine competitive edge. This is the mirror-image of the historic assumption that retirement is a powerful and inexpensive instrument of social reconstruction. A new myth replaces the old.

2 Retirement and the Origins of Age Discrimination

Age discrimination,[1] of which retirement is a particular variant, dates from the last quarter of the eighteenth century. Not until a century later, however, did either the larger phenomenon of age discrimination or the specific mechanism of retirement come to affect large numbers of persons.[2] In the two decades before 1900, age discrimination grew virulently, as the owners and managers who made personnel decisions for American corporations redefined the work force to achieve increased efficiency. Osler's valedictory, part of this virulence and yet responsible for the first major public discussion of it, could not have been conceived in the milder climate of age relations characteristic of Jacksonian America.

Between 1885 and 1940, age discrimination went through two major historical stages. Before 1915, age discrimination was born and nurtured at the hands of a capitalist economy that, relative to its twentieth-century counterpart, was very competitive and committed to a high level of productive efficiency in the pursuit of short-term profit. The competitive structure of the economy was primarily a product of the rise of national markets caused by the growth in the rail system and urbanization, but competitive conditions were exacerbated, in a

1. I am grateful to Tom Cole for pointing out the pitfalls of using the term *age discrimination*. These words carry a liberal bias, for they imply that the problem might be solved by the elimination of unenlightened prejudice against the employment of older workers, when, in fact, what happens to older workers, including their forced retirement, can hardly be described as the product of ignorance or misunderstanding. Nonetheless, I see no reasonable alternative. As I use the term, it describes policies and actions that gradually redefined the position of the middle-aged and elderly in the work force.

2. While it is possible to appreciate the differences that mark the historical frameworks of W. Andrew Achenbaum and David Hackett Fischer, these differences may be less important than Fischer believes. Achenbaum's work suggests a dramatic transformation in age relations in the 1880s; Fischer, while positing a "revolution" in age relations between 1770 and 1820, acknowledges in several places in his book that change was slow until late in the nineteenth century. W. Andrew Achenbaum, *Old Age in the New Land: The American Experience Since 1790* (Baltimore, 1978), chap. 3; David Hackett Fischer, *Growing Old in America* (New York, 1977), chap. 2, and pp. 128, 142–43.

visible way that led directly to age discrimination, by the increasing popularity of the shorter workday. Economists and physicians constructed an ideology that reinforced and rationalized this discrimination; scientific managers carried it out in shop, factory, and office.

Employers sought to recover the costs attendant on a shorter workday by utilizing available technology to obtain more product from each worker. The preponderance of evidence indicates, however, that it was not the technology itself, but rather the speed at which it was operated, which brought grief to older workers. Employers apparently felt that the high capital costs of new machinery could be justified only if that machinery were operated at speeds that led inevitably to the obsolescence of workers too old to maintain required levels of productivity. In the printing industry (the data base for many of my conclusions), this entire process was the subject of negotiations between labor and management. As labor lost control of the work process, trade unions succumbed to the temptation to bargain away the rights of older workers.

It is also possible that employers introduced new technology and insisted on high-speed operation in order to force older workers out of the labor force. In the late nineteenth century, the effort to develop a more stable, more tractable, and more disciplined working class was sometimes defined in terms of eliminating older workers with seniority, influence in the union, or preindustrial work habits. Certainly there is evidence for the general case that technology was often introduced for some other purpose than increased efficiency, narrowly defined.

In the two decades after 1915, age discrimination worsened absolutely because of continued technological change, an intensification of the youth cult during the 1920s, and the unemployment of the Depression. By 1930, it had become a subject of study by social workers, fraternal organizations, labor unions, business trade groups, and committees of the House and Senate. In a political sense, the issue had arrived.

At the same time, however, age discrimination had begun to change with the changing face of American capitalism. As business increasingly sought to trade immediate profit for future security (economic efficiency for social efficiency, in other words), older workers became valuable for their stability and conservatism. Some capitalists discovered that older workers could meet traditional demands for efficiency by contributing to reduced rates of work-force turnover and by servicing particular product markets. Having succeeded before 1920 in creating a less tradition-bound industrial working class, post-1920 employers often experienced the most difficulty with younger workers. The older worker of 1930 (say, thirty-five years old in 1900) belonged to the first generation of workers to reach old age under the full-blown pressures of ageism. Made cautious and cooperative through pension plans and threats of job loss, this older worker had become a reasonable ally for certain employers.[3]

THE PROBLEM OF TECHNOLOGY

Lee Welling Squier's *Old Age Dependency in the United States*, published in 1912, was an angry book. In it, Squier challenged the right of the individual employer to "engage men in an occupation that exhausts the individual's industrial life in ten, twenty, or forty years; and then leave the remnant floating on society at large as a derelict at sea."[4] Squier implied that it was justifiable for an industry to wear out its workers (having done so, it must simply make provision

3. Achenbaum demonstrates rather convincingly that the withdrawal of older males from the labor force was minimal before 1890, significant in the next three decades, and especially rapid after 1920. "This suggests," he concludes, "that age discrimination in the marketplace significantly increased *after* negative notions about the aged were already commonplace." Achenbaum explains this discontinuity in two ways. First, bureaucratization of American business and government in the late nineteenth century curiously enhanced the position of the elderly, allowing older employees to reach positions of authority by climbing new promotional ladders. Second, "ideas about the worth and functions of the elderly have a life of their own: the unprecedented denigration of older Americans arose independently of the most important observable changes in their actual status" (Achenbaum, *Old Age in the New Land*, pp. 74, 86).

The second of these explanations is not really an explanation at all; it is simply a conclusion from observed facts. Ideas and functions do not move together in a given time frame; hence, they must be separate entities, unrelated in any demonstrable way. The first explanation assumes idea and function *are* generally related and seeks to explain why at any particular time one might be independent of the other. This explanation is viable as far as it goes. Late-nineteenth-century civil service regulations, for example, clearly helped create and protect an aging bureaucracy. Achenbaum's interpretation, however, stops with the ability of older workers to protect themselves; it assumes that without such protection, their removal would be imminent, idea and function reunited. As I hope to show in later chapters, this assumption that the aged had only their own devices to rely on is incorrect. They could also depend on a highly developed sense of community and comradeship in most bureaucracies, a sense shared by those who had to make personnel decisions. Managers might feel an older worker was inefficient and should be separated from the organization but still feel obligated not to carry out that separation. Retirement allowed the resulting gap between idea and function to be closed. Significantly, it was a marginal institution in 1890, an important one after 1920.

Michel Dahlin accounts for the rise of old-age unemployment by the "transformation of America from an agricultural to an industrial economy" and the consequent changes in occupational structure and employment opportunities. Industrial employment, she argues, prevented older workers from accumulating property as they had done under an agricultural economy; it also created dependence by making it difficult for workers to be self-employed. See Michel Dahlin, "The Economic Crisis: Unemployment and Ageism," Paper presented at the Mississippi Valley Historical Conference, 10 March 1977, pp. 2, 3, 4. However, it is entirely possible to conceive of an industrial system under which workers were allowed to accumulate property in anticipation of old age and even to remain self-employed (or cooperatively employed) in substantial numbers. It is not so much the existence of industry, but the way in which the industrial revolution was pursued under American capitalism, which explains age discrimination. See Fischer, *Growing Old*, pp. 101–02; and Carole Haber, "Mandatory Retirement in Nineteenth-Century America: The Conceptual Basis for a New Work Cycle," *Journal of Social History* 12 (Fall 1978): 78.

4. Squier, *Old Age Dependency in the United States: A Complete Survey of the Pension Movement* (New York, 1912), p. 272.

for them, presumably through some form of retirement); that work was inherently consuming, damaging, and destructive; and that technology was the central agent in the work experience of middle-aged and older employees. By the late 1920s, technology was one of the most common explanations of the employment problems of older workers. Herbert Hoover's Committee on Recent Economic Changes found the essence of the problem in a new job mix that placed a premium on youthful vigor. Labor-saving machinery, commented the *Commercial and Financial Chronicle*, had displaced men and reduced opportunity. Even in the midst of the Great Depression, when one would expect such an analysis of unemployment to have been overthrown by the sheer numbers of those without jobs and the collapse of the world economy, the technological argument remained influential, prompting a 1936 investigation of unemployment and technology by the House of Representatives. By 1960 the centrality of technology had emerged as an article of faith among social gerontologists.[5]

The only legitimate early study of the problem, by English economist William Beveridge in 1909, took a diametrically opposed point of view. Machinery, Beveridge said, did not cause unemployment, for if machinery had been making labor superfluous, the price of labor would have fallen with the advance of technology. In fact, the opposite had happened. Although Beveridge reduced unemployment to "specific imperfections of adjustment," including regular changes in industry, fluctuations in industrial activity, and the need for reserves of labor to meet incidental fluctuations in trade, he was well aware that older workers were not absorbed as easily as younger workers. Since technology was not involved, the problem must reside in some characteristic of the older worker which served to inhibit his employment. Older workers, Beveridge reasoned, lacked a quality essential in a rapidly changing society—adaptability.[6] Beveridge had, in effect, reversed the technological argument, moving from an inflexible technology to the inflexible worker.

The printing industry offers some opportunity to test the technological theory in an historical context. As late as 1885 there was apparently no discrimination in the printing industry, a classic craft in which type was set by hand in thousands of small shops. Ottmar Mergenthaler built his first direct-linecasting

5. *The Index*, September 1929, p. 136; Don D. Lescohier, *Working Conditions*, in John R. Commons, ed., *History of Labor in the United States, 1896–1932*, 4 vols. (New York, 1935) 3:146–48; *Commercial and Financial Chronicle* 129 (26 October 1929): 595–96 (editorial); U.S., Congress, House, Subcommittee on Labor, *Investigation of Unemployment Caused by Labor-Saving Devices in Industry: Hearings* on H.R. 49, 13, 14, 17, 20 February and 2, March 1936, 74th Cong., 1st sess. (Washington, D.C., 1936), hereafter referred to as House, Subcommittee on Labor, *Investigation of Unemployment: Hearings*; Fred Cottrell, "The Technological and Societal Basis of Aging," in Clark Tibbitts, ed., *Handbook of Social Gerontology: Societal Aspects of Aging* (Chicago, 1960), p. 95.

6. *Unemployment: A Problem of Industry* (London, 1909), pp. 12 (quotation), 116–17, 120.

machine in 1884. When the problem of correcting errors was solved the next year, the success of his machine was assured. By 1892 the inevitability of the Mergenthaler, or Linotype, had been conceded by the few remaining skeptics.[7] A seventy-four-year-old charter member of the Dayton Typographical Union No. 57, then a resident in the Union Printers' Home in that city, captured something of the impact of the change in "The Old Way and the New":

> The typo's old pick from the case
> Has changed to machine's rapid pace—
>> To iron and steel,
>> To shafting and wheel,
> And the keyboard has taken his place.
>
> The clinking old rule and the stick,
> With their time-beating, rattling click,
>> Are now laid away,
>> And slow "prints" and gray
> Are "out" by a Linotype trick.
>
> Adieu to the "strings" and the paste,
> To the longest we often have raced;
>> Old-timers are "out,"
>> But the young comp.'s about
> And filling up columns with haste.[8]

This is one view. The Linotype had resulted in the replacement of the older, slower workers, as well as the traveling, or "tramp," printers, as they were called. Other sources confirm the coincidence of the Mergenthaler and age discrimination. Between 1895 and 1915, older workers were phased out for younger men with better eyesight, more speed, and more endurance. Age limits in hiring became commonplace in the industry, and some firms were willing to take the more unusual and unpopular action of releasing older employees.[9] Mike Bachman, a seventy-eight-year-old traveling printer, was a figure of some fame precisely because he had managed to grow old and remain independent while operating the Linotype. His arrival in Urbana, Illinois in 1922 for a "sit" on the campus newspaper, the *Daily Illini*, was a major event. "But can he print," said the union report. "Advancing age has not slowed up his nimble fingers, and

---

7. John S. Thompson, *History of Composing Machines* (1904; reprint ed., New York, 1972), pp. 100–103; E. L. Marsters, "Routine of a Mergenthaler Office," *Inland Printer* 9 (June 1892): 776; ibid., 9 (August 1892): 955–56; ibid., 3 (September 1886): 749 (editorial).

8. *Inland Printer* 47 (July 1911): 606, stanzas 1, 2, 7.

9. *Typographical Journal* 13 (15 August 1898): 155; ibid., 26 (March 1905): 258.

when he sits down to a linotype machine, the foreman is kept busy providing galleys fast enough for Mike to 'dump' on."[10]

For reasons on which masters and journeymen disagreed, Mike Bachman and his kind had become rare. The *Inland Printer*, voice of the employers, was torn between what it saw as the absurdity of superannuation in an industry in which brains, skill, and experience played such a major role and strength and endurance such a minor one, and the inevitability and rationality of the whole process. The latter viewpoint was dominant. Acknowledging that labor had been intensified and that intensification was in some measure responsible for the problems of the older worker, owners located the source of this intensification in two factors: first, technology, which they labeled at once as benign and a mark of the "advance of civilization"; second, the reduction in working hours, for which, of course, the workers were responsible. Technology produced superannuated workers because "the daily task is more exacting."[11]

Shop owners had also developed a more tractable labor force. The "'old-time prints'" were irrepressible drinkers, who might at any moment quit work and leave the shop for the companionship of the saloon; the "sober," "well-educated," and "quick-witted" young men who replaced them had lost the drinking habit.[12]

The victims of this reorganization shared with the owners a sense of the inevitability of what was happening to them, but their resignation emerged from an analysis of capitalist modes of production rather than technology itself. They understood that not the machine but the demands placed on its operator by the shop owner were behind "the 'grind' the 'old boy' has to undergo today in order to hold his job."[13] Although printers agreed that good eyesight and supple fingers were requisites of Linotype operation, they would not accept the master's argument that the mere operation of typesetting machines damaged the nervous systems and general health of the worker. It was, wrote one typesetter, "the unnatural pace that kills."[14] Employees did, however, acknowledge the claim of their employers that the capital requirements imposed on the industry by typesetting machinery entailed certain operating requirements. A $3,500 piece of ma-

10. Ibid. 61 (October 1922): 497.
11. *Inland Printer* 39 (August 1907): 691–92 (editorial); ibid. 47 (June 1911): 385 (editorial).
12. "Passing of the Old-Time Printer," *Inland Printer* 34 (December 1904): 400; Christopher Lasch, "The Corruption of Sports," *New York Review of Books* 24 (28 April 1977): 26–27; Herbert Gutman, "Work, Culture and Society in Industrializing America, 1815–1919," *American Historical Review* 78 (June 1973): 531–88.
13. *Typographical Journal* 61 (October 1922): 429.
14. Herbert W. Cooke, "The Machine Operator and His Nerves," *Typographical Journal* 26 (January 1905): 2; ibid. 22 (April 1903): 367–68.

chinery, the Mergenthaler had to be operated efficiently (extensively and intensively) to be economical.[15]

By the early 1920s the system that had ousted the older workers was beginning to produce concern among their more youthful replacements. A Memphis machine operator predicted that the "'speeding-up' system is going to put a whole lot of us on the bench at a much younger age than the limits of the pension now allows and we had each better be preparing for that time."[16] In Reading, Pennsylvania, apprentices were in short supply because the word was out that employers wanted speed and continuous productivity. Rather than become "speed hounds," young apprentices applied for positions in the quieter atmosphere of the ad room. The *Inland Printer*, on the other hand, believed (and with some logic) that the shortage had been artificially induced by journeymen who belittled and discouraged apprentices because they saw in them potential future competitors.[17]

Aging machinists faced the same problems as their counterparts in printing and arrived at similar conclusions. Faced with the competition of younger men and liable to dismissal at the first sign of age, machinists who had not yet reached middle age felt compelled to deceive their employers by dyeing their hair. As employers demanded more from their workers and increased the speed of their tools, the older machinists who could not keep pace were replaced by boys. Like the junior printers, these younger employees were often trained outside the apprenticeship system, in part because the increased divison of labor made broad-based training unnecessary; and in part because veteran employees would no longer tolerate an institution that produced their competitors and accelerated their superannuation.[18] A Works Progress Administration study of Philadelphia machinists revealed that machinist skills were not, as commonly believed, transferable from one industry to the next, and that once fired, older machinists had much more difficulty in finding new employment than did younger ones.[19]

IMPERATIVES OF THE WORKDAY

Technological imperatives and labor-force modification are part of an answer to the conundrum of age discrimination. But why the speedup? Why, in the

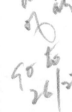

15. Ibid. 13 (15 August 1898): 155–56.

16. Ibid. 61 (October 1922): 430.

17. Ibid. 61 (July 1922): 80; *Inland Printer* 36 (February 1906): 698–700 (editorial).

18. James O'Connell, "The Manhood Tribute to the Modern Machine," *Machinists' Monthly Journal* 18 (May 1906): 409–11; Roger C. Dickey, "After 50—What Then?" *American Machinist* 81 (14 July 1937): 637–38.

19. "Ten Years of Work Experience of Philadelphia Machinists," reported in *New York Times*, 9 October 1938, p. 12.

last years of the nineteenth century and the first decade of the twentieth were American employers so interested in squeezing the most from their labor?

Behind the speedup was a set of interrelationships that revolved around the shorter working day. Historians who have studied the politics of the working day have centered their inquiries on the Haymarket Riot of 1886 and questions of social order. For most employers and workers, however, the shorter working day was important largely for its economic implications.

The modern phase of the agitation for a shorter working day began in 1886, when the ten-hour day and the six-day week were the common experience of American labor. A national strike in that year failed, but agitation continued, pushed by national unions.[20] In the printing industry, working-day politics had their beginnings in 1887, and within four years the International Typographical Union (ITU) had secured agreements covering limited numbers of the nation's newspaper workers. At the 1898 Syracuse conference, representatives of management and labor agreed to extend the nine-and-a-half-hour day to most of the industry as of November 21, 1898, and the nine-hour day a year later. Through a strike initiated in 1905, the ITU and its companion unions reduced the working day to eight hours in some areas of the industry.[21] Aggregate data for other industries indicates that the printing experience was typical. Nationally, the decline in the working day was gradual from 1892 through about 1915. For eleven selected industries, a *major* decline of .6 percent occurred in 1892–93, and another, of .9 percent, in 1901–02.[22]

In presenting its case for the shorter working day, labor offered a number of rationales; shorter hours would mean more time for recreation, leisure, and education as well as less toil before the machine. For the most part, however, these considerations were peripheral. The shorter working day was a work-sharing program that the printers (capital *and* labor) believed would help solve the threatening problem of technologically induced unemployment. This analysis was shared at least by cigar makers, painters, engineers, blacksmiths, machinists, iron molders, and silk weavers.[23] Work sharing was a goal of the major

20. Henry David, *The History of the Haymarket Affair: A Study in the American Social-Revolutionary and Labor Movements* (New York, 1936), p. 160.

21. Leona M. Powell, *The History of the United Typothetae of America* (Chicago, 1926), pp. 25, 39–41, 51, 54, 75; United Typothetae of America, "A Shorter Workday," Conference at Syracuse, New York, 10, 11, 12 October 1898 (Boston, 1898), bound with United Typothetae of America, *Proceedings of the Twelfth Annual Convention of the United Typothetae of America*, held in the city of Milwaukee, Wisconsin, 23–26 August 1898 (Boston, n.d.).

22. Lazare Teper, *Hours of Labor*, Johns Hopkins University Studies in Historical and Political Science, series L, no. 1 (Baltimore, 1932), pp. 32–48.

23. David, *Haymarket Affair*, pp. 164, 167–68, 170–71; U. M. Weideman, *The Great Struggle of the Masses Against the Classes: The Conflict of the Ages and the Physiology of Overwork* (South

unions of typesetters and printing pressmen in 1898. In Dayton and New York City, for example, machinery installation had left a surplus of printers, and union officials expected the shorter workday to at least contribute to their reemployment.[24] Labor organizations were seeking to aid their unemployed (presumably an older group) through the mechanism of the shorter working day. There is also some evidence that particular groups of workers sought to share directly and personally in the productivity of labor-saving machinery. This was especially likely to occur in occupations, such as newspaper typesetting, where work was naturally concentrated in one period of the day; in this situation, compositors argued, a longer working day would only mean additional hours of idleness.[25]

No matter how benign the intent of the labor organizations, the major impact of the shorter working day was to intensify the pressures on older workers. The Syracuse agreement inaugurated a decade of industry interest in cost cutting. Employers who could neither pass their costs on to consumers nor reduce wages sought to lower operating expenditures by eliminating less efficient older employees. The *Inland Printer*, in an editorial that may have been only self-serving, cautioned in 1907 that the eight-hour day would only "serve to intensify labor—the capable workman will be in greater demand than ever, while the indifferent one will be shunned as never before."[26]

The union printers must share responsibility for the speedup and its consequences for older workers. Pressed by owners at their 1898 convention about potential increases in labor costs, union spokesmen *offered* the speedup. An organizer for the ITU said he was "satisfied that so far as the compositors are concerned that a man can do in nine hours what he can do in ten. . . . I know I can do in eight hours what I can do in ten."[27] Railroad workers pressing for the eight-hour day made the same argument in 1916.[28] Employers would discover that this was not simply talk, that output could be maintained during a shortened workday. When the steel industry switched to the eight-hour day from the

---

Manchester, Conn., 1897), pp. 24, 34; Marion Cotter Cahill, *Shorter Hours: A Study of the Movement Since the Civil War* (New York, 1932), p. 13; New York State, Bureau of Statistics of Labor, *Thirteenth Annual Report of the Bureau of Statistics of Labor for the Year 1895*, 2 vols. (Albany, 1896), 1: 259–65.

24. United Typothetae, *Proceedings*, 1898, pp. 19, 24, 68; United Typothetae, "Shorter Workday," p. 107.

25. Powell, *United Typothetae*, p. 51; David, *Haymarket Affair*, p. 164.

26. *Inland Printer* 39 (September 1907): 852 (editorial); Powell, *United Typothetae*, pp. 89–91; L. H. Prescott, "The Economic Outlook in Printing," appendix 4 of United Typothetae, *Proceedings*, 1898, p. 173.

27. United Typothetae, *Proceedings*, 1898, p. 98.

28. Onward Bates, "What is the Significance of the Eight-Hour Working Day?" *Railway Review* 59 (16 September 1916): 384–85.

twelve-hour day in 1922, for example, the jump in productivity was prodigious.[29] By inviting the speedup in return for the shorter working day, labor organizations bargained away the job rights of older workers who could not produce at higher speeds and of the unemployed, who could be absorbed only if output levels remained stable.

Older workers may have suffered because the shorter working day ultimately brought more machinery into workshops and factories. Owners who could not speed up their machinery and whose employees could not produce more because of the limitations of their machines made this argument. They insisted that the speedup would not help increase productivity. Amos Pettibone of the United Typothetae, the employers' trade group, said: "While certain gentlemen will claim that they can do as much work, or more work, in eight or nine hours than they can in ten, we will concede that it is true . . . but it is not so with our machines—they are manufactured and geared to run at a certain speed."[30] A reduction in working time, said the owners, was equivalent to a reduction in capital investment. The union representatives countered by pointing out that the argument had validity only when a plant was operating at full capacity; otherwise, the operation of previously idle machinery would benefit capitalists by increasing the ratio of variable to fixed costs. It seems likely that one impact of the working-day reductions was to encourage ongoing mechanization of the industry as, in the years to follow, individual enterprises approached full operating capacity.[31]

✓ AN ECONOMIC RATIONALE

During the late nineteenth century, economists labored to develop a theoretical framework that would tie the seemingly harmful industrial realities of the shorter working day and higher wages to the desirable goal of increased productivity. Where capitalism had experienced these phenomena at an early date, as in England and Germany, the economic rationale was most developed. Gerhart von Schulze-Gävernitz used the classic case of the English cotton textile industry as evidence that high wages and falling work hours could be reconciled with productivity, through the mechanism of age discrimination.[32] In an 1871 work

29. *Iron Age* 95 (4 March 1915): 537–38; United States, Department of Labor, Bureau of Labor Statistics, "Productivity of Labor in Merchant Blast Furnaces," *Bulletin* 474, misc. series (Washington, D.C., 1929), p. 47. See also Fischer, *Growing Old*, p. 143.
    30. United Typothetae, "Shorter Workday," p. 75.
    31. United Typothetae, *Proceedings*, 1898, pp. 99–100; United Typothetae, "Shorter Workday," pp. 105–06.
    32. Lujo Brentano, *Hours and Wages in Relation to Production*, trans. Mrs. William Arnold (London, 1894), p. 17.

on factory legislation, Ernest von Plener for the first time raised the issue of the age of the work force. Following the introduction of shorter hours, he wrote, "the operatives, *especially the younger ones*, no longer exhausted by excessive bodily effort, produced the same amount, and frequently even turned out more in the shorter time, having, owing to the almost universal system of payment by the piece, a special interest in doing so."[33]

The conviction that the modern workman must be a superior being was especially strong in the classic work of Lujo Brentano, a German economist whose *Hours and Wages in Relation to Production* was published in 1894. Brentano grounded this belief (which one also finds in the work of Frederick W. Taylor) in the liberal classicism of Adam Smith, who had emphasized that the well-fed worker, hopeful of a secure future, would "exert [his] strength to the utmost."[34] But Brentano went well beyond Smith in articulating a theoretical relationship between high wages, shorter hours (which together formed the standard of living), and productivity. A higher standard of living, Brentano suggested, changed the outlook of the workman, who under its influence renounced his home and his "accustomed surroundings." His energy awakened, this new worker was capable of more intensive labor. Meals and rest periods could be eliminated. Employers, now possessed of "superior workmen, well paid, well fed, intelligent, strenuous, and eager," would install "faster, more delicate machines," as the English had done in their cotton mills. Aware that the labor-force modifications his theory predicted were already taking place in the industrializing nations, Brentano pronounced these modifications beneficial. "To work of that kind," he suggested, "children [are] no longer equal. The perfected machine, on the other hand, makes the father once more the family bread-winner, and restores the child to the school to which he properly belongs." Brentano concluded with a sentence that foreshadowed the difficulties of older and middle-aged workers: "Henceforward, grown men are wanted for the work, and indeed, only such are of any use whom a higher standard of living has fitted to meet the higher demands made on them by machinery." More than any other single work published in the late nineteenth century, Brentano's *Hours and Wages* provided the capitalist class with a powerful rationale for eliminating older workers who were inefficient and tradition-bound, and for hiring younger workers with more muscle, more energy, and fewer ties to the past.[35]

33. Italics mine. From *Die Englische Fabrikgesetzgebung (Vienna, 1871)*, quoted in Brentano, *Hours and Wages*, pp. 29–30.

34. Quoted in Brentano, *Hours and Wages*, p. 4; Taylor, *Principles of Scientific Management* (New York, 1915).

35. Brentano, *Hours and Wages*, pp. 37, 40, 43, 48, 57–58, 51–52, 61, 61–62. See also Joseph A. Litterer, "Systematic Management: The Search for Order and Integration," *Business History Review* 35 (Winter 1961): 465. Between 1899 and 1939, almost every industry reduced man-hour

Several American economists contributed to this flowering ideology. Three years into the severe depression of the 1870s, Francis Walker suggested relieving the pressure on labor markets through legislation "prohibiting labor for all classes beyond the term which physiological science accepts as consistent with soundness and vigor."[36] An interest in productivity rather than unemployment informed Jacob Schoenhof's *Economy of High Wages*, published in 1892. A laissez faire economist and low-tariff Democrat, Schoenhof traveled the world for the Department of State, comparing wage rates and productivity and concluding that productivity increases depended upon rising living standards. As an example of the relationship between low wages and low productivity, Schoenhof pointed to the English nail industry, where "old and young, husbands, wives, and daughters, all work at nail making from four or five in the morning until late at night."[37] An economy that offered labor to inefficient workers was not functioning properly.

It remained only for the theory to be incorporated into the mainstream of American economics. That task fell to Alfred Marshall, dean of turn-of-the-century economists and author of a number of popular textbooks. In *Principles of Economics*, Marshall, with Oslerian detachment, tied elemental physical characteristics to profit. Health and strength were the basis of industrial efficiency: "In estimating muscular strength, or, indeed, any other kind of strength, for industrial purposes, we must take into account the number of hours in the day, the number of days in the year, and the number of years in a lifetime, during which it can be asserted." Discussing Marshall's physical emphasis in an article written in 1906, well-known statistician Frederick Hoffman concluded that for the nation to maximize its productive potential, given the present capacities of its population, work should normally begin at age fifteen and cease at sixty-five. Economic theory was linked to the workplace in an alliance detrimental to older workers and mandating retirement.[38]

SUPPORT FROM SCIENCE AND MEDICINE

Science came to the support of capitalist economics in late-nineteenth-century studies of work and fatigue. Prevailing theories originated in the work of

requirements per unit of product (Solomon Fabricant, "Labor Savings in American Industry, 1899–1939," National Bureau of Economic Research, *Occasional Paper* 23 [New York, 1945] pp. iii–iv).

36. Quoted in Haber, "Mandatory Retirement," p. 86.

37. Jacob Schoenhof, *The Economy of High Wages: An Inquiry into the Cause of High Wages and Their Effect on Methods and Cost of Production* (1892; reprint ed., New York, 1974), pp. 225, 5–6, 10–11.

38. Frederick L. Hoffman, "Physical and Medical Aspects of Labor and Industry," *Annals of the American Academy of Political and Social Science* 27 (May 1906): 3.

George Beard, a physician who in the 1870s popularized the idea of "neuras-thenia," a catchall illness with an endless list of symptoms, including anxiety and fatigue. The disease was hereditary and cumulative. "No two persons," writes historian Charles Rosenberg, "would be born with the same amount of nervous force; no two persons would be subjected to the same external pres-sures. Only those individuals whose endowment of nervous force was inade-quate to the demands of daily life succumbed to neurasthenia."[39] The closer one's contact with the new technology of the nineteenth century—the steam engine, the Linotype, the sewing machine, even the telegraph—the faster one's supply of nervous force would be consumed, never to be replenished.[40]

Work became associated with nervous strain, tension, anxiety, stress, and nerves; workers were "burned out," "used up," "exhausted," and "prematurely aged." During debates over retirement legislation, each occupation, from rail-roading to teaching to mail delivery, would claim to be the most tension-produc-ing and energy-consuming. In his 1912 study of old-age dependency, Squier opened a chapter on transportation with a description that might well have been written by Beard:

> There is no part of the great national labor machine that wears out men more rapidly or subjects them to greater hazard than that which we call "transportation." Especially is this true of those engaged in the operation of trains and vessels on time schedules, which require by day and night the strictest attention to duty and rules. Every moment is fraught with danger. Brain, nerve and muscle are all subject to the severest and most unexpected strain. . . . The locomotive engines are of the most intricate device and require the keenest intelligence, quickest action and oftentimes the most prolonged tension of mind and body.[41]

During their campaign for pensions, the public-school teachers argued a similar case:

> The severe mental strain and high nervous tension under which faithful teachers work tend to make them apprehensive of the future. Small and insufficient salaries preclude those frequent and necessary relaxations which preserve health and elasticity of mind and body. . . . Work itself rarely kills, but worry often does.[42]

39. Charles E. Rosenberg, "The Place of George M. Beard in Nineteenth-Century Psychiatry," *Bulletin of the History of Medicine*, 36 (May–June 1962): 249.
40. Ibid., pp. 246–47, 254, 256–57.
41. Squier, *Old Age Dependency*, p. 109.
42. From the *Official Report* of the Teachers' Annuity Guild of Massachusetts, quoted in Mary D. Bradford, "Teachers' Pensions and Insurance," *Journal of Education* 51 (11 May 1905): 512.

Even bureaucracies not involved in the competitive economy shared this concept of work. Writing to Pierre S. Du Pont in an attempt to recruit youthful members for his National Civic Federation, John Hays Hammond explained his inquiry with reference to the "high tension and complexities of our Twentieth Century civilization."[43]

The import of such statements is independent of their scientific validity. In their various forms, these work-related ideas encouraged employers in their proclivity to select younger workers, whose contact with the technological sources of nervous tension had heretofore been limited; they led logically to the notion of a "work life," which naturally ended well before death, perhaps even in middle age; and they defined the older worker as one who had used up a considerable portion of his allotted nervous force.

LINKS TO THE WORKPLACE: SCIENTIFIC MANAGEMENT

The crucial figure linking the theoretical and empirical constructs of the economists and the physicians to the workplace was the corporate manager—and, increasingly after 1885, the "scientific" manager. Here the economist found a resolute ally. Forged in the same competitive and technological environment that had produced the work of Brentano and Marshall, scientific management shared with economics a variety of assumptions and attitudes concerning the relationship between labor and industrial efficiency. Applied to the workplace, scientific management contributed to the displacement of older workers.

From the very first, Frederick W. Taylor and his fellow managers had as their central aim an increase in labor productivity, whatever the state of technology.[44] As the working day decreased during the late nineteenth century, Taylor's phrase "an honest day's work" took on new meaning, and his lifelong interest in "soldiering" was heightened.[45] Searching for methods to increase the intensity

---

43. Hammond to Du Pont, 17 November 1914, in Pierre S. Du Pont Papers, the Longwood Manuscripts, Eleutherian Mills Historical Library, Greenville, Wilmington, Delaware, group 10, series A, no box number, file no. 769.

44. In recent years, historians have subjected scientific management to a searching reexamination. As instructive as these studies have been, their evolution in the economic environment of midcentury has resulted in a historical reconstruction that, while enormously valuable in understanding certain aspects of scientific management, is tangential to its central purpose. Samuel Haber, for example, sees Taylor's interest in productivity as a function of a deeper concern for social order and harmony of interest (*Efficiency and Uplift: Scientific Management in the Progressive Era, 1890–1920* [Chicago, 1964], p. 27). See also Harry Braverman, "Labor and Monopoly Capital: The Degradation of Work in the Twentieth Century," *Monthly Review* 26 (July–August 1974), 1–134.

45. Haber, *Efficiency and Uplift*, pp. 2, 67; Milton J. Nadworny, *Scientific Management and the Unions, 1900–1932: A Historical Analysis* (Cambridge, Mass., 1955), p. 6. "Soldiering" described workers who presumably would consciously work at less than optimum levels of effort.

of labor, scientific managers concentrated on two areas: wage incentives and work-force selection. While the second is often ignored or misunderstood, it was central to Taylor's outlook. In "Shop Management," written in 1903 and one of his most influential papers, Taylor noted that the system owed its success to the rejection of ordinary workmen and the employment only of unusual ones.[46] Eight years later, in *The Principles of Scientific Management*, Taylor reemphasized the point in his famous example of Schmidt, a laborer selected for intensive effort in large part because of his superior strength.[47]

Practitioners of scientific management in the Progressive Era were understandably sensitive to the charge that their art required supermen and would result in a merciless weeding out of the inefficient. Harrington Emerson insisted that efficiency "comes to assure standard wages to each according to age, experience, and class of work." If so, even the inefficient would be employed, if at reduced rates of compensation. On the other hand, for Emerson the most efficient shop was one that "eliminates from its force inefficient men." Perfectly willing to admit that child labor would be "curtailed because it is inefficient," Emerson had nothing to say about the likely analogous impact on the aged members of the work force.[48] Beard's idea of cumulative fatigue essentially justified the central concern of the scientific managers—an increased work pace—for if one's nervous force was inherently limited, it could make little difference at which portion of the work life it was expended. This may explain why the early practitioners of scientific management were interested in fatigue only as a daily problem associated with a particular task rather than as a cumulative yet attenuable affliction.[49]

Scientific management demanded more of its workers than a heightened level of intensity; it also required a certain kind of flexibility. If not exactly scientists, these managers and those to follow were experimenters, with the factory as their laboratory. Labor must be willing to cooperate, first in the process of experimentation, then in a reconstruction of its work habits. In the early nineteenth century, capitalists staffed their factories with children, in part because, as Englishman Andrew Ure wrote, "it is found nearly impossible to convert persons past the age of puberty, whether drawn from rural or from handicraft

46. Horace Bookwalter Drury, *Scientific Management: A History and Criticism*, Studies in History, Economics and Public Law, ed., Faculty of Political Science of Columbia University, vol. 65, no. 2 (New York, 1915), p. 66.

47. See the discussion in Braverman, "Labor and Monopoly Capital," pp. 28–34.

48. Harrington Emerson, *Efficiency as a Basis for Operation and Wages* (New York, 1909), pp. 193, 222.

49. Robert Franklin Hoxie, *Scientific Management and Labor* (1915; reprint ed., New York, 1966), p. 90; Braverman, "Labor and Monopoly Capital," pp. 23, 31; Nadworny, *Scientific Management*, pp. 72, 77–78.

occupations, into useful factory hands. After struggling for a while to conquer their listless or restive habits, they either renounce the employment spontaneously, or are dismissed by the overlookers on account of inattention."[50] A similar obstacle confronted the aggressive management movement and, to a lesser extent, most late-nineteenth and twentieth-century capitalists. They used the same solution as their predecessors: recruit a young, flexible labor force, willing to play the guinea pig, unfettered by craft traditions and dysfunctional work routines. William Osler would have applauded the virtual unanimity with which older workers were labeled unadaptable. An industrial psychiatrist for the Metropolitan Life Insurance Company wrote of five kinds of employee crises. The fifth was the crisis of the older employee:

> He is a touchy individual, and criticism of his actions is always hampered by the very human warmth and respect his long record generates. Yet it is true that to grow old gracefully is a very difficult art. Time does indeed "march on." Old ways give place to new, and the old employees cling to their timeworn ways, suspicious of the young men and their newfangled methods.[51]

Paul Cherington, professor of marketing at the Harvard Graduate School of Business Administration, argued that American business was being strangled by a surfeit of old men in young men's jobs. The approach of middle age, Cherington said, could be observed in the appearance of such qualities as lack of adaptability, devotion to routine, reluctance to adventure, chronic impatience, and rigidity.[52]

The Blackford system of character analysis was something of a second cousin to scientific management, having no interest in how work was carried on, but sharing with the larger movement a fascination with objective standards and the belief that just as there was one right way to do every job, so also was there for every job one right type of worker. Ostensibly, Katherine Blackford had little to say about older workers. Her work contains only one extended reference to age, and that a warning to employers to avoid rigid age regulations: "Years, as we have seen, are not always the test of a man's age. Youthfulness is

50. Quoted in Stephen A. Marglin, "What do Bosses Do? The Origins and Functions of Hierarchy in Capitalist Production," *Review of Radical Political Economics* 6 (Summer 1974): 100.
51. Lydia G. Giberson, "Emotional First-Aid Stations in Industry," *Personnel* 16 (1939–40): 14. See also, Philadelphia Industrial Relations Association, Employment Problems Committee, "Report on Older Workers," *Personnel Journal* 17 (1938–39): 104.
52. "Why Can't We Modernize Manpower?" *American Business* 6 (May 1936): 34. For dissident voices, see Richard S. Schultz, "Abilities and Attitudes of Older Employees," *Personnel* 15 (1938–39): 42–43, and Otto Pollak, "Conservatism in Later Maturity in Old Age," *American Sociological Review* 8 (April 1943): 175–79.

of the spirit and is not measured by calendars and birthdays. The man who looks young for his years is usually advancing. He who looks older than he should be is slipping backward."[53] As the statement indicates, however, physical appearance was fundamental to the Blackford system, the exterior a sound measure of inner qualities. Employers should never expect successful physical effort from the "frail"; "rigidity of joints" was evidence of obstinacy; an aggressive type had "firm, elastic or hard flesh" rather than "soft, or flabby flesh"; and so on.[54]

Certain physical characteristics were better than others. An organization survived, according to Blackford, to the extent that the employment supervisor insured that it was not built of "soft, weak human material." Aggressive types were essential for almost every white-collar function, including specialty selling, wholesale selling, insurance selling, real estate selling, bond selling, advertising, soliciting, newspaper reporting, law (trial of cases), promotion of enterprise, organizing, politics, collecting, foremanship, superintendency, sales management, advertising management, general management, and the company presidency.[55]

In spite of Blackford's caveat about age restrictions, her work was saturated with a youth bias. Industrial disturbances, she claimed, occurred when workers were imperfectly suited to their jobs because employers selected men unfitted for their tasks. This was rhetoric, of course, designed to sell the system; but for older workers it was rhetoric with a vengeance, for it implied that the existing, older (as opposed to the potential, younger) work force was composed of misfits. When Blackford suggested the need for society to begin early in youth to develop and determine attitudes and abilities, when she discussed the "young person's" inclinations and preferences, the point was clear: concentrate on the young, for the old are beyond redemption.[56]

This focus on matching worker and job was also present in the industrial health and safety movements. Although these movements originated in part in Progressivism's concern for social justice, each was also generated by several

53. Katherine M. H. Blackford, *Employers' Manual: Instructions to Employment Supervisors and Other Executives in the Use of the Blackford Employment Plan* (New York, 1912), p. 29. Samuel Haber links Blackford to scientific management through Harrington Emerson (*Efficiency and Uplift*, p. 56).

54. Katherine M. H. Blackford and Arthur Newcomb, *Analyzing Character: The New Science of Judging Men; Misfits in Business, The Home and Social Life*, 2d ed. (New York, 1916), pp. 134, 405; Katherine M. H. Blackford and Arthur Newcomb, *The Right Job: How to Choose, Prepare for, and Succeed in It, A Treatise for Parents, Guardians, Teachers and Vocational Counselors*, 2 vols. (New York, 1924), 1: 146–47.

55. Blackford, *Employers' Manual*, p. 21; Blackford and Newcomb, *Right Job*, 1: 148.

56. Blackford and Newcomb, *Analyzing Character*, pp. 9, 10, 13, 36–37. See also Alfred Rossiter, *A Pocket Manual for Character Analysts and Employment Managers: Based on the Blackford System* (n.p., 1915), pp. 7, 20.

notions of efficiency. Insofar as this was true, older workers did not fare well. Employers in the railroad industry found in the rapidly developing system of seniority a convenient explanation for the shameful accident situation in the first decade of the century.[57] Older workers were also held responsible for higher accident rates in industries in which the installation of piecework systems had resulted in a premium on speed.[58] In each case there was just enough truth to the charge for it to have some impact. Insurance companies warned employers of the wide variety of occupations considered dangerous for those over sixty or even fifty years of age. One insurance list contained: driving and caring for horses, trucking, loading or unloading cars or trucks, piling and handling raw material, lumbering and logging, moulding, carpentry on scaffolds or buildings, milling, painting from ladder or scaffold, washing windows, work on any elevated platform or which required climbing, any machine or production work that required stooping, lifting, or handling of heavy objects, pick-and-shovel work, work in yards or around tracks, any jobs where there was an occupational disease hazard or excessive heat, sweeping in heavy machine shops or hazardous plants, oiler, and nightwatchman.[59]

POST-1915: THE VALUE OF THE OLDER WORKER

Before 1915 managerial activity had been dominated by efficiency motivation, and older workers were seen largely as inefficient burdens; after 1915, although age discrimination in hiring continued to worsen, a number of firms, supported by scientific managers and industrial psychologists of the twenties, came to see older employees as valuable for their potential contributions to reduced labor turnover, work-force control, and social conservatism.

Two analyses of scientific management published in 1915 reflect a nascent ambivalence about the appropriate role of the older worker. Horace Drury, though familiar with Taylor's statements on the need to hire superior individuals, pointed to the Watertown arsenal, where no discharges had taken place when scientific management was instituted, and to the Tabor and Link-Belt plants, where "the old employees . . . were retained under the new system."[60] Writing for the United States Industrial Commission in 1915, Robert Hoxie repeated the

57. *Railroad Trainmen's Journal* 21 (December 1904): 907 (editorial).

58. John Wrench, "Speed Accidents: A Study of the Relation Between Piecework and Industrial Accidents," Birmingham, England, University, Faculty of Commerce and Social Science, *Discussion Papers, Series E: Social Science Methodology*, no. 17 (May 1972), pp. 3, 7, 10.

59. L. C. Carey, "Safe Occupations for the Aged Worker," *National Safety News* 13 (April 1926): 21.

60. Drury, *Scientific Management*, pp. 160, 66–67.

arguments of organized labor: scientific management "tends to displace all but the fastest workers, . . . shortens the tenure of service, . . . tends to undermine the worker's health, shortens his period of industrial activity and earning power, and brings on premature old age." Although reluctant to concede Taylor's claim that the system protected workers against the speedup and exhaustion, Hoxie found that older, inefficient workers had not been turned out of plants operating under scientific management.[61] The disparate policies that Drury and Hoxie observed in the hiring and maintenance of older workers illustrate that the economic system was a sophisticated mechanism, for which the older worker was not one entity but several, to be manipulated as circumstances would dictate, as the needs of the system changed, and to the extent that existing notions of community and friendship would allow.

Turnover, a factor of some importance in the relationship between age and work, first became a serious problem on Detroit assembly lines in the years after 1914 and for a large proportion of American industry during the First World War, when firms had to train large numbers of new workers.[62] Corporate planning departments (the counterpart of government efficiency commissions) usually recommended transferring older employees to new jobs rather than discharging them when they became relatively inefficient; superannuated employees were to be transferred to a "reserve department," where they would be employed in work of a " 'fill-in' character."[63]

As studies of turnover began to reveal that workers over twenty-five were more likely to stay with their employers, the older worker became, for a limited number of companies, a money-making proposition. To some extent, the new interest in turnover was a function of advances in cost accounting, for it was now much easier to isolate any particular cost and its relationship to the total cost of the product. An older, less efficient worker might be tolerated and kept on if, in an accounting sense, his work, relative to that of a hypothetical replacement, was efficient. But decreased labor turnover was also conceived as a method of building conservative values into one's work force, an exercise that assumed special importance in the years immediately following World War I and in the late 1930s. Employers knew that a strike posed a whole range of different

---

61. Hoxie, *Scientific Management and Labor*, pp. 15–17, 97.
62. Fred H. Colvin, *Labor Turnover, Loyalty and Output: A Consideration of the Trend of the Times as Shown by the Results of War Activities in the Machine Shops and Elsewhere* (New York, 1919), p. vii; Lillian Erskine and Treadwell Cleveland, Jr., "New Men for Old: The Hiring and Firing Problem in Industry," *Everybody's Magazine* 36 (April 1917): 424.
63. Harry A. Hopf, "The Planning Department as a Factor in the Modern Office Organization," *Efficiency Society Journal* 4 (November 1915): 8.

questions for older workers than for younger ones, and that their responses to those questions were more likely to be conservative.

Management must have learned a great deal from the 1915 Hartford strike, where Pratt and Whitney employees went out for the eight-hour day without a reduction in wages. Of 3,000 employees, only 1,152 struck, and a substantial proportion of those who remained at work were older.[64] Although it is possible that in this case, the issue, the eight-hour day, did not have much appeal for older workers, other evidence suggests another explanation. Older workers *had* taken part in much of the shorter-hour agitation; for many of them, the result was an inability to secure employment when the strikes were over. They remained on the strike rolls of their locals, drawing whatever benefits fellow workers could provide.[65] For some, the frustration of unemployment became so great that they were tempted to break with the union. During the 1922 Denver printing strike, union correspondent Harry Rapp reported his astonishment that a seventy-three-year-old man had "ratted" (scabbed). "When a man that old backslides and deserts his fellows," said Rapp, "you can arrive at but one conclusion: His extreme age has affected his mentality. No sane man could be persuaded to play a renegade's part at 73 years of age."[66]

According to Peter Friedlander's recent study of class and culture in a United Automobile Workers' local in the late 1930s, the conservatism of the older workers was a product not of fears of unemployment but of their continuing ties to European peasant culture. These first-generation immigrants were fearful, submissive, and therefore laggards in the union movement, because of their reluctance to challenge constituted authority—in this case, management. Friedlander's argument that these attitudes were built into these men, rather than situational, is based on the observation that when the union had organized the Detroit plant and signed the contract, submissiveness persisted, only its object was now the union, as the first-generation workers became deeply loyal to their new leaders.[67]

A version of Friedlander's generational explanation was a part of business ideology. Employers realized that older workers had a different set of values than younger workers, and that social stability could be enhanced by maintaining, or reestablishing, links for the transmission of the older generation's social

64. *Iron Age* 96 (7 October 1915): 850–51; Marion A. Bills, "Stability of Office Workers and Age at Employment," *Journal of Personnel Research* 5 (April 1927): 476.

65. *Typographical Journal* 31 (July 1907): 84.

66. Ibid. 61 (September 1922): 322.

67. Peter Friedlander, *The Emergence of a UAW Local, 1936–1939: A Study in Class and Culture* (Pittsburgh, 1975), pp. 46, 73, 98.

conservatism. Testifying before a Senate committee investigating unemployment in the late 1920s, James T. Loree, general manager of the Delaware and Hudson Company, emphasized how his railroad often employed three generations of the same family because the older generations, though less efficient, had a positive influence on the younger men. An Indiana mine superintendent found that by maintaining a reasonable quota of workers over forty-five he had improved the morale of the entire work force and eliminated wildcat strikes. In 1917, a family-owned and operated sawmilling company sought to maintain older workers for their loyalty and pride in their work, as well as for the stability these values implied for the company's operations. The company could avoid "an irresponsible working force. . . . The boys they trained as apprentices are working side by side with them and absorb the traditions of the shop."[68] At the same time, the White Motor Company of Cleveland was in the midst of an analysis of the age distribution of its work force which would reveal that its average worker was only twenty-six years old. Seeking some compromise between order and efficiency, the company concluded that the relative youth of its work force was responsible for its costly turnover problem, for younger workers were restless and changeable. Within three years the company had raised the average age of its employees to over forty. Turnover was down, and the shop was managed through committees. According to one observer of the changes at White Motor, the experience of the older workers "makes a most effective balance wheel and aids greatly in securing a safe interpretation of the newer ideas and methods of management. The younger men prevent the management from staying in a rut, and the older men keep the changes within commercial bounds."[69]

During the 1930s, anxiety over social upheaval brought increased attention to potential sources of stability. Excessive radicalism, associated in the public mind with youth and immaturity, could be countered with age. Research, none of it of lasting scientific validity, supported the perception of old age as a period of conservatism. In 1930 and 1931, E. K. Strong pointed out that likes, dislikes, interests, and ambitions changed less from age twenty-five to sixty-five than from fifteen to twenty-five. Three years later, social psychologist Floyd L. Ruch presented data that he believed demonstrated that older people not only per-

68. Frank Disston, "How We Hold Our Men," *System* 31 (February 1917): 118, and 116, 120, 122; Senate, *Hearings on Unemployment, 1928–29*, pp. 101, 115–16; letter from Indiana miner, *Coal Age* 35 (February 1930): 11.

69. Colvin, *Labor Turnover*, p. 41, and vi–vii, 39–40; Hoxie, *Scientific Management*, p. 97; Ralph E. Heilman, "Do You Keep Your Men Too Long?" *System* 33 (April 1918): 539–41. See also Tamara K. Hareven, "Family Time and Industrial Time: Family and Work in a Planned Corporation Town, 1900–1924," in Tamara K. Hareven, ed., *Family and Kin in Urban Communities: 1700–1930* (New York, 1977), pp. 187–207.

formed less well than younger people on learning tests, but had "greater difficulty in learning those materials which demand a tearing down of old habits." Ruch concluded that the physical deficiencies found among the elderly were the result of changes in the neuromuscular tissues, and he reasoned that these physical changes were likely to induce social conservatism: "The further a proposed change or reform deviates from their past experience the harder it is for them to grasp its significance or appreciate the need of it."[70] For employers this meant that older workers would be more likely to resist "outside influences and agitation," a prospect of considerable importance, especially after the economy turned downward in 1937.[71]

That employers were receptive to and influenced by such considerations is evident in a 1938 survey carried out by the National Association of Manufacturers (NAM). This massive study revealed that employers thought older and younger workers substantially alike in every area but one—cooperation. Over half of the respondents found workers over age forty more cooperative; only about 5 percent found them less so. Of 604 supplemental statements submitted, 223 praised the work habits of their older employees. Ninety-three of these stressed the loyalty and cooperation of older workers, 88 their stable viewpoint and general understanding of management's problems and needs.[72] This analysis had its analogue even among New Deal liberals like Secretary of Labor Frances Perkins, who in late February 1938 announced that American industry had an "overabundance of youth. They have the courage and energy of youth in their dealings with industry and none of the wisdom and practical common sense of those older men with families to support, homes to keep up and children to send to school." A number of industries, Perkins said, would be better off negotiating with older workers. "More could be accomplished," she said, "through the stability of people who have gone by youth and can think in terms of their whole range of experience."[73]

By 1935, a number of studies of health problems as a function of age had demonstrated that older people made reasonably good workers. One of the first, a 1925 study of 1,819 factory workers of the Norton Company in Massachusetts, concluded that for every worker not able to work after age sixty, there were two

70. Floyd L. Ruch, "The Differential Decline of Learning Ability in the Aged as a Possible Explanation of Their Conservatism," *Journal of Social Psychology* 5 (August 1934): 331, 335.
71. Philadelphia Industrial Relations Association, "Report on Older Workers," p. 105.
72. National Association of Manufacturers, *Workers Over 40*, A Survey by the National Association of Manufacturers of its Member Companies to Determine the Status of Workers 40 and Over (New York, 1938), pp. 7, 20.
73. Perkins speech at Private School Teachers Association, quoted in *New York Times*, 20 February 1938, pt. 2, p. 1.

that could. Older workers were generally in good health, and few had signs of degenerative disease.[74] Four years later, another study concluded that a worker's highest earning capacity could be significantly prolonged by medical supervision and skillful placement after age fifty.[75] In 1930, employers who would use illness rates as an explanation for age discrimination had to contend with statistical evidence that employees between twenty-five and forty years old were more likely to be sick (defined as two or more days out of work) than those between forty and sixty. The lowest incidence of sickness was found in the fifty-five-to-sixty-four age group. A public-service company in Massachusetts considering compulsory retirement for those over seventy found that the illness experience of that group compared favorably with that of younger employees.[76] Research published in 1935 showed that up to age sixty-three, disabling diseases occurred most often among employees in their early thirties.[77] Moreover, in the late 1920s studies began to appear indicating that older workers suffered fewer, if more costly, accidents.[78]

CONTINUED DISCRIMINATION

Neither the demands of social stability nor the new health studies suddenly made an anachronism of age discrimination. Most employers continued to prefer younger to older workers. Even the NAM survey reveals as much.[79] In the broadest sense, the choice was usually between a stable, conservative work force that blended youth with age and produced moderate short-term efficiency, and a more mobile, potentially more radical and militant work force made up largely of highly productive younger workers. The choice was between two kinds of efficiency—productive and social—and between two attitudes toward future profits, one more immediate than the other. Within this continuum compounded of control and productivity, employers were sometimes able to achieve one without sacrificing the other. This was the case with turnover reduction, for here the older worker offered both efficiency and stability. Group incentives,

74. W. I. Clark and E. B. Simmons, "Old Workers in Industry Remain in Good Health," *Nation's Health* 7 (December 1925): 812–14.

75. W. Irving Clark, "The Fate of Old Employees," *Journal of Industrial Hygiene* 11 (January 1929): 2.

76. Dean K. Brundage, "The Incidence of Illness among Wage Earning Adults," *Journal of Industrial Hygiene* 12 (December 1930): 385–86.

77. U.S., Treasury Department Public Health Service, "A General View of the Causes of Illness and Death at Specific Ages," by Selwyn D. Collins, in *Public Health Reports* 50 (22 February 1935): 245.

78. C. S. Slocombe, "The Dangerous Age in Industry," *National Safety News* 22 (July 1930): 68–69. This study is of workers on the Boston Elevated Railway.

79. NAM, *Workers Over 40*, p. 12.

popular after Elton Mayo's Hawthorne experiments of the early 1930s, were similarly attractive, for they allowed corporations to maintain an older work force by stimulating slower workers to acceptable levels of productivity.[80] For the most part, however, the corporation operated on the efficiency end of the continuum, and personnel managers, unconvinced of the viability of an older work force, consistently practiced various forms of discrimination.

In the health movement, older workers remained pawns in larger games, their needs ancillary to industrial efficiency and control. Full of the typical Progressive passion for order and standards, statistician Hoffman had in 1906 called for the establishment of physical requirements for entry and continuance in different trades and occupations, as an aid in "eliminating the physically unfit from recognized unhealthful or injurious employments." He recommended applying the physical and medical theories then used by the army, navy, police, and fire departments to industrial employments.[81] A half century later, however, no such standards had been developed, largely, one suspects, because they would have functioned at cross purposes to compulsory retirement programs.[82]

The absence of job-performance standards did not deter government and industry from developing and applying the physical examination, even though the technique implied that standards existed and workers were affected as if they did. Examinations were apparently first used in the 1890s; by the late 1920s about one firm in five put its workers through a physical.[83] These examinations served several purposes. They played a role in the administration of retirement and pension systems, for some employers used the exams to exclude unreasonably large numbers of older applicants from employment.[84] Railroad workers believed that their employers were using the physical to enforce age restrictions, neglecting its administration when labor requirements dictated, and as a weapon against labor organizations. During the 1930s, twenty-seven railroad employees in the vicinity of Council Bluffs, Iowa petitioned the president of the United

80. C. C. Balderston, *Group Incentives: Some Variations in the Use of Group Bonus and Gang Piece Work*, Industrial Relations Department, Wharton School of Finance and Commerce, University of Pennsylvania, Research Studies, vol. 9 (Philadelphia, 1930), pp. 92–93.

81. "Physical and Medical Aspects," pp. 18, 17.

82. A. G. Kammer, "Optional Retirement Plans: Their Implications for the Industrial Physician," *Industrial Medicine and Surgery* 21 (July 1952): 343.

83. *Railroad Trainmen's Journal* 17 (November 1900): 959–63; U.S., Congress, Senate, Committee on Education and Labor, *Unemployment in the United States: Hearings Pursuant to S.R. 219, A Resolution Providing for an Analysis and Appraisal of Reports on Unemployment and Systems for Prevention and Relief Thereof, Together with Senate Report No. 2072,* 11, 12, 13, 14, 17, 18 and 19 December 1928, 9 and 14 January, 7, 8 and 9 February 1929 (Washington, D.C., 1929), p. 14.

84. New York State, Senate, Committee on Civil Service, *Second Report of the Senate Committee on Civil Service in Relation to the Standardization of the Public Employments of the State,* no. 29 (Albany, 1917), pp. 20–21; A. A. Graham, "Old-Age Civic Pensions," *Machinists' Monthly Journal* 23 (September 1911): 855–56.

States to sign the railroad retirement bill recently passed by Congress. They argued that railroads without pension plans were "at the present time giving a rigid physical examination and in many cases taking the old men out of service mostly on account of their eyes."[85] The Mid-Continent Oil Company admitted that it was one of many enterprises that applied the physical examination more rigidly to older applicants than younger ones, a practice justified, it said, because of "unjust claims" against the company by employees with physical defects. Through the rigid physical examination, the company availed itself of the protection available under state law, according to which claims were not allowable if the employer could show that the employee had the physical ailment before employment. The problem, concluded a company official, "is not so much with age as it is with physical condition."[86] Thus, older workers were often victims of an open-ended device that was seldom applied in the interests of health.

Supported by the familiar pillars of efficiency and profit, age discrimination received additional aid from the youth cult of the twentieth century. By the 1920s, this focus on youth was an inescapable aspect of the national experience. American culture demanded that its women return, via the shortened skirt, to adolescence. It found in Charles Lindbergh's spectacular achievement at twenty-five a cause for self-congratulation; it allowed the young the freedom to set their own standard of conduct or morality. But why did the youth cult exist at all? What accounts for its potency in the third decade of the century? With his phrase "technological filiarchy," historian Gilman Ostrander has given us cause and effect. The changing relationship between age and youth was the product of the advanced stages of the Industrial Revolution, characterized by the decline of the farm and the rise of the factory and, especially in the 1920s, by the extraordinarily rapid development and spread of technology, particularly the automobile and the assembly line, which had a major impact on American culture. This was, according to Ostrander, "an era of technological progress," in which "it was expected that the sons and the daughters would enjoy advantages that the parents had not been able to enjoy, in a mechanically better world than the parents had known." Ostrander concludes: "The Roaring Twenties consisted of nothing less than the blanket repudiation of the traditional farm-oriented, church-oriented, somewhat patriarchal moral order of the Protestant Republic,

85. Letter with petition, 19 August 1935, Franklin Delano Roosevelt Papers, Franklin Delano Roosevelt Library, Hyde Park, New York, Official Files, 1095, "Railroad Retirement Board" (hereafter referred to as FDR-OF); *Railroad Trainmen's Journal* 17 (November 1900): 959; ibid. 18 (February 1901): 150; ibid. (October 1901): 834.
86. A. S. James, "No Hiring Age Limit is Fixed by Mid-Continent Companies," *National Petroleum News* 28 (25 November 1936): 23–24.

and the crux of the revolution was the reversal of the order of authority in a society from age to youth. . . . American society looked to youth for guidance."[87]

To Ostrander, then, rejuvenation was a natural process, emerging from economic change, age turning over the reins of power to a new generation of youthful technocrats. But why, if the process was natural and inevitable, was it carried on so artificially, so self-consciously? It seems possible that the youth cult of the 1920s was not so much a recognition of a new order as it was one stage in a long-term crisis in Western and American culture. At the center of the American version was the fear that the culture was, as psychologist G. Stanley Hall insisted, in the throes of senescence:

> In fine, not only has the Western world now lost the exhilarating sense of progress that has for generations sustained and inspired it but civilization faces to-day dangers of decay such as have never confronted it since the incursion of the barbarians and of the Moslems into Europe. Other more disastrous wars are possible. Class hatred and the antagonisms of capital and labor, national and individual greed, race jealousies and animosities, the ferment of Bolshevism, the ascendancy of the ideals of *kultur* over those of culture in our institutions for higher education in every land, industrial stagnation and unemployment, the crying lack of leaders and the dominance of mediocrity everywhere, the decay of faith and the desiccation of religion, the waning confidence in democracy: these are the prospects we must face.[88]

Faced with declining natural resources (the close of the frontier), with what was perceived as a weakening of the immigrant pool, aware that with every year the population grew older,[89] Americans seemed bent on proving that their culture was, in the analogy popularized in Hall's earlier work, only in its adolescent stage, looking forward to maturity rather than back on it. The attempt partook of farce and tragedy, with no better symbol than the aging Babbitt of Sinclair Lewis, romping with the youthful "bunch" as if by returning to play he might

87. Gilman M. Ostrander, *American Civilization in the First Machine Age: 1890–1940* (New York, 1970), pp. 238–39, 273, and chap. 6. See also Loire Brophy, "New Perspective in.Advertising and Personnel," *Advertising and Selling* 26 (21 November 1935): 28; Paula S. Fass, *The Damned and the Beautiful: American Youth in the 1920s* (New York, 1977); Gilbert Osofsky, "Symbols of the Jazz Age: The New Negro and Harlem Discovered," *American Quarterly* 17 (Summer 1965): 229–38; and Thomas R. Cole, "Patriarchal Prolongevity: The End of Old Age in America, 1890–1925," Paper presented at the Annual Meeting of the Organization of American Historians, New Orleans, April 1979.

88. G. Stanley Hall, *Senescence: The Last Half of Life* (New York, 1923), p. 432. See also Margaret Mead, *Blackberry Winter: My Earlier Years* (New York, 1972), p. 139.

89. Hall, *Senescence*, p. 31; Ira S. Wile, "'Youth Waneth by Increasing,'" *Mental Hygiene* 12 (July 1928): 516–20.

undo the cultural knots that strangled him.[90] The corporations, apparently in need of regular transfusions to avert stagnation, required, in the personnel language of the day, "fresh blood," "new blood," and "young blood."[91] From the staid Du Pont companies to the efficiency societies, employees had to be more than competent; they had to be "bright" and "snappy"; they had to have "bustle." Should a worker's output decline, his "pep" was in question; a medical examination, the obvious solution. A change in diet or living habits might work wonders: "He recovers his 'pep,' his producing ability increases, and his accidents decrease. He has his old fire and carefulness. He is a profitable employe and not a drag."[92]

The Salesman: A Case Study

The experience of the salesman—the foremost occupational symbol of the twentieth-century economy of consumption, distribution, and mass markets—illustrates a variety of these phenomena. It also provides evidence for the hypothesis that older workers were more likely to suffer employment handicaps in industries where the development of new methodologies was abrupt and sporadic.[93] Neither an executive nor a member of the working class, the salesman remained outside the corporate and union bureaucracies, which by 1920 were beginning to protect minimal numbers of workers from unemployment and old age. He was uniquely vulnerable to changes in fashion and consumer taste, to

90. Sinclair Lewis, *Babbitt* (New York, 1942).

91. Heilman, "Do You Keep Your Men Too Long?" p. 540; letter Ernest McCullough, *New York Times*, 4 August 1929, pt. 3, p. 5.

92. L. A. Phelps, "Employment, Medical Supervision and Safety," *Efficiency Society Journal* 6 (April 1917): 213; Irénée Du Pont to A. Felix Du Pont, 8 May 1915, Irénée Du Pont Papers, Eleutherian Mills Historical Library, Greenville, Wilmington, Delaware, Vice-President Files, ID-13, file "Employment, 1914–1917."

93. This hypothesis was developed by Elliott Dunlap Smith, professor of industrial engineering at Yale University and a member of the Taylor Society. In several forums, including an important meeting of the American Management Association in 1930, Smith argued that the obsolescence of older workers was not, as others had said, a function of the psychological deficiencies incident to the aging process, but in fact followed from management's own failure to apply its principles scientifically. Continuity was crucial. Forced unemployment was most likely to occur "when periods of managerial and engineering stagnation are followed by spurts of intensive progress." Where basic job requirements had remained stable, as for carpenters, machinists, executives, and engineers, workers prospered in middle age; where development of new methods was abrupt and sporadic, as in selling, managing, and paper-box manufacturing, older employees suffered from unnecessary layoffs. See Smith statement in "Employment Age Limitations," Abstract of Discussions at a Meeting of Eastern Section of the Taylor Society, Boston, 5 April 1929, in *Bulletin of the Taylor Society* 14 (October 1929): 223–24; *Iron Age* 125 (6 February 1930): 453; James H. Gildea testimony, in House, Subcommittee on Labor, *Investigation of Unemployment*, p. 69.

the competitive markets of the early twentieth century and the business cycle. Although the salesman's skills would seem to have been relatively easily transferable from one industry or firm to another, this aspect of the occupation was circumscribed by the increasingly sophisticated nature of products and sales training.

Between 1900 and 1930, salesmen, particularly those over forty, were victimized by changing definitions and requirements of their occupation, a revolution as real and disruptive as simultaneous developments in the technology of automobile manufacture. This revolution began in 1903 with the publication of *Salesmanship*, a self-styled first attempt to establish a literature on the science of selling. The effort began innocuously enough. Salesmen had to know their goods and have an affable and courteous disposition. A knowledge of psychology and human nature was considered of some importance, as was the related and, for the time, clever idea of "suggestibility," or inducing purchases through suggestion. Almost from the first issue, however, there was some recognition in the journal that older salesmen might be ill suited to this new professionalism. These early pieces at once denied that a problem had to exist and warned of its coming:

> Let me say that a man is only as old as he acts, and it is his own fault if he is shelved for a younger man. There is no profession where experience is more needed than in the practice of salesmanship, and the one who in middle life keeps up with the procession in thoughts, customs and habits, is of more value to the house he represents than any youth, no matter how active or brilliant he may be. But if he foolishly relies on past individual experiences and does not make an effort to assimilate the ideas of the progressive element, he is sure to be pushed aside.[94]

In little more than two years, the journal had dropped its tentative approach and had taken up a full-scale attack on the unambitious men in the "Used-to-Be class," the old men with their anecdotes of crucial big sales. Every organization had its "imitation fighting man," who corrupted the better elements of the sales force and collapsed under pressure:

> Their salesmanship is not genuine tried and proven gold, like that of the other veterans, but only tinfoil made up to resemble it. They are stage salesmen, all show and no reality—stuffed figures without life—mere scarecrow bluffs. Bluff and a certain outward appearance is their entire

94. R. N. Hull, "The Fourth Profession," *Salesmanship* 1 (November 1903): 143; *Salesmanship* (July–August 1903): 24, 31, 36, 47; (September 1903): ibid. 66 ("Our Creed").

stock in trade. They bluff their way into a position, hold onto it with bluff, and let go of it only when their stock of bluff is played out.[95]

The type was usually identified with the older age groups.

The critique focused on the inability of older salesmen to adopt the methods of the modern corporation or to adapt to a changing economic and technological environment. These deficiencies were variously ascribed to a natural stubbornness that comes with age, to learning disabilities, and to prejudice against anything new. At the Du Pont Company, a sixty-five-year-old salesman named Elder confronted reality rather than theory when the assistant director of sales and the vice-president requested his retirement under the company's new pension plan because he was "too old a man to adopt our present methods" and because he was not sufficiently active to adequately cover his large territory.[96] Older salesmen were further disadvantaged when, after 1920, corporations seeking people with technical training turned increasingly to colleges. Rather than educate thirty- and forty-year-old workers to market the new technology, General Electric hired engineers and Bristol-Myers recruited college graduates with training in pharmacy, medicine, or dentistry. It was commonly believed that older salesmen could be trained and retrained only with recently developed techniques designed to overcome inherent resistance.[97]

These policies reflected real changes in marketing methods which emerged with chain stores, retail consolidations, industrial concentration, and scientific buying. As chemists, mechanical engineers, and other technical personnel replaced shop superintendents as buyers of industrial products, and as chain-store buyers, aided by statistical departments and laboratories, replaced the grocer and the druggist as purchasers of consumer goods, the old-time salesman who had succeeded on the basis of personal contact and the force of personality became an anachronism. Another technical consideration—the tendency, par-

95. W. C. Holman, "Ginger Talks," ibid. 6 (May 1906): 190–91; (April 1906): 143–44.

96. Norris A. Brisco, "Selecting Salespeople," *Salesmanship* 4 (November 1916): 386; Frank L. Scott, "What is the Older Man's Place on the Sales Force?" *Printers' Ink* 127 (19 June 1924): 33; J. W. Hamilton, "Getting Salesmen to See It Your Way," *Sales Management* 1 (October 1918): 7; *Sales Management* 6 (January 1924): 382; Assistant Director of Sales to J. A. Haskell, 16 February 1905; J. A. Haskell to T. C. Du Pont, 27 January 1905, in E.I. Du Pont de Nemours & Company Papers, Eleutherian Mills Historical Library, Greenville, Wilmington, Delaware, series II, part 2, box 816, folder 59, "Pensions."

97. Earl A. Means, "Why Bristol-Myers' Men Stick," *Sales Management* 32 (15 May 1933): 507; W. A. Sredenschek et al., *Sales Personnel Techniques*, American Management Association, Marketing Series, no. 39 (New York, 1940), pp. 15–17; Joyce Oliver, "Does It Pay to Attempt to Train Seasoned Salesmen?" *Sales Management* 33 (20 October 1933): 410, 414; R. C. Hay, "How American Radiator Gives Old Men New Sales Ideas," *Sales Management and Advertisers' Weekly* 14 (26 May 1928): 853.

ticularly after 1920, to market products toward youth—also induced employers to sell through younger personnel.[98]

The sales publications were never free from an emphasis on ambition, energy, determination, and industry as the critical ingredients of the first-rate salesman. But in 1905, and for some time thereafter, this reasonable reconstitution of the work and success methodology had been perverted by an overpowering focus on the physical requirements of salesmanship. *Salesmanship* initiated this development with its prominent features on the rhetoric of Theodore Roosevelt ("I wish to preach, not the doctrine of ignoble ease, but the doctrine of the strenuous life—the life of toil and effort, of labor and strife") and Harvard President Charles W. Eliot ("There is real pleasure and exhilaration in bodily exertion. . . . There is pleasure in mere struggle").[99] The first volumes of *The Salesman*, which began publication in 1909, pursued the theme relentlessly. In the intensely competitive world of sales and business, one was either a winner or a loser, weak or strong, one of the fittest or a misfit. Only perfect health could make possible the tireless physical effort required to achieve complete success in life. Occasionally the older salesman was singled out for explicit attention. "Some of you fellows," bellowed a sales manual published in 1913, "allow age to disqualify you! You sit around and groan and pine and whine. Quit that! Get busy and hustle and think! Use the Pompeian of Energy and get Youth-i-fied!"[100] A similar, if less strident concern with the physical demands of the profession was behind the efforts to pension Elder, the aging Du Pont salesman.[101]

Although stamina and endurance continued to be perceived as important qualities in the 1920s and 1930s, they were never as important as in the decade after 1905. After about 1915, however, the older salesman was faced with a related obstacle, one for which he could not prepare, even with regular exercise. Convinced of the crucial importance of matching person and task, and lacking

98. *Sales Management and Advertisers' Weekly* 16 (29 December 1928): 798 (editorial); M. A. Dean, "What Experience has Proved," *Salesmanship* 6 (February 1906): 63; Andrew L. Carmical, "To Sell Today—Appeal to Youth," *Sales Management and Advertisers' Weekly* 15 (22 September 1928): 645, 674–75.

99. *Salesmanship* 6 (January 1906): 8; ibid. (February 1906): 69; E. Ray Speare, "The 'Extra Ounce' Required," *Salesmanship* 6 (January 1906): 25–26; *Salesmanship* 1 (November 1903): 117. See also William O. Douglas, *Go East, Young Man, The Early Years: The Autobiography of William O. Douglas* (New York, 1974), p. 35.

100. James Withers Elliott, *Salesmanship: An Artistic Science* (New York, 1913), pp. 29–30; Harry Willis, "Are Salesmen Born or Made?" *Salesman* 1 (September 1909): 29–30; *Salesman* 2 (July 1910): 134–35; Roy Alden, "Building Mental Efficiency by Physical Exercise," *Sales Management* 5 (August 1923): 1011–12; Walter F. Wyman, "Mistakes I have Made in Hiring Salesmen," *Sales Management and Advertisers' Weekly* 16 (October 13, 1928): 126; Burton Laird, "Age-Limit for Salesmen," *Printers' Ink* 181 (7 October 1937): 80.

101. See note 96.

objective standards to guide the process, personnel managers were drawn for at least a decade to a group of pseudoscientists who claimed that character (and therefore ability to sell) could be inferred from physical appearance. After Katherine Blackford, whose theories had considerable influence in the personnel field, Grant Nablo, with superb photos designed to demonstrate relationships between size and shape of the head and behavior, was perhaps the best known. Although not all employers felt comfortable selecting their employees according to similarity with basic head or facial prototypes, opinion in the sales journals would indicate that opposition was limited and usually premised on the need to consider other factors as well as physiognomy. Speaking before the Chicago Managers' Association, Dr. J. M. Fitzgerald argued for the existence of three segments of personality—mental, spiritual, and physical. The last was the product of age, health, height, weight, and athletic tone of muscles. "We are," he concluded, "first of all things affected profoundly by the *physical* personality. More people are thus affected than by the other elements of personality."[102] Generally, the focus was on the face, and the analysis was usually such as to call age into question. The best salesmen were those with severe facial lines and full, rather than sunken, faces. Best of all was the aggressive type, identified by the slight hump on the nose, about one-quarter of the way down.[103]

At the retail level, applicants who survived the initial contact with the personnel manager because of an unusually well-preserved countenance faced another, also presumably scientific, variant of age discrimination. The age of the employee was expected to be suited to the department within the establishment. This could benefit the aging job-seeker: "mature" women, for example, were considered ideal for selling infants' wear, coats, dresses, suits and expensive fabrics; toiletries salespeople, on the other hand, were expected to be young enough to reflect "youth, attractiveness, and all the other qualifications that the buyers of this merchandise hope to gain through its use."[104] In the prosperous year of 1927, a Texas woman with fifteen years' retail sales experience was

102. J. M. Fitzgerald, "Ridding Your Personality of Its Minus Quantities," *Sales Management* 1 (June 1919): 175; R. M. Farmer, "The Selection and Training of Salesmen," *Sales Manager* 1 (October 1919): 59; Nablo, "The Value of Character and Ability Analysis in the Selection of Salesmen," *Salesmanship* 4 (1916): 448–52; Eugene Whitmore, "A Character Analyst Takes a Whirl at the Photographs," *Sales Management* 6 (October 1923): 25–26; Whitmore, "Sales Executives Criticise Reports of the Character Analysts," *Sales Management* 6 (November 1923): 153–54, 210.

103. Charles W. Alexander, "If You Need Salesmen Who Think and Stick," *Sales Management* 6 (November 1923): 189–90; Stanley Gibson, "Can You Pick Men Successfully?" *Opportunity* 1 (November 1923): 17–18.

104. James W. Fisk, "Organization of Retail Selling Force," *Salesmanship* 4 (November 1916): 380. This article contains results of a survey conducted by employers of the National Association of Corporation Schools, which indicates that age was, next to previous employment, the most important factor in selecting employees.

refused employment at a number of department stores; at one, she was informed that the work "would be too much of a tax for a lady of your age."[105] Discrimination in the retail trades was apparently particularly severe because the relatively simple nature of the work meant that stores could not justify even the minimal additional expense of retaining experienced salespeople.[106]

Discrimination in sales began to ease after 1924. Customers as well as personnel managers were put off by too much vigor, enthusiasm, confidence, and pep. Employers found older salesmen less likely to irritate difficult customers and more likely to succeed with the abusive customers called "hardshells." Corporations increasingly desired career men, willing to remain with the enterprise and learn the new, often complex product lines.[107] Sales executives in the printing trades seemed to agree that the more technical the product, the older the salesman could be and retain his efficiency; by the late 1930s they had also become firmly convinced of the excessive turnover costs that accrued to firms hiring younger salesmen. When *American Business* published its survey findings in 1937, demonstrating that the average age of "star" salesmen was forty-two and that older salesmen were the best producers in a number of lines, the problem would seem to have come full circle.[108]

AGE DISCRIMINATION BECOMES A SOCIAL AND POLITICAL PROBLEM

There were those, even in the late 1920s and early 1930s, who too easily dismissed age discrimination as a function of the youth fetish and pronounced its imminent demise[109] and others, of greater influence, who denied that a problem existed. Among the latter were Glenn A. Bowers and Murray Latimer, leading spirits behind Industrial Relations Counselors, Incorporated, a prestigious business advisory agency with links to major corporations. Bowers and Latimer shared the view that although hiring limits existed, they were related to demonstrable and legitimate job requirements.[110] In 1930 the Associated Industries argued that there was no general discrimination against workers over forty. Two years later the Bureau of the Census released a report based on 1930 figures which (given the massive problems with unemployment statistics) offered some

105. H. Sidney Smith, Jr., "'Too Old for a Store,'" *Opportunity* 21 (October 1933): 22.
106. Heilman, "Do You Keep Men Too Long," p. 541.
107. *Advertising and Selling* 18 (16 March 1932): 46; *New York Times*, 8 November 1930, p. 16; Scott, "Older Man's Place on the Sales Force," p. 36.
108. *Printers' Ink* 180 (15 July 1937): 65; ibid., 201 (4 December 1942): 17; ibid. 180 (8 July 1937): 49; *American Business* 7 (March 1937): 20–21; ibid. 7 (April 1937): 21, 37.
109. See, for example, *New York Times*, 18 May 1930, pt. 3, p. 10.
110. Glenn A. Bowers, "Employment, Wages, and Industrial Relations," *Factory and Industrial Management* 79 (February 1930): 327–28.

legitimate evidence that age discrimination between thirty-five and forty-five was less severe than had been thought. Unemployment for the group was estimated at less than 2.5 percent. But the Bureau's statistics also revealed unemployment among the fifty-five-to-fifty-nine age group of 7 percent, and over 13 percent for those between sixty and sixty-four.[111] Those who argued that age discrimination should not be taken seriously because the forty-five-to-sixty-four age group was a larger percentage of the labor force in 1930 than in 1890 were misguided; the increase, though real, would have occurred naturally, for the population itself was aging. It was, moreover, in part the product of the elimination from the work force of those over sixty-five and under twenty; child-labor legislation and retirement had, for the moment, eased the pressure on the middle-aged.[112]

Nonetheless, in the five years after 1925, age discrimination came to be perceived as the serious social problem it had been for more than two decades. A study by the New York State Committee on Old Age Security, completed in 1932, found hiring discrimination began at age thirty-five for men, thirty for women. The first bulletin of the California Department of Industrial Relations concluded that arbitrary discharge of workers because of age was becoming general policy in the late 1920s. A problem that might have been tolerated had it remained within the industrial working class and the unorganized middle class of salesmen, had by this time aroused concern in the increasingly organized public sector and in those professions, such as accounting and engineering, most dependent on the private sector.[113] As the economic system either released older workers or refused to hire them, organizations with an interest in old-age dependency came to share the sense of urgency. The American Association for Labor Legislation and the American Association for Old Age Security saw age discrimination as a problem to be met through the fuller development of public pension systems.[114]

This ferment produced the first intensive studies of age discrimination.

111. *New York Times*, 12 October 1932, p. 20.
112. *Dun's Review* 47 (February 1939): 39; *New York Times*, 19 November 1932, p. 14 (report of a study by Ralph G. Hurlin of the Russell Sage Foundation); *Automotive Industries* 73 (10 August 1935): 157, 174–77, 185.
113. *New York Times*, 19 November 1932, p. 17; *National Safety News* 21 (June 1930): 48; statement by Arthur W. Berresford, president of the American Engineering Council, in *New York Times*, 12 January 1930, p. 16; H. A. Wagner, "Forty and the Future," *Professional Engineer* 14 (October 1929): 13–15; letter from accountant, *New York Times*, 29 March 1930, p. 18.
114. Mss. paper by John B. Andrews, January 1922, in American Association for Labor Legislation Papers, Labor-Management Documentation Center, Labor and Industrial Relations Institute, Cornell University, Ithaca, New York, microfilm reel 65; American Association for Old Age Security Papers, Labor and Industrial Relations Institute, box 33, file "Old Age-Middle Age-Employment Handicaps, etc."

These inquiries, lacking in historical insight, pointed to the technological environment of the 1920s and to a variety of short-term factors, particularly pensions, group insurance, and workmen's compensation, which as explanations of age discrimination conveniently ignored the historical needs of a capitalist economy for efficiency and control. Even the data generated by the NAM demonstrated that these short-term factors were less important in the decision to establish an age limit than the perceived physical problems of the older worker.[115] Insurance company figures, less reliable because the companies had a vested interest in demonstrating that the underwriting of group life policies did not lead to discrimination, produced the same conclusion. Nonetheless, the social insurance argument had considerable appeal. The American Federation of Labor, eager to shift pension controls from the private corporations to the more neutral hands of the state and national governments, and unwilling to come to grips with the potential long-term divisiveness of the age discrimination issue for its members, leaned heavily on the contention that private benefit programs were conducive to discriminatory practices. A major segment of the corporate community also welcomed the opportunity to trace social dislocation to welfare policy.[116]

EASY SOLUTIONS

Unable to approach the real sources of discrimination within the corporations and government bureaucracies, Americans turned their attention to the distributive mechanism of the employment agency, much as farmers had once attacked the grain exchanges and as consumers in the 1970s would seek to explain rising food prices through reference to wholesale and retail elements in the food trade. Norman Thomas, in 1929 the Socialist party candidate for mayor of New York City, attacked dishonest private employment agencies and advocated a municipal agency to give special attention to placing men and women over age forty-five. Though Thomas's solution at best would only have shifted unemployment from one group to another, it could not be denied that agencies participated in the climate of discrimination.[117] A fifty-one-year-old New York City accountant, unemployed since the depression of 1920–21, wrote of his experience nine years later with two of the largest employment agencies in the city. At one

115. See results of NAM survey in *New York Times*, 21 March 1929, p. 23. Pensions, group insurance, and workmen's compensation and their relationship to age discrimination are treated in Dahlin, "The Economic Crisis."
116. *Iron Age* 134 (5 July 1934): 46; *New York Times*, 2 October 1929, p. 33; ibid., 7 October 1929, p. 27; ibid., 10 November 1929, pt. 2, p. 6.
117. *New York Times*, 11 October 1929, p. 4.

his interviewer, "making a circle with his blue pencil around my age, said: 'Mr.————, this will be your greatest drawback.'" At a small, exclusive office in midtown Manhattan, he was informed that the agent would "have to go by specifications."[118] Public agencies in Massachusetts enforced hiring age limits of fifty-five in general employment, forty-five in clerical and office positions. After 1915, some public employment agencies developed specialized departments to deal with the vocational problems of minors (often called "junior workers"), but there were no equivalent services for older workers.[119]

One cannot expect of an age that it possess a coherent, historically and culturally informed overview of its institutions; but one can expect that a society seriously interested in exploring the work problems of a major segment of its population would center its inquiry on the workplace. This did not occur. Instead, analysis focused on a series of short-term institutional factors that, once accepted as the cause of age discrimination, could and did serve as a vehicle for a critique of social legislation. The considerable interest in the 1920s in technology came closer to explaining discrimination, but the dominant view made of technology a liberating force, the progenitor of the "new leisure." Contemporary analyses ignored the matrix of conditions that had generated age discrimination in the late nineteenth century: a competitive economic system, primarily concerned with the intensification of labor and therefore in the speed of its technology, driven by market structures and a critical externality, the shorter working day; and depending for profit on superior workmen. The perspective of the late 1920s or early 1930s could not reveal that the new interest in middle-aged and older workers emerged as well from the economic system, as its compelling drive for efficiency was attenuated and supplemented by the desire for stability and control. It helped that research showed that older workers were not so terribly inefficient and that Americans had, by 1925, recovered from their worst fears of cultural senescence.

Summary

This analysis implies a good deal about the reform movement of the late 1920s: it was generated within the economic system; it served at least some employers; and the solutions implied in its own analysis were superficial and peripheral to the sources of age discrimination. The battle for reform, as it was first joined in the late 1920s, was not so much a real contest, with the outcome

118. Ibid., 29 March 1930, p. 18; ibid., 14 July 1931, p. 24.
119. "Employment Age Limitations," *Bulletin of the Taylor Society*, p. 227; Lescohier, *Working Conditions*, pp. 196–196n.

in doubt, as a ritual struggle, with both sides aware of the identity of the ultimate victor. It could be no other way. The solutions that might have made a difference, and made[120] the conflict real—massive job creation; a willingness to continue production with older forms of technology; a reduction in the operating speed of the technology—were not considered viable options. As William Osler had so clearly seen, a society that is dedicated to progress and allows its economic institutions to define its terms must learn to sacrifice the older generation for the younger.

Retirement and age discrimination emerged as important phenomena at the same time, and not coincidentally. Retirement was one of several means available to a business culture committed to restructuring the age components of the work force. Workers might be fired outright, of course, but (as later chapters indicate) such a policy was difficult for most public and private employers to carry out. Retirement was impersonal and egalitarian in its application. It allowed the powerful turn-of-the-century impulse toward efficiency to coexist with a system of labor-management relations that was still permeated with personal and human relationships. After 1915, a minority of employers found older workers attractive. Overall, however, discrimination did not diminish. Most employers continued to favor younger workers, and after 1925 retirement came to be seen as a realistic antidote to unemployment in depressed industries and in the economy at large.

120. See Margaret Mead, *And Keep Your Powder Dry: An Anthropologist Looks at America* (1942; reprint ed., New York, 1965), p. 42.

PART TWO CASE STUDIES IN THE EARLY
HISTORY OF RETIREMENT

3 Efficiency, Security, Community: Retirement in the Federal Civil Service

The first general piece of retirement legislation for federal employees was passed by a Republican Congress and signed into law by Democrat Woodrow Wilson in May of 1920. Amended many times, the measure remains the core of federal civil service retirement. It was the product of twenty-five years of public discussion, initiated by the ad hoc retirement program of Secretary of the Treasury L. C. Gage in 1897, nourished by the activities of the United States Civil Service Retirement Association and a number of other organizations of government employees, and sustained by the continued interest of the executive branch in bureaucratic efficiency. Theodore Roosevelt's Keep Commission, William Taft's Commission on Economy and Efficiency, and Woodrow Wilson's Bureau of Efficiency probed the relationship between superannuation and productivity and advocated a retirement program, but for some years their activity was insufficient to overcome divisions within the ranks of the retirement movement, fears of massive future public burdens, and the continued strength of the southern wing of the Democratic party, which stood to benefit from the status quo.

The 1920 legislation was designed to induce efficiency. Personal mechanisms for dealing with older employees were to be replaced by impersonal ones; the firing process was to be bureaucratized. The act was also intended to bring some measure of security to those retiring. On this, the pension recipient and the efficiency expert could find common ground, for what was for one an incentive to retire in favor of a more productive younger person was for the other relief from future anxiety. However, neither of these objectives—efficiency or security—was fully realized with the 1920 legislation. The minimal pension available under the act restricted its ability to break down the peculiar version of community that existed in most federal agencies well into the twentieth century. Discretion continued in the determination of employees to be retained. Reluctant to discharge employees to lives of poverty, agency heads took advantage of an optional extension provision in the law to allow even superannuated workers to remain at their posts. In 1926, the law was amended and annuities increased in order to provide an incentive sufficient to overcome the informal but powerful bonds between older employees and their superiors which for years had protected aging bureaucrats from the Progressive impulse toward efficiency.

AGING IN THE FEDERAL BUREAUCRACY

In 1903, the Treasury was one of several executive departments employing older personnel in substantial absolute numbers. Of 6,003 Treasury employees in the District of Columbia, 954 (15.9 percent) were between fifty and fifty-nine years of age; 660 (11 percent), between sixty and sixty-nine; 114 (1.9 percent), between seventy and seventy-nine; and twelve (0.2 percent), over eighty. The percentages were all close to the averages for District of Columbia departments. Older personnel were heavily concentrated in low-income clerical and subclerical occupations.[1] Chief Clerk Wallace Hills, responsible for hiring minor functionaries, was especially solicitous of those associated with the Civil War. Charwomen, he wrote one aspirant for the position, usually came from the ranks of widows and orphans of Union soliders, "and when departures are made in appointing others, the necessity therefor must be very urgent in its character." When a shortage in watchmen forced Hills to remove an ill major from the payroll, the chief clerk was maudlin in his apologies, promising to restore the Civil War veteran to the status to which his loyal service entitled him.[2]

Aging was inherent in late-nineteenth-century bureaucracies, for the population itself was growing older with each decade. The problem worsened as Civil War veterans came to pensionable age in large numbers between 1893 and 1903. Because of preferences granted under civil service legislation, these veterans were found in large numbers in every government agency. As late as 1919, when many of the veterans were dead, Commissioner of Pensions Gaylord M. Saltzgaber claimed that 90 of his 878 employees had served in the Civil War.[3]

1. U.S., Department of Commerce and Labor, Bureau of the Census, *The Executive Civil Service of the United States*, Bulletin No. 12 (Washington, D.C., 1904), 28 (table 24), 35 (tables 31, 32).

2. W. H. Hills to Mrs. Ida V. Hendricks, 19 April 1892, Record Group 56, "Records of the Treasury Department," National Archives, Washington, D.C., Office of the Secretary (OS), Books of Letters sent by the Assistant Superintendent; Wallace H. Hills to My dear Major, 23 September 1898, Private Book of W. H. Hills, Chief Clerk.

3. Charts I and IV, Record Group 51, "Records of the Bureau of Efficiency, 1913–1933," National Archives, Washington, D.C. 61 (file "Pension Office"), box 405; U.S., Congress, Senate, Committee on Civil Service and Retrenchment, *Retirement of Civil Service Employees: Hearings Before the Committee on Civil Service and Retrenchment on S. 1699, A bill for the Retirement of Employees in the Classified Civil Service and for other purposes*, 66th Cong., 1st sess. (Washington, D.C., 1919), pp. 10–11; Memorandum, Clerk in Charge of Tenth St. Branch to Chief Clerk, Adjutant General's Office, 27 October 1913, RG 94, "Records of the War Department," National Archives, Washington, D.C., Office of the Adjutant General, Doc. File No. 2093958.

These aged veterans were considered untouchable for political reasons. At the Patent Office, Civil War personnel were "permitted to hold their present positions without disturbance, irrespective of the work done by them." In some agencies, incapacitated veterans were even protected from salary reductions. Taft, who more than any president was responsible for public interest in governmental efficiency, felt compelled to act contrary to his efficiency principles where aged veterans were concerned.[4]

Compounding the problem were the general conditions of employment and removal under the Pendleton Civil Service Act of 1883, as amended. Reform had, on the one hand, not worked well enough; on the other hand, too well. It had not eliminated the intense pressures brought to bear on bureau chiefs and department heads who attempted to reduce or discharge an employee who had become useless or inefficient. Once the employee was discharged, pressures for reinstatement mounted. The more inefficient (and, therefore, the more unemployable) the affected bureaucrat, the more intense the campaign for reinstatement.[5] Ironically, civil service reform may also have contributed to inefficiency by depriving the system of a mechanism—regular and arbitrary removal, through spoils—that prevented superannuation by insuring turnover. Security of tenure implied a relatively permanent, and therefore aging, bureaucracy. This, at least, was the conventional wisdom of the Civil Service Commission and retirement advocates, who found the argument ideally suited to making the case that government pensions were not only not irresponsible but were in fact the logical result, perhaps even the capstone, of a popular and benign civil service system. Employees were not, of course, bound into the system; anyone could leave the government for other employment. But security of tenure encouraged employees to remain, and at some point the job became a matter of "devotion" to government service. No person so devoted, claimed retirement proponents, "no man who serves faithfully . . . shall end his days in an almshouse."[6]

4. Edward B. Moon to Chief Clerk, Department of Interior, no date; J. L. Davenport to Secretary of Interior, 20 April 1912, Record Group 48, "Records of the Department of the Interior," National Archives, Washington, D.C., Office of the Secretary, Personnel Supervision and Management, 1907–1942, File 15–15–4. Hereafter referred to as RG 48, OS-PSM.

5. F. C. Ainsworth to John R. Proctor, 14 July 1900, Record Group 94, AGO, Document File No. 466269, box 677.

6. William R. Willcox, Chairman of the Public Service Commission, quoted in *Civil Service News*, 29 June 1909, pp. 1–3; *Postal Record* 38 (April 1925): 144; Ainsworth letter, cited note 5. The National Civil Service Reform League, committed to the civil service system, was sharply critical of a viewpoint that it considered inimical to continued reform. In a series of reports issued between 1900 and 1910, the league argued that the spoils system had allowed influential politicians and their supporters to foist useless and needless cronies onto a hapless government and presented a limited statistical argument that emphasized how minor had been the accretions to superannuation in the federal service over the ten years after 1893.

See National Civil Service Reform League, Special Committee, *Superannuation in the Civil Ser-*

In the spring of 1897, Gage found his administration at Treasury subject to the charge that political influence had resulted in the removal of reasonably efficient personnel because of their political or religious characteristics. In response to this accusation and to the mounting evidence of general inefficiency in his department, Gage appointed a special committee of three, including his private secretary, Frank A. Vanderlip, to investigate the "character, habits and efficiency" of his subordinates.[7] Gage soon announced that employees over seventy years of age would be paid a nominal salary of seventy-five dollars per month; in return, considerably less work would be expected. This proposal generated the first serious discussion of a civil pension. Opposition to Gage's informal "pension" system (for it was perceived as such) came from the affected employees themselves and from the supporters of Civil War veterans, who found the action an affront to those who had rendered loyal service and were worried lest this be the entering wedge for a genuine pension system. The next year, efficiency advocates anxious to save public monies succeeded in attaching a rider to an appropriation bill for Treasury which provided that no part of the appropriation could be paid in salaries to superannuated employees. Having defined a large group of men and women as superannuated, Gage had to drop them altogether.[8]

THE POLITICS OF RETIREMENT

Opponents of early pension proposals, most of which called for contributions by employees only, anticipated that the public would ultimately be called upon to contribute. Taxpayers, acutely aware at this very moment of the budgetary consequences of the commitments made years earlier to Civil War veterans, shuddered at the thought of creating yet another army of clerk pensioners.[9]

---

vice: 1910 (n.p., n.d.), pp. 1, 4–5, in National Civil Service League Papers, Pendleton Room, U.S. Civil Service Commission Library, Washington, D.C., box "National Civil Service League Publications, 1882–1916," and other reports in this box. Hereafter referred to as NCSL Papers.

7. L. C. Gage to Frank A. Vanderlip, Maj. Fred. Brackett, and Theodore F. Swayze, 23 April 1897, RG 56, OS, box 5, labeled "Report of Committee, Feb. 1889–Sept. 1912." Vanderlip was later to play a role in private-sector retirement.

8. *Brooklyn Daily Eagle*, 9 March 1900, in Record Group 146, "Records of the United States Civil Service Commission," National Archives, Washington, D.C., U.S. Bureau of Pensions Scrapbook, materials 1900–1940; clippings, *Milwaukee Sentinel*, 18 December 1897; *Minneapolis Times*, 25 January 1899; *Ottowa Free Press*, 6 December 1899, all in Civil Service Clipping Collection, U.S. Civil Service Commission Library, Pendleton Room, Washington, D.C. (hereafter referred to as CS Clippings).

9. Clippings, *Rochester* (New York) *Union and Advertiser*, 16 December 1897 (editorial); "Clerks' Retirement Fund," *Washington Star* (no date); *Concord* (New Hampshire) *Monitor*, 24 January 1900; *Toledo Blade*, 25 March 1900; *Philadelphia Press*, 25 February 1900; *New York Evening Post*, 28 January 1901, in CS Clippings.

At the same time, government employees were measured against the standards traditionally applied to pensioners and found wanting. Though bureaucrats cultivated the image of sacrifice, the general public did not see civil employees in this light. Unlike soldiers, police, and firemen, they risked nothing. Unlike teachers, they were considered well paid, and their hours were neither long nor especially arduous. Many, because they had secured their positions through patronage, were not particularly bright, talented, or well qualified. It was widely believed that the average government clerk lived an uncommonly secure, relatively soft life and could very well look out for his own future. The *Binghampton Republican* perceptively criticized the whole notion of a civil "servant" and its implications: "It is presumed that a person in office for twenty-five years holds it for the salary, and because it is as much or more than he can get at anything else. At all events he holds it because he wants it, and for what there is in it, and not because the State holds him or needs him."[10] A population that had recently experienced the insecurity of a major depression was not ready to grieve for one of the few groups that had been reasonably well insulated from it.

In the ground swell created by the Gage action, government workers in several District of Columbia offices became aware of their common needs, of the power of the political arena, and of the necessity of organizing to achieve their goals. Clerks and others who had once taken their future in a federal agency for granted now had to consider the possibility of a forced retirement, without salary. The clearinghouse for these fears was the United States Civil Service Retirement Association (USCSRA), founded in early 1900 in, appropriately, the Treasury Department. Its first president was Charles Lyman, chief of the Appointments Division in Treasury, whose cautious approach protected the organization in its first year. Into Lyman's office came requests for information on the new association, inquiries about the association's position on some recently introduced retirement bill, or suggestions for legislation. But at this point, neither Lyman nor the USCSRA was prepared to take advantage of the surge of interest. The association had not prepared its own bill, and Lyman was convinced that many of the new proposals were based on inadequate data. He spent the first year gathering statistics and working with actuaries.[11]

10. Clippings, *Binghamton* (New York) *Republican*, 2 March 1899; *Brooklyn Citizen*, 29 January 1900; *Concord* (New Hampshire) *Monitor*, 24 January 1900; *Philadelphia Bulletin*, 29 January 1901; *Baltimore Herald*, 19 December 1900 (editorial); *Philadelphia Inquirer*, 26 February 1900, in CS Clippings; poem, Lindsay S. Perkins, "Squash Center Discusses Civil Service Retirement," *Civil Service Advocate*, July 1915, p. 1240, copy in RG 146, Civil Service Records, Bureau of Pensions Scrapbook.

11. M. Brosius to Lyman, 27 March 1900; Employees of Customs Service, New York Port, to

Jacob W. Starr acceded to the presidency of USCSRA in June 1901. In 1920, after two decades of leadership, he would be reverently known as "Captain" Starr; in 1901, however, he was a thoroughly middle-class third-class clerk earning $1,400 a year. To secure necessary information on which to base retirement legislation, the association had attempted to circulate cards through the executive branch, requesting data on age, salary, and length of service. When resistance to these tactics developed, Starr in February 1901 secured from the Senate a resolution calling on the heads of departments to provide necessary information. Outside of Washington some federal employees charged the new association with discriminating in favor of the particular age mix found in the District and with contemplating legislation that would favor District employees.[12]

Starr's aggressive leadership was equal to the obstacles thrown up against a union of government employees that solicited information, organized, and, by some definition, lobbied. Although Roosevelt had approved the organization's request to obtain information upon which to base retirement legislation, the president carefully circumscribed other activity in an executive order of January 31, 1902, forbidding officers and employees of the government "either directly or indirectly, individually or through associations, to solicit an increase in pay or to influence or attempt to influence in their own interest any other legislation whatever, either through Congress or its committees, or in any way save through the heads of the Departments in or under which they serve."[13] Aimed directly at the USCSRA, the order was made less severe only by Roosevelt's personal commitment to Starr to allow association committees to continue their work.

Development of a legislative program was also inhibited by the difficulties of financing a retirement program entirely through employee contributions. Not until February 1909 would a retirement bill be favorably reported from a congressional committee.[14] The Roosevelt administration's contribution to civil

Lyman, 24 March 1900; Duncan Veazy to Lyman, 30 August 1900; Lyman to Veazy, 20 September 1900; Lyman to Veazy, 30 August 1900, in RG 56, Appointments Division, General Correspondence Relating to the Civil Service Retirement Association, 1882–1910 (one box only).

12. Excerpt from the *Washington Times*, 8 August 1920, printed in the *Annuitant* 1, no. 1 (1922): 6–7; John Doyle to Ella Loraine Dorsey, 28 January 1902, RG 146, Bureau of Pensions Scrapbook.

13. George B. Cortelyou to Gentlemen, 21 February 1902, in United States Civil Service Retirement Association, *Report: March 9, 1903* (Washington, 1903), p. 45, bound in *Publications, etc., National C. S. Retirement Association: 1906–9* (binding title) in U.S. Civil Service Commission Library, Washington, D.C. The large volume contains materials on the USCSRA back to 1903 and is referred to hereafter as USCSRA *Materials*. Copies of the *Washington Investigator* are located inside its back cover. Memorandum from three civil service commissioners to president, 24 April 1915, Woodrow Wilson Papers, Manuscript Division, Library of Congress, Washington, D.C., series 4, file 2, reel 160. Excerpt from *Washington Times*, 8 August 1920, printed in *Annuitant* 1 (1922): 7.

14. USCSRA, *Report: March 9, 1903*, p. 42; Herbert D. Brown, "Savings and Annuity Plan

service retirement was the Keep Commission, formally known as the Commission on Departmental Methods. Appointed in 1905 and headed by Assistant Treasury Secretary Charles H. Keep, the commission emerged from an environment of fears of national bankruptcy and was charged with improving government business methods. Its work was carried out by twelve subcommittees, each with its own sphere of activity: personnel, hours of labor, and so on.[15] Although its mandate clearly transcended the issue of retirement, it also encompassed it, and from 1906 through 1908 the Keep Commission provided advocates of retirement with a forum for their views and generated the first reliable information on superannuation and treatment of older employees in federal agencies. Appearing before its Subcommittee on Personnel, Starr said his group was willing to support any retirement bill acceptable to Congress. The opposition of younger employees could be easily overcome by returning their contributions when they left the civil service.

Charles Lyman, former officer of the USCSRA and now a member of a Keep Commission subcommittee, argued that support of younger elements could be secured only by making percentage contributions rise with salary increases.[16] More important, Lyman was convinced, philosophically and empirically, that the entire proposition of retirement involved clear dangers for the larger community. He found "the great corporations" willing to make provision for their old men, but the government bent on dismissal. By insisting on a moral right it did not have—the right to make the very young and old a charge on community and friends—the government would only help to create a parasitic mass that consumed without working. Although Lyman was willing to countenance retirement on grounds of inefficiency, he resented a resolution of the subcommittee, passed in his absence, that tied inefficiency to age and pressed retirement as the remedy. "It is probable," he lectured his colleagues,

---

Proposed for Retirement of Superannuated Civil-Service Employees," S. Doc. 745, 61st Cong., 3d sess., submitted 21 May 1911, printed as appendix A in U.S., Congress, House, *Retirement from the Classified Civil Service of Superannuated Employees: Message from the President of the United States*, Transmitting Report of the Commission on Economy and Efficiency on the Subject of Retirement from the Classified Civil Service of Superannuated Employees, Doc. No. 732, 62d Cong., 2d sess. (Washington, D.C., 1912), p. 27. Hereafter referred to as House, *Retirement: Message from the President, 1912.* See also, John Black and John [Unknown] to James R. Garfield, 16 October 1908; J. I. P. to Mr. Secretary, 15 October 1908; M. F. O'Donoghue to Garfield, 14 October 1908, in RG 48, OS-PSM, file 15–14–3.

15. Oscar Kraines, "The President Versus Congress: The Keep Commission, 1905–1909: First Comprehensive Presidential Inquiry into Administration," *Western Political Quarterly* 23 (March 1970): 5–6, 9–10.

16. Minutes of Subcommittee on Personnel, 43d and 42d meetings, RG 56, Keep Commission, Information for Commission on Departmental Methods, box 1, file "Minutes of Subcommittee on Personnel."

that in its present temper any scheme, to meet the approval of congress, would have to provide for compulsory retirement at a given age; but this would be compromising a principle to secure action . . . there can be no justification of putting one efficient person out of the service in order to put another presumably competent person in the service simply because the person who goes out is older than the one who comes in.[17]

Some of Lyman's position found its way into the subcommittee's final report on the question of superannuation. Although the report linked retirement and efficiency, it emphasized not so much the elimination of the inefficient older employee as the role of the pension in attracting and keeping competent personnel who might otherwise be tempted by business and by the new Carnegie-financed university pension programs. Its suggested retirement bill contained provision for those who might wish to remain after reaching the standard retirement age (providing they continued to be efficient), and for the younger employees it provided for distribution of contributions upon separation from the service.[18]

Lyman could find this common ground with other members of the subcommittee because his background in Treasury had convinced him that the alternative to legislation was abrupt separation. He did not believe—nor did the data then available demonstrate—that Treasury was inefficient because its clerks were getting old. He confronted his subcommittee with Keep Commission data on the quality and quantity of work produced by the 457 employees (7.4 percent of the total work force of 6,201) over sixty-five years of age.[19]

Did Lyman have proof that older clerks were efficient? It would seem so, for only ten employees received "poor" quality ratings and only nine received a four or below on the quantity scale. But there are other possibilities. The numerical quality ratings were based on general comments by supervisors. These comments indicate that those rated "good" or below were not thought of as "first-class" employees. A carpenter rated "good" had the following written after his name: "work not equal to a first-class carpenter." The work of a mechanical employee, rated "excellent," was described as "equal to younger employee in regard to time and workmanship." If this standard holds, then only those 137 employees rated "excellent" were considered capable of some reasonable approximation of the standards set by younger employees. Assuming that the nu-

17. Ibid., 41st meeting of Subcommittee on Personnel; ibid. 40th meeting, 6th meeting.

18. Typescript report of the Subcommittee on Personnel of the Committee on Departmental Methods, RG 56, Keep Commission, Subcommittee on Personnel, box 2, file, "Correspondence, etc., Subcommittee on Personnel," pp. 1–4, 9–10, 14–15, 17–18.

19. Minutes of Subcommittee on Personnel, 18th meeting, RG 56, Keep Commission, Information for Commission on Departmental Methods, box 1, file "Minutes of Subcommittee on Personnel."

Table 2.1 Rating Quantity and Quality of Work of 457 Employees Sixty-five or Over

Number of Persons	Quantity Rating, on Scale of 10	Quality Rating				
		Excellent	Good	Fair	Average	Poor
2	1					2
	2					
	3					
7	4		2	2	1	2
19	5	1	5	8	1	4
27	6	2	7	14	4	
48	7	3	12	14	19	
81	8	4	54	8	15	
73	9	12	48	6	7	
200	10	115	69	4	10	2
Totals 457		137	197	56	57	10

merical ratings on the quantity scale can be converted by the same idiom, only employees receiving ratings of 9 and 10 could be considered the equal of their younger counterparts. In short, something like half of the sixty-five-year-olds were found generally inefficient.[20]

COMMUNITY AND EFFICIENCY

Why, then, did supervisors describe an inefficient labor force as efficient? The answer seems to be that these supervisors actively sought to protect older employees within their jurisdictions. If incidents such as the Gage efficiency campaign and the March 1907 firing of Post Office mailbag employees were now a part of the federal scene, they were still unusual events, shocking to the protective sensibilities of many bureaucrats. Responses to Keep Commission inquiries make this clear. Like other department heads, each of the assistant postmasters was asked to state how many reductions in salary had been made in the past two fiscal years for general inefficiency, old-age inefficiency, and all other causes. One postmaster reported that of 145 employees, he had reduced only one older employee and had fired no one. Another, with 295 clerical employees (and some others), reported two reductions, both for old-age ineffi-

20. Ratings are available in RG 56, Keep Commission, Subcommittee on Personnel, box 2, file "Records of Sub-Com. on Personnel." Records of other departments are similar. A good many of the older employees were watchmen, and the relevance of these ratings and this line of argument to them is questionable.

ciency and both in the Rural Free Delivery Service, and one general dismissal. The postmaster general, with over 250 employees, reported three reductions and fifteen dismissals for general inefficiency, and seven reductions for miscellaneous causes, but no reductions or dismissals related to old age.[21] The postmaster and his assistants would perhaps have agreed with the claim of the War Department's J. C. Scofield, who joined Lyman in defending the efficiency of the aging civil servants. Ninety-nine percent, he said, had "a special claim, growing out of long service in the Departments."[22] Victorian notions of order and community had not yet been completely altered.

Nonetheless, at the highest levels of the executive branch, retirement was gradually becoming acceptable. In 1904 superannuation had become sufficiently important to warrant mention in one annual agency report; between 1909 and 1911, almost every major agency made some allusion to it. At the Interior Department, the secretary discovered superannuated employees dropped to lower grades and retained because of political pressure or sympathy for those involved. The government, said the secretary of war, was operating a pension system "without retirement."[23] These expressions reflected the views of the chief executive under whom they were issued, for Taft, with his strong ties to business and his distaste for bureaucracy, found the concept of retirement congenial. In May 1909 he received USCSRA convention delegates at the White House and granted the executive committee of the association permission to present its views to Congress and to participate in the preparation of retirement legislation. Three years later, at least two executive agencies allowed association officials to collect funds within the departments to finance a committee's travel to the Democratic and Republican national conventions. Although the administration stopped short of allowing the group to advocate particular political candidates, it had significantly expanded the ability of the USCSRA to press its case.[24]

Taft institutionalized his commitment to retirement by creating the five-member Commission on Economy and Efficiency (CEE) and by accepting its recommendations on civil service retirement. Consumed by the desire to provide precise measurements of the relationship between age and efficiency, the CEE took estimates of efficiency from supervisory reports and developed charts that

21. "Answers to the Keep Commission," a bound volume, in RG 28, "Records of the Post Office Department," National Archives, Washington, D.C., Office of the Postmaster General (PGO), series 19 (Records Relating to the Keep Commission, 1906–1907).

22. Minutes of Subcommittee on Personnel, 6th meeting, RG 56, Keep Commission, Information for Commission on Departmental Methods, box 1, file "Minutes of Subcommittee on Personnel."

23. House, *Retirement: Message from the President, 1912*, pp. 9, 11, 12.

24. John C. Black to Secretary of Interior, 1 April 1911; Llewellyn Jordan to W. L. Fisher, 3 June 1912; Fisher to Jordan, 5 June 1912, in RG 48, OS-PSM, file 15–14–3; Paul P. Van Riper, *History of the United States Civil Service* (New York, 1958), pp. 217, 224.

presumably indicated how much of the salary of employees was actually earned. Commission figures demonstrated the decline in efficiency to be marginal (less than 1 percent) up to age forty-five and only 3 percent up to age sixty. At age seventy the loss from superannuation was labeled "considerable" (over 14 percent). Only at age eighty-five, the commission concluded, did the loss from superannuation cleary justify forced retirement.

From these figures, the commission should have determined that a retirement program was an unnecessary and unreasonable expense. It did not. Instead, it went on to advocate compulsory retirement at age seventy, the annuity to be financed entirely at employee expense. Taft correctly labeled this a "compulsory savings plan" and affirmed that retirement plans would be justifiable only by increases in efficiency in the public service. And having read the report, he, too, felt compelled to justify conclusions that did not emerge from the data. "The loss [in efficiency] shown as the result of the investigation," he said, "is undoubtedly much less than the actual loss from superannuation."[25] While unpleasant to observe, this awkward juggling of the facts was not entirely without reason. Dependent on the votes of veterans and the support of the GAR, Taft had somehow to justify policies that risked alienating these constituencies.[26]

Encouraged by official interest, the retirement movement expanded rapidly. Beginning in 1907, the USCSRA held a series of mass meetings, drawing from three hundred to (by one estimate) six thousand people. Its ability to reach potential members was augmented with the publication, in 1909, of its own *Civil Service News* and the support of another new journal, the *Washington Investigator*. The USCSRA began to have some success outside of Washington, especially in the New York City area (Fiorello LaGuardia later recalled the organization of a small branch in the Ellis Island Division of the Immigration Service), but District of Columbia clerks remained its basic constituency.[27] Robert Alcorn, who later became well known as the national representative and president of the National Association of Retired Federal Employees, was the inspiration behind the powerful retirement movement that developed in the Naval Gun Factory after his arrival in the District in March 1910. Calling itself the Retirement Committee, this group made contact with interested parties in stations and government arsenals.[28] The National Association of Letter Carriers (NALC), a na-

25. House, *Retirement: Message from the President, 1912*, pp. 3–4, 39–42, 46–47, 59.
26. Taft to Mr. Secretary, 18 April 1912, RG 48, OS-PSM, file 15–15–4.
27. *Washington Post*, 30 January 1907, p. 5; *Civil Service News*, 29 June 1909; *Washington Investigator* 1 (March 1909) and (April 1909); typescript of LaGuardia address, Civil Service Papers, U.S. Civil Service Commission Library, box 11. Unless otherwise noted, cited numbers of the *Civil Service News* and *Washington Investigator* are available in the Civil Service Commission Library.
28. *Annuitant* 20 (April 1945): 1–2; Xerox of Robert H. Alcorn, "The Fight for Retirement," *Retirement Life*, August 1955, p. 4, in National Association of Retired Federal Employees Papers,

tional union with its greatest strength in the New York City Post Office, existed independently of the USCSRA but also participated for a time in its activities. A strong supporter of civil service retirement, the NALC was responsible for a very successful series of mass meetings held in major cities on Retirement Day, October 1, 1910.[29] In a speech before hundreds of government employees in April 1911, one pension advocate called the clerk's campaign for retirement "the most popular issue ever started in the United States" and claimed that civil service personnel were on the verge of an important mass movement that could lead to retirement legislation and Robert LaFollette's election to the presidency.[30]

This vision fell short of fulfillment and retirement suffered a serious setback when the two major advocates of civil service retirement, the USCSRA and the NALC, became bitter enemies. The primary source of conflict was a difference of opinion over the kind of pension system the government should maintain. The self-consciously pragmatic leaders of the USCSRA, anxious to overcome the deep hostility to bureaucrats and fears of pension costs, wanted a "contributory" plan, financed in large measure out of salaries. They also expected that contributions would be facilitated by salary increases for federal employees. The USCSRA had the support of the CEE, which favored a contributory system for its cheapness and because employees would be likely to think of the alternative—called a "straight" plan—as part of the employment contract, a deferred salary requiring compensation upon dismissal. In Congress, these interests found expression in the Gillett-Perkins retirement bill, which also provided for retirement at specified ages.[31]

national office of the National Association of Retired Federal Employees, 1533 New Hampshire Avenue, N.W., Washington, D.C. (hereafter referred to as NARFE Papers). An organization called the Civil Service Council, which advocated retirement of superannuated employees, existed in the Washington area and circulated petitions in May 1910. See RG 48, OS–PSM, file 15–4–4 for petition, bylaws, and constitution of the organization. Washington machinists were a part of the USCSRA after 1908. See clipping, *Washington Times*, 23 November 1936, in CS Clippings, file "Retirement-History."

29. *Postal Record* 23 (September 1910): 200 (editorial); (November 1910): 246 (editorial); (December 1910): 260.

30. Copy of speech by Fulton Gordon, delivered at a testimonial dinner given by the Business Men's Association, Washington, D.C., 12 April 1911, in RG 94, AGO, Doc. File No. 466269 (box 677); David P. Thelen, *Robert M. La Follette and the Insurgent Spirit* (Boston, 1976), chap. 5.

31. *Washington Investigator* 1 (March 1909): 4, 10, 12–13; ibid. (April 1909): 1, 52, 55; *Washington Post*, 30 January 1907, p. 5; Frank Mann Stewart, *The National Civil Service Reform League: History, Activities, and Problems* (Austin, 1929), pp. 190–91, 194; House, *Retirement: Message from President, 1912*, pp. 14, 17; *Civil Service News*, 29 June 1909, pp. 1, 3 (other page numbers not decipherable). For a general assessment of the depth of feeling against a civil pension list, see "Speech of Senator Carter of Montana, at meeting held by the U.S. Civil Service Retirement Association, February 24, 1906," in RG 48, OS, a grey box containing materials on the Keep Commission, file "Superannuation and Retirement." The 80 percent figure is based on a poll taken by the *Washington Star* and published 3 June 1915, reprinted in the *Civil Service Advocate*, July 1915, p. 1229, copy in RG 146, Bureau of Pensions Scrapbook.

The letter carriers found the contributory scheme unsatisfactory. The idea that Congress could control their salaries indirectly, through deductions for pensions, was itself disturbing. "No compulsory deduction plan can be operated with justice," wrote Edward J. Cantwell, who edited the NALC's *Postal Record*. "Government employees need protection against the Gillett Bill more than they do against old age."[32] Dispersed throughout the country rather than concentrated in Washington like the clerks, the carriers were pessimistic about their ability to exert sufficient influence on salary levels to help finance the pension through contributions; they did not believe that the principle of the Gillett bill—which covered only persons in offices and departments in Washington—could be successfully applied outside the District. There was a technical as well as a political problem; the Gillett bill's system of annuity payments from assessments on salary increases that accompanied promotions would have prejudicially affected the letter carriers, whose promotions were automatic for a certain number of years. Cantwell also claimed that even District of Columbia clerks seldom earned enough to allow regular contributions to a pension fund; many took in boarders, and some 75 percent contributed to the support of parents or other relatives.[33]

These differences proved difficult to reconcile. By 1910, letter carriers within the USCSRA could no longer tolerate the domination of the retirement association by a limited group of men employed in Washington executive departments. Determined to take control of the association, and with it the valuable exemptions from political restrictions issued by Roosevelt and Taft, a group of dissidents led by Michael O'Donaghue of the NALC set themselves up as the leadership of the USCSRA. For more than two years there were two retirement associations of the same name, each taking dues and pursuing entirely different goals.

In February 1910, USCSRA president Llewellyn Jordan and the advocates of contributory pensions filed suit in the Supreme Court of the District of Columbia seeking an injunction against the activities of the group now calling itself the United States Civil Service Retirement Association. In court, plaintiffs made much of the fact that Cantwell, as president of the new association, was fraudu-

32. *Postal Record* 23 (September 1910): 201 (editorial).

33. *Civil Service News*, 29 June 1909, pp. 1–3; *Postal Record*, 23 (February 1910): 34 (editorial); ibid. 23 (April 1910): 85 (editorial); ibid. 23 (June 1910): 121; ibid. 23 (July 1910): 152–53 (editorial); ibid. 23 (August 1910): 176 (editorial); ibid. 23 (December 1910): 260; George T. Morgan, "Facts About Civil Pensions," *Civil Service News* 23 (December 1910): 262–63; *Civil Service News* 24 (January 1911): 15 (editorial). The USCSRA estimated its own strength at thirty thousand, that of the NALC at twenty-six thousand. See *Solomon E. Faunce et al., v. Michael F. O'Donoghue, et al.*, Bill in Equity No. 29154, filed to Supreme Court of the District of Columbia on February 25, 1910, pp. 19–20. For the USCSRA I have seen membership estimates as low as five thousand.

lently using monies sent in by advocates of contributory plans. The defendants emphasized the stifling atmosphere Jordan had created within the old USCSRA, taking dues from postal employees and others but failing to provide them with commensurate representation and voice, refusing, they claimed, to allow reasonable expression of the straight pension alternative. Andrew McKee, a New York City carrier who gave testimony in the civil suit, said he was inclined to assist in Jordan's reelection to the presidency in 1910 until he learned that Jordan had told a joint congressional committee holding hearings during the USCSRA convention that "he believed the great mass of federal employees approved of [a contributory plan]. . . . That statement," McKee told a hearing auditor, "was absolutely untrue."[34]

The court could give control of the association to the plaintiffs, but it could not heal the breach between the two parties. Less than a year after the June 18, 1912 decree restraining the defendants from representing themselves as the USCSRA and from soliciting funds under that name, they had formed a new organization, the National Association of Civil Service Employees (NACSE). It was designed to extend civil service, to disseminate information on superannuation, and to devise plans for retirement—along straight pension lines of course.[35]

Continued division might have been anticipated, for the original dispute was a serious one, built on major issues. It was, on the one hand, a classic jurisdictional dispute between two unions interested in organizing the same personnel. The USCSRA was dominant in the critical Washington, D.C. area and possessed decided advantages in its historical control of the retirement issue and its exemption from restrictions on political involvement. As the NALC sensed, control of the organization was a worthy prize. But even when the jurisdictional matter had been resolved by the courts, the original issue—contributory versus direct pensions—remained and would continue as a disruptive factor for more than a decade.

Why did these groups care so much about the shape of the system? Professional differences—in pay scale, promotion ladders, even ability to effect pay increases—seem incapable, in and of themselves, of sustaining profound division. Two distinct approaches to politics were involved. The USCSRA was born of the need to protect the very old from the spread of the new managerial mentality; in outlook, it was less union than benevolent institution. Its leaders,

34. This account is based on Equity Case No. 29154 (see note 33), including Bill of Complaint, legal brief for defendants, legal brief for complainants, testimony before auditor, exhibits, and copy of decree.
35. Clipping, *Washington Post*, 6 April 1913, in CS Clippings, file "Retirement-History, 1912–1915."

middle aged and older, increasingly vulnerable to age discrimination and in sight of their own retirement, wanted the Congress to act now rather than later and were willing to accept less in return. The contributory program would have less appeal for younger bureaucrats, but then this group was not the USCSRA's central constituency. What the USCSRA might call a pragmatic approach, the letter carriers would describe as unnecessary compromise of basic principles. A traditional union group with broader age-group support, the NALC could more easily wait. Its skepticism of retirement through employee contributions was, moreover, justified. As Taft had publicly proclaimed, such a system was only a mechanism for compulsory savings. Should something of that kind prove necessary, the union, rather than the state, could provide it. The direct pension was something else; a real gain, unlikely to come out of wages. At stake was nothing less than the future contours of the welfare state and, in fact, whether a real welfare state, providing benefits out of general revenues, would exist at all. The decision to construct a surrogate welfare state, premised on individual rather than social responsibility, was made not in 1935, but in the decade after 1910.

THE WILSON PRESIDENCY; THE CIVIL SERVICE RETIREMENT ACT

The early years of the first Wilson administration brought no closing of the breach. Meetings of USCSRA and NASCE leaders resulted only in agreement to disagree. The younger association was encouraged in its position by a heightened interest in the economic costs of turnover and by the beginning of a major effort by Representative James A. Hamill of New Jersey to move a straight pension bill through Congress. Supported by Secretary of Labor William B. Wilson, the Hamill bill was the subject of a major petitioning campaign and was also advocated by a surprising number of small businessmen—wholesalers, suppliers, and manufacturers.[36] The major stumbling block to a favorable committee report on the Hamill bill appeared to be Martin Dies of Texas, who feared the implied deferred salary would all too quickly become a benefit payable to widows.[37]

Between 1913 and 1916, the major pension organizations benefited from escalating threats to job security in the federal bureaucracy. A broad-ranging

36. Clipping, *Washington Star*, 17 May 1913, CS Clippings, file "Retirement-History, 1912–1915." Information on the petition movement is located in John J. Deviny to Wilson, 13 March 1915; Order of Railway Conductors of America, Detroit Division no. 48 to Wilson, 8 April 1915; and other materials in Wilson Papers, series 4, file 431, reel 272.

37. Lathrop Brown to Herbert D. Brown, 20 February 1914, RG 51, "Records of the Bureau of Efficiency," National Archives, Washington, D.C., .33, file "Separation and Retirement of Employees."

inquiry into the impact of superannuation, initiated in 1913 by Tennessee senator John Shields of the Committee on Civil Service and Retrenchment, produced a series of defensive replies not unlike those provided Taft's Commission on Economy and Efficiency. At the War Department, most department heads simply denied the existence of older bureaucrats unable to do a full day's work; a number acknowledged the declining stamina and vigor of employees at or near seventy but insisted on the compensations of knowledge and experience.[38] An organization called the Army Field Clerks Association petitioned the adjutant general to restore to the retired list a group of 210 clerks who in 1894 had been discharged from the army and rehired as civilian or "headquarters clerks," on the same salaries as enlisted men but without their retirement benefits. Although the field clerks association made the right arguments—that the aged clerks could not save money, and that retirement would promote efficiency in the service—the War Department rejected the appeal as a case of special legislation.[39]

The Post Office Department was the scene of one round of firings and a good deal of threatening talk. A reporter for the *Washington Times* covered the May 1914 severance of seventeen employees from the District of Columbia Post Office as the emotional event it was for at least two very old postal workers. One of those released was John J. B. Lerch, a Civil War veteran who had entered the Post Office on Lincoln's recommendation fifty-one years earlier. His wife was in need of constant medical attention. Among the organizations protesting the dismissal were the GAR and two German-American groups of which Lerch was a prominent member. The seventeen also included Augustus Ridgely, another Civil War veteran with fifty-one years of government service. Perhaps aware that her husband had received a "good" efficiency rating, Mrs. Ridgely attributed his firing to the new administration's prejudice against GAR men. Although this charge overlooked the growing prejudice against age in the federal bureaucracy, it was an accusation to which Woodrow Wilson, with his southern ties, was all too vulnerable. Ridgely's case was taken up by the GAR and his fraternal organization, the Masons. The USCSRA used the publicity surrounding the May episode to endorse a proposed House Joint Resolution calling for the payment of emergency pensions until regular legislation could be moved through Congress.[40]

38. See the small file, generated by Shields to Lindley M. Garrison, 19 September 1913, in RG 94, AGO, Doc. File No. 2093958.

39. Memorandum, Walton H. Bush to Col. Henry O. S. Heistand, 6 December 1913; memorandum, unsigned and undated, RG 94, AGO, Doc. File No. 1705066.

40. J. R. Hildebrand, "Men Cast on Scrap Heap by U.S. Show Need for Pensions," *Washington Times*, 19 May 1914; Hildebrand, "Veteran, Dean of Postoffice, Among Those Thrust Aside," *Washington Times*, 20 May 1914, in CS Clippings, file "Retirement-History, 1912–1915"; copy of House

In October 1914, a convention of postmasters from Maryland, Delaware, Virginia, and South Carolina listened as the first assistant postmaster general announced a campaign against age-related inefficiency. Employees would be retained in their present positions only as long as they were capable of earning the money paid them. Older clerks and carriers would have their salaries scaled to conform to declining efficiency. The first assistant informed his audience that he was not sympathetic with postmasters who retained aging employees for humanitarian reasons. "The law," he explained, "does not provide for pensions, and neither does it provide for permanence of tenure in the civil service. On the contrary it states that incompetent employees shall be removed." Detroit resident Henry Duffield (not a Post Office employee) sent a report of the address to Woodrow Wilson, sure that this "misrepresents the position of our good president and his administration. . . . I saw several employees of the govt. who are in really desperate circumstances. These same men, had their employer been the Standard Oil Co. instead of Uncle Sam, would today be enjoying liberal pensions."[41] Later in the year Daniel Goldschmidt, the new president of the USCSRA, informed Wilson in unusually frank terms that the removal of older postal workers and the probable removal of others had contributed "to a feeling of unrest, that borders on actual mental distress among the employes of the Federal Government."[42]

The political difficulties inherent in operating a civil service without retirement came to a head in 1916, an election year. Saltzgaber, commissioner of the Pension Bureau, an agency expected to handle an especially large quota of aged employees, served notice that the bureau could be forced to drop sixty-seven employees by July 1, the beginning of the fiscal year. Saltzgaber's cold-blooded disregard for the needs and abilities of older workers was not then a matter of record, nor was the commissioner willing, as he would be four years later when a retirement program existed, to make it so. Instead, he informed the press that his action had been precipitated by recently imposed budget restrictions. He had attempted to secure positions for those to be released, only to discover that other offices did not want the older employees and did not have the funds to attract the younger ones.

Joint Resolution, transmitted to Wilson by Llewellyn Jordan; Jordan to president, 25 May 1914, Wilson Papers, series 4, file 431, reel 272. The NASCE made a similar proposal in March 1915 (John J. Deviny to Wilson, 13 March 1915, Wilson Papers, series 4, file 431, reel 272).

41. Clipping, *Detroit Free Press*, 7 October 1914, enclosed with Duffield to Wilson, 18 October 1914, in Wilson Papers, series 4, file 431, reel 272. Duffield's last point was well taken, for by 1915 the general public believed that pensions were widespread in the private sector. While inaccurate, that often-repeated argument threatened the entire progressive antibusiness line by making it seem as if business was more socially conscious than government.

42. Goldschmidt to Wilson, 3 December 1914, Wilson Papers, series 4, file 224, reel 242.

The administration's response to Saltzgaber's action came from Herbert D. Brown, chief of the Bureau of Efficiency and for almost a decade one of the nation's leading pension actuaries. Brown believed, with Democratic party leaders, that Saltzgaber had intentionally sought to injure the party by making it liable to the charge that it had abandoned the old soldier. The Saltzgaber action had other ramifications. By revealing that parts of the federal bureaucracy continued to shelter old people, it made the Democrats for the first time active if begrudging participants in this commonly acknowledged form of inefficiency. Conversely, the firings could be seen as part of a larger effort to eliminate the superannuated and, by southerners especially, as the beginning of a much-needed severing of the traditional relationship between the GAR and the national government.[43]

None of these disparate viewpoints would have been compromised by a civil pension, yet for the better part of his two terms, Wilson refused to provide the civil service retirement movement with even the mildest succor. During his first term he followed the Democratic platform of 1912 and studiously avoided the issue, no easy task considering the numerous requests for aid that poured into the White House each year. For four years after 1914, pension advocates were unable to gain even a reasonable hearing from the president. Hamill managed a personal meeting on the subject in 1914 but could generate no satisfying response in the following years. When he suggested in 1915 that Wilson mention the pension in his upcoming message to Congress, Wilson pathetically replied that organizational complications would prevent it: "I am going to group all the topics of my message around a single theme and, having adopted that plan for it, it would not be possible for me to put in disconnected topics."[44]

The divisions within the pension movement seriously hampered its efforts to push an unwilling administration into action, and the depression that began in 1913 and continued through 1914 must have undercut the pension movement and been especially detrimental to progress of the presumably more costly Hamill legislation. But this does not explain Wilson's rebuff of Hamill in late 1915, when the fiscal crisis had passed.

Wilson's opposition was basic, not ephemeral. Better than most, he understood what the Democratic party was in the years after 1912 and why a civil pension was likely to be divisive. The issue had first been raised under William

43. Memorandum, Brown to Mr. REA, 22 May 1916, enclosing clipping, *Washington Times*, 17 May 1916; draft of a proposed letter to be sent by Senator Thomas Martin or Joseph W. Byrns, 23 May 1916; Brown to Joseph W. Byrns, 11 July 1916, in RG 51, 61., box 405, file "Pension Office."
44. Wilson to Hamill, 24 November 1915; Hamill to Wilson, 22 November 1915, Wilson Papers, series 4, file 43, reel 272. See also, circular letter, 22 January 1915, Wilson Papers, series 4, file 431, reel 272.

McKinley and was, thereafter, firmly identified with the Republican party. In 1912 both conservative and progressive wings of the party installed a pension plank in their platforms. The interests of these wings were somewhat different: the Taft group was more concerned with efficiency, and less with social justice, than was Roosevelt's entourage. Yet both wings had shared the administration of the civil service system (Roosevelt for a time as civil service commissioner in the 1890s) and experienced the frustrations of trying to modernize a civil service that had also to serve as a holding agency for Civil War veterans and others with a claim on the state and the party.[45] Although individual Democrats, like Secretary of Labor Wilson and Secretary of Commerce William Redfield, were outspoken proponents of civil pensions, the issue was not yet dominant in party counsels nor central to its concerns. There was hostility within the party to Republican support of its old soldier constituency through the "persistent special legislation" of the military pension, and rural and small-town Democrats—the source of the party's strength—remained unconvinced that they should be financing the retirement of urban clerks.[46] "What Senator or Member [of Congress]," asked a Patent Office official of delegates to a 1915 convention of the USCSRA, "can go back to the wheat fields and cotton belt, and say to his constituents: 'I am working to put a new tax on you and your children, so as to give a pension to government clerks who are getting too old to work and want you to support them?' "[47]

Wilson's term was the beginning of a lengthy process that would culminate in the urbanization and nationalization of the Democratic party. In 1912 or 1916, however, he could maintain his party as a viable institution only by deferring to its southern component. He did so regularly—over race, child labor, women's suffrage, and other issues. Southern Democrats, long isolated from the executive branch, were most in need of a healthy spoils system. In early 1914, their attempts to withdraw some offices from the civil service through the Moon rider to the Post Office appropriation bill were defeated by the president. He could hardly risk further alienation of this group by supporting a civil pension list. His acquiescence to the demands of the southern wing took the classic Wilsonian form manifested as well in the child labor and suffrage questions: inaction.[48]

45. *Washington Times*, 16 December 1913; *Washington Star*, 25 September 1912; in CS Clippings, file "Retirement-History, 1912–1915."

46. B. J. Read, Red Jacket Consolidated Coal and Coke Co. to Patrick J. Tumulty, 19 April 1913, Wilson Papers, series 4, file 431, reel 272.

47. Copy of *Civil Service Advocate* 6 (July 1915): 1237, Wilson Papers, series 4, file 431, reel 272.

48. Joseph P. Annin, "Mr. Wilson Not to Raise Issue," clipping, *Washington Herald*, 3 February 1914, CS Clippings, file "Retirement-History, 1912–1915"; Arthur S. Link, *Woodrow Wilson and the Progressive Era: 1910–1917*, The New American Nation Series (New York, 1963), pp. 59, 64.

This constellation of obstacles to a civil pension list was considerably modified after 1915. Employee organizations in the federal service grew rapidly in strength and size. The AF of L moved into the District of Columbia in March 1916 to organize employees protesting a House bill designed to save money by increasing working hours. Within the year, its new Federal Employees Union had, according to its organizers, three thousand members. It pressed hard for pension legislation on the grounds that younger workers were more efficient and that low salaries had prevented older workers from providing for their own retirement. The National Federation of Postal Employees also gained increased authority through affiliation with the AF of L. The war encouraged organization everywhere, but the effect was particularly dramatic where strong unions had already existed. By March 1919, for example, the Navy Yard Retirement Association could advocate the McKellar-Keating retirement bill with the authority of its eighteen thousand members.[49] Even in 1915, the Civil Service Commission counted thirty-four organizations with outside affiliations and fifteen that were independent. Its outlook was influenced by events in France, which had recently experienced a general strike by postal employees, and by similar troubles in Italy and Great Britain. The commission was convinced that the organization of government employees in the United States had reached a dangerous point: "The manifest tendency of organizations, unless carefully restricted and supervised, is to lead to political activity and to political assessments, contrary to the express provisions of the civil service law and rules." Among many examples, it noted an effort by the postal workers to prevent the dismissal of older employees.[50] Organization for pension purposes was perfected in late 1916, when Alcorn, from the Joint Retirement Committee of the Naval Gun Factory, succeeded in creating an umbrellalike policy-formation and lobbying institution called the Joint Conference Committee on Civil Service Retirement. Advocates of retirement could approach Congress with some semblance of unity.[51]

49. "Excerpts from Circular Heretofore Issued with Amendments," *Bulletin of Federal Employees' Union No. 15007, AF of L*, 23 March 1916, copy in RG 48, OS-PSM, file 15–4–5; Federal Employees Union to president, 19 May 1916, enclosing resolutions adopted at meeting of 19 May 1916; Francis Black to Wilson, 1 March 1919, in Wilson Papers, series 4, file 431, reel 272.

50. Memorandum, three commissioners to president, 24 April 1915, Wilson Papers, series 4, file 2, reel 160.

51. C. Eder Reed to Wilson, Wilson Papers, series 4, file 431, reel 272. In November 1917 the group was made up of the officers, and represented the employees, of eight government unions: T. F. Flaherty's National Federation of Postal Employees (AF of L); N. P. Alifas's International Association of Machinists; Jordan's USCSRA; John J. Deviny's NASCE; Florence Etheridge's National Federation of Federal Employees; John Beach's Federal Employees Union of Washington, D.C. (AF of L); Alice Deal's High School Teachers Union of Washington, D.C.; and Alcorn's own organization at the Naval Gun Factory.

The Democratic party was also in flux. Nationally, it had begun to accommodate organized labor to its ranks and to enact a variety of programs previously identified with the 1912 Progressive party platform. The pension followed the same script. The 1916 Democratic platform contained a pension plank, justifying legislation entirely on the narrow grounds of efficiency. Wilson, however, continued to parry all attempts to initiate executive or congressional activity that might lead to its implementation.[52]

The World War affected the issue of civil service retirement in several ways. It made the aging veteran respectable again, vitiating some of the southern antagonism toward the protection granted old soldiers by government agencies. It also aged the civil service, as young men left government employment and were replaced by the unemployed and voluntarily retired. For those who defined the war as a contest between the autocratic efficiency of Germany and the democratic efficiency of the United States, retirement seemed a natural weapon of combat. The return to peacetime conditions was responsible for an unusually high estimated yearly postwar turnover in government of 41 percent, for which retirement seemed a likely antidote.[53]

The immediate cause of Wilson's decision to support civil service retirement is not evident. He may have been influenced by an important study of public-employee retirement written by Lewis Meriam for the Institute for Government Research (IGR). Chaired by Frank Goodnow, the IGR was interested in the application of scientific method to business and government, and it made the study available to Wilson in June 1918. Meriam focused on what retirement could contribute to efficiency and morale in the government service, but he also emphasized what retirement could do to prevent the future grievances of new entrants into the system. A pension was important not so much for what it would do for older employees as for its influence on younger ones. A system had to be devised for the young, and modified as need be for the old. Wilson may well have been intrigued by Meriam's conviction that the pension could be more than a housekeeping device.[54]

Sometime in the last half of 1918, Representative Edward Keating and Senator Kenneth McKellar got the ear of the president. According to Keating,

52. Copy of Democratic platform plank on retirement, in Wilson Papers, series 4, case 3249, reel 346; Josephus Daniels to My dear Mr. President, 21 August 1916, and Wilson to My dear Daniels, 23 August 1916, in Wilson Papers, series 4, file 431, reel 272.

53. Van Riper, *History of Civil Service*, p. 261; Civil Service Reform Association, *Can a Democracy be Made Efficient?* (n.p., n.d.), in NCSL Papers, box "New York Civil Service Reform Association, 1882—."

54. Lewis Meriam, *Principles Governing the Retirement of Public Employees* (New York, 1918), pp. 4–5, 7, 18–20, 25, 294, 300; W. F. Willoughby, Director, IGR to Wilson, 13 July 1918, Wilson Papers, series 4, file 431, reel 272.

Wilson's response was entirely enthusiastic. He read their retirement bill and said: "I have just one criticism. The maximum is too low."[55] His support, and the return of a Republican Congress in the fall 1918 elections, increased the likelihood of legislation. Few surprises emerged from hearings held in 1918 and 1919. Alcorn's joint conference testified in favor of the original Keating-McKellar bill, objecting only to the small sum of money ($180 per year) the legislation provided for a retired couple. Led by Saltzgaber, agency heads recounted the problems of superannuation in their bureaus. Redfield and William Wilson perpetuated a popular misconception by insisting that "a very large percentage of the private employing corporations have inaugurated retirement pension systems."[56] When the McKellar bill reached the floor of the Senate in September 1918, it faced opposition from southern conservatives, led by Mississippi senators John Sharp Williams and James Vardaman, who were opposed to the principle of granting valuable pension rights to a special interest that should have had no particular claim on federal funds. Others found the measure too complex and unpredictable in terms of future costs and revenues. They neither trusted the cost accounting nor felt the measure appropriate to a wartime economy.[57] Opposition coalesced around Atlee Pomerene of Alabama, who managed to delay passage for almost two years while professing his desire to secure retirement legislation.[58]

In early 1920, Pomerene attempted to work his magic on the Sterling-Lehlbach bill, similar in most respects to the defunct McKellar proposal. Although he could not prevent the bill from emerging from committee and being reported to the Senate, he employed a variety of obstructionist tactics. Pomerene had enough support from progressive Republicans like George Norris, who spoke eloquently against the legislation as an unnecessary and untimely addition to bureaucracy and government spending, to make a vote on recommitting the bill very close, but in early April the measure passed.[59]

55. Keating to Harry B. Mitchell, 17 May 1940, Civil Service Papers.

56. U.S., Congress, Senate, *Retirement of Civil Service Employees, 1919*, pp. 37, 10–11, 24, 34–35; U.S., Congress, Senate, Committee on Civil Service and Retrenchment, *Retirement of Employees in Classified Civil Service: Hearing Before the Committee on Civil Service and Retrenchment on S. 4637*, Bill for the Retirement of Employees in the Civil Service, 65th Cong., 2d sess., 28 August 1918 (Washington, D.C., 1918), p. 64 (hereafter referred to as Senate, *Civil Service Retirement, 1918*).

57. U.S., Congress, Senate, *Congressional Record*, 65th Cong., 2d sess., 1918, 56, pt. 11: 11241; 65th Cong., 3d sess., 1918, 57, pt. 1: 41–42, 138; 65th Cong., 2d sess., 56, pt. 11: 11194, 11450, 11572.

58. *Congressional Record*, 65th Cong., 3d sess., 1918, 57, pt. 1: 33–34, 133–34, 143 (vote to substitute).

59. *Congressional Record*, 66th Cong., 2d sess., 1920, 59, pt. 3: 2442–44, 2445, 2498–2508, 2548, 2755 (Norris); pt. 4: 3397; 66th Cong., 2d sess., 1920, 59, pt. 5: 5164–72.

In the House, the Lehlbach companion measure was reported unanimously and generally celebrated on the floor for what it would do for old government workers who had no savings and no homes they owned outright, as well as for its anticipated impact on bureaucratic efficiency. Straight-pension advocate Hamill spoke on its behalf. Representative Louis Fairfield was applauded when he interpreted the pension bill as a radical departure, indicative of the nation's ability to adapt to urbanization, the closing of the frontier, and "all the perplexing problems of social, economic and industrial unrest."[60]

It is difficult to assess the extent to which the legislation was intended as an antiradical device. This kind of notion was not generally articulated in the Congress. But these were special times, in which organizations of public employees in Boston and Seattle were exercising some of the strength and authority that had accrued to them during the war. Brown argued from his Bureau of Efficiency that union affiliation of government employees reduced efficiency and morale. Like police and firemen, government personnel had to be separated from "strike organizations." Colorado senator Charles Thomas's attempt to use the pension list to directly undercut government unions by amending the Sterling-Lehlbach bill to exclude any employee belonging to a labor organization was, however, not taken seriously. It received only three votes. Nonetheless, it seems unlikely that the Congress was unaware of the conservative purposes that pensions had served in private industry and the professions. Several months after the pension bill became law, the *Washington Herald* acknowledged the tradeoff implicit in the system: "If the government employe is to draw pay after he quits work, he must submit to standardization of his labor while he is active, and he must be the servant of the state and not a dictator to it through massed action."[61] Thomas's amendment was summarily rejected because it was too blatant and too straightforward, a signal of confrontation in a retirement movement rooted in the more subtle soil of welfare capitalism.

There is scattered evidence of an undercurrent of opposition to compulsory retirement which was not articulated in the Congress. An official of the Frick and Lindsay Company of Pennsylvania responded to the appeals of the American Association for Labor Legislation. "Our government," he wrote, "is not a competitive one and it should take care of its old employees when they become incapacitated from [sic] work, but if an employee is capable of performing his

60. *Congressional Record*, 66th Cong., 2d sess., 1920, 59, pt. 6: 6310, 6299, 6294–95.
61. Clipping, *Washington Herald*, 21 August 1920, in CS Clippings, file "Retirees, Individual Stories (1920)." The Thomas and Brown comments are in *Congressional Record*, 66th Cong., 2d sess., 1920, 59, pt. 5: 5163–64. American Association for Labor Legislation stationery for this period carried the slogan "Social Justice is the Best Insurance Against Social Unrest" (John B. Andrews to president, 19 May 1920, Wilson Papers, series 4, file 431, reel 272).

duties and desires to keep at work he should not be deprived of that prerogative by legislation." Better, perhaps, to chloroform all employees at seventy than to "commit them to the slow death of starvation and want by putting them on a parsimonious pension list."[62] P. J. McNamara, vice-president and national legislative representative of the Brotherhood of Locomotive Firemen and Enginemen, supported the bill only reluctantly. He had talked personally with a number of government workers who did not want to be pensioned. He spoke of one old woman, "hardly able to waddle around and when you mention retirement to her she feels worse about it than some of the younger ones there would feel if you want to rub some of the paint off their faces."[63] It was too little and too late. The Lehlbach bill passed the House with fewer than sixty dissenting votes.

IMPLEMENTING THE NEW LAW

The act of May 22, 1920 provided for the retirement of civil service employees aged seventy and with at least fifteen years service. Mechanics, letter carriers, and post office clerks were eligible for benefits at age sixty-five, railway clerks at sixty-two. Annuities were determined by years of service. The maximum, for those with more than thirty years service, was $720 per year. The minimum payment of $360 per year went to those with fifteen to eighteen years service. Except for a government contribution to fund the retirement of older personnel who would be unable to contribute much to their pension, the plan was financed entirely through a 2.5 percent deduction from salary. Retirement was neither voluntary nor immediately mandatory, but a hybrid of the two. An employee who had reached the retirement age under the act would normally be retired. He might, however, ask to be retained for a two-year term, at the end of which another request could be made. The act required, however, that by 1930 no employee could be retained more than four years beyond the listed age of retirement.[64]

For thousands of federal employees in the District of Columbia and elsewhere, August 20, 1920 was the last day of work. In most agencies the atmosphere was morose, the separations sad and dramatic. Secretary of War Newton

62. H. M. Barlett to American Association for Labor Legislation, in American Association for Labor Legislation Papers, Labor-Management Documentation Center, Labor and Industrial Relations Institute, Cornell University, Ithaca, New York, microfilm reel 21. Hereafter referred to as AALL Papers.

63. McNamara to Timothy Sheaz, 12 March 1920, AALL Papers, reel 21; *Congressional Record*, 66th Cong., 2d sess., 1920, 59, pt. 6: 6381 (final vote).

64. U.S., Laws, Statutes, *Civil Service Retirement and Salary Classification Laws*, comp., Elmer A. Lewis, Superintendent, Document Room, House of Representatives (Washington, D.C., 1927), pp. 1–5.

D. Baker found himself apologizing for the meager annuities provided in the legislation. In Chicago, 135 postal workers retired under protest, claiming their pensions were not sufficient to support them.[65] In Washington there was intense concern for the fate of more than ten thousand local and forty thousand national unclassified civil service employees who had not been specifically included in the retirement system. Another immediate problem involved those who had reached the retirement age but were not eligible for pension because they had less than fifteen years of government service. "Great leniency," said the *Washington Star*, "is being exercised by department heads in these cases, and officials expect the cases of separation without annuity to be few and far between."[66]

The Congress had not passed a compulsory retirement measure, but this did not prevent several agency heads in positions of influence from attempting to make it so. Postmaster General Albert Burleson believed the act could be interpreted to compel the dismissal of all employees who had reached retirement age; he was warned by the president to issue extension certificates to efficient personnel until the cabinet had arrived at a uniform policy.[67] The worst culprit was efficiency zealot Saltzgaber, still head of the Pension Bureau. Although Saltzgaber was willing to acknowledge that employees of retirement age did the best they could and that many were reasonable workers, he refused to grant a single extension to any of the eighty-eight persons who applied. "I do not believe there

65. Clipping, *Washington Post*, 21 August 1920, CS Clippings, file "Retirees, Individual Stories (1920)"; clipping, *Washington Star*, 26 August 1920; *Washington Times*, 20 August 1920, CS Clippings, file "Retirement Act, 1920."

66. Clipping, *Washington Star*, 17 August 1920, CS Clippings, file "Retirement Act, 1920"; clipping, *Washington Star*, 18 August 1920, ibid. The classification issue was most easily resolved. By June 1920, before the act went into effect, the Civil Service Commission had included 118 positions under the label "mechanic," including boxmakers, diemakers, bricklayers, glaziers, plumbers, and steamfitters. Unskilled laborers, however, were for some time specifically denied coverage in spite of "insistent demand" because of the administrative problems created by the intermittent and uncertain duration of their employment. By the end of 1921, the Civil Service Commission and the president had agreed that unskilled laborers who fulfilled the fifteen-year service requirement were eligible for an annuity at age seventy. Legislation to include laborers making less than $600 per year was successfully pursued by the Warren Harding administration and the National Association of Post Office Laborers. The original legislation was also amended in 1922 to provide eventual annuities to employees over fifty-five, fulfilling the service requirements, who had been involuntarily separated from the service for reasons other than misconduct. See Memorandum, U.S. Civil Service Commission, 12 June 1920, Wilson Papers, series 4, file 431A, reel 272; memorandum, Helen Gardener, G. R. Wales, and John H. Bartlett to The President, 23 December 1921, Warren Harding Papers, Manuscript Division, Library of Congress, Washington, D.C., file 419, folder 1, reel 204; John H. Bosche to Will H. Hays, 22 May 1922; Hays to George B. Christian, Jr., 29 May 1922; The White House to Senator Thomas Sterling, 9 June 1922; Helen Gardener to The President, 6 June 1922, in Harding Papers, file 419, folder 1, reel 204; U.S., Laws, Statutes, *Civil Service Retirement*, comp., Lewis, p. 13.

67. Memorandum, 2d Asst. Postmaster General to Postmaster General, 15 July 1920; Tumulty to Burleson, 17 July 1920, in Wilson Papers, series 4, file 431A, reel 272.

is one [older person in the pension bureau]," he wrote, "whose work may not be better done by a younger person and generally at a lower initial salary; consequently I do not see how I can honestly certify that the continuance of any of them would be advantageous to the public service."[68] This unpopular policy was soon repudiated by Interior officials, and by 1923 the Bureau of Pensions, minus Saltzgaber, was making extension decisions like other agencies. This meant that while department heads usually recommended for continuance only those employees capable of maintaining a high level of efficiency, they were vulnerable to an occasional sentimental lapse. Margaret C. Towles, for example, was recommended for continuance by the chief of the Certificate Division of the Bureau of Pensions. Towles was not only efficient; she had also for many years been the sole support of an invalid sister, and "the enforced reduction to the amount of [the] retirement allowance would prove a very great hardship indeed." A less needy case involved an employee in the Congressional Division whose request for continuance received a positive recommendation because "he, his daughter and wife are buying a home on the installment." Extension reports often contained information on marital relations, property holdings, earning capacity of spouse, and dependents.[69] The 1920 legislation had not yet depersonalized the bureaucracy.

AMENDING THE LAW TO MAKE IT WORK

Before his retirement in the first days of 1921, Jacob Starr was among those charged with administering the Sterling-Lehlbach legislation in the Office of the Adjutant General. He was immediately impressed with the inequities among retired federal employees, especially the discrepancy between civil service and military annuities, and the genuine deprivation that faced some recent retirees who were living on a good deal less than the sixty-dollar monthly maximum payment provided in the legislation. When he left government service, Starr managed to secure a list of persons who had retired up to December 31, 1920, including where they lived, when they had retired, and how much annuity they were receiving. Hundreds of invitations brought thirteen men, including pension

---

68. Saltzgaber to John Barton Payne, 30 June 1920, Wilson Papers, series 4, file 431, microfilm reel 272; U.S., Congress, Senate, Committee on Civil Service, *Retirement of Employees in the Classified Civil Service: Report No. 604, to Accompany S. 786*, April 5, 1926, 69th Cong., 1st sess. (n.p., n.d.), p. 16.

69. See file "Retirement at 70," RG 15–D, "Records of the Veterans Administration," Bureau of Pensions, Office of the Chief Clerk, Miscellaneous Personnel Records, 1884–1930, box 7, which consists largely of responses to Chief Clerk Hays Haymaker, who had requested from various department heads reports on employees over seventy.

movement veterans Robert Armour and Theodore Swayze, to the first meeting of the National Association of Retired Federal Employees (NARFE).[70]

Products of the chaotic organizational situation that had divided federal employees for two decades, Starr and his colleagues in NARFE were self-conscious about the need for unity and therefore reluctant to pursue causes that might prove disruptive or distracting. When Alcorn was demoted at the Navy Yard, for example, the executive committee considered an action for reinstatement but deferred to a stronger spirit of noninterference. In spite of some opposition within NARFE to the then prevalent demand for retirement after thirty years service, the organization was content to allow other groups to work their legislative will except to the extent that the passage of legislation might prevent or delay an increase in annuities. NARFE remained independent of any political party and refused even direct requests for aid to candidates for public office. Caution also prevailed in structuring and organizing NARFE. Although there was some early talk about the need for building on a foundation of decentralized auxiliaries, Starr and his successors recognized the natural, easy unity of the retired Washington bureaucrats who, together wih a small number of local people still employed in government agencies, provided the organization's essential strength.[71]

NARFE remained entirely unconcerned with the relationship between retirement and efficiency in government. It would later take on a broad social function, entertaining, educating, and providing a limited sense of community for retired government employees through its magazine, the *Annuitant*.[72] In the 1920s, however, the organization was concerned only with annuitants whose retirement incomes would not buy decent shelter, clothing, and food. These people wrote of their troubles while remitting the one-dollar membership fee and, as the cost of living rose during the 1920s, a good many wrote the president of the United States. Sixty-six dollars a month, wrote the "Wife of a long service man," would pay the rent on about one room in New York City. Calvin Coolidge incurred the animosity of hundreds of pensioners who found his economy cam-

70. "NARFE History," typescript of an unsigned address, p. 1; Xerox copy of minutes of 19 February 1921 meeting; NARFE, Executive Committee, Minutes, Meeting of 15 October 1921, in a handwritten and typewritten volume, "Permanent File of the Minutes of the Executive Committee, October 1921 through December 1922," in NARFE Papers.

71. NARFE, "Permanent File," meetings of 12 November 1921; 19 November 1921; 16 November 1921; 10 December 1921; 25 March 1922; typescript of meeting of executive committee, 26 February 1923; joint meeting of committees of the association, 25 September 1923; joint meeting of committees, 17 December 1923; and executive committee, 23 October 1928, in bound volume of minutes of meetings of various committees of NARFE, in NARFE Papers. By late 1921 NARFE had over seven thousand members.

72. *Annuitant* 14 (January 1939): 12.

paign disgusting and demanded an increase in annuities from the swelling pension fund. Erastus Williamson, eighty-three years old and retired from the pay department of the Navy Yard, wrote that he and his wife had suffered on the government's maximum civil service pension: "If I had not owned my house I don't know what we could have done." As for the legislation that would have increased payments, he wrote, "It seemed *wicked* that it failed last session."[73] A Chicago postal worker with thirty-seven years' experience had deferred his retirement for three years because the pension would put him in the Cook County poorhouse. Many who were recently retired were living with their children or on charity of some kind. Several Customs Service employees from Rockland County, New York, firm Republicans all, hired a broker to communicate their disappointment with Coolidge's official penury. Just now, wrote the broker, they "have the impression that you have gone out of your way to make life a little more miserable for them and their fellow workers."[74]

NARFE also represented those who were better off but were suffering from the shock of a suddenly reduced standard of living. This point of view is present in "GOODBYE, PAY ROLL: Wail of a Retired Federal Clerk," published in the *Annuitant*:

Twice a month in rain or shine,
You've turned up so slick and fine,—
Pay envelope, good and true,
How I dread to part with you.

You met my needs from day to day,
And helped to keep the wolf away,—
Pay envelope, good and true,
How can I live apart from you?

Butcher, baker, candy maker,
And other traders by the acre,—
Pay envelope good and true,
How they'll dread my cut with you.

Friends in office I adore,
But love the pay envelope even more,—
Manila jacket,—hue or buff,—
How I hate to lose your "stuff."

73. Ibid. 1 (1922): 1; Wife of, to President, no date, Harding Papers, file 419, folder 1, reel 204; Williamson to President, 7 April 1926; H. F. Frink to President Coolidge, 9 March 1925, Calvin Coolidge Papers, Manuscript Division, Library of Congress, Washington, D.C., file 43, reel 43.
74. George D. James Co., brokers, to Coolidge, 19 May 1926; G. W. Ford to Coolidge, 25 April 1926, Coolidge Papers, file 43, reel 43.

> But Uncle Sam, the ruthless guy,
> With scarce a bat of either eye,—
> Pay envelope good and true,—
> He's knocked the spots clean off of you.[75]

The poem illustrates as well the dangers in sentimentalizing the relationship between older workers and their jobs; money may not have been a substitute for the workplace, but neither was it of marginal importance. The Congress recognized this, as well as the power of NARFE, when in 1926 it increased the maximum benefit to one thousand dollars. NARFE was largely responsible for insuring that benefits went to employees already retired.[76]

The other major legislative effort of the 1920s, the campaign for retirement by years of service rather than age, ended in failure in spite of the considerable pressures brought to bear. Retirement after thirty years' service was particularly popular with workers who classified their jobs as especially exhausting and enervating. Postal workers who experienced the mechanization and speedup in the federal postal service claimed their shortened work lives justified retirement after thirty years. Navy Yard employees argued that ship construction was characterized by such a high level of nervous tension that a fifty-year-old worker with thirty years' experience was generally "a physical wreck and ready for retirement."[77] Neither Alcorn of the joint conference nor John Beach of the Pension Bureau argued for thirty-year retirement. Instead, each backed a provision in the bill for retirement at age forty-five with fifteen years' service for employees separated from the service because of some necessary reduction in force. Beach was responding to an ongoing problem of layoffs in his agency, Alcorn to Navy Yard unemployment caused by disarmament.[78] Thirty-year retirement

---

75. By A. P. R., in *Anuitant* 1, no. 2 (1924): 19.

76. *Ibid.*, July 1949, p. 11. The National Federation of Federal Employees, founded during World War I, was also an effective petitioner for the increased annuity and early retirement. See Luther C. Steward to President, 2 March 1925, and undated 110 page petition, in Coolidge Papers, file 43, reel 43.

77. Quoted from "article," sent to Harding by the Navy Yard Retirement Association, in Harding Papers, file 419, folder 1, reel 204; *Union Postal Clerk* 22 (February 1926): 8; George Eleutler to Coolidge, 16 December 1924, Coolidge Papers, file 43, reel 43; U.S., Congress, Senate, Committee on Civil Service and Retrenchment, *The Civil Service Retirement Act: Joint Hearings before the Committees on Civil Service of the Senate and House of Representatives*, 69th Cong., 1st sess., 14, 15, and 16 January 1926 (Washington, D.C., 1926), pp. 65–69, 123, 178, 185 (hereafter referred to as Senate, Committee on Civil Service and Retrenchment, *Civil Service Retirement Act: Joint Hearings, 1926*.

78. U.S., Congress, Senate, Committee on Civil Service and Retrenchment, *Civil Service Retirement Act: Joint Hearings, 1926*, pp. 22–23, 53, 55, 58–59; Eleutler letter, cited note 77; typewritten "Report of Survey of the Bureau of Pensions," 17 September 1923, RG 15-D, Bureau of Pensions, Office of the Chief Clerk, Miscellaneous Personnel Records, 1884–1930, box 7, file "Old Age Pension Report at Survey," p. 45.

also appealed to individual employees who had begun work at an exceptionally early age and found, under the present system, that they would not be eligible for retirement until they had accumulated forty, forty-five, and even fifty years' service. "Why," wrote a woman in the printing trades of the Government Printing Office who had thirty-five years' experience and was eight years from retirement, "*should anyone be discriminated against because he was so unfortunate as to have to go to work young?*"[79]

What Congress rejected and accepted in 1926 tells us a good deal about what that body intended in relationship to retirement. It also confirms that retirement legislation was designed to increase efficiency, but that this could not be accomplished independent of the social needs of employees. Several provisions of the new law were essentially unemployment measures, in which Congress recognized the growing problems of mechanics in the federal service and the increasing difficulty middle-aged employees were having finding any kind of work after they were dropped from government jobs. In slightly modified form, the Congress accepted the Beach-Alcorn proposals; an employee forty-five to fifty-five years old, separated because of necessary force reductions and with fifteen years' service, was entitled to an annuity at age fifty-five. Any mechanic with thirty years' service, separated under like conditions, was eligible for an annuity at age sixty-two.[80] Across-the-board thirty-year retirement, however, was seen as excessively costly and unlikely to return commensurate benefits in efficiency. Still, the system was not working properly. Because of inadequate annuities, the impact of the 1920 law had been seriously circumscribed. Faced with a bleak economic future upon retirement, employees preferred to work and applied for the continuance; administrators, often aware of the straitened circumstances of their subordinates, refused to turn out the inefficient. The increased annuity under the 1926 act was designed to shore up the old legislation and make it the instrument of efficiency it had been expected to be.[81]

SUMMARY

It would be a mistake to see the retirement movement as a comfortable or equal alliance between the advocates of retirement as security—as a form of social justice—and the proponents of retirement as efficiency. Retirement as a

79. Sarah C. Cromelian to Calvin Coolidge, 20 November 1923, Coolidge Papers, file 43, reel 43.

80. U.S., Laws, Statutes, *Civil Service Retirement*, comp., Lewis, pp. 41, 46; Senate, Committee on Civil Service, *Retirement: Report No. 604*, p. 11.

81. U.S., Congress, Senate, Committee on Civil Service and Retrenchment, *Civil Service Retirement Act: Join Hearings, 1926*, pp. 41, 65.

method of caring for the aged became necessary and popular when business-oriented reformers decided that superannuation in the government service was too costly to endure. Government bureaucrats created organizations to press for retirement legislation only when the existing, informal retirement mechanism (i.e., employment within the bureaucracy) was threatened by efficiency advocates. The organizational and legislative efforts of the United States Civil Service Retirement Association and the National Association of Retired Federal Employees insured that the laws of 1920 and 1926 were more generous and humane than they would otherwise have been, but these organizations represent not so much the demand for a new life-style called "retirement" as a defensive reaction against proponents of economic efficiency.

Those who favored increased efficiency were the dominant component in the political history of retirement. They created commissions to study the larger problem of efficiency and the smaller one of superannuation; ultimately, they secured legislation. Yet these successes were not achieved without a curious kind of opposition. Supervisors and bureau chiefs refused to certify the inefficiency of their older employees—though the evidence indicates they believed these employees to be inefficient. In the wake of the 1920 legislation, many remained sensitive to the personal needs of their employees, jeopardizing the basic purpose of the law. When, in 1897, L. C. Gage set in motion the forces leading to retirement legislation, his Department of the Treasury was a caretaking agency, a kind of informal retirement institution; like other federal bureaus, it did not easily shed this character. Even in the mid-1920s, the federal bureaucracy was not yet the fully rationalized instrument that some desired. It was still laced with personal ties and informal bonds that often transcended increasing pressures for purely contractual relationships. It was the function of retirement legislation to sever these ties, break the bonds of informality, and usher in the contractual society. The difficulty with which this process was carried out testifies to the ongoing presence of community under difficult conditions and to the continued hold of nineteenth-century values in a twentieth-century culture committed to modernization.

4 Retirement in Education: The Economic and Social Functions of the Teachers' Pension

THE PUBLIC SCHOOLS

In April 1891, the *Journal of Education* published a symposium on teachers' pensions, the first national attention the issue had received. The honor of opening the symposium went to U.S. Commissioner of Education W. T. Harris, who presented the case against pensions—even then, a minority view, shared by only six of the fifteen symposium participants. A general system of teachers' pensions, Harris argued, would bring undesirable persons into the profession, prevent the formation of habits of thrift, and reduce salaries, which were, Harris emphasized, rising. "Consequently," the commissioner said, "the teacher with an equal amount of thrift or personal economy may provide for his old age just as well as the mass of the community."[1]

This last remark must have seemed as hollow to public-school teachers as it did to a number of symposium participants, for at no time in the half century after 1870 did teachers receive more than minimal compensation. Chicago teachers argued before the Board of Education in 1895 that their salaries were much the same as they had been in 1877.[2] A deflationary economy eased the teachers' plight somewhat through most of the late nineteenth century, but after 1900 this protection was not available. In 1905, E. G. Kimball, president of the District of Columbia Teachers' Annuity and Aid Association, appealed to Andrew Carnegie for subsidy. The situation he depicted might have been that of any of hundreds of school districts across the nation: low salaries, a rising cost of living, a heavily female population bound to the city by family ties and thus unable to pursue higher salaries elsewhere. Several years later, the National

1. *Journal of Education* 33 (2 April 1891): 211.
2. Don T. Davis, "The Chicago Teachers' Federation and the School Board," statement of February 1917, in Chicago Teachers' Federation (CTF) Papers, Chicago Historical Society, Chicago, Illinois, box 1; symposium statement by John E. Bradley, *Journal of Education* 33 (2 April 1891): 211.

Education Association (NEA) presented data revealing that in forty-four of forty-eight cities, salaries of elementary teachers were below those of laborers. Averaging only forty years of age in 1913, urban teachers had become bitter over their inability to save.[3] Active or retired, Boston's women teachers were predominantly unmarried, burdened by the need to spend a portion of their earnings in the care of dependents, and had very limited savings or none at all.[4]

During the Progressive Era, the profession remained relatively young, because most teachers, in light of salary levels, could not afford to make the public schools a career. Young women left teaching to marry (an act prohibited women in many school systems), and both men and women were attracted by more lucrative parallel opportunities in growing state and national government bureaucracies. Only during the World War, when general work-force shortages forced school boards to recruit older teachers and to reinstate some previously retired, were students taught by larger numbers of teachers in their fifties, sixties, and seventies. For several years thereafter, an unusually severe teacher shortage aroused interest in higher salaries but produced no significant gains, because the war had only intensified a condition of limited supply which was characteristic of the market for teachers throughout this period.[5] School administrators regularly complained of shortages and lamented the intense interurban and interstate competition for those available. Educators, like industrialists, found high turnover rates expensive and socially undesirable.[6]

3. Kimball to Carnegie, Andrew Carnegie Papers, Manuscript Division, Library of Congress, Washington, D.C., box 118; U.S., Congress, Senate, *Teacher's Retirement Fund: Address Given at Washington, January 16, 1909, before the College Women's Club*, by Lyman A. Best, Secretary of the Board of Retirement of the Department of Education of New York City, S. Doc. 541, 61st Cong., 2d sess. (n.p., 1910), p. 2; National Education Association (NEA), *Report of the Committee on Teachers' Salaries and Cost of Living* (Ann Arbor, Mich., 1913), pp. 49, 229; U.S., Congress, House, Committee on the District of Columbia, *Retirement of Public School Teachers in the District of Columbia: Hearings before the Committee on the District of Columbia on H.R. 2076*, 66th Cong., 1st sess., 5 and 6 June 1919 (Washington, D.C., 1919), pp. 6, 50–51.

4. Women's Educational and Industrial Union, Department of Research, *Old-Age Support of Women Teachers: Provisions for Old Age Made by Women Teachers in the Public Schools of Massachusetts*, Studies in Economic Relations of Women, vol. 11 (Boston, 1921), pp. 11–12, 47, 51, 54, 57.

5. House, Committee on District of Columbia, *Retirement of Public School Teachers: Hearings*, p. 9; NEA, *Teachers' Salaries and Cost of Living*, pp. 212–15; California, *Report of the California Public School Teachers' Retirement Salary Commission* (Sacramento, 1929), p. 21; Lester Dix, *The Economic Basis for the Teacher's Wage* (New York, 1931), pp. 11, 87.

6. Jesse Crawford Waller, *Tenure and Transiency of Teachers in Kentucky*, George Peabody College for Teachers Contributions to Education No. 60 (Nashville, 1929), p. 50; Lester Ward Williams, "Turnover Among Secondary Teachers in Illinois" (abstract, Ph.D. Diss., University of Illinois, 1931). The problem seems to have been less one of teachers moving from one state to another than of the early age of withdrawal from the profession. See Reuben T. Shaw, *A Study of the Adequacy and Effectiveness of the Pennsylvania School Employes' Retirement System* (Philadelphia, 1926), chap. 2.

If school districts were not generous with their funds, they were also reluctant to approach older teachers of declining ability with the full force of which they were contractually capable and which, on grounds of reason and logic alone, they might have applied. When dismissal meant starvation or the almshouse, school boards would not dismiss. James MacAlister, who had recently completed eight successful years as Philadelphia's superintendent of schools, chose the 1891 convention of the NEA as a forum for disseminating his views on caring for superannuated teachers.

> Many good and faithful women there were, incompetent and inefficient indeed, but still teaching the best they knew how and up to the standard required of them when appointed many years ago. Will you turn these women out upon the streets, send them to the poor-house? So long as we have no pensions to give them, shall we not keep them in the schools? We must do so, and make the best we can of them.[7]

In Philadelphia, MacAlister had refused to remove an excellent teacher who, because of age, twice a day left her class to a student monitress and took a nap. He was spared excessive guilt when a woman he felt compelled to dismiss because she was too feeble even to come to school became the charge of wealthy retailer John Wanamaker.[8] Nor was MacAlister the only practitioner of this ad hoc form of community assistance. John Swett, superintendent of the San Francisco public schools, claimed to have seen many women who were allowed to remain in schools after they were "broken in health, and long after they ought to be retired."[9]

David Snedden, well known for his progressive approach as commissioner of education for Massachusetts, believed that school systems shared this tendency with other public-sector bureaucracies. "No public employment," he said, "will resolutely dismiss faithful servants who have become incapacitated, if these possess no resources to fall back upon."[10] As Snedden, MacAlister, and others realized, however, this caretaking function was not as well suited to schools as it was to other institutions. A corporation might shift an older worker to some less demanding task, or a government agency, existing outside a market framework, could absorb a limited number of older employees who did nothing

7. In the discussion following William E. Anderson, "Qualification and Supply of Teachers for City Public Schools," *Journal of Proceedings and Addresses of the National Education Association*, Session of the Year 1891, Held at Toronto, Canada (New York, 1891), pp. 422–30, 431–43 (discussion), p. 438 (quotation).

8. Elizabeth A. Allen, "Teachers' Pensions,—The Story of a Women's Campaign," *Review of Reviews* 15 (June 1897): 701.

9. *Journal of Education* 33 (April 2, 1891): 213.

10. Charles A. Prosser and W. I. Hamilton, *The Teacher and Old Age*, intro. by David Snedden (Boston, 1913), p. vi.

at all; the result might not be productive, but neither was it particularly difficult to achieve physically nor was it of much negative impact. The teacher's work, on the other hand, was perceived as an indivisible unit—one teacher, before one class, all day. That a teacher of declining skills or energies might teach less than a full day or assist in another's classroom seems not to have been considered.[11] The school could be maintained as a retirement institution, therefore, only if officials were willing to allow superannuated teachers to be completely function-less (at home or in the school), or if they were retained in their normal classroom responsibilities. The first option was not entertained; the second, for reasons explored later, was considered potentially damaging to the student. "A school-teacher's work," noted a Senate report on public education in the District of Columbia, "is personal, direct, and positive. It works for the good or the ill of each pupil. To retain a superannuated teacher in the service is a positive harm to her pupils and a manifest injustice to the rising generation."[12]

In the thirty years after 1890, educators adopted a variety of mechanisms, including tenure, certification, and higher salaries, to deal with the economic and social problems explicit and implicit in this description. But it was the pen-sion, in 1890 a device associated largely with Civil War veterans, which had the broadest appeal and the widest application. From the very first, the pension was seldom perceived only as a weapon against old-age dependency; it was, indeed, a multiedged tool, designed and engineered to modify the sex and age compo-sition of the teaching force, the market for teachers, and the climate of the profession, and to achieve a number of other aims under the rubrics of economic efficiency, social efficiency, and social justice. Because the pension was ex-pected to do so much, its advocates were not always in agreement; teachers and administrators sometimes differed, and teachers often split along age and in-come lines. Nonetheless, the teachers' pension was a mechanism by which American culture sought to reshape its educational institutions to achieve eco-nomic progress and social order. This objective was limited and compromised by a desire to perpetuate nineteenth-century concepts of community and to main-tain the teachers as a symbol of cultural stability.

When the NEA came to consider the pension question in 1891, no teacher pension legislation existed anywhere in the United States. Most of the other developed nations, on the other hand, had for some time maintained state or municipal superannuation benefit systems. Russia's was inaugurated in 1819; Italy's began in Genoa in 1854. Typically, Americans had relied on voluntary

11. Lillian C. Flint, "Pensions for Women Teachers," *Century Magazine* 79 (February 1910): 618.
12. U.S., Congress, Senate, Committee on the District of Columbia, *Teachers' Retirement*, S. 1064, 64th Cong., 2d sess., 14 February 1917 (Washington, D.C., 1917), p. 2.

associations to which teachers contributed in return for assistance during illness or in old age. The first of these institutions was created in the late 1860s. They tended to be concentrated in eastern cities, where teachers were older and more plentiful. Between 1879 and 1891, as the teaching staffs of the newer midwestern cities aged and prepared themselves for retirement, associations were formed in Cleveland (1879), Detroit (1888), St. Paul (1890), and Chicago (1891). Some of these had permanent funds, while others raised money when they needed it, often by passing the hat. All these early groups provided what was essentially ad hoc aid, for annuities were not available until 1887, and then only within the New York City association. Boston teachers supplemented their city pensions with an annuity from a teachers' association retirement fund established in 1900.[13]

The first pension legislation was introduced in 1879, at the behest of the Brooklyn Teachers' Association. That bill, and another introduced two years later, failed to pass. New Jersey was the scene of the next pension drive, initiated in 1890 by three female public-school teachers who had found themselves standing on a street corner, unable to discover any convincing reason why police and firemen, and not teachers, should have pension coverage. The next year the movement took a crucial turn when several events demonstrated that pensions had the support of the educational establishment. At Philadelphia, in February of 1891, the Department of Superintendence of the NEA recommended retirement with thirty years' service. That April, the *Journal of Education* conducted its pensions symposium. The 1891 Toronto convention of the NEA considered retirement at some length.[14]

Pension advocates in a number of states now found a more receptive climate. Brooklyn teachers and principals succeeded in selling the idea to a skeptical board of education; in 1895 the New York state legislature passed a bill enabling Brooklyn to inaugurate a pension program. The New Jersey teachers found their task complicated by the breadth of their goal—legislation providing potentially for all teachers in the state—and the hostility of the governor who, in 1895, met with a pension committee of fifteen women and one man, listened intently, and according to descriptions that filtered back to the teachers after they

---

13. A. Reichenbach, "The Superannuation of Teachers," *Education* 16 (March 1896): 386–87; Lucy Edith Hobbs, *History of the Teachers' Annuity Movement in Iowa*, University of Iowa Extension Division, *Bulletin* 145, College of Education Series No. 20, 1 April 1926 (Iowa City, 1926), pp. 5–6; Mary D. Bradford, "Teachers' Pensions and Insurance," *Journal of Education* 61 (11 May 1905): 512; Women's Educational and Industrial Union, *Old-Age Support of Women Teachers*, p. 39.

14. Senate, *Teacher's Retirement Fund*, pp. 6–7; Allen, "Teachers' Pensions," p. 700; Reichenbach, "Superannuation of Teachers," p. 388; Anderson, "Qualification and Supply"; Shaw, *Pennsylvania Retirement System*, pp. 11–12.

had departed, received the report "with great laughter." The next year, when the New Jersey State Teachers' Federation entered the fray, the teachers abandoned their efforts at state pensions in favor of mutual old-age and invalid insurance under state law. Their bill became law—though without the governor's signature.[15]

Chicago's women matched New Jersey's in aggressiveness. Preliminary drafts of teacher-pension legislation were written by Arvilla C. DeLuce, who also managed to secure the written support of all but one teacher in the system. Although the teachers would not organize in the powerful Chicago Teachers' Federation until March 1897, they had pension legislation by 1895. The Chicago Board of Education proved remarkably cooperative, offering the teachers the use of the board room for meetings. Catherine Goggin, whose career in Chicago teachers' politics was just beginning, made a speech of some reknown to a House committee in Springfield ("Mr. Chairman I want the pension"). And the state's governor, John Peter Altgeld, helped construct the bill to protect teachers' tenure.[16]

For fifteen years, the states did little about teachers' pensions, principally because of actuarial difficulties. Then, between 1911 and 1915, twenty-three states enacted legislation, and by 1916 a total of thirty-three states had some system of retirement for public-school teachers. Of these systems, twenty-one, most in the Midwest and Northeast, were statewide, and the same number were contributory—supported by both public and private (teacher) contributions. The Massachusetts legislation of 1913 followed an actuarial investigation; it has been called the first "scientific" teachers' pension law.[17]

This was the age of efficiency. In passing these laws and in their administration, legislatures, school boards, and superintendents naturally found themselves concerned with the hard, financial realities of public-school operations. Proponents and opponents of the pension recognized immediately that, depending on one's philosophical outlook, the pension might be either a bounty, granted, much like the waiter's tip, in appreciation of past service but conceived as a gift, discretionary and noncontractual; or a deferred wage, earned in the

15. Senate, *Teacher's Retirement Fund*, p. 6; Allen, "Teachers' Pensions," pp. 703–04.
16. Arvilla C. DeLuce, "Brief Account of the Pension Movement," handwritten statement, CTF Papers, box 1, file "Historical Data"; Catherine Goggin, "Brief History of Chicago Teachers Federation," statement, November 3, 1906, ibid.; recollection of Margaret Haley, in "Stenographic Report of the Regular Meeting of the Chicago Teachers Federation, October 12, 1935," CTF Papers, box 19, p. 78.
17. U.S., Department of Interior, Bureau of Education, *State Pension Systems for Public-School Teachers*, by Carson Ryan, Jr. and Roberta King, Prepared for the Committee on Teachers' Salaries, Pensions, and Tenure of the National Education Association, *Bulletin* 14 (Washington, D.C., 1916), pp. 5–9; Hobbs, *Teachers' Annuity Movement*, pp. 7, 22.

process of one's regular work, and therefore an entirely contractual obligation. Teachers usually felt more secure with the deferred wage concept, and contributory plans made this definition a necessity.[18]

The pension was a wage, deferred into retirement. At once a theory and a description of reality for school boards and teachers, this idea had some interesting implications. When the subject first received national attention in 1891, objections came largely from those who feared that pensions would reduce compensation by siphoning off funds from the small pool that nineteenth-century taxpayers grudgingly made available for teachers' salaries. This seems not to have been an appealing prospect even to state legislators and school administrators, who perhaps understood how easily the wage issue could trigger teacher resistance and organization. Progress toward the first New Jersey legislation was dependent upon the ability of the teachers to convince the legislature that this would not occur.[19]

There was, of course, another possibility: salaries might be reduced, but without incident. After all, what was the value of a deferred wage? On this, one could only speculate. In a letter to Frank Vanderlip, formerly active in retirement matters with the Treasury Department and now a member of the Board of Trustees of the Carnegie Foundation for the Advancement of Teaching (CFAT), life insurance executive Charles D. Norton explored the problem: "If teachers (and other workers) are to be provided with pensions gratis by employers the wage scale can and will remain lower than it can remain if the teachers are to pay for their own old age and disability pensions."[20] This implied that a dollar placed in a pension plan by the school board was worth more than a dollar in salary; that teachers placed a higher valuation on future income than present, and on security rather than immediate consumption. This was also the consensus of the NEA. It seems likely, then, that pensions had particular appeal to school administrators at a time when inflation threatened school budgets and increased the difficulties of maintaining teacher salaries, and when, for the same reason, the promise to pay became cheaper every year. The early pension plans, moreover, were often so poorly constructed that the promise could become completely worthless. Having deferred the wage, the schools could refuse to pay it.[21]

Pension legislation also served as a way of reaching the rural areas and the

18. "Stenographic Report of Monthly Meeting of the Chicago Teachers' Federation, March 10, 1928," CTF Papers, box 8, p. 84.

19. Allen, "Teachers' Pensions," p. 701; *Journal of Education* 33 (2 April 1891): 211–14.

20. Norton to Vanderlip, 1 February 1908, Frank A. Vanderlip Papers, Rare Book and Manuscript Library, Columbia University, New York, N.Y., box 11, file "CFAT. Misc. Correspondence."

21. Ibid.; William McAndrew, "Some Suggestions on School Salaries," *Educational Review* 27 (April 1904): 383.

small towns, where salaries were especially low. Reluctant to extend direct financial aid to local school districts, state officials concerned about the quality of education in relatively isolated regions could force some improvement through the pension. Norton went so far as to suggest a $10 million national endowment which, in conjunction with a semipublic corporation, would affect every teacher in the United States through a system of standard old-age pensions. "Any plan," he wrote, "which enables a community to eliminate superannuated teachers, without working any hardships would be enormously valuable. Small towns and rural districts are helpless in this respect."[22] The danger, which California faced in the 1920s when it considered including counties and school districts among the contributors to retirement funds, was the old one that these jurisdictions would take the costs out of salaries.[23]

Once established, the pension tempted school boards into policies that may have been economically justifiable but were only marginally ethical. The prospect of all those future obligations encouraged age discrimination in hiring, since older teachers would be eligible for pensions sooner, perhaps before they had contributed sufficiently to the fund. There is evidence that the celebrated dismissal of sixty-eight Chicago teachers in 1916 was linked to the bankrupt pension fund. Teachers charged that an ongoing probe of teacher competency was in part designed to eliminate older teachers, "thereby saving a salary that is a maximum salary and thereby saving a pension that would have to be paid were that teacher retained in the system, and retired in accordance with the intent of the law."[24]

The Great Depression of the 1930s intensified the pressures to institute such policies. Early in the decade, Cleveland school officials calculated that a simple change in the retirement age from seventy to sixty-five, by making possible the replacement of higher salaried teachers by lower salaried ones, would enable the system to save $100,000 while maintaining the size of its staff. One large system reportedly brought local pressure to bear on those eligible to retire, urging them to do so to make jobs available for new teachers at lower salaries. Wherever funding was a problem, school districts used retirement regulations to remove older teachers from the payrolls.[25]

22. Norton letter, cited note 20; Illinois, The Illinois Educational Commission, *Tentative Recommendations in Regard to Minimum Salaries for Teachers*, Proposed by the Educational Commission of Illinois, *Bulletin* 7 (Springfield, 1909), p. 24.

23. California, *Teachers' Retirement Salary Commission Report*, p. 26.

24. Statement of William E. Grady, in "Addresses at Teachers' Union Mass Meeting," 6 July 1916, CTF Papers, box 45, file "July–October 1916," p. 28; Walter A. Jessup, *The Teaching Staff* (Cleveland, 1916), p. 65.

25. T. C. Holy, *Cleveland Teachers' Salaries*, A Study Sponsored by the Cleveland Teachers Federation in Co-operation with the Cleveland Board of Education (Columbus, Ohio, 1932), pp.

School boards learned quickly that one concomitant of retirement was capital accumulation; and as the funds grew, so did the benefits to be derived from control and the conflicts over administration. In Illinois, few problems developed as long as teachers were the sole contributors. When, in 1907, small amounts of public money were pumped into the system, the Chicago Teachers' Federation (CTF) was able to secure control of the new fund only with difficulty. By 1913 accumulations reached almost one million dollars, and the board of education turned to the state legislature for legislation to transfer control from the teachers to the board. Though some teachers were concerned that control of the fund would give the board influence over the crucial decisions about length of service then made by the pension plan's board of trustees, it seems more likely that school officials simply wanted control of the money. With the backing of the Illinois State Federation of Labor, the teachers defeated the board's bill and control remained with the teachers. In return for contributions to the pension system, the board was granted additional influence on the existing pension board of trustees.[26] Other teacher groups were not so fortunate; in twenty-five of thirty-three cities, teachers had less than a majority on the board controlling the fund.[27]

No one would have denied that a fundamental purpose of teacher retirement was efficiency. Administrators, teachers, and the courts as well accepted this point of view. Goggin, a resolute defender of teachers' rights, was willing to commit the CTF to the proposition that "the only test of a teachers efficiency is in the work in the school room and that any scholarship which does not manifest itself in efficiency is of a kind which is of no benefit to the system . . . that inefficient teachers should be eliminated and efficient ones allowed to work without constant dread of what she is being marked."[28] While retirement of superannuated teachers was usually ancillary to some larger purpose, it was also often justified on its own terms, as a technique compelled by the development of bureaucracy. In spite of the general youth of the profession, the focus of

161–62; National Education Association, Committee on Retirement Allowances, Anna Laura Force, Chairman, "Retirement Systems in the Depression," Record Group 47, "Records of the Committee on Economic Security," Subject File, National Archives, Washington, D.C., box 38, file "Old Age Retirement-Teachers System," pp. 3, 4, 14.

26. David statement, CTF Papers, box 1, p. 7; "Pension Delegate Convention, Meeting April 12, 1913," typescript, CTF Papers, box 41, file "Jan–April 13, 1913," pp. 13–14, 20–21, 24–25, 35; "The Chicago Teachers' Pension Situation," CTF Papers, box 41, file "April 14–September, 1913"; "Points for March 13, 1917 on Teachers' Tenure Bill (House Bill 394) in House Committee on Education," typescript, CTF Papers, box 46, file "Jan.–March, 1917."

27. "Pension Delegate Convention, Meeting April 12, 1913," typescript, CTF Papers, box 41, file "Jan–April 13, 1913," p. 17.

28. Goggin, "Chicago Teachers Federation," CTF Papers, box 1, file "Historical Data"; "The Chicago Teachers' Federation," CTF Papers, box 1.

complaints of inefficiency was the older teacher. Administrators justified their superannuation programs with reference to the similar problems faced in the railroad bureaucracies, the larger industrial establishments, the army, and the federal civil service.

Conveniently, teaching became the most exhausting of occupations. Its confining nature was held to be more corrosive of vitality than carrying mail in the open air. Instruction of the young took its toll in nervous and mental strain. Teachers pointed to the unique disciplinary problems caused by unruly elements in the classroom and to the right of the students to appeal to administrators over the heads of their teachers. The Teachers' Annuity Guild of Massachusetts argued that the pressures of the profession could only be alleviated by larger salaries, which would make possible "those frequent and necessary relaxations which preserve health and elasticity of mind and body. . . . Work itself rarely kills, but worry often does."[29] Before a House committee in 1919, District of Columbia administrators and officials united in this critique of the older teacher. Suprintendent of Schools Earnest L. Thurston found in retirement a means of "securing a regular inflow of new blood, young, and efficient and full of energy." For the teachers, Rebecca E. Shanley actively defended a provision in the bill under consideration which allowed the board of education to retire teachers at age sixty-two. "We felt that at that age the teacher who had been in the schoolroom with 40 or 50 children for so many years will have lost much of her efficiency. . . . We felt that a teacher—a great majority of the teachers in the schoolrooms in the graded schools—at the age of 62 ought to be retired for the good of the service."[30] In 1923, the Supreme Court of Wisconsin held that a teachers' pension law did not appropriate public funds for a private purpose since its real purpose—efficiency through continuous service—was publicly and generally acknowledged.[31]

Chicago teachers witnessed a transformation in the application of efficiency, as the school board moved from notions of efficiency circumscribed by community to its purer forms. In 1901, the president of the school board, Graham H. Harris, had been apologetic in defending the right to retire teachers for reasons of efficiency. By 1924 the board was reviewing the Strickler Report, an authorized investigation of the public schools by a University of Chicago stu-

29. Bradford, "Teachers' Pensions," p. 512; "Stenographic Report of the Mass Meeting of the Chicago Teachers Federation Held at the Studebaker Theatre on Tuesday, November 25, 1924, at Four-thirty O'Clock P.M.," CTF Papers, box 4, p. 74; Allen, "Teachers' Pensions," pp. 701, 703; Senate, *Teachers' Retirement Fund*, pp. 3–4; Snedden, introduction to Prosser, *Teacher and Old Age*, p. vi.

30. House, *Retirement of Public School Teachers: Hearings*, pp. 42 and 9.

31. *State ex rel. Dudgeon v. Levitan, State Treasurer*, 181 Wisc. 326 (D. Wisc. 1923).

dent, Robert Strickler. Its content could have led to the dismissal of over six hundred teachers. For the most part a young group made younger by their own retirement programs, teachers seem not to have been much interested in the dangers presented by presumably scientific definitions of superannuation.[32] Yet in 1928, Isaiah T. Greenacre, for years legal counsel to the CTF, eloquently summarized those dangers at a monthly meeting of the union. Employers, he said, began with the fact that the average person of seventy was less efficient. "They take advantage of that [fact] and they attempt to create a class . . . the way in which they work it is to classify." The process, Greenacre pointed out, was insidiously open-ended. "If they can classify all over 70 or all over 65 or over 50, who shall know where the limit of that would be. The limit in law, I can tell you, is when they become unreasonable, but that, of course, has to be thrashed out in a court of law on the facts and circumstances."[33]

The board's abiding interest in retirement-induced efficiency was revealed in a bitter controversy over emeritus status in the mid-1920s—the immediate cause of Greenacre's remarks. The Strickler Report made clear that the pension system, designed to encourage the retirement of teachers and principals over seventy, had not worked. In the absence of compulsory retirement provisions, the older employees had stayed in their jobs, preferring the salary and environment of work to retirement with a minimal pension. On December 9, 1925, the board created a branch of educational service known as emeritus service, to which all teachers, principals, and superintendents (except the chief superintendent) would be automatically assigned at age seventy, provided only that they had been with the schools for at least twenty consecutive years. Those transferred to the new status would receive approximately half of their normal salary.[34] Three days later the CTF convened to consider the new ruling. Leading the attack was Margaret Haley, the strong-willed leader of the federation and publisher of her own partisan educational journal, *Margaret Haley's Bulletin*. Haley searched for the meaning of the emeritus ruling. She was concerned that the incompetency charges filed years ago against sixty-eight teachers over seventy would constitute a break in service and make them ineligible for emeritus benefits under the twenty-year rule; she also feared that the ruling would have destructive consequences for her union and for the privileges of its members. "It might just develop in the courts," she said, "that this is just an excuse for

32. Harris to Lucius E. Fuller, 7 October 1901, CTF Papers, box 36, file "Sept–Dec 1901"; "Stenographic Report Meeting November 25, 1924," pp. 63ff.
33. "Stenographic Report of Monthly Meeting of the Chicago Teachers Federation, March 10, 1928," CTF Papers, box 8, pp. 99–101.
34. *Margaret Haley's Bulletin* 3 (30 January 1926): 187–88. A similar phenomenon was taking place among federal employees in the 1920s.

accomplishing indirectly what the Board did not try to accomplish directly, or could not accomplish directly. They are attempting to separate teachers from the service, in violation of the tenure law."[35] Haley and others were also apprehensive that the ruling, by modifying the principle of uniformity—to every member the same pension—would prove divisive, eventually undermining the pension system itself. But it was the tenure issue that continued to disturb the union. Almost a year later, Haley wrote in her bulletin that "Chicago teachers' tenure is being attacked under the guise of soft 'retirement' phrases."[36]

Three principals went to court in the interests of all seventy-two persons affected by the emeritus ruling. The teachers pressed their view that the order was an illegal attempt to bypass established retirement procedures, a position the board perhaps had strengthened inadvertently by referring in the original ruling to "retirement" of teachers (changed to "transferred" after the suit was initiated). The board argued that emeritus service was not retirement with a pension but "removal to another branch of the service," and it insisted on the right to pass regulations relevant to productivity. "They in their wisdom," said the board's attorney, "have determined that efficiency begins to be impaired at the age of seventy years." Federation counsel Greenacre was well aware of the board's interest in efficiency and of its use of a statistical argument that violated the well-established practice of measuring efficiency on an individual basis. None of the principals had received poor ratings or been subject to written charges. The board, Greenacre told the CTF several years later, had violated life-employment contracts "not because on a trial they would find them inefficient, but because they belong to a class which they say as an average is at least known to be inefficient."[37] This was the essence of mandatory retirement.

Although the courts eventually upheld the emeritus ruling, the case was actually settled in 1927 in the state legislature, with a new pension law allowing earlier retirement (at age sixty-five) and providing for a gradual phase-in of mandatory retirement provisions—first for seventy-five-year-olds, then seventy-four-year-olds, and so on.[38] Haley found this approach compatible with the federation's desire to protect the pension and especially tenure. In fact, neither she nor CTF legal counsel disputed the *idea* of retiring superannuated (genuinely inefficient) employees; they were accomplices in the development of mandatory

35. "Stenographic Report of Meeting of Chicago Teachers' Federation, December 12, 1925," CTF Papers, box 6, p. 46.
36. *Margaret Haley's Bulletin* 4 (25 October 1926): 55; "Stenographic Report Meeting December 12, 1925," p. 47.
37. "Stenographic Report Meeting March 10, 1928," p. 101; *Margaret Haley's Bulletin* 3 (30 January 1926): 188–89; ibid. 4 (16 November 1926): 66–67; ibid. 3 (30 January 1926): 187.
38. *Margaret Haley's Bulletin* 4 (15 June 1927): 293; ibid. 3 (17 May 1926): 329.

retirement standards. Until 1927, the CTF had succeeded in keeping the advocates of efficiency at arm's length and had at least defended the rights of all its members to be judged as individuals. The emeritus ruling forced the union to reconsider this position and ultimately to sacrifice both an ideal and a generation of older teachers.

School officials were willing to press an issue as potentially divisive as emeritus status because retirement was often part of a larger process of restructuring the teaching profession to suit changing educational needs. Younger teachers were valued not only because they were cheaper, healthier, and more energetic, but because older teachers might relate inadequately to the modern world. Walter Jessup's 1916 report on Cleveland's teaching staff found age important. "Are they so young that they are unable to bear properly the responsibility of training the future citizens of Cleveland? Are they so old that they have lost sympathy with the ideals of childhood and are out of touch with the ideals of modern citizenship?" He found a "striking contrast" (not further defined) in the professional attitudes of elementary principals over and under age fifty.[39]

Older teachers were not disliked so much for their senility as for their backwardness, for the fact that they were trained in the old ways of the nineteenth century. MacAlister found Philadelphia's teachers inefficient and incompetent in spite of the fact that they were teaching "up to the standard required of them when appointed many years ago."[40] In typical fashion, the 1909 report of the Illinois Educational Commission committed the state to adjusting its schools to new industrial conditions and to employing teachers who would understand the need to deemphasize old scholastic ideals and concentrate instead on shaping youth to perform the tasks of an industrial and bureaucratic society.[41] While the Illinois authorities thought of this process largely in terms of the modernization of rural and small-town school systems, which were increasingly sending their students into the cities rather than the countryside, others, particularly in the postwar years, equated modernization with Americanization. Advocating a District of Columbia retirement measure in 1919, NEA field secretary Hugh S. McGill spoke of the need to bring the "ablest and best" into the teaching profession, lest the finest instructors be lost and children educated by teachers who had foreign accents "and a foreign manner of living."[42]

Retirement was also expected to contribute to this educational restructuring

39. Jessup, *Teaching Staff*, pp. 49, 52–53.
40. Discussion following Anderson, "Qualification and Supply," pp. 438, 440.
41. Illinois, Illinois Education Commission, *Preliminary Report to the Forty-Sixth General Assembly of the State of Illinois*, Submitted in Accordance with an Act Approved May 25, 1907, *Bulletin* 9 (Springfield, 1909), p. 41.
42. House, *Retirement of Public School Teachers: Hearings*, p. 24.

by bringing more men into teaching. In the ten years after 1898, the percentage of male teachers in Illinois' elementary schools, for example, had declined from 28 to 19 percent; for many, the trend was alarming.[43] Two factors were at work here. First, and perhaps most important, men were considered essential to the development of a professional teaching community, and unmarried women were seen as the cause of the failure to create such a community. As long as the teaching force remained "shifting and impermanent," teaching would remain a bastard profession. One solution was to encourage men to become or to remain teachers by raising wages and providing retirement benefits.[44] Second, it seems likely that the call for an end to female dominance mirrored the interest in modernization. Perhaps, as education became less concerned with integrating youth into the ethnic, religious, and moral "island" communities of the late nineteenth century, and more the vehicle of industrial progress in the twentieth, the female teacher came to be associated with an earlier order. Because educators never wanted teaching to be fully integrated into the market economy, they would continue to value women for this tie and would never have recommended an abrupt turn to male dominance. But they were willing to acknowledge that the pendulum had swung too far and that there was some need to recruit men, who might be more aggressive and more acquisitive in outlook. Retirement would sever the ties of ethnicity, age, and sex which bound the educational system to a preindustrial culture.[45]

Retirement might save money and create a more productive work force; it might restructure education to meet industrial needs. But the central goal of retirement policy may have been neither productivity nor modernization, but social stability. The first steps in the process, and the first stages in the argument, were simple enough and straightforward. Educators wanted to retain qualified teachers, to reduce turnover and transiency and improve continuity of service, and to attract highly qualified people into the profession. The new industrial society would require a teaching force capable of preventing social upheaval. During the original debate over pensions in 1891, the superintendent of schools at Springfield, Massachusetts, Thomas M. Balliet, developed this idea:

> The present social unrest among all classes of people—especially the ignorant,—coupled with universal suffrage, will before long force upon us,

---

43. Illinois Educational Commission, *Minimum Salaries for Teachers*, p. 18; Jessup, *Teaching Staff*, p. 41.

44. House, *Retirement of Public School Teachers: Hearings*, p. 10; Prosser, *Teacher and Old Age*, p. 35; Illinois Educational Commission, *Minimum Salaries for Teachers*, p. 18.

45. I am indebted here to Robert H. Wiebe's *Search for Order: 1877–1920* (American Century Series, New York, 1968), and Herbert Gutman's "Work, Culture and Society in Industrializing America: 1815–1919," *American Historical Review* 78 (June 1973): 531–88.

in a very practical way, the necessity of securing men and women of first-rate ability to direct the work of the public schools,—probably the greatest single force in modern society. Good salaries, better social recognition, permanency of tenure, and a certainty of being above want after the years of efficient service are over, are the only means by which such talent can be secured for this work.[46]

By instituting a pension system and admitting that its teachers had been underpaid, Balliet concluded, a community could make a forceful impression on "the minds of the vulgar and the ignorant."[47] Destitute teachers were uncomfortably proletarian, potential radicals, at the very least likely candidates for organization by the rising teachers' federations or the American Federation of Labor. The well-rewarded teacher was less likely to be radical and more likely to be capable of handling the disciplinary problems linked to general social unrest and of maintaining academic standards appropriate to the preservation of a "republican form of government" under "precarious social condition[s]."[48]

It is common to think of professionalization as a self-interested and individualistic attempt by an occupational group to increase its economic and social standing in the culture. Professionalization in teaching was that, but it was also something wished on teachers from without, the culture's attempt to create a profession suited to its needs. The German schoolmaster who remained in one place, his influence increasing with his permanency, was the ideal. He had dignity, independence, and an honorable place in the life of his community—qualities, wrote the president of a South Carolina industrial and teachers' college, "attributable more to tenure of office and to pensions than to high salaries."[49] Others agreed. One did not create a professional class, devoted to public school teaching and capable of fulfilling the sometimes contradictory demands for stability and growth, by offering higher salaries alone. Instead, one held out security, a future reward, which in 1890 or 1910 was believed to, and perhaps did,

46. *Journal of Education* 33 (2 April 1891): 211.

47. Ibid., p. 212.

48. Senate, *Teacher's Retirement Fund*, p. 2; Dix, *Economic Basis*, p. 11; Mrs. William D. Cabell, "Is the Teacher a Proletarian?" *Education* 20 (September 1899): 35; Charles Richmond Henderson, "Municipal Pension Systems and Pensions for Teachers," *American Journal of Sociology* 13 (May 1908): 846; Davis statement, CTF Papers, box 1, p. 9; NEA, *Report of the Committee on Salaries, Tenure, and Pensions of Public School Teachers in the United States to the National Council of Education*, July 1905 (n.p., 1905), p. 466.

49. Quoting D. B. Johnson, president of Winthrop Normal and Industrial College, in discussion following "Statement of the Work and Proposals of the Committee on Teachers' Salaries and Cost of Living for 1912–13," *Journal of Proceedings and Addresses of the NEA*, Fifty-first Annual Meeting, Salt Lake City, Utah, 5–11 July 1913 (Ann Arbor, Mich., 1913), p. 413; John E. Clark, "Shall Teachers Be Pensioned?" *Journal of Proceedings and Addresses of the NEA*, Thirty-fifth Annual Meeting, Buffalo, N.Y., 3–10 July 1896 (Chicago, 1896), pp. 989–90. On professionalization, see Richard Hofstadter, *The Age of Reform: From Bryan to F.D.R.* (New York, 1955), pp. 154–55.

possess enormous potential for control. "There are men and women every-where," wrote Aaron Marcus, a member of the Pennsylvania Board of Education, "who would gladly dedicate their lives to the cause of childhood if they might be assured of but one thing,—that they will not be obliged to end their days as an object of charity."[50] It was widely believed that by eliminating anxiety and worry from the mind of the teacher, the prospect of ultimate security in old age would improve the quality of the classroom performance and increase efficiency.[51]

Yet this unusual grant of security was not just another efficiency mechanism. Its essential thrust, in fact, was in a diametrically opposed direction. Far from immersing the teacher further into the cultural nexus of growth, change, and efficiency, the pension—this offer to retire—was intended to mold the teaching profession into an island of stability, as isolated as possible from the agitation of economic forces. L. R. Klemm suggested no less in the 1891 pension symposium:

> The stability of state institutions demands that the teachers who prepare the young generation for future citizenship form a profession that in itself represents stability. Anything that will insure the teacher security in his position and make it pay him to devote his life to his profession is a state consideration. Hence, a pension makes it unnecessary for the teacher to devote attention to the accumulation of property. He need not be a money maker, nor yet a money-saving person. He is free from that gnawing emotion, "fear of the future and of old age."[52]

Ten years later, Lucy Flower presented a report of the legislative committee of the CTF to the Illinois State Federation of Teachers. She emphasized that the teacher who received a fair wage and had reasonable tenure in office should be expected to practice ordinary economy and to secure her own future.[53] Common enough among those who opposed public expenditures for funds, Flower's suggestion cut against the grain of the pension movement. School districts could, after all, have followed Flower's advice, raised teachers' salaries, and observed as teachers tried to make the kinds of savings and investment decisions that

50. Marcus Aaron, *A State System of Retirement Funds for Teachers: From the Viewpoint of a Business Man and a School Teacher*, Address Delivered Before the State Educational Association, Harrisburg, Pa., 29 December 1916 (n.p., n.d.), p. 4.

51. Senate, *Teacher's Retirement Fund*, p. 6; House, *Retirement of Public School Teachers: Hearings*, p. 9; Graham H. Harris to Richard Yeates, 7 May 1901, in CTF Papers, box 35, file "Jan–May 1901"; *Journal of Education* 33 (2 April 1891): 211.

52. *Journal of Education* 33 (2 April 1891): 212. See also McAndrew, "School Salaries."

53. Flower to President and Members of the Illinois State Federation of Teachers, CTF Papers, box 36, file "Sept–Dec 1901."

would guarantee them an income in old age. As appropriate as such an exercise might have been for the factory worker, the salesman, or the local merchant— whose essence lay in participation in the market economy—it was increasingly inappropriate for the teacher. Interestingly, one of the few educators of national stature to remain uncommitted to pensions, New York's commissioner of education, Andrew S. Draper, not only believed that teachers should take responsibility for their old age, but that a skilled teaching force would be most likely to emerge from an aggressive, competitive environment: "There must be no leveling down for the sake of helping the weaker teachers. The conditions must be so set that the stronger and more ambitious ones would be encouraged to do their best."[54] Most educators wished to remove the teacher from the vagaries of the marketplace, just as their contemporaries in the world of business wished to bring that marketplace under control. For the latter, the tools were the trade agreement, price fixing, and the merger; for the former, the pension.

In *Social Limits to Growth*, Fred Hirsch argues that even a system as geared to private acquisition and gain as the American economy must withhold such license from those who control the system. Though they might indirectly serve the interests of those they regulate, the regulators are not expected to profit in any direct sense from their positions of influence. They are, indeed, expected to possess a number of religiously derived values, including truth, restraint, and obligation. The market system, says Hirsch, is "at bottom, more dependent on religious binding than the feudal state, having abandoned direct social ties maintained by the obligations of custom and status." Although Hirsch's concern is with religion, it seems likely that education served a similar function for the society. Like the government bureaucrats, teachers would show the way to the future but guard the past, educate future capitalists but remain outside the marketplace. The pension would make them the mechanism of restraint as well as the engine of progress. This was the essence of social efficiency.[55]

There was, finally, a social justice component to the teachers' retirement movement. If teachers were to feel something besides manipulation, there had to be. Single, female, and poor, the average public-school teacher was a perfect candidate for aid; even a society interested in retirement chiefly for its contributions to social and economic efficiency could hardly fail to appreciate both the plight of the teacher and the benefits to be derived from conceptualizing

---

54. NEA, *Report on Salaries, Tenure, and Pensions, 1905*, p. 466. Draper was not a member of the committee; his statement is part of a brief discussion appended to the report.

55. The quotation is from Robert Heilbroner's review of the Hirsch book in *New York Review of Books*, 3 March 1977, p. 11; Hirsch, *Social Limits to Growth* (Cambridge, Mass., 1976), pp. 119, 122, 128–29, 137, 139, 143–44, 175.

retirement as a movement with humanitarian origins. There is evidence of genuine solicitude in the efforts of several cities, including Cincinnati, Philadelphia, and St. Paul, to permit retired teachers to return to the system in order to become eligible for the pension. During the 1930s, when the teacher population became particularly destitute, the idea of the pension as a mechanism for dealing with a serious social problem was revived; school authorities then at least justified their right to efficiency on fulfillment of a parallel obligation to provide for teachers in their old age.[56]

Yet the ideology of social justice developed in a backhanded way, as industrial education specialist Charles Prosser observed in 1913. "The cause of teachers' pensions," he said, "has of late years gained additional support from the growing recognition that, after all, they are only one phase of the world-wide movement toward the social insurance of all workers against the great risks of life."[57] Had insurance against risk for its own sake, for social justice, been intrinsic to the pension movement, that would hardly have been worthy of "growing recognition" or of Prosser's own sense of discovery. Even in the 1930s, school boards felt compelled to make all the efficiency arguments as well as the argument from social justice, and they were all too willing to take advantage of the pension systems and hard times to strengthen their schools by getting rid of old teachers.[58]

So varied in function and flexible in application, the pension held some potential benefit for each element it touched. For this reason, the politics of teachers' pensions were seldom characterized—at least not for long—by struggles between rigid, polarized interest groups. Easily convinced of the benefits to their systems, school boards and principals generally supported the pension movement and often, as in Cleveland, played an initiating role. Their attitude of cooperation is in striking contrast to the conflict engendered by matters of salary.[59] While school officials were likely to be divided over means rather than ends, accepting the dominant ideologies of social and economic efficiency,

56. Aaron, *Retirement Funds for Teachers*, pp. 3–4; Allen, "Teachers' Pensions," p. 702; Flint, "Pensions for Women Teachers," p. 619; John Edward Seyfried and DeWitt Grady Robinson, "New Mexico Retirement System with Model Plan and Laws," *University of New Mexico Bulletin, Education Series* 8 (15 October 1934): 7–8; "Teacher Retirement Legislation for Kentucky," *Bulletin of the Bureau of School Service*, College of Education, University of Kentucky 9 (September 1936): 11–12, 24.

57. Prosser, *Teacher and Old Age*, p. 19.

58. "Stenographic Report of the Regular Meeting of the Chicago Teachers Federation, June 15, 1935," CTF Papers, box 19, p. 73.

59. Graham H. Harris to Richard Yeates, 7 May 1901, CTF Papers, box 35, file "Jan–May 1901"; Senate, *Teacher's Retirement Fund*, pp. 6, 7; fragment of undated letter from Catherine Goggin (c. 1897), CTF Papers, box 35, file "1868–1899"; Jessup, *Teaching Staff*, pp. 38–39; "The Chicago Teachers' Federation" and other statements in CTF Papers, box 1, file "Historical Data."

teachers sometimes found themselves at odds over what for them was the end result of the pension—the retirement of older teachers—and what that result implied. Income, age, sex, and position within the system provided the major lines of division. In Chicago and New Jersey, retirement plans financed through a regressive 1 percent deduction from salaries of teachers and supervisory personnel drew criticism from principals and supervising teachers, who thought their contributions excessively large, and praise from teachers drawing small salaries, who liked the idea that their benefits would be subsidized by those with higher incomes. Income also explains why high-school teachers were more reluctant to support pensions than their grade-school counterparts, and why better-paid, more secure urban teachers in New Jersey preferred to establish their own plans rather than rely on a statewide system that would entail subsidies to rural and small-town teachers.[60]

Age, however, proved most divisive, contributing to some disagreement over almost every feature of the plans. Although one would expect the younger teachers to have welcomed programs that functioned through a form of age discrimination, youthful elements often provided the only major opposition. They were likely to be opposed to systems in which they forfeited all or most of their contributions upon leaving the system; to length-of-service provisions over twenty years; and to financing the immediate retirement of older teachers who had made no contributions. In Buffalo, young women who expected to marry before they reached old age opposed the pension.[61] The support of younger teachers, vital to the movement's success, was secured through appeals to conscience and by adjustments of the plans to the requirements of their opponents. Younger teachers were, of course, fully aware that the departure of their older colleagues through retirement would bring promotions and pay increases.[62]

For older teachers, the choice was not so difficult. Often they did not wish to be forced to retire. Many Chicago teachers, not faced with a mandatory retirement provision, did not retire at seventy, and in Pennsylvania, a survey conducted in the 1920s revealed that a majority of those retired desired to continue in the service. The resources of older teachers, however, were often so meager as to preclude other options. And most wanted the security that others, for their

60. Allen, "Teachers' Pensions," p. 705; Goggin statement and DeLuce statement, CTF Papers, box 1, file "Historical Data"; Lee Welling Squier, *Old Age Dependency in the United States: A Complete Survey of the Pension Movement* (New York, 1912), p. 140.

61. California, *Teachers' Retirement Salary Commission Report*, p. 28; Allen, "Teachers' Pensions," p. 706; Senate, *Teacher's Retirement Fund*, p. 8; Clark, "Shall Teachers Be Pensioned," p. 995 (discussion); Women's Educational and Industrial Union, *Old-Age Support of Women Teachers*, p. 40.

62. Allen, "Teachers' Pensions," p. 706; Senate, *Teacher's Retirement Fund*, p. 8.

own reasons, were offering. The oldest teachers had to leave their jobs, but in return they received an annuity, often at minimal personal expense.[63]

For the most part, the conflicts generated by the pension and retirement questions were sideshows, and opposition a holding action in a losing cause. The pension was, after all, largely a methodology, a recently discovered device for exerting cultural leverage, and one that seemed to offer some reasonable prospect of achieving growth without sacrificing order, efficiency without sacrificing community. Growth and order proved compatible, in the short run at least. The two goals were pursued on such different axes (growth in the factories and mines, in the business schools, in the advertising profession, and in the economics of consumer demand; order in the public schools, in the prisons and courts, and in the burgeoning field of private and public social welfare) that incongruence would become visible only decades later in a declining rate of growth and increasing inability to compete in international markets. Retirement seemed a remarkably inexpensive device in 1915 or 1925. By the 1970s, there was some question whether the society could afford to make good on the costly commitments of an earlier generation. With other mechanisms designed to shape conduct and control behavior, the pension was becoming a factor of importance in the economics of the firm and the nation.

Efficiency and community existed on the same axis, and visibly so, within the person of the older or retired teacher. There was to be no place within the schools for the older teacher who had been labeled unproductive or whose release was considered essential for recruitment or some other purpose. The issue of the incompatibility of efficiency and community was joined at an April 1925 meeting of the Chicago Board of Education. Before the body was a proposed Illinois state law providing for compulsory retirement for teachers and principals, beginning at age seventy-five in the first year, so within five years seventy-year-old teachers would face compulsory retirement. Board members discussed the proposal. What Mrs. W. S. Heffernan found a humane, farsighted effort on the part of the superintendent, J. Lewis Coath found unreasonably protective. "Let's make it seventy," he said, "and stick to it, let them go at the same time. Seventy is too old to teach school, anyhow." Superintendent William McAndrew replied that Chicago's teachers, unlike the employees of railroads and other corporations, had not been forewarned: "Our school family in Chicago has not had any intimation whatever of an attempted compulsory retirement law." The five-year phase-in would give teachers an opportunity to make plans and put their affairs in order before their separation. Board president Charles M. Moderwell,

63. Shaw, *Pennsylvania Retirement System*, p. 30.

a prominent coal operator, thought some employees might have an easier time adjusting than others, and that the board might properly take an individual's property holdings into account. "Put it through at seventy-one," Coath replied, "and if that kid at eighty-three is in hard luck his grandparents can take care of him." Debate ended, and the board passed a motion calling for mandatory retirement at seventy with a year's notice—in some limited sense a compromise. Even then, Coath had the last word: "I do not think these boys and girls can adjust themselves in a year's time to meet this situation if they are not already adjusted."[64] Efficiency and community were not compatible, because one was immediately destructive of the other. Retirement meant separating teachers from their jobs, and therefore from their personal histories and roots. That the pension should have this impact was entirely consistent with its primary origins as a device for achieving economic efficiency and social control.

THE COLLEGES

In March of 1901, Andrew Carnegie retired. To "the Good People of Pittsburgh" he described his feelings on leaving the world of work:

> My resolve was made in youth to retire before old age. From what I have seen around me I cannot doubt the wisdom of this course, although the change is great, even serious, and seldom brings the happiness expected.
>
> But this is so because so many, having abundance to retire upon, have so little to retire to. The fathers in olden days taught that a man should have time before the end of his career for the "making of his soul." I have always felt that old age should be spent not, as the Scotch say, in "making mickle mair," but in making good use of what has been acquired.[65]

As part of the occasion, he gave $5 million in bonds to the Carnegie Company, the income to be spent on three Pennsylvania libraries, on injured employees and their dependents, and on pensions for those employees who, in Carnegie's words, "after long and creditable service, through exceptional circumstances need such help in their old age and who make a good use of it."[66] Taken together,

---

64. "Stenographic Report of the Proceedings of the Regular Meeting of the [Chicago] Board of Education, April 8, 1925," CTF Papers, box 5, pp. 20–27.
65. Clipping, *Pittsburgh Post*, 14 March 1901, quoting letter in *Pittsburgh Dispatch*, 12 March 1901, Carnegie Papers, Manuscript Division, Library of Congress, Washington, D.C., box 269, scrapbook, "Misc. Clippings, 2/4/01–4/17/01."
66. Quoted in clipping, *Pittsburgh Dispatch*, 14 March 1901, in scrapbook, Carnegie Papers, box 269.

the two statements reveal Carnegie's own ambivalence, and even confusion, over the nature of retirement. He is convinced his is the right decision, yet he fears for his future happiness; he affirms that the problem is not one of means but of attitude, yet his actions suggest an awareness of the limitations imposed by class. An outstanding plutocrat and immigrant, he addresses his comments as if to a classless, communal society.

Carnegie had always been attracted to scholars, and as his interest in pensions deepened during the next few years, it focused on college professors. Convinced that teachers were not sufficiently rewarded for their labors, he maintained a number of private pensions for them while he weighed the relative merits of pension and salary adjustments. In January 1905 he asked Henry S. Pritchett, president of the Massachusetts Institute of Technology, to develop estimates of the amount necessary to support an insurance or pension system in major collegiate institutions free from denominational control. The officious Pritchett gathered the data with the help of banker Frank A. Vanderlip and applauded Carnegie for his thoughtfulness. "The more I think of it," he wrote, "the more feasible the plan seems."[67] When Pritchett's report indicated that a system of free pensions might be applicable only to forty or fifty institutions, and impressed by Dr. William Osler's February address on retirement, Carnegie decided to go ahead with the project. In April he officially deeded the funds to the new foundation and participated in the selection of trustees.[68]

Almost immediately, the founder's conception of the role and purpose of the foundation began to diverge from Pritchett's. As Carnegie's charge to the trustees made clear, his aims were limited. Teaching, he began, was the least rewarded of all the professions; as a result, not only teachers but education had suffered. Because few colleges provided pensions, "able men hesitate to adopt teaching as a profession and many old professors whose places should be occupied by younger men, cannot be retired." But for expected opposition from state governments, he would have included state systems in the program as well. The sectarian restrictions, he believed, were limited and precise: "Only those [institutions] which are under control of a sect or require Trustees (or a majority

67. [Pritchett] to Carnegie, 6 February 1905, in Frank A. Vanderlip Papers, Rare Book and Manuscript Library, Columbia University, New York, N.Y., Henry S. Pritchett file (name file); "The Carnegie Foundation for the Advancement of Teaching: Its Present Situation, its Policy and Its Needs, a Confidential Report," typescript, Nicholas Murray Butler Papers, Rare Book and Manuscript Library, Columbia University, New York, N.Y., Pritchett files, folder 4, p. 3; Pritchett to Vanderlip, no date, Vanderlip Papers, Pritchett file, Abraham Flexner, *Henry S. Pritchett: A Biography* (New York, 1943), pp. 87, 88, 91, 93–94.
68. "CFAT," Butler Papers, p. 3.

thereof), Officers, Faculty or Students, to belong to any specified sect, or which impose any theological test, are to be excluded."[69]

Although it is exceedingly difficult to separate Carnegie's motives from those of Pritchett, the trustees, and the institutional recipients of Carnegie aid, it seems that these elements from the beginning expected the Carnegie Foundation for the Advancement of Teaching (CFAT) to be more than Carnegie did. Pritchett, as self-effacing as he might be in his contacts with Carnegie, was an aggressive, opinionated man for whom the CFAT came to be a tool for reshaping higher education. At MIT he had advocated a pension system to keep younger men in service and, therefore, to stimulate "the development of the research spirit," which he considered vital to "national progress."[70] When, in May of 1905, college presidents Nicholas Murray Butler of Columbia and William Rainey Harper of Chicago appealed to him to resign from MIT to head the foundation, Pritchett wrote to Vanderlip. "I tried to be modest & shy," he said. "Does the thing appeal to you as one capable of being made into an influential plan & one which might count for a large influence in the educational problems?"[71]

The divergent interests of Carnegie and Pritchett are also apparent in an exchange of letters in December 1905, ostensibly over the name for the new organization. Pritchett thought the "Carnegie Foundation for Education" would include the primary purpose—pensions—yet reflect the breadth of the charter. "Now my belief," he wrote, "is that one of the great benefits of this Foundation is to be the educational unity established by having a single agency which is representative of the whole country deal with all these institutions. . . . our activities may cover a far greater range with respect to education than that of the present problem which we are undertaking." Carnegie replied that he preferred "Carnegie Professional Pension Fund" or the "Carnegie Education Pension Fund" and concluded: "I don't think you should disguise the fact that it is first and foremost a pension fund. The closer union it may bring about is incidental, though important."[72] A goal Pritchett defined as central was to Carnegie "incidental"—at least to be achieved inadvertently, perhaps unimportant (in spite of

69. Carnegie to CFAT Trustees, 16 April 1905, Carnegie Papers, box 114. Another version of this letter, dated 18 April 1905 (box 115) contains a line, crossed out, stating that state institutions can be included if state officials agree.

70. Clipping, "Teachers' Pensions," *Boston Globe*, 20 February 1904, Henry S. Pritchett Papers, Manuscript Division, Library of Congress, Washington, D.C., box 18, "Scrapbooks—1904 Miscell."

71. Pritchett to Vanderlip, 16 May 1905, Vanderlip Papers, Pritchett file.

72. Pritchett to Carnegie, 9 December 1905; Carnegie to Pritchett, 11 December 1905, Carnegie Papers, box 122.

his letter's conciliatory ending), and probably obscure. Carnegie seems never to have been interested in this "unity" idea.

Under Pritchett's guidance, the CFAT incorporated Carnegie's emphases on efficiency, relief of age dependency, and antisectarianism. Like Carnegie, Pritchett was impressed with the destructive impact of church influence on higher education. Both men must have appreciated the efforts of sectarian institutions like Queen's University (where regulations required that a majority of the trustees be Presbyterian) to disavow their origins and natures in order to participate in Carnegie largesse. This aspect of the CFAT program received the support of the American Unitarian Association and of educators who expected sectarian education to respond with a new sense of liberalism and higher standards of efficiency.[73]

Pritchett and Carnegie also found common ground in the need to invigorate higher education with a spirit of enterprise and efficiency, qualities that had contributed to Carnegie's success in steel and railroading and seemed relevant to other bureaucracies. College presidents accepting foundation trusteeships usually noted their own problems with superannuated professors and the difficulties of attracting competent personnel to such an unremunerative profession. Smith's president, L. Clark Seelye, expected pensions to enable poorer colleges to attract and retain high-quality personnel by eliminating the temptation to depart for higher salaries. E. Benjamin Andrews, chancellor of the University of Nebraska and president of the American Association of State Universities, seemed untroubled by the prospect of private money in public universities. Convinced of the particular relevance of pension-induced efficiency in the state schools, he asked Carnegie to extend his program to these institutions. The public, he said, would not be opposed to private "cooperation" in caring for professors. Pritchett found higher education too competitive, too oriented toward college athletics, and altogether too democratic, too devoted to "the average member of society," as he put it.[74]

In his search for a great university devoted to research interests, Pritchett was less concerned with the pension as a retirement than as a recruitment device. Retirement's major contribution was to eliminate the inefficient. Greatness

73. Daniel M. Gordon to Andrew Carnegie, 24 August 1905, Carnegie Papers, box 119; Charles E. St. John to Carnegie, 8 June 1905; Geo. Crothers to Carnegie, 7 June 1905, Carnegie Papers, box 117. Sectarianism and details of the establishment of the CFAT and its programs are well handled in Joseph Frazier Wall, *Andrew Carnegie* (New York, 1970), pp. 871–80.

74. Seelye to Carnegie, 20 April 1905, Carnegie Papers, box 115; Samuel Lantz to Carnegie, 29 April 1905, Carnegie Papers, box 116; W. Peterson to Carnegie, 19 April 1905, Carnegie Papers, box 115; E. Benjamin Andrews to Carnegie, 19 April 1905, Carnegie Papers, box 118; Pritchett to Carnegie, 21 January 1908, Pritchett Papers, box 2, file "Andrew Carnegie, 1901–1913."

would emerge when the society's talented young individuals entered the universities rather than the corporations and law firms, when the university could draw to it "a fair proportion of the brains and the energy of the race."[75]

Nonetheless, the Carnegie pension system was also designed to encourage research through the selective retirement of those especially suited to such work. Under a 1909 CFAT regulation, professors in Carnegie institutions could apply for retirement after twenty-five years of service to one or more institutions. The grant was not automatic, however. The CFAT could exercise "discretion," voting allowances to those who had done noteworthy work as administrators, had made definite preparation for early retirement under an older CFAT rule, or "who have shown marked fitness for research." Columbia professor James McKeen Cattell wrote Pritchett that it was "not clear how the executive committee [of the foundation] will decide on the merits of professors or that it is desirable for it to exercise such a function."[76]

Pritchett envisioned a role for the CFAT which went well beyond anything Carnegie articulated. The CFAT would spearhead an organizational revolution, binding teachers into a new professional relationship and linking colleges to public secondary schools. At the apex of this vertically integrated structure, shaping all instruction through its influence on higher education, would be the CFAT.[77] Although Pritchett knew, even early in 1905, that interference in the determination of college policies would be controversial, he pushed the foundation in that direction. Standards of admission were subject to particular scrutiny. By 1911, Pritchett sensed the growing authority of the organization. Work at the foundation, he wrote his friend Vanderlip, "has just begun to ripen into the most interesting developments. I have before me from a half dozen states the whole question of their educational organization. For example the governor of Kansas at my advice vetoed a wild and dogmatic scheme for the reorganization of the state educational institutions."[78]

75. Carnegie Foundation for the Advancement of Teaching, *Eleventh Annual Report of the President and of the Treasurer*, October 1916 (Boston, n.d.), p. 62; Morris Llewellyn Cooke, *Academic and Industrial Efficiency: A Report to the Carnegie Foundation for the Advancement of Teaching, Bulletin 5* (New York, 1910): 23.

76. Pritchett to Cattell, 26 November 1910; Cattell to Pritchett, 8 November 1910, James McKeen Cattell Papers, Manuscript Division, Library of Congress, Washington, D.C., box 35, Henry S. Pritchett file.

77. CFAT, *Eleventh Annual Report*, p. 62; Carnegie Foundation for the Advancement of Teaching, *Tenth Annual Report of the President and of the Treasurer*, New York City, October 1915 (Boston, n.d.), p. 49; "CFAT," Butler Papers, p. 12.

78. Pritchett to Vanderlip, 10 April 1911, Vanderlip Papers, Pritchett file; Pritchett to Vanderlip, 27 June 1905, Vanderlip Papers, Pritchett file; "CFAT," Butler Papers, pp. 7–8, 12; Clyde Furst to Edward P. Currier, 21 September 1911, Vanderlip Papers, box 11, file "CFAT. Clyde Furst, 1911–1927"; Henry S. Pritchett, "The Moral Influence of a University Pension System," *Popular Science Monthly* 79 (November 1911): 512. On the use of the private foundation as an instrument of

Pritchett maintained an extensive, personal correspondence with figures identified with the right wing of the Republican party: Butler, Vanderlip, Elihu Root, and particularly William Howard Taft. Pritchett and Butler were Taft supporters in 1912, Republicans in 1920, and in the 1930s mutual critics of the Townsend pension plan, which they criticized as both impossible and immoral (a scheme, Pritchett wrote Butler, "which promises to give a man a living at somebody else [*sic*] expense").[79]

This and the general environment of professional activism and threats to academic freedom that characterized the period from 1890 to 1920 is the context in which CFAT efforts to operate directly on the professor must be interpreted. Organized in the Carnegie pension system, the college professor would achieve a heightened sense of his place in the social order, and this would in turn affect what he taught. That seems to be the import of this section from the annual report of the CFAT for 1916:

> Men must be a part of a political or social régime for many years in order to come to political or social consciousness. The political and economic history of every country illustrates this truth, but it is not so evident that the plan of organization of the teaching profession here proposed . . . carries with it such consequences. . . . We are taking the first steps in an organization of the teaching body of English-speaking North America which, when it becomes incorporated into the profession of the teacher and into the college administration, will in large measure determine the quality *and the aims* of the teacher and his college.[80]

Pension benefits would also, of course, bring security, a release from anxiety, and independence. But one could have too much independence, and so the professor would hopefully also attain a greater feeling of "responsibility." Teachers, like workers, would respond to the pension not with profligacy and irresponsibility, but with an awakened appreciation of what they literally had invested in the system. "The security given by a pension system," wrote Pritchett in 1911, "is really the acquisition of a certain equity which will result in benefit to those who participate in it."[81] To Pritchett, then, the pension was akin to a

---

social control, see Barry D. Karl, "Philanthropy, Policy Planning, and the Bureaucratization of the Democratic Ideal," *Daedalus* 105 (Fall 1976): 131–35 and cf. Henry Steele Commager, "The American Style of Giving," *Mainliner* 20 (December 1976): 41, 43.

79. Pritchett to Butler, Butler Papers, Pritchett files, folder 7; Butler Papers, Pritchett files, folder 3; "CFAT," Butler Papers, which contains a list of the executive committee of the CFAT in 1915; Walter P. Metzger, *Academic Freedom in the Age of the University* (New York, 1955), chaps. 4 and 5; Carol S. Gruber, *Mars and Minerva: World War I and the Uses of the Higher Learning in America* (Baton Rouge, La., 1975); Hofstadter, *Age of Reform*, pp. 152–55.

80. CFAT, *Eleventh Annual Report*, p. 62 (italics mine).

81. Pritchett, "Moral Influence," pp. 508, and 507, 503, 509; CFAT, *Tenth Annual Report*, p. 49; CFAT, *Eleventh Annual Report*, pp. 26, 29; "CFAT," Butler Papers, p. 13.

stock option or bonus, or to the savings clubs, which were expected to stabilize the social outlook of workers by tying them to gradually increasing bank accounts.[82]

If gratitude reflected influence, the CFAT had a good deal of the latter, particularly in its first decade. Unable to save in years of inflation, the nation's professoriate considered Carnegie a kindly benefactor. In letters full of deprivation and unhappiness, the teachers applauded foundation efforts. "It would seem that you intended to throw out a plank for us poor devils to cling to," wrote a Rutgers College professor of romance languages in April 1905. "It is something to have made a man feel more reconciled to his lot. I thank you again."[83] Department heads, deans, and presidents found the pension a convenient mechanism for effecting the separations heretofore rendered too difficult by personal and historical relationships. Free from "hesitation and embarrassment," administrators could now guiltlessly retire the old, the infirm, and those who had remained on the faculty only because they were known to have resources inadequate for retirement. The claims of teachers who had served "ungrudgingly through long periods of depression," heretofore so difficult to square with efficiency, need no longer be tolerated; the Carnegie program seemed to exact no cost, to offer an efficient and yet humane society.[84]

These techniques of influence and control disturbed a number of educators and public figures. Harvard's Charles W. Eliot immediately disliked the provision in the original articles of incorporation enabling the CFAT to make general grants for educational purposes, and he had to be reassured that this section would become operative only if, in the distant future, the trustees should find it absolutely necessary to go into some field other than pensions.[85] Some professors objected to receiving a pension directly from a private foundation, and a great many would have preferred to receive income in the form of salary increases. When Carnegie trustee Charles Thwing approached Radcliffe professor L. B. R. Briggs to secure his support for a testimonial honoring the founder, Briggs refused. "My own feeling," he wrote, "has long been that the Carnegie pension system, though wonderfully helpful, is in some ways pretty dangerous. As I understand it, one man, Mr. Pritchett, has, with a money power behind

82. See Festus J. Wade, "How Bankers Can Help to Solve Labor and Industrial Problems: Turning the Workman into a Capitalist Via the Savings Pass Book Route," *Trust Companies* 37 (September 1923): 267–69.

83. Edwin B. Davis to Carnegie, 28 April 1905, Carnegie Papers, box 115; P. H. K. McComb to Carnegie, 28 November 1910, Carnegie Papers, box 183; Clyde Furst to Pritchett, 25 August 1915, Pritchett Papers, box 8, subject file "Carnegie Foundation for the Advancement of Teaching."

84. L. Clark Seelye to Carnegie, 20 April 1905; W. Peterson to Carnegie, 19 April 1905, Carnegie Papers, box 115; Samuel Lantz to Carnegie, 29 April 1905, Carnegie Papers, box 116.

85. Carnegie to Eliot, 22 August 1905, Carnegie Papers, box 119.

him, a certain control over the universities of America, a control, it seems to me, such as no one man ought to have; but perhaps I am wrong about this."[86] In 1919, Cattell accused the CFAT of having pressured the University of Illinois to alter "the conduct of its medical school at Chicago" or risk losing pensions payable to academic employees at Urbana, and of having informed Ohio administrators that its universities must be "reconstructed."[87]

A first-rate psychologist, Cattell's controversial opinions and abrasive personality made him vulnerable to removal under the standards of academic freedom then generally applied. Cattell used the pages of the journal *Science*, which he edited, to make his case against the foundation. Colleges would now be tempted, he said, to use the pension to get rid of teachers over sixty-five in order to hire younger and cheaper replacements; they would also pay lower salaries. But most important, Cattell defined an annuity as a withholding of salary "to be paid ultimately after good behavior."[88] The professor's freedom of speech and action would be severely limited. In 1914, in large part because of Cattell's attacks, the National Education Association declared the CFAT a threat to academic freedom.

Convinced that discretionary administration of the twenty-five-year provision was potentially destructive of the independence of the teaching profession, Cattell decided to challenge the CFAT on its own terms. In 1910 he made written and public application to the foundation for such a pension, noting that he would be eligible in 1913 and looked forward to retiring then. Pritchett rejected the application. "The foundation," he added, "would view with grave concern the possibility of your withdrawal from editorial duties. We should find it difficult to get along without the aid of your kindly and encouraging editorial scrutiny." Cattell replied, "Your last paragraph is presumably only legitimate irony; but it is open to the unfortunate interpretation that beneficiaries of the foundation may not criticize its conduct or the educational schemes it promotes."[89]

Paranoia? Perhaps, but Cattell must have felt vindicated when Columbia, seeking an excuse to rid itself of the troublesome professor, attempted, unsuccessfully, to retire Cattell in May 1913, using the 1910 application as justifica-

86. Briggs to Thwing, 14 March 1913, Charles F. Thwing Papers, Case Western Reserve University Archives, Cleveland, Office Files, box 14, folder "Correspondence of University professors concerning an address honoring Andrew Carnegie"; Joseph Jastrow to Carnegie, 26 May 1905, Carnegie Papers, box 117; Pritchett to Thwing, 16 December 1905, Thwing Papers, Office Files, box 10, file "The Carnegie Foundation."

87. James McKeen Cattell, *Carnegie Pensions* (New York, 1919), p. 6.

88. J. McKeen Cattell, "The Carnegie Foundation for the Advancement of Teaching," *Science*, N.S. 29 (2 April 1909): 533, and 535n, 536; Pritchett to Butler, 10 July 1914, Butler Papers, Pritchett files, folder 3; Metzger, *Academic Freedom*, p. 197.

89. Cattell, *Carnegie Pensions*, p. 10.

tion.[90] Four years later, the Columbia trustees fired Cattell on a wartime disloyalty charge. When Cattell's request for retirement was subsequently denied by university officials on the grounds that dismissal had deprived him of the right to apply for benefits, Cattell took his case to the AAUP, which appointed a committee of three to investigate. The committee declined to take up the legal question as it had been posed by the university, preferring to treat the issue in the context of academic freedom. Retiring allowances were a form of deferred wages or salary, the committee claimed. Their use for other purposes, "like decreasing the danger of frequent changes in the group of employees or preventing recalcitrant or insubordinate conduct is likely seriously to impair the usefulness of the system and to increase the danger of friction between employer and employee."[91]

The CFAT became embroiled in two other controversies, each indicative of the suspicion with which the organization was regarded. The first arose in the last days of 1912, when Norman Hapgood in *Collier's* accused the CFAT of attempting to injure Woodrow Wilson's political prospects by revealing that he had applied to the foundation for a pension on the basis of his prior presidency of Princeton University. Although such an act would have been consistent with the CFAT's political sympathies, Pritchett's correspondence indicates that the story originated elsewhere, and that Pritchett had, in fact, warned Wilson of possible repercussions upon his application in December 1910.[92]

The second controversy occurred over the incorporation in 1918 of the Teachers' Insurance and Annuity Association of America (TIAA) by the same conservative elements then in control of the CFAT, including Root, Butler, Pritchett, and Yale University's president, Arthur Twining Hadley. The free pension system had proven too costly for the foundation; it was to be replaced and supplemented with a system of compulsory, contributory annuities administered by TIAA. The Carnegie Foundation would underwrite the corporation's administrative expenses.[93]

90. Cattell to Pritchett, 26 April 1918, Cattell Papers, box 143, Henry S. Pritchett file.

91. American Association of University Professors, *Bulletin* 4 (November–December 1918): 44. Columbia interpreted as treasonous a Cattell letter to members of Congress protesting the sending of conscientious objectors into combat duty overseas. W. B. Pillsbury, "Biographical Memoir of James McKeen Cattell, 1860–1944," *National Academy of Sciences Biographical Memoirs* 25 (Autumn 1947): 3.

92. Pritchett to Vanderlip, 22 January 1912; Pritchett to Wilson, 18 January 1912; Pritchett to Hapgood, 20 January 1912, Vanderlip Papers, Pritchett file.

93. "Report on the Handbook of Life Insurance and Annuity Policies for Teachers," 14 March 1919, including a report on the Carnegie Foundation by Ira C. Edwards, in Record Group 51, "Records of the Bureau of Efficiency," National Archives, Washington, D.C., 33 (file "Separation and Retirement of Employees"); Pritchett to editor, *Nation*, 20 December 1918, rough draft, Pritchett Papers, box 8, Subject file "Carnegie Foundation for the Advancement of Teaching."

When the transition was being planned in 1916 and 1917, the AAUP regularly reviewed CFAT proposals through its Committee on Pensions and Insurance (known as Committee P) and had some direct, if limited, input into the new system. Still, Committee P and the association withheld approval from TIAA. Committee members were disturbed at what they interpreted as a cavalier attitude toward teachers receiving or anticipating CFAT free pensions. Although the foundation emphasized its intent to honor past obligations, the committee would have preferred a contractual arrangement. CFAT plans to make teacher contributions compulsory were ultimately dropped owing to AAUP opposition.

Committee P also found that CFAT plans failed to provide for sufficient teacher participation in the management of the company, and this criticism was linked to fundamental questions of educational policy. Time and again, AAUP officials returned to the problems inherent in uniting a pension system with an institution interested in policy. The absence of a contractual obligation with regard to the free pensions would allow the CFAT to influence the substance of education by threatening to withdraw benefit payments from institutions who refused to join TIAA; even under the proposed new arrangements, CFAT officials would be able to exert influence by altering the terms by which institutions became eligible. The AAUP had no argument with an independent, disinterested organization capable of evaluating higher education. It insisted, however, that "the criticism and advice of such an institution [be] supported only by the influence to which their merit entitles them."[94] Thus, when Cattell polled the profession in 1918, asking for opinions on the CFAT's plans for life insurance and annuities, only 13 of 670 respondents (perhaps a biased sample) acknowledged those plans to be "satisfactory."[95]

Despite their differences on the role of the CFAT, Carnegie and Pritchett could coexist, because each understood, in some fashion, that Pritchett was doing for higher education what Carnegie had done for steel—imposing unity on a chaotic structure through vertical integration, experimenting with social welfare to develop a more cooperative labor force, and honing the enterprise

94. AAUP, *Bulletin* 3 (November 1917): 34, also 13, 32–33; ibid. 2 (November 1916): 62–63, 68; ibid. 2 (December 1916): 8–9; ibid. 4 (November–December 1918): 35–36, 39; ibid. 5 (March 1919): 7; ibid. 5 (October 1919): 20, 29. Harlan F. Stone chaired Committee P.

95. Memorandum, Cattell Papers, 4 December 1918, box 168, AAUP file. The poll asked repondents to check one of three alternatives. The alternatives, with numbers selecting each, were:

> The plans of the Carnegie Foundation for life insurance and annuities seem to be satisfactory.   13
>
> It seems to be desirable to consider alternative plans under control of the teachers concerned.   561
>
> The recipient is not prepared to express an opinion at the present time.   94
>
> (Mixed ballots)   2

into a high state of efficiency. Responding to Cattell in 1911, Pritchett seemed acutely aware of these analogies and of the dangers inherent in a centralized pension system.

> Every modern state is really engaged in the effort to reconcile the problem of the freedom of the individual with the efficiency of the large agencies which modern society has called into being. The question is whether both causes cannot be served, whether in fact our society will not be compelled to find a means for safeguarding the freedom of the individual up to all reasonable limits and at the same time to secure the advantages of the tremendous agencies which have been organized in the last fifty years, such . . . as trusts and other industrial combinations. I apprehend that the problem of the centralized pension system is really only a small part of the larger question. My own view is that the ultimate solution lies not in wiping out the large organization in order to ensure the freedom of the individual, but rather to control the large organization in such way as to safeguard the freedom of the individual. It is quite as possible to allow one's devotion for individual freedom to become a danger as it is to allow one's advocacy of centralized power to become a danger. Is there not, after all, a fair adjustment under which both may be preserved?[96]

Cattell's own career in the next decade would offer compelling evidence that a "fair adjustment," if possible at all, had not yet been achieved.[97] Rejected in his application for a twenty-five-year pension, almost fired under the guise of retirement, finally denied a pension for political reasons, Cattell had felt the full force of the Carnegie pension system.

But if Cattell's position made his case unique (he was, after all, the CFAT's most vocal and most powerful critic), his problems were only those of the system, writ large. Carnegie's naive protests notwithstanding, Pritchett never intended to resign MIT's presidency in order to preside over an objective fact-finding agency or a surrogate old-age home. His goal was to use the foundation and its primary tool, the pension, to exert influence over the process and content of American education.

Pritchett's defense of the foundation—large organizations, perhaps dangerous but justified by their efficiency, could be controlled rather than eliminated—conveniently skirted the central issue of the right of an economic and social elite to shape education to its own configurations. Just as the core problem in indus-

---

96. Pritchett to Cattell, Cattell Papers, box 143, Henry S. Pritchett file.
97. For a different evaluation of the Carnegie program, see Wall, *Andrew Carnegie*, p. 879. Wall concludes that the free pension system was "a noble experiment," without which "we should not have had the kind of national evaluation of higher education that we sorely needed."

trial relations was not the size of the corporation but the relationships between owners, managers, and workers, so the issue facing educators was not the size of the foundation, not even its centralized character (though structure cannot be divorced from the exercise of power), but rather its oligarchic form and its commitment to class-biased definitions of social progress. To argue, as Pritchett did, that such institutions could be controlled, was to imply that the CFAT's excesses were aberrations from a larger, socially benign purpose of "efficiency." In fact, the thrusts that wounded Cattell and threatened the integrity of teachers and educational institutions (especially sectarian ones) were not incidental to the CFAT, but its reason for being.

5 Capital and Labor:
Retirement and the Reconstruction of Community

It was no accident that Huey Long, one of the great political entrepreneurs in American history, had once traveled the small towns of Louisiana, Oklahoma, and Tennessee as a salesman. This most demanding of occupations offered independence and, for the talented and fortunate few, the prospect of substantial earnings through commissions on sales. For the majority, the reward for long nights in strange hotel rooms was a plain but still entrepreneurial existence. This was the world of Arthur Miller's Willy Loman, the conscientious but sixty-year-old salesman whose declining productivity ended in his firing by thirty-six-year-old Howard Wagner, the son of "Old Man" Wagner, who had hired Willy decades before.[1]

Although Willy is usually seen as the archetypal victim of a callous, commercial society, David Riesman questioned that conclusion. "Howard Wagners," he wrote in *Individualism Reconsidered*, "are hard to come by."[2] A substantial body of evidence indicates that Riesman's point was well taken. Howard Wagners were, if not exceptional, at least not commonplace, and the American corporation, in 1949 when *Death of a Salesman* appeared and to a much greater degree a half century earlier, confronted superannuation and its own needs for efficiency with mixed feelings and inconsistent policies.

Within most turn-of-the-century enterprises, hiring and firing functions remained with foremen and supervisors; not until 1925 would any substantial proportion of American business transfer these duties to the impersonal and "scientific" hands of a separate personnel department. Although, as the history of age discrimination demonstrates, the business system was clearly capable even at the turn of the century of firing older workers in the cause of efficiency, that system continued to harbor significant countervailing tendencies, inherited from

1. Thomas Harry Williams, *Huey Long* (New York, 1969); Arthur Miller, *Death of a Salesman* (New York, 1949).
2. *Individualism Reconsidered: And Other Essays* (Glencoe, Ill., 1954), p. 223.

the less rationalized business environment of the nineteenth century.[3] The impulse toward efficiency was regularly tempered by the personal relationships that continued to exist between employers and employees, particularly in the smaller corporations and communities. Even in the larger institutions, employers often were simply incapable of making decisions they knew would likely have tragic results; of firing, for example, a sixty-year-old worker who might never find another job. It is essential to realize that retirement was not a part of this countervailing matrix; it was not part of the paternalistic, caretaking side of the corporation. Its function, in fact, was precisely the opposite. The pension was expected to free those who made personnel decisions from the fetters of personalism, to transform a human situation into a bureaucratic one, to make the Howard Wagners the norm. Socially, retirement heralded a period of funded leisure, clearly preferable to its unfunded equivalent, the helpless, unemployed, older worker; for the corporation and for the trade union, it was this and much more.

CAPITAL: THE FUNCTION OF RETIREMENT

A series of incidents at the Du Pont Company, manufacturer of explosives, illustrate the internal stresses that the older worker placed on the corporation in pre-pension days. One case involved Fred Fisher, a Du Pont employee with fourteen years' service and salaried at $100 per month, who had been informed of his separation. To Alfred Du Pont, Fisher wrote, "There is but one thing I know anything about now and that is powder, both in my working hours and in my dreams. Mr. Alfred, I do not feel that I can possibly go out into the world at this late date. My body and soul is in this business." He pleaded with Alfred Du Pont to find him a place in his department. More than a month later, Alfred Du Pont received a letter from his cousin. "Nobody connected with the company," it read, "regrets to see an old employee leave or old employees stand still more than I do and nobody likes to see an old employee go to the front more than I do." But Fisher was a special case, a slow employee who made mistakes. His salary and work load had been reduced the year before. He had been transferred to sales, then to accounting, and had continued to perform so poorly that it would not have been difficult to locate a more efficient replacement. The letter closed, however, on another note. The author had no objection to Fisher being placed in sales or accounting. "I think we would all be glad to see him get

3. Alfred D. Chandler, Jr., *Henry Varnum Poor: Business Editor, Analyst, and Reformer* (Cambridge, Mass., 1956); Tamara K. Hareven, "Family Time and Industrial Time: Family and Work in a Planned Corporation Town, 1900–1924," in Hareven, ed., *Family and Kin in Urban Communities: 1700–1930* (New York, 1977), pp. 187–207.

something to do."[4] There are other examples. One Bidwell, a bookkeeper who apparently served no useful function, was kept on by one of the Du Pont divisions "to avoid too sudden a change." Although it was expected that he would soon leave of his own will, he was not dismissed.[5] With the acquisition of the Hazard Powder Company early in the century, the Du Pont people had also acquired a Mr. Lentilhon, who by the time of his death in 1911 had been shifted many times in an attempt to find him work in which his deficiencies would be minimized. The company felt responsible for Lentilhon and would not release him.[6]

The paternalism did not extend to Lentilhon's widow, nor did the company's solicitous attitude encompass older workers who were not connected with the Du Pont organization. In 1915, H. M. Barksdale, general manager of E. I. Du Pont, was approached by a personal friend seeking employment for his father. Barksdale held firm. "It is an exceedingly difficult thing," he wrote, "to secure a position for a man of your father's age—To those of us who have reached or passed that period in life this seems most unfair and very hard, but the fact remains that the trite saying 'this is the age of young men' is nearly 100% true when it comes to an employer filling vacancies in his organization."[7]

Other evidence of the ties binding business and older employees is scattered but of some collective significance. Textile mills, whether in New England or the South, often recruited labor through family connections in small communities. It was not uncommon, even in the 1930s, for father and son to work in the same weave room—a situation that protected some older workers. Employers were willing, for a time at least, to operate with a presumably less efficient family labor system in return for its benefits in recruiting an adequate labor force.[8] Sarah Louise Proctor studied eighteen large retail dry-goods and clothing

4. 31 January 1905, E. I. Du Pont de Nemours & Co. Papers, Eleutherian Mills Historical Library, Greenville, Wilmington, Delaware, series 2, part 2, Vice-presidential files, box 806, file "Personnel, 1905–07"; Your affectionate cousin to Alfred I. Du Pont, 9 February 1905, ibid. Hereafter referred to as Du Pont Papers.

5. Eugene Du Pont to J. C. Du Pont, 9 January 1902, Du Pont Papers, box 812, file "Personnel, 1902–04."

6. Memorandum, President to H. A. Du Pont, 7 March 1911, E.I. Du Pont de Nemours Powder Co. Papers, Eleutherian Mills Historical Library, Greenville, Wilmington, Delaware, series 2, part 3, Presidential Files, box 123, file "Corres. re Employees, 1911–1914." Hereafter referred to as Du Pont Powder Co. Papers.

7. Barksdale to Harcourt P. Burns, 5 October 1915; William H. Phinney to H. M. Barksdale, 27 July 1915, Du Pont Papers, series 2, part 2, Vice-presidential files, box 1004, file 13.

8. U.S., Congress, House Committee on Labor, *Unemployment, Old Age and Social Insurance: Hearings Before a Subcommittee of the Committee on Labor on H.R. 2827*, A bill to provide for the Establishment of Unemployment, Old Age and Social Insurance and for Other Purposes, and H.R. 2859, H.R. 185, and H.R. 10, 74th Cong., 1st sess., 4–8, 11–15 February 1935 (Washington, 1935), pp. 196–97, testimony of Walter L. Pickard; Hareven, "Family Time."

stores around 1920 to ascertain their policies toward older women employees. Although few of the women had been with their stores long enough to establish a strong claim to protective benefits, Proctor found that six stores aided older women with gifts of money, five had some form of pensioning, six made "consistent" efforts to shift older women into easier jobs, nine allowed older women to come in for shorter hours, and all but one paid full wages to working employees.[9] In the machinist trade and elsewhere, the maintenance of inefficient older employees was a well-established practice which by the late 1920s was associated with payroll leaks and the "hidden pension." In one machinery company, older employees received half of their salary whether they worked or not; if they managed to work more than half a normal schedule, the company paid them what they had earned.[10] Robert Hoxie found in 1915 that even in plants using scientific management techniques, older employees were often retained well beyond the point of greatest usefulness to the company.[11]

Companies kept their older workers for a variety of reasons. Some, as I have indicated elsewhere, were attracted by the prospect of reduced turnover and a rising level of cooperation with management policies. Some only acquiesced in seniority provisions, an increasingly important element in collective bargaining agreements after 1925. Others, like canning executive William Powers Hapgood of the Columbia Conserve Company of Indianapolis, felt some genuine sense of moral obligation to care for older workers as long as they were capable of doing something useful in the plant.[12] Similar conditions persisted in the fourth and fifth decades of the century. On the basis of an American Youth

9. "Care of Older Women Employees by Boston Retail Stores," Women's Educational and Industrial Union, Department of Research, *Old-Age Support of Women Teachers: Provisions for Old Age Made by Women Teachers in the Public Schools of Massachusetts*, Studies in Economic Relations of Women, vol. 11 (Boston, 1921), appendix, pp. 103–04. See also Charles R. Manley, Jr., "The Migration of Older People," *American Journal of Sociology* 59 (January 1954): 324–31.

10. *American Machinist* 66 (7 April 1927): 590; ibid. 72 (27 March 1930): 533; ibid. 72 (20 March 1930): 474–75.

11. Robert Franklin Hoxie, *Scientific Management and Labor* (1915; reprint ed., New York, 1966), p. 97.

12. U.S., Congress, Senate, Committee on Education and Labor, *Unemployment in the United States: Hearings Pursuant to S. Res. 219*, A Resolution Providing for an Analysis and Appraisal of Reports on Unemployment and Systems for Prevention and Relief Thereof, Together with Senate Report No. 2072, 11–14, 17–19 December 1928, 9 and 14 January, 7–9 February 1929 (Washington, D.C., 1929), p. 49 (Hapgood testimony). On seniority, see Dan H. Mater, "Effects of Seniority Upon the Welfare of the Employee, the Employer, and Society," *Journal of Business* 14 (October 1941): 384–418; Frederick H. Harbison, *Seniority Policies and Procedures as Developed Through Collective Bargaining*, Princeton University, Department of Economics and Social Institutions, Industrial Relations Section (Princeton, N.J., 1941), pp. 52–54; Arthur R. Porter, Jr., *Job Property Rights: A Study of the Job Controls of the International Typographical Union* (New York, 1954), pp. 17–23; David Montgomery and Ronald Schatz, "Facing Layoffs," *Radical America* 10 (March–April 1976): 15–27.

Commission study of unemployment carried out in the late 1930s, the *New York Times* charged that employer humanitarianism—the maintenance of older workers with dependents—was in part responsible for massive unemployment among workers under twenty-five years of age. An analysis of pension plans in the gas industry undertaken at the same time concluded that in spite of the added stimulus of social security, many plans were still so insufficient that employers were reluctant to recommend retirement.[13] During the Second World War, the problems presumably posed by an aging work force were exacerbated by the drafting of youth and the middle-aged for military service. Thomas Midgley, Jr. shaped his presidential address to the American Chemical Society around this theme, emphasizing how the aging of corporate structures in the chemical industry through retention of old employees would place limits on efficiency and originality. The chairman of the Board of Trustees of the New York State Bankers Retirement System found similar conditions in his industry. Not only did bank employees remain at their jobs long after age had impaired efficiency; in many cases, full-salaried older employees were physically unable to report for work.[14]

The private corporation, in short, was doing no more and no less for the older worker with service ties than the colleges and high schools were doing for teachers, the police departments for patrolmen, and the national government for clerks and other bureaucrats. Each of these institutions, some more reluctantly than others, cared for their aged dependents in some minimal fashion. Like these public institutions, the private sector became increasingly uncomfortable with this role after the turn of the century. The pension system—institutionalized retirement—appeared to be the solution.

At Du Pont, the pension plan was being revised in part to effect the involuntary retirement of older men no longer considered fit for promotion. Two Du Pont departments were somewhat overzealous in their use of the companywide plan as a device for the release of inefficient workers.[15] At the Black Powder Department, 119 of 176 employees were pensioners in 1914, prompting a critical inquiry from an officer of the powder company. The pension plan, he concluded, "was taken advantage of in order to get rid of some men who were undesirable . . . [it] was worked over time for the first few years of our history

---

13. *New York Times*, 15 December 1939, p. 24; Roland S. Child, "An Analysis of Employee Pension Plans," *American Gas Association Monthly* 20 (February 1938): 57.

14. Midgley, "Accent on Youth," *Chemical and Engineering News* 22 (10 October 1944): 1646–49; Joseph E. Hughes, "A Retirement System as Manpower Insurance," *Banking Law Journal* 60 (August 1943): 622; Laurence G. Hanmer, "Are Employees 'Expendable'?" *Trusts and Estates* 76 (February 1943): 137; foreman's round table, *American Machinist* 65 (30 December 1926): 1068.

15. Memorandum, J. A. Haskell to T. C. Du Pont, 19 January 1914, Du Pont Powder Co. Papers, series 2, part 3, Presidential Files, box 123, file "Salaries, 1908–14."

in the Black Powder Department." He was informed that the pension had been used as a dumping ground for poor workers only in a limited number of cases; in any event, the sales department had been doing the same thing, only more of it.[16]

The use of social insurance to break the ties binding older employees to companies was of particular import in the urban utility companies. Hybrids of public and private forms, the utilities had some of the characteristics of public agencies and often maintained close ties to urban political systems. As such they were usually more responsive to the needs of older workers than were private corporations, and their needs for pension relief were correspondingly acute. Utility executives, claimed the vice-president of a Baltimore power company, tended to keep on inefficient older employees "out of sheer good-heartedness." He advocated the pension as the best means of eliminating a condition that sapped the energies of the organization.[17] By 1930 a number of employers had become disenchanted with attempts to place older workers in positions of re-duced responsibility. Even at lower salaries, older workers in new positions were paid more than younger employees; on line jobs, where production was depen-dent upon the weakest link, the maintenance of an inefficient worker, young or old, could be detrimental to productivity.[18] The problem was particularly great in smaller communities, where a released older worker was not the anonymous figure he or she might be in a larger city. Corporations usually looked to the private pension to systematize the retirement decision, but the state, of course, could also contribute. Princeton economist J. Douglas Brown, investigating the problems of older workers for Franklin D. Roosevelt's Committee on Economic Security in 1934, concluded that employers could best be freed from the "moral pressure" imposed by fellow employees of older workers by a general system of old-age insurance.[19]

Just how a pension system might aid a local company in a small town in

16. Unsigned memorandum to F. L. Connable, 24 April 1914 (quotation); memorandum Conna-ble to Coleman Du Pont, 27 April 1914, Du Pont Powder Co. Papers, series 2, part 3, Presidential Files, box 123, file "Salaries, 1908–14."

17. Charles M. Cohn, "The Gas Man Comments on the Subject of Pensions," *American Gas Journal* 129 (July 1928): 32; J. J. Berliner, "Pension Systems," *American Gas Journal* 128 (May 1928): 28; L. A. Smith, "A Pension System for Water Works Employees," *Journal of the American Water Works Association* 21 (1929): 31; Murray Webb Latimer, *Industrial Pension Systems in the United States and Canada*, 2 vols. (New York, 1932), 1: 35–36.

18. *American Machinist* 72 (27 March 1930): 533; N. Wallis Streat, "The Problem of the Old Employee," *American Water Works Association Journal* 23 (January 1931): 85; Stuart Brandes, *American Welfare Capitalism: 1880–1940* (Chicago, 1976): 103–05.

19. Memorandum, Mrs. [Barbara] Armstrong to Mr. Witte, 13 October 1934, Record Group 47, "Records of the Committee on Economic Security," Special Staff Reports, box 23, file "Old Age Security Staff Report."

dealing with superannuation is illustrated by an event in the textile mill of the New Freedom Products Company in 1916. Located in Simsbury, Connecticut, a river-valley community of about four thousand, this family-owned and managed enterprise of only three hundred employees had maintained close employer-employee relationships well into the twentieth century. After 1900, although there was no marked change in employee relations, the burdens of administration made this personal relationship more and more difficult to sustain. In this transitional period, a foreman described the retirement of one of the firm's older workers:

> I remember not long after I went to X room. Old Mr. McGuire, Jim McGuire's father, used to make spools, and he was getting to be a pretty old man. He'd go over to the storage bin, and sometimes he'd only bring one spool at a time. And he'd kind of stagger, and I was afraid he would fall into one of the machines. Used to carry one of them red bandana handkerchiefs sticking out of his side pocket, and more than once I picked up one of them blue tipped matches. Didn't have signs up all over the way they have today. Well finally I spoke to Franklin [one of the two superintendents], and I guess he mentioned it in the office because Mr. Shields' come out. He got me and Mr. McGuire together, and he said, "We have decided that you have worked long and hard. And you always done good work too. And we think it is time you had a rest. So we have decided to pension you, and we will give you $55 a month, and you can have your house free as long as you live. But that doesn't mean that your wife can have it free after that."
>
> "Now," he says to me, "Johnny, is that a fair proposition?"
>
> "Yes, it is," I says, "very fair."
>
> So the old man was pensioned off. You know, it's a funny thing about them pensions. Practically everybody that gets one dies pretty soon after.[20]

One could argue that nothing had changed at New Freedom, that old Mr. McGuire was simply experiencing benign nineteenth-century paternalism, albeit in a new form. But one must consider how differently this incident might have been reported had the company been unable or unwilling to offer the pension. It seems unlikely that the company could have carried off the action at all. The personal approach is a gloss; the pension is real. The company could release McGuire in an ostensibly personal and gracious way only because it had bureaucratized retirement through the impersonal mechanism of the pension system.

20. John S. Ellsworth, Jr., *Factory Folkways: A Study of Institutional Structure and Change* (New Haven, Conn., 1952), p. 46, and chap. 1. The company name is fictitious.

McGuire's separation was the predecessor of the retirement dinner, replete with gold watch. Ostensibly personal, it was, in fact, impersonal.

Beyond the introduction of a bureaucratic atmosphere, companies also expected retirement systems to provide economic benefits. For corporations interested in reducing wage costs, the pension offered some intriguing possibilities. "In your opinion," Du Pont's treasurer, J. J. Raskob, asked his assistant Charles Copeland, "would a man work for you for 15¢ an hour on account of some pension plan you might employ, rather than work for me for 16¢ an hour with no promises of any kind in regard to pension?"[21] The question is revealing. Neither Raskob nor Copeland had any idea what the answer was nor how to find out. What they did know was that it was a common practice, at that time validated by the courts, for a corporation to legally disavow any contractual obligation to retain an employee or pay a pension, provided the employee had not contributed to the fund. Until the actual payment of the benefits, said a New York court, the pension was an "inchoate gift" to which the employee had no contractual right, even though the pension might have been instituted or increased in lieu of additional wages.[22]

The possibility of such a windfall, however, had to be balanced against liabilities. Refusal to pay was a monumental breach of goodwill in an age conscious of the value of public approval. Moreover, as the accountants pointed out, the wage was a sharp instrument of reward and punishment; the pension, in comparison, was a rough device that might enrich an employee who had made only a minimal contribution to the firm's welfare and yet not benefit a more valuable employee who, perhaps because of some unfortunate break in service, had failed to qualify.[23]

Nonetheless, in 1913 and 1914 Du Pont officials were concerned about rising salary levels and convinced that the pension could help them secure employees at lower wages and reduce their total wage bill by eliminating expensive and relatively inefficient older workers. Coleman Du Pont was encouraged in this by his personal friend, retired banker George W. Perkins, who wrote: "I never heard of any plan except one that would assist in regulating salaries and that is a pension plan. If you people have not any such plan in operation, I

21. Memorandum, 22 December 1914, ACC 152, 228, Irénée Du Pont Papers, Eleutherian Mills Historical Library, Greenville, Wilmington, Delaware, Vice-presidential files, ID 10, "Bonus Pension Plans, 1914–1915."

22. Albert deRoode, "Pensions as Wages," *American Economic Review* 3 (June 1913): 287–88; Roy Lubove, *The Struggle for Social Security: 1900–1935* (Cambridge, Mass., 1968), p. 243, n. 70.

23. John Whitmore, "Industrial Pensions and Wages," *Journal of Accountancy* 47 (April 1929): 244, 246–52.

strongly urge you to get busy and adopt one. The right sort of pension plan comes pretty near being a panacea for most of the ills that exist between employer and employee."[24]

Consistent with the growing emphasis on psychology among employers, workers were expected to respond to the pension with a new efficiency born of a reduction in anxiety. This would be achieved in several ways. The employee who could look forward to security in old age would be more content in his job, more comfortable in his work surroundings, and presumably that much more productive. The proverbial "shadow" that haunted older workers would be dissipated. The security of tenure that the pension implied (but did not guarantee) would allow some employees the luxury of thinking of their jobs as permanent arrangements, which was expected to result in a pleasant and stable domestic existence conducive to more effective service.[25] Employers who looked forward to the pension's contribution to the removal of older workers also anticipated a reduced accident rate and the energizing impact of the flow of promotion within the organization.[26] The promotional problem was especially prominent in older industries, such as textiles, railroads, and iron and steel, which by the twentieth century had begun to experience reduced growth rates and to suffer from varying degrees of labor impaction.

Employers have always been concerned about losing first-rate workers, skilled or unskilled. But not until the second decade of the century did labor turnover become central to management. Although unusually prominent during the world wars, the origins of turnover lie in more basic conditions of labor and industry. One was an immigrant labor force, guided in its job decisions by family ties and religious affiliations rather than loyalties to task, firm, or plant.

24. Perkins to Coleman Du Pont, 2 February 1914, Du Pont Powder Co. Papers, series 2, part 3, Presidential Files, box 123, file "Salaries, 1908–14"; memorandum, Irénée Du Pont to Accounting Committee, 16 April 1913, Du Pont Papers, series 2, part 2, Vice-presidential files; memorandum, J. A. Haskell to T. C. Du Pont, 19 January 1914, Du Pont Powder Co. Papers, series 2, part 3, Presidential Files, box 123, file "Salaries, 1908–14." Murray Latimer is not impressed with the argument that pensions influence wages, but his data is economic rather than historical. See Latimer, *Industrial Pension Systems*, 2: 781–82.

25. Smith, "Pension System," p. 32; J. Edward Tufft, "Making Laborers Capitalists: How Joslyn Plan Works," *Steel* 101 (15 November 1937): 24; Gerard Swope, "Stabilization of Industry," *General Electric Review* 34 (October 1931): 547; Berliner, "Pension Systems," p. 28; Miles M. Dawson, "Service Pensions and Employes' Insurance as an Aid to Efficiency," *Greater Efficiency* 3 (December 1913): 19; "Keeping Workers Contented," *The Automobile* 36 (15 March 1917): 576; Daniel Nelson, *Managers and Workers: Origins of the New Factory System in the United States, 1880–1920* (Madison, Wis., 1975), p. 153. The Ford Company was well known for its interest in family matters. See Roger Burlingame, *Henry Ford: A Great Life in Brief* (New York, 1955), pp. 87–88. On the family's redefinition as a provider of basic emotional needs in the 1920s, see Paula S. Fass, *The Damned and the Beautiful: American Youth in the 1920's* (New York, 1977): 97.

26. Charles L. Dearing, *Industrial Pensions* (Washington, D.C., 1954), p. 39; Cohn, "Gas Man Comments," p. 32; Streat, "Problem of Old Employee," p. 85.

Another was the increasingly stultifying nature of industrial labor; some of the most serious turnover problems were in the new automobile assembly plants of the Ford company.[27] Workers were also, to some extent, encouraged in their mobility, expected to follow the steel industry, for example, as it developed new plants near power sources. With the decline of rail transport costs in the late nineteenth century and the dramatic improvement of roads after 1910, workers were more likely to move. Still, turnover was not so much created as discovered, a by-product of the interest in scientific management. By 1918, the General Electric Company was keeping track of a variety of employee data on age, nationality, education, family relations, length of employment, number of times employed, number leaving, and reasons for leaving, using the Hollerith machine, a primitive punchcard system.[28] Between 1913 and 1919, several scholarly treatments of turnover appeared.[29]

The pension was only one of a number of devices, including higher wages, psychological testing, job analysis and classification, and the service bonus, that corporations adopted or contemplated to rationalize and reduce turnover.[30] By increasing identification with the company, the pension would encourage valuable employees to forego higher wages elsewhere to stay with the enterprise. It would reward character-building "steady work," discourage the "floaters" who undermined social stability in the urban labor markets, and enable the company to recruit and hold a superior work force.[31] Turnover was clearly the dominant consideration in Du Pont deliberations over a new pension plan in 1914. Raskob, the treasurer, had some difficulty even with the notion of the pension as a manipulative device, questioning whether it was "proper" to use the pension to keep employees with the company, or whether a pension plan should be designed "to take care of old employees who, through misfortune, ignorance or

27. Nelson, *Managers and Workers*, pp. 84–86.

28. Charles M. Ripley, "Life in a Large Manufacturing Plant," *General Electric Review* 21 (August 1918): 580.

29. Hughes, "Retirement System," pp. 619–20. Nelson, *Managers and Workers*, p. 150; copy of Du Pont *Bulletin* No. EMD-1, from H. G. Haskell, Du Pont Papers, series 2, part 2, Vice-presidential files.

30. Nelson, *Managers and Workers*, pp. 149–51; Ripley, "Life in a Manufacturing Plant," p. 581.

31. Smith, "Pension System," p. 2; Tufft, "Making Laborers Capitalists," pp. 23, 25; memorandum, Irénée Du Pont to Accounting Committee, 16 April 1923, Du Pont Company Papers, series 2, part 2, Vice-presidential files; *Iron Age* 95 (22 April 1915): 902; *Iron Trade Review* 52 (10 April 1913): 870; Ripley, "Life in a Manufacturing Plant," p. 579; William Lodge, "Pension Plan for the Machinery Industry," *Iron Age* 91 (17 April 1913): 948; Brandes, *Welfare Capitalism*, p. 105; Frank A. Vanderlip, "Insurance for Workingmen," reprinted in U.S., Congress, House, *Retirement from the Classified Civil Service of Superannuated Employees: Message from the President of the United States*, Transmitting Report of the U.S. Commission on Economy and Efficiency on the Subject of Retirement from the Classified Civil Service of Superannuated Employees, Doc. No. 732, 62d Cong., 2d sess. (Washington, D.C., 1912), p. 19.

other causes, find themselves without resources when incapacitated after a certain number of years' service."[32] J. A. Haskell, informed by a superintendent that the company's bonus and pension system would keep him at Du Pont even if he were offered a 50 percent wage increase elsewhere, felt no such ambivalence, nor did Copeland, Raskob's assistant. Like other Du Pont officials, Copeland was aware of the company's high turnover rate and convinced that a carefully designed retirement plan would significantly increase stability in the service without undue cost. His focus, however, was distinctive and forward-looking in its emphasis on the necessity for early vesting in order to attract and hold younger workers. The older elements in the work force, he believed, would naturally stay; in an increasingly discriminatory labor market, many had no place else to go. Younger workers, on the other hand, were freer to shift occupations; they could be held within the company only by offering some early reward for service. To this end, Copeland favored some vesting after five years with the company. "A plan which merely contemplates reward after a lifetime of employment," he argued, "while it might be better for the employees themselves on the average, is not the best suited to the interests of the Company."[33]

By the mid-1920s, the pension's contributions to general efficiency and reduced turnover were under scrutiny. Employers were more aware of the imprecision of the instrument than they had been fifteen years before and more informed of its limited impact on service stability. Growing labor surpluses had reduced the need for a mechanism to restrict the mobility of the work force.[34] Yet retirement continued to be valued for its contribution to the elimination of superannuation, and employers had new expectations emerging out of the changing economic and social climate of the late 1920s and 1930s.[35] In some sense, the new pensions were a function of prosperity, a way of capitalizing the profits of the 1920s and the expected growth of the next decade. It seems likely, too, that pension funds may have appealed to some employers as an easily con-

---

32. Raskob to Mr. Charles Copeland, 22 December 1914, ACC 152, 228, Irénée Du Pont Papers, Vice-presidential files, ID 10, "Bonus Pension Plans, 1914–1915."

33. Memorandum, Copeland to Irénée Du Pont, 28 December 1914, ibid.; memorandum, Irénée Du Pont to J. J. Raskob, 23 November 1914, ibid.; memorandum, Haskell to T. C. Du Pont, 19 January 1914, Du Pont Powder Co. Papers, series 2, part 3, Presidential Files, box 123, file "Salaries, 1908–14"; Carole Haber, "Mandatory Retirement in Nineteenth-Century America: The Conceptual Basis for a New Work Cycle," *Journal of Social History* 12 (Fall 1978): 82–83. For another point of view, see Latimer, *Industrial Pension Systems*, 2: 753–54. When pension funds are vested, they become the employee's legal property.

34. Whitmore, "Industrial Pensions," pp. 246–52; Berliner, "Pension Systems," p. 28; Lubove, *Struggle*, p. 131; Michel Dahlin, Ph.D. dissertation in progress, chapter "The Problem of the Older Worker."

35. Latimer, *Industrial Pension Systems*, 2: 787; H. B. Bergen, "Personnel Policies in the Light of the New Deal," *Personnel* 11 (August 1934): 22.

trollable source of investment capital.[36] But the uneven prosperity of the 1920s, spilling over into the Depression in late 1929, was of more importance in conceptualizing the role of retirement and the pension. In 1935, a New York City consulting accountant argued that just as unemployment reserve funds were a reserve for unemployed workers, so were pensions an analogous reserve for superannuated employees. A Chicago company, blessed with a work force averaging only thirty-eight years of age, actually used its pension fund for unemployment relief. Solomon Barkin, then serving with the New York State Commission on Old Age Security, advocated early retirement—to be achieved in part through the pension—to relieve labor-market pressures.[37]

The pension served other Depression-related purposes. The Packard Motor Car Company's plan was intended to stabilize the employment of the older working population by providing for the transfer of partially superannuated employees to a specially organized department that recognized declining energies and abilities. This form of pensioning, in which retirement began within the factory, was apparently designed to prevent the wholesale dismissal of older workers.[38] Others believed that the pension could stimulate consumption, either by making consumers more willing to purchase goods by reducing anxiety about the future or by distributing income to older, poorer elements of the population, who were more likely to spend it. The latter idea was also basic to the Townsend program and served to counter fears that an aging population, out of touch with consumer habits, was itself contributing to the depressed state of the economy.[39]

The case for the pension plan as a form of labor control was first articulated at some length by Frank A. Vanderlip of the National City Bank of New York, in the December 1905 issue of the *North American Review*. One of the early architects of civil service retirement, Vanderlip came to the defense of the straight pension plan (under which the employer provided the entire sum) for its contributions to regulating the conduct of the work force. He attributed the railroads' interest in the straight pension to its role in establishing "military discipline." For the sake of a pension an employee would, he believed, "sacrifice much of his personal liberty, including his right to strike for better wages or

36. H. S. Person, "Shorter Work Week Or Shorter Work Life?" *Factory and Industrial Management* 79 (January 1930): 56; Tufft, "Making Laborers Capitalists," pp. 24–25.

37. H. C. Hasbrouck, "Reserves for Jobless and Aged," *Electrical World* 105 (2 February 1935): 262–64; Rogers A. Fiske, "Flexible Pension Fund Used for Unemployment Relief," *Iron Age 130 (14 July 1932): 49;* Solomon Barkin, *"Economic Difficulties of Older Persons," Personnel Journal* 11 (April 1933): 400.

38. *Machinery Magazine* 37 (October 1930): 102 (editorial).

39. Gerard Swope, "Stabilization of Industry," *General Electric Review* 34 (October 1931): 543–47; G. Chauncey Parsons, "If the Next Congress Requires Pensions: Here are Ways to Set Them Up," *Food Industries* 6 (October 1934): 442; Person, "Shorter Work Week," pp. 57–58.

shorter hours."[40] Much of the early opposition to pensions was predicated on the assumption that the institution would restrict independent action.[41] By the 1930s, this philosophy of conflict between capital and labor had been replaced by an ethic that emphasized the possibilities of cooperation, but the message was only rhetorically different: sharing in the bounties of capitalism, a satisfied, secure working class would resist dangerous agitators and take a responsible attitude toward the strikes that by the late 1930s were the bane of the capitalist economy. Chauncey Parsons, an insurance broker who made dozens of speeches in behalf of pensions in the 1930s, never failed to use this argument.[42]

The evidence that pensions were actually used to control radical activity is limited but interesting. During a 1916 strike of 1,600 employees at the Worcester and Providence plants of Crompton and Knowles, a weaving enterprise, the company installed an extremely liberal old-age pension plan. It announced that former employees of the company (the strikers) would be given full credit for prior service toward the twenty-five-year service qualification, provided that they were reinstated before August 15, then about a month away. Although the company claimed to have taken this action in recognition of the needs of its operatives, its aggressive nature was patent.[43] In 1922, pensioners of a rail line in western Maryland were deprived of their annuities when they refused to come back to work as scabs during a strike of enginemen and firemen. Much the same thing happened on a Canadian road several years later, but the Maryland incident was the most famous of its kind and for years served well those who wished to discredit the pension system.[44]

A Brief Chronology

To date there is no adequate study of the chronology of pension systems before 1935. Scholars agree that the first American corporation to adopt a pen-

---

40. U.S., Congress, House, *Retirement from the Classified Civil Service of Superannuated Employees: Message from the President of the United States*, Doc. No. 732, 62d Cong., 2d sess. (Washington, D.C., 1912), p. 20, also p. 19.

41. DeRoode, "Pensions as Wages," p. 288; speech by Victor Berger, *Congressional Record*, 62d Cong., 1st sess., 1911, 47, pt. 4, p. 3699; Haber, "Mandatory Retirement," pp. 83–84.

42. Tufft, "Making Laborers Capitalists," p. 23; *Iron Age* 91 (17 April 1913): 948; Dearing, *Industrial Pensions*, p. 39; *Iron Trade Review* 52 (10 April 1913): 870; G. Chauncey Parsons, "How and Why Annuity and Other Pension Plans Have Failed: The Alternative," *Annalist* 43 (8 June 1934): 910; Parsons, "Next Congress," p. 442.

43. *Textile World Journal* 51 (15 July 1916): 20.

44. U.S., Congress, House, Committee on Labor, *Old Age Pensions: Hearings before the Committee on Labor*, 71st Cong., 2d sess., 20, 21, 28 February 1930 (Washington, D.C., 1930), pp. 140–41, 152; Latimer, *Industrial Pension Systems*, 2: 756, 760; U.S., Congress, House, Committee on Ways and Means, *Economic Security Act: Hearings on H.R. 4120*, 74th Cong., 1st sess., 21 January and 12 February 1935 (Washington, D.C., 1935), p. 666 (Dingell testimony).

sion system was the American Express Company, in 1875, and that until 1910 the railroads, public utilities, banks, metal industries, and the larger industrial corporations accounted for most of the approximately sixty plans effected. The year 1910 was a benchmark, for in the decade that followed new plans were established at a rate of at least twenty-one per year. Among the factors accounting for this spurt, three related ones are particularly relevant: the general popularity after 1910 of scientific management; the recognition of labor turnover; and the attention given to bureaucratic efficiency and superannuation by the William H. Taft administration. The rate of plan creation rose substantially in the 1920s to perhaps forty-five per year, a product of the decade's conservative industrial environment and of tax advantages first available in 1916. Pension activity continued strong through 1935 and may even have intensified during the early years of the Depression.[45] As in the pre-1910 period, plans continued to be concentrated in the larger firms, where risk could effectively be spread throughout the organization and impersonal, bureaucratic arrangements were least disruptive. In the metal trades, however, and probably in other industries, second-echelon firms of from three hundred to one thousand employees were much more likely to have a retirement plan than were firms with more than one thousand employees.[46]

By any estimate, corporation retirement programs failed to deal adequately with the swelling problems of old-age dependency. As of 1932, only 15 percent of American workers were potentially covered under the plans, and perhaps 5 percent of those who needed benefits were actually receiving payment. The corporate systems seldom provided benefits for spouses of workers, usually required fifteen to thirty years' service, and only 10 percent of the plans legally obligated the company to any kind of payment. Because few of the plans were contributory, most did not even offer the advantages of accumulated forced savings. Actuarial weaknesses and a general disregard for the necessity of reserve funds (money accumulations to finance future retirements) made it unlikely that the system would adequately protect the aged poor.[47] According to one estimate, the average plan in 1920 paid the retiring worker about $360 per year, about half what the lowest-paid government worker received under civil service retirement legislation passed that year and a sum inadequate for the support of two persons without savings. Most plans graduated payments according to income, so that lower-paid employees received considerably less than this average.[48] By 1930

45. Latimer, *Industrial Pension Systems*, 1: 39; Lubove, *Struggle*, pp. 127–29; David Hackett Fischer, *Growing Old in America* (New York, 1977), pp. 165–67.
46. *American Machinist* 72 (10 April 1930): 615–17; B. F. Timmons, *Personnel Practices Among Ohio Industries* (Columbus, Ohio, 1931), p. 120.
47. Lubove, *Struggle*, pp. 128–29; *Textile World* 84 (August 1934): 1606.
48. *Iron Age* 104 (17 July 1919): 182; ibid. 99 (24 May 1917): 1265.

the typical industrial plan retired employees voluntarily at age sixty or sixty-five with twenty or twenty-five years' service. Compulsory retirement was not yet considered necessary for the promotion of continuous service nor, given the right of the corporation to release employees for inefficiency under incapacity clauses written into most plans, was it essential to the elimination of superannuated workers. Plans generally covered all employees within the firm, regardless of function and salary.[49]

Industrial pensions received the formal sanction of the tax system beginning in 1916, when corporations were allowed to deduct, as "ordinary and necessary expenses," the actual payments to retired employees or their families or dependents. At that time, Internal Revenue regulations specifically denied deductions for contributions to pension funds but implied that this limitation applied only to funds controlled by the corporation, as opposed to fiduciary-managed employee pension trusts.[50] This was made explicit in early 1919 in a new regulation, according to which corporate "donations" to an employee pension trust that was "entirely separate and distinct from the corporation" were considered contributions to a charitable institution and therefore deductible from gross corporate income in arriving at net income subject to taxation.[51] Contributions to employer pension reserve funds not independent of the corporation were not deductible. In 1928, corporations secured legislation allowing deductions over a period of years for monies transferred from pension reserves to trusts, and for reasonable contributions to newly created pension plans. The revenue act of 1926 extended to pension trusts the distribution provisions applied to stock-bonus and profit-sharing plans since 1921. Under these provisions, employees were not taxed on amounts accumulated to their credit until they were actually distributed, and then only to the extent that payments exceeded amounts paid in. This meant that most benefits were taxed at the lower income-tax rates usually applying to older taxpayers and that taxpayers received the substantial benefits of deferral.[52] By 1930 the pension offered employer and employee alike important financial advantages not available even fifteen years earlier.

49. Latimer, *Industrial Pension Systems*, 1: 101, and 63 (table 10).

50. U.S., Treasury Department, Department of Internal Revenue, Regulations No. 33 (revised) Governing the Collecting of the Income Tax, Imposed by the Act of September 8, 1916 as Amended by the Act of October 3, 1917 (Washington, D.C., 1918), p. 73 (Art. 136).

51. U.S., Treasury Department, Bureau of Internal Revenue, *Income Tax Rulings Nos. 1–655, Inclusive, Cumulative Bulletin*, no. 1, April–December 1919 (Washington, D.C., 1922), p. 224.

52. J. S. Seidman, *Seidman's Legislative History of Federal Income Tax Laws: 1938–1861* (New York, 1938), pp. 516–17, 604–05; Commerce Clearing House, *U.S. Tax Cases*, vol. 74–1 (Chicago, 1974), pp. 83,573 (*Trebotich v. Comm.*); Earl L. MacNeill, "Trends in the Pension Field," *Trusts and Estates* 80 (January 1945): 65–68; Rainard B. Robbins, *Impact of Taxes on Industrial Pension Plans*, Industrial Relations Monograph No. 14 (New York, 1949), chap. 2.

Although the legislation and Treasury regulations make much of the importance of maintaining

LABOR: THE TRADE-UNION PENSION PLAN

Trade-union pension plans were of much less statistical significance than their industrial counterparts. As of 1930, only about fifteen internationals and a few locals had pension programs. The first was established in 1900 by the Pattern Makers' League of North America. Within ten years pensions were in force for select groups of workers, including jewelry workers, printers, carpenters and joiners, machinists, journeymen plumbers, gas fitters, steam fitters, and street and electric railway employees.[53] These were, on the whole, working-class elites, middle-class workers with skills that freed them from the almost total insecurity that hounded the unskilled, especially in the new mass-production industries, and gave them incomes that made retirement deductions tolerable. They were workers who could reasonably accept the pension as the risky proposition it was. Some 90 percent of the American work force remained outside the trade unions and therefore removed from trade-union pension systems, and most of those who did belong were fighting more primitive battles for existence and using more basic weapons, such as the strike.

Nonetheless, the debates within the trade unions over the establishment and maintenance of these plans reveal much about the function of retirement in a trade-union bureaucracy. Most striking is that the pension plan was expected to have functions akin to the corporate programs. First, it was a security device. In the International Typographical Union (ITU), the scene of an extensive debate over the pension in the first decade of the century, it was generally recognized that revolutionary technological changes in printing had destroyed or severely undermined the ability of older printers, particularly typesetters, to perform satisfactorily. A more gradual change in production techniques, though equally destructive of the earning power of the older worker, had taken place among the machinists. In each case, the pension was a logical response to superannuation brought on by changes in technology and by the high speeds at which capitalists chose to operate the new machinery. There seemed nothing to do but provide the released employee with something to live on. The secretary-treasurer of the International Association of Machinists, George Preston, defended a pensionable age of sixty on the grounds that few men over that age were physically capable of working in the trade.[54]

---

legal distance between the corporation and the trust, there is reason to doubt whether the criteria designed to achieve separation were sufficient to produce independence. Especially in the period of unrest following World War I, corporate fiduciaries were notoriously biased in their defense of private property through harmonious labor relations. See, for instance, James G. Smith, "Rôle of Corporate Fiduciary in the New Industrial Revolution," *Trust Companies* 46 (February 1928): 201–04.

53. Dearing, *Industrial Pensions*, p. 31; *Typographical Journal* 35 (August 1909): 172–73.
54. International Typographical Union (ITU), *Reports of Officers and Proceedings of the 53d*

Unions felt responsible for older workers separated from their trades as a result of participation in strikes, especially those leading to the eight-hour day. This was the most emotional issue raised during the ITU's discussion of pensions. "For these benefits lasting and positive to the young men," said its Committee on Benefit Features, "the old men have sacrificed their all."[55] Union leaders recognized that these early and crucial strikes could easily have been defeated had older workers succumbed to the temptation to remain in the shop; the pension was a just reward for what in retrospect was an act of occupational suicide. The issue retained some potency even in the early 1920s, when pensioners claimed their earlier contributions to organizational successes justified increased benefits. Interest in the pension as a form of social justice was also fueled by the increasingly burdensome cost of one of the alternatives, the insurance that a number of trade-union members held from fraternal orders.[56]

The union's concern with justice was linked to its own financial needs. Recognizing the plight of older workers who had sacrificed themselves in strikes, the machinists had since 1903 made provision for these victims on the strike roll, sometimes paying benefits for more than two hundred weeks. Preston found this custom expensive and anticipated that a new pension system would at least aid in distinguishing between those who needed assistance and those who preferred to "remain on the pay rolls for reasons best known to themselves."[57] As he must have realized, however, the problem was not so much one of those who could work and would not, as it was one of general unemployment among middle-aged and older machinists. Few could dispute that benefits should not go to shirkers and those working as machinists or in some other trade, but that did not remedy the situation created when industry had redefined old age by adjusting the relationship between the worker and technology. By industry standards, these workers were superannuated and should have been treated as pensionable.

The printers worked out the relationships between the pension and unemployment at the 1925 Kalamazoo convention, where union officials succeeded in raising the retirement age from sixty to sixty-five. Consulting actuary H. C.

Session of the ITU, Hot Springs, Arkansas, August 12 to 17, 1907, supplement to *Typographical Journal* 31 (October 1907): 159; George Preston, "Superannuation," pt. 2, *Machinists' Monthly Journal* 22 (March 1910): 270, Dahlin, Ph.D. dissertation in progress, chapter entitled "Company Pensions: The Private Solution."

55. ITU, *Report of 53d Session*, p. 235; George Preston, "Superannuation," pt. 3, *Machinists' Monthly Journal* 22 (April 1910): 367–68.

56. *Typographical Journal* 61 (December 1922): 682; ibid. 31 (August 1907): 157–58. A Kansas printer claimed that the pension was particularly necessary because of the large percentage of wage-earners who were homeless. See *Typographical Journal* 31 (July 1907): 33–34.

57. Preston, "Superannuation," pt. 1, *Machinists' Monthly Journal* 22 (February 1910): 153.

Marvin bore the brunt of this controversial effort. He argued first that sixty was an uncommon age in union and corporate plans. Of seventeen steam railway funds he had reviewed, none permitted retirement at sixty, and only one permitted it before sixty-five. Sixty was actuarially unsound (i.e., too costly) and, just as important, not justified by the nature of the work, for, in his opinion, sixty-year-old printers were not superannuated. "The man of seventy at this time," he said, "is fully as capable of securing sustaining employment as the member of 1907 was at the age of sixty." Since printers between sixty and sixty-five were not really old, retired workers in this age group, Marvin reasoned, were really unemployed, and the fund had become a mechanism for relieving unemployment, often of a voluntary nature. This last problem—printers voluntarily leaving their jobs to take the pension—seemed to Marvin a violation of the principles on which the original plan had been established eighteen years earlier. The system had been designed to care for those unable to secure work because of age, and the test of physical disability was whether the individual had tried and failed to secure employment. The chairman of the union's pension committee buttressed Marvin's viewpoint by pointing out that the larger printing houses were taking advantage of the union pension to retire employees the day they reached sixty. An increase in the retirement age would prevent this and thus eliminate unemployment among men perfectly capable of functioning at their jobs. The union voted to adopt the proposal.[58]

The main import of this incident is clear. The pension had originally been designed, in some measure, to deal with superannuation—that is, with old age as defined by industrial requirements, which was no more than a form of unemployment. In 1925 the union was still willing to operate by this definition; it wished only to ensure that the definition had itself been adjusted to new occupational requirements. If, however, Marvin was mistaken in assuming a change in the age structure of the profession (and there is reason to believe he was),[59] the action of the convention takes on an entirely different meaning, signifying a turn away from its past attitude of responsibility toward the superannuated.[60]

Union officials also expected retirement programs to perform a variety of tasks associated with organizational strength and efficiency. With its older ma-

58. ITU, *Proceedings of the 70th Session of the ITU, Kalamazoo, Michigan, August 10–15, 1925*, supplement to *Typographical Journal* 67 (September 1925): 64–66, 68.

59. *Typographical Journal* 67 (August 1925): 183; ibid. 61 (November 1922): 615; ibid. 61 (July 1922): 80; ibid. 61 (October 1922): 429.

60. The pension as a response to the unemployment problems of the middle-aged and older worker is discussed in Senate, *Hearings on Unemployment, 1928–29*, p. 63 (William Green testimony); U.S., Congress, Senate, Committee on Pensions, Subcommittee, *Old Age Pensions: Hearing on S. 3257, A Bill to Encourage and Assist the States in Providing Pensions to the Aged*, 24 February 1931, 71st Cong., 3d sess. (Washington, D.C., 1931), p. 94.

chinists secure in their pensions, the machinists, for example, need not reduce their strike effectiveness by leaving the old men on the shop floor during a conflict with management. If the union was vulnerable because of its older workers, one eliminated the older workers and with them the vulnerability. Benefits would also serve as a bonding mechanism, forging member loyalty to the larger organization. This effect would be achieved in part indirectly, as a result of association of the pension with the union rather than with the company; a union plan offered a solution to old-age dependency without the threat to union solidarity posed by a company plan designed to tie the worker to management. At the ITU, the pension was sold to the union membership at the 1907 convention as a device to hold somewhat reluctant workers in the fold. The twenty-year continuous service rule, President James M. Lynch told assembled delegates, "will cause many to consider well before severing their connection with the organization for any of the trivial reasons which now influence them."[61] Preston of the machinists expected the superannuation benefits to attract the "in and out" workers then troubling his organization. Whether the pension could make members of those who might not otherwise join is problematical. The printers, and to a greater degree the railroad unions, expected the pension to aid, or at least not hinder, attempts to invigorate their aging organizations by bringing in younger men. Retirement itself accomplished this, of course, but the trainmen were also aware that superannuation benefits based on age rather than continuous service could prove enough of a burden to the younger generation to prevent their joining.[62] Among the printers, the hope was that a larger pension would bring in the "open shoppers" and the country practitioners of the art, who historically had remained aloof from the union. A 1915 report from the Buffalo, New York local of the ITU indicates some success in attracting older recalcitrants, who sometimes became "enthusiastic workers in the cause of unionism, particularly in relation to the benefit features."[63]

For all the anticipated benefits, retirement programs were not universally popular even within the unions that could most easily afford them. Reasons are not hard to discern. To the union the pension was an aggregate activity that could be justified because it promised so many rewards. Individual union members, actual and potential, cared little for these aggregate benefits; for them the retirement system was personal, its impact on them simple and direct, not an

61. *Typographical Journal* 31 (September 1907): 286; ibid. 35 (October 1909): 387; A. A. Graham, "Old-Age Civic Pensions," *Machinists' Monthly Journal* 23 (September 1911): 855–56.

62. Preston, "Superannuation," pt. 3, p. 368; *Railroad Trainmen's Journal* 19 (September 1902): 734–35 (editorial); *Typographical Journal* 61 (December 1922): 757; ibid. 47 (July 1915): 20.

63. *Typographical Journal* 47 (September 1915): 366; ibid. 67 (August 1925): 183; ibid. 31 (October 1907): 387.

average but a unique quantity. Many members of a Boston local of the ITU—and the case must have been replicated all over the nation—belonged to the Franklin Society, a fraternal association that paid them five dollars per week for life upon disability and old age. They feared this minimal benefit would disqualify them from participation in the proposed union plan, which held out benefits only to those who had no other income or means of support. Others found the ITU's twenty-year continuous service rule too severe. If the average age of ITU members at death was forty-five and a half years, as one correspondent claimed, a pension not available until age sixty hardly seemed worth paying for, especially to younger recruits.[64] The raw vote figures on the ITU pension plan are not very instructive. By a margin of 17,177 to 9,194, the membership approved the benefit package. Among the larger locals, the New York vote was extremely close; the Chicago local, on the other hand, voted almost four to one in favor of the plan. Most of the smaller locals, even some that were clearly rural or small town, voted to establish the pension.[65]

A rising cost of living throughout the Progressive Era and the 1920s reduced benefits and created political problems (the need, for example, to come back to the membership to ask for benefit increases) that would not have existed in a period of stable prices. Because they seldom employed actuaries and might not even know the age distribution of the membership, union leaders were constantly, and legitimately, concerned about the costs of their plans. Officials of the ITU fund must have been alarmed when a 1909 study of fund usage revealed that sixty-year-old applicants (the youngest eligible) were the largest single age group. That the fund should insure against unemployment was an anathema.[66]

LABOR: THE OLD-AGE HOME

The old-age home has been of even less importance than the pension in caring for the nation's aged. In 1910, only a small percentage of America's four million persons sixty-five and over lived in old-age homes. After a half century of late-nineteenth-century growth in these institutions, less than one older person in twenty had taken up residence. The great majority of homes had been established, beginning in the mid-nineteenth century, by fraternal and religious groups. The few old-age homes established by organized labor housed perhaps

64. Ibid. 31 (October 1907): 386; ibid. 47 (July 1915): 13–14; ibid. 35 (August 1909): 172–73.
65. From the "Report of the International Canvassing Board," *Typographical Journal* 31 (December 1907): 627–32.
66. Preston, "Superannuation," pt. 1, p. 154; ITU, *Reports of Officers and Proceedings of the 55th Session of the ITU, Held in St. Joseph, Missouri, August 9–14, 1909*, supplement to *Typographical Journal* 35 (September 1909): 61.

one thousand workers; they counted for little in terms of caring for a dependent population.[67]

Union members, however, did not dismiss the homes, real or potential, as insignificant. From 1880 to 1930, and particularly at the turn of the century, the old-age home was pondered often and profoundly. The pages of the journals of the machinists, the railroad trainmen, and the printers and typesetters bear witness to the intensity of the exchange, as workers in these occupations tried to explain why they wanted, or did not want, an old-age home. Faced with the prospect of a new retirement institution that could radically alter their lives, they described what they expected from home, family, friends, city, and the old-age home. An aging segment of the prosperous working class explored the meaning of community.

The focus of much of the attention was the union printers' home, constructed in 1894. Such an institution was first seriously considered in 1886, when George W. Childs and Anthony J. Drexel gave the ITU $10,000 to erect a home at Colorado Springs. Some thought the donation, rumored the largest ever made to any body of organized wage-earners, might better be used to establish a life insurance plan, but this suggestion was rejected by a vote of the membership. As the union debated, the fund grew from additional contributions. When $22,000 had been accumulated in 1889, the annual convention committed the union to a home and to Colorado Springs, where the local board of trade had donated an eight-acre plot. In 1894, four years after the erection of the main building and in accordance with a Colorado law requiring a separate edifice for the treatment of contagious disease, the convention unanimously adopted an assessment of fifty cents on each member to finance construction of a hospital on the grounds. The central structure of the completed facility was two stories high and had one hundred rooms, with bay windows, surrounded by porches to make sun and air accessible to the residents. If it resembled a home, it was, as the membership realized, a magnificent, almost regal one.[68]

The printers' home at Colorado Springs was watched carefully by other unions considering establishing or expanding facilities for their older members. In 1913–14, in response to rank-and-file members who wished to see their union

67. Lee Welling Squier, *Old Age Dependency in the United States: A Complete Survey of the Pension Movement* (New York, 1912), p. 6; Frank D. Loomis, "On the Care of Old People in Chicago and Vicinity," typescript report, March 1923, for the Chicago Community Trust, in Chicago Welfare Council Papers, Chicago Historical Society, Chicago, Illinois, box 23, folder "Aged, 1922–29."

68. *Typographical Journal* 12 (15 April 1898): 337; ibid. 13 (1 August 1898): 96–101; *Machinists' Monthly Journal* 25 (February 1913): 162–64. Drexel and Childs were close associates of James MacAlister, the Philadelphia educator and Drexel Institute of Art president who played an important role in teacher retirement.

erect something similar, the general executive board of the machinists' union undertook an inquiry into the Colorado Springs operation. Three machinists thought the printers had done a splendid job. But the union's secretary-treasurer was less impressed. The printers' home, he reported, cared for only 127 inmates out of a total membership of 60,000. The yearly cost of $100,000, or $541 per resident, exceeded the ordinary cost of care in an average hospital. Financial factors alone forced his conclusion that the "home does not appear to be a good form of benefit to adopt."[69]

This was also the logic of the members of the Brotherhood of Railroad Trainmen (BRT), who in 1900 were considering establishing a larger home to replace the one then shared with other railroad brotherhoods. Many union members believed that the financial problems associated with home management could sap the strength of the organization and even destroy it. As evidence of the danger of branching out into unfamiliar areas, they cited the earlier failure of a brotherhood printing plant. Others insisted that a home be self-supporting and resented anticipated increased assessments.[70] The printers voiced similar fears about the Colorado Springs facility. One inmate, in fact, wrote that he had always opposed the establishment of a home in favor of a pension, and he suggested reducing expenses of operation by putting inmates to part-time work as printers.[71]

Who lived in these old-age homes? Which groups were they expected to house? The first question may be answered more easily than the second. The small railroad workers' facility, opened in Highland Park, Illinois in 1890, was designed essentially for disabled employees incapable of earning a living in the market economy. In an industry as physically destructive as railroading at the time, this qualified a great many men. Yet in June 1894 the Highland Park structure housed only twenty persons; in July, only four. Most of these were physically disabled, though the home was also intended to aid those who were helpless because of age and lacking other sources of care. In these early years the home turned away several men who in the judgment of the proprietor were capable of earning a living if willing. It took in an eighty-year-old former engineer "who had out-lived all his relations and friends."[72]

69. *Machinists' Monthly Journal* 25 (February 1913): 162; Preston, "Superannuation," pt. 2, p. 270; George Preston, "Can We Afford It? [Machinists' Home]," *Machinists' Monthly Journal* 26 (March 1914): 292–93; *Machinists' Monthly Journal* 26 (March 1914): 294.
70. *Railroad Trainmen's Journal* 22 (July 1905): 501–03; ibid. 23 (January 1906): 53–54; ibid. 16 (September 1899): 841; ibid. 18 (April 1901): 307–09; ibid. 22 (October 1905): 789.
71. *Typographical Journal* 22 (March 1903): 283; ibid. 12 (15 April 1898): 338–39; J. W. Bramwood, "The Union Printers' Home," *Typographical Journal* 22 (January 1903): 18.
72. *Railroad Trainmen's Journal* 11 (June 1894): 509, and 510; ibid. (August 1894): 744; ibid. 22 (April 1905): 284.

Printers were less often victims of serious injury, and therefore their old-age home did not experience the anomaly of harboring the really young. With no age minimum, however, it did care for a number of middle-aged union members. In the first six years of the home's operation, 209 inmates were admitted. Of these, the cause of entry for 60 percent can be identified. Forty percent of those entering were admitted for consumption. At least thirty-six, or 17 percent, were classified as either "superannuated" or for "general debility." Of the super-annuated, the youngest was sixty-two, the oldest seventy-six, and the average slightly over sixty-seven. The thirteen printers admitted for general debility were younger, mostly in their fifties, the youngest forty-four. Those in this category were no doubt expected to regain their strength and leave the home. Superannuation, on the other hand, was defined as a permanent condition, a function of fitness rather than chronological age.[73] Inmates were expected to be physically capable of benefiting from living in the home. The admission committee claimed that some locals had used the home as a refuge for undesirable members.[74] Taking into account the differences in the two industries, the homes of the trainmen and printers were similar institutions, open to unfortunates who for reasons of sickness, physical disability, old age, or unusual family situations could not care for themselves. Each home served only a small percentage of those eligible in any of these categories.

If it seems obvious in retrospect that these old-age homes could only with great difficulty and at great expense have been expanded to care for *all* the disabled and otherwise unfortunate, it was not so clear in 1900. Within the BRT, the home issue coincided with, and was related to, the rise of age discrimination on the railways. Would the home be a refuge for this rapidly growing group of middle-aged unemployables who were ready, by industry's definition, for retirement? To those familiar with the costs of institutionalization, the idea was unsettling. Age limits would force these workers out of the brotherhood, wrote one trainman, "for not even the most enthusiastic member will declare that they can be taken to a Home."[75] By 1910 the printers and the machinists also had to consider whether the home, like the pension, would function as a retirement institution for the middle-aged, in effect as a form of unemployment relief. Officials at Colorado Springs were receiving a growing number of applications from members under age sixty, seeking admission because they could not make a living at printing or any other vocation. Because the claim was difficult to

73. ITU, Report, *Proceedings of the ITU, Forty-fourth Session, Syracuse, New York, October 10–15, 1898*, supplement to *Typographical Journal* 13 (15 November 1898): 79, 85–87.
74. "Report of Admission Committee," ibid., p. 80.
75. *Railroad Trainmen's Journal* 18 (April 1901): 308.

disprove and within the guidelines established for the facility, such people had in the past been allowed to enter. But as their numbers increased, so did doubts about the ability of the institution to survive this open-ended commitment.[76]

The disability problem was certainly most critical among the railroad work-ers. Although common sense suggested the difficulty of establishing a central agency large enough to care for these victims, this was an emotional issue for many who worked on the roads. Those already receiving union disability pay-ments were apprehensive lest they be taken away; others simply believed that disabled workers deserved the security a home could provide. Among the latter was L. S. Coffin, seventy-one years old in 1894, committed to the home concept to the extent that several years later he would, by purchasing one of its two buildings, rescue the brotherhoods' small institution at a time of financial crisis. For Coffin the home was "a most sacred trust." In 1901, when the BRT was on the verge of a vote to join with the engineers and the conductors to create a larger institution, Coffin used the pages of the *Railroad Trainmen's Journal* for an impassioned plea that readers trust his judgment on a matter to which he had devoted the last twelve years of his life. Brushing aside the difficult related questions of scope and finance, he asked the brotherhood to support a home "that is a refuge, a haven of rest, for every distressed and helpless railroad man in the Brotherhoods."[77]

Coffin and other old-age home advocates labored also against the wide-spread feeling that in addition to serving a potentially dangerous number of unfortunates, these institutions would, as other welfare institutions reputedly did, also create them. When it learned of the Drexel-Childs grant to the ITU, the *Printers' Circular*, a local Philadelphia publication, predicted that a home would be abused by lazy members of the trade.[78] Inmates at Colorado Springs were often publicly reproached for improvidence by those who had visited the facility, prompting one resident to reply that "if someone were willing to super-vise their efforts and give to them intelligent direction, most of the abused in-mates might be found more than willing to do their little best [toward maintain-ing the facility by gardening and farming]."[79] The few who took advantage of the Highland Park home were subject to the same kind of abuse, based on the presumption that their confinement would, as one trainman expressed it, "create a careless way of living among some of the men." One member of the brother-

76. ITU, *Report of 55th Session*, p. 15; Preston, "Superannuation," pt. 2, p. 270.
77. *Railroad Trainmen's Journal* 18 (December 1901): 1017; ibid. (May 1901): 389; ibid. 11 (June 1894): 510. For a brief biography of Coffin, see W. G. Edens, "How We Care for Our Aged and Disabled," *Railroad Trainman* 56 (September 1939): 410.
78. *Inland Printer* 4 (December 1886): 165.
79. *Typographical Journal* 12 (15 May 1898): 424.

hood, W. A. Wheeling, was typical in linking the old-age home and the alms-house. Wheeling affirmed that his wife and children would never enter this "side show to a poor farm."[80]

The strident, moral tone of this criticism suggests an underlying personal meaning that transcended concern for cost and inmate work habits. For these men, the enemy was the ultimate insecurity of joblessness and poverty, and the union home was its symbol. Shocked at the begging he had observed, Joseph Greig cautioned his fellow printers to take care that in their old age they would have no need to file application to Childs-Drexel "or be so weak as to lean upon the arm of society for support." Better by far, he said, to "own a home bearing one's own title, that it may stand as a fit monument of honor for posterity to look upon."[81]

For many, the old-age home was the antithesis of what they wanted in their old age, a visible reminder not only of the possibility of poverty but of how easily the old might be denied their community. But community did not mean the same thing to all workers. For the railroad worker, whose job might remove him physically from his small town or city for days at a time, the central elements in his community tended to be geography and home. Home meant a return to one's geographical community, a canceling out of one's basic occupational mobility. It would also, of course, include family; but the railroad worker really missed the whole community—friends, acquaintances, neighbors, familiar physical environs. "Brothers," wrote one trainman, "how many of us would leave our family and friends and homes of our childhood days and go to a Brotherhood Home, perhaps far distant, and end our days in a strange place with strangers?"[82] The same writer who had insisted on the BRT home's contribution to moral degeneration maintained a more complex vision of his own future: "When I am old and worn out, even if I am not married, I would not leave my people and the place or country in which I had lived all my life to go to the 'Brotherhood Home,' possibly in some distant part of the United States or Canada. If the single men would not want it isn't it safe to say the married men would not take advantage of it."[83] When one trainman wrote "be it ever so humble, there is no place like home," he most certainly did not mean the union old-people's home. The *Railroad Trainmen's Journal* was flooded with articles and letters on the subject of "home" at precisely the period in the mid-1890s that

80. *Railroad Trainmen's Journal* 22 (July 1905): 500; ibid. 18 (April 1901): 321.
81. *Typographical Journal* 12 (15 June 1898): 542.
82. *Railroad Trainmen's Journal* 22 (September 1905): 682.
83. Ibid. 22 (July 1905): 500.

Coffin's Highland Park facility was having trouble surviving because the membership would not support it with voluntary contributions.[84]

Machinists and printers, on the other hand, most often contrasted the old-age home with family. They expressed these families ties not as powerful emotional bonds but as rational connections that somehow could not be cast away, however positive the alternative might seem. It was common to argue against the old-age home on the ground that old workers could not take advantage of it "on account of family ties" or because of their "inability to separate themselves from their families."[85] Because they slept and worked in their communities, they neither felt nor expressed the kind of longing for home so common among the more mobile trainmen.

The old-age home might also violate family in another sense—marriage. Wives could not reside in either the trainmen's or the printers' home, which made separation the inevitable result of a worker's entrance into either institution. In 1915, when this issue was first seriously discussed within the ITU, the most common reaction was that opening the home to wives or constructing a separate facility for them would be inordinately expensive as well as a violation of the traditional restriction of benefits to union members. At the same time, however, local union districts were taking up the possibility of establishing cottages for wives at the Colorado Springs site. By the mid-1930s the ITU women's auxiliary was internally divided over whether to continue raising monies for a separate wives' home or to abolish the project and throw the accumulations of some $11,000 into a pension fund. The trainmen's ladies auxiliary achieved a partial solution much earlier by constructing their own facility at Glencoe, Illinois, near the men's home.[86]

Coffin had difficulty selling his railroad colleagues on the home, because he tried to make it into a family substitute, a genuinely homelike home, where an old engineer could live "as happily as he would have been had he been living with a son worth thousands of dollars."[87] It was not that and could not be. But the old-age home did have characteristics very appealing to certain union members. First, it offered ultimate security. Though some thought of the home as a

84. Ibid. 22 (September 1905): 682; ibid. 11 (May 1894): 434–35.

85. *Typographical Journal* 27 (July 1905): 41; "Report of Secretary-Treasurer of Machinists' Union on Printers' Home," *Machinists' Monthly Journal* 25 (February 1913): 162, 164; ITU, *Report of 53d Session*, p. 235.

86. *Typographical Journal* 47 (July 1915): 20–21; ibid. (August 1915): 181–82; International Typographical Union of North America, Woman's International Auxiliary, *Proceedings of the Thirtieth Annual Convention, Held at Palmer House, September 10–14, 1934* (Chicago, n.d.), pp. 15, 38; Edens, "How We Care for Our Aged," p. 410.

87. *Railroad Trainmen's Journal* 11 (June 1894): 509.

poorhouse, for others, perhaps the more secure, it was one of a number of ways of conceptualizing one's future in a world characterized by industrial accidents and technological change. Expressions of support for the home came from a printer with a religious sense of fate, for whom the home was protection against a completely unpredictable future; from a railroad worker who believed that his contribution to the institution had removed the taint of charity; from a poor trainman with a large family whose monetary contributions to the home were matched by his insistence that he would never set foot inside; and from a homeless man who had no other place to go. "If we all had homes," he wrote, "there would be no need to build."[88]

The home also served as a symbol of occupational fraternity, centered around both job and union. Strong fraternal feelings existed among printers and trainmen, and each group used the home to express, preserve, and intensify those feelings. An ITU candidate for home trustee campaigned by placing the home in the context of the general aims and purposes of the union: cooperation, self-protection, unity, fraternization, friendship. A trainman supported mandatory home contributions so that "our disabled brothers could live like kings."[89] A printer called the Colorado Springs home "a figurative shading oak, the most wonderful example of fraternity and brotherhood among those who toil that the world has known."[90] Said an enthusiastic machinist, "Outside of mother, I know of no sweeter word than comrade."[91] If some of this was rhetoric, there was a good deal of truth in it, as union officials were well aware. By 1925 the ITU had produced a film, largely about the printers' home. Entitled *His Brother's Keeper*, it was circulated widely to enthusiastic audiences.[92]

The printers particularly had a remarkably powerful notion of themselves as a unique occupational group. In the 1880s, for example, veterans of Chicago's printing establishment—printers, pressmen, and typographers who had been in the area for twenty-five years or more—were part of a social organization, the Old-Time Printers' Association.[93] Although technology would modify the printing business dramatically and reduce the degree of occupational cohesion, in 1900 much of it remained, especially among older and retired printers.

88. Ibid. 22 (December 1905): 959; ibid. 21 (September 1904): 679; ibid. 18 (May 1901): 385–86; *Typographical Journal* 39 (August 1911): 196.
89. *Railroad Trainmen's Journal* 17 (February 1900): 145; *Typographical Journal* 12 (15 April 1898): 339.
90. *Typographical Journal* 47 (December 1915): 767.
91. E. Farrington Wilcox, "A Machinists' Trade-Union Home," *Machinists' Monthly Journal* 23 (July 1911): 538.
92. *Typographical Journal* 67 (November 1925): 708; report of *Boston Globe*, reprinted ibid., p. 783.
93. *Inland Printer* 3 (March 1886): 422.

A former printer and resident of the National Military Home near Dayton described for readers of the *Typographical Journal* the kind of community he had found on his retirement. There were a number of old-time printers at the home, staffing two printing offices. He was aware of who worked in each shop and the regiments in which they had served. Some printers he knew personally, others only by sight, but in each case he seemed informed of the area from which a printer had come and was, as he put it, "known" in. A few printers continued to maintain an interest in the union, but the usual tie was less formal. "The old boys of the craft," he explained, "occasionally get together and 'talk shop,' for we have not lost our interest in it." (The printers of Dayton, on the other hand, were not particularly outgoing, preferring to remain distant from the "uniformed inhabitants of the home.")[94]

Perhaps not as pervasive, the trainmen's own sense of fraternity appears to have been based on comparatively narrow ties to other trainmen rather than to the larger group of railroad workers. In fact, much of the opposition within the BRT to a more elaborate home was based on this occupational definition; many trainmen—the Chicago lodge, for example—wanted an old-age home open only to members of their brotherhood.[95]

The Reconstruction of Community

In the 1930s, it became fashionable to point out that modernization had destroyed community in the United States, isolating individuals from the most vital of their social frameworks. Daniel Bell sought to correct this impression in his *End of Ideology*, published in 1955. While admitting that "urbanization, industrialization, and democratization have eroded older primary and community ties on a scale unprecedented in social history," Bell argued that these ties had been effectively replaced by voluntary associations, which provided "real satisfactions for real needs."[96] As a sociologist interested in the condition of American culture in the 1950s, Bell could be content with his discovery of voluntarism, secure in the knowledge that these voluntary institutions helped their members and that, short of an attempt to measure satisfaction under primary and secondary associational situations, his theory was unassailable. Using their own more dynamic techniques, historians have fleshed out the static picture developed by the sociologists. Robert Wiebe's *Search for Order* describes the

94. *Typographical Journal* 13 (1 December 1898): 477–78. See also ibid. 22 (February 1903): 149.

95. *Railroad Trainmen's Journal* 10 (June 1893): 478; ibid. 18 (January 1901): 52.

96. Bell, *The End of Ideology: On the Exhaustion of Political Ideas in the Fifties* (Glencoe, Ill., 1960), p. 31.

late-nineteenth-century decline of the geographically based "island communities" and their replacement by regional and national associations based on occupation and function. The historian and the sociologist agree, therefore, that primary ties were shattered, and that they were replaced by some necessary and positive mechanism of social adjustment.[97] For Wiebe this is some kind of centralizing institution, such as a trade union; for Bell, it is a voluntary association on any level.

One must question how well this approach applies to the aged or those ready to retire from work. Voluntary associations of the aged were few before 1930. Occupational and functional associations were designed to facilitate the career goals of a younger, upwardly mobile population. Where older workers were close together and numerous, as in the civil service in Washington, D.C. in 1900, they would form their own special-interest groups, based on the needs of aging workers in a particular labor market. But the printers, machinists, and trainmen were not so centralized, and special-interest old-age groups were not feasible for them. Instead, they worked within their existing structures, the unions, and within a more limited range of options. Faced with two basic sources of community—the national community of occupation, represented by the old-age home, and the local community of family, friends, and town, represented by the pension—these workers rejected the old-age home and chose the pension.[98]

Among the printers, the pension was seen as a way of avoiding the home and allowing the retired worker to live within his local community. Four years after the printers' pension plan went into effect, the union's president announced that applications to the home had declined as older printers decided to remain in their communities, and he hoped and predicted that the pension would depopulate that portion of the home assigned to the aged.[99] Perhaps the most poignant evidence comes from William A. Smith, a forty-seven-year-old, completely incapacitated resident at Colorado Springs. Although he affirmed how important the home had been to him, how he had, indeed, loved it, he was deeply affected by the fact that he was not eligible for the pension. "Why," he asked, "should I

97. Wiebe, *The Search for Order: 1877–1920* (New York: American Century Series, 1968), p. 111.

98. After 1915, advocates of state old-age pensions regularly offered up a version of this argument: old-age pensions would strengthen the family and preserve the home. What I am suggesting is that at an early date, workers came to a like decision on the basis of positive ideas they held about what community was and how they desired to experience it. Cf. Dahlin, Ph.D. dissertation in progress, chapter entitled "The Pension Debate: Search for a Public Solution."

99. *Typographical Journal* 26 (January 1905): 37–38; ITU, *Reports of Officers and Proceedings of the 57th Session of the ITU, San Francisco, Cal., August 14–19, 1911*, supplement to *Typographical Journal* 39 (October 1911): 46; *Typographical Journal* 67 (August 1925): 183.

not be given a chance to change the scene, or to spend my last days with my people?"[100] Except, perhaps, for those without friends or family ties, the home was not enough. Fraternal spirit and security, real or symbolic, would not suffice. Old age, said one printer who believed strongly that the home should exist, is a time when "men long to mingle with old friends, to feel the sympathy and companionship of those bound to him by blood or long association, to view familiar scenes and surroundings."[101] This was not Colorado Springs, and it was not Highland Park. Threatened but not destroyed, the island communities held firm.

SUMMARY

When management discussed the pension, and labor the pension and old-age home, their reference points were organizational and financial, their interest focused on efficiency and control. For the corporation and the union, the pension was a device for recruiting and holding personnel and for prosecuting the ongoing struggle for survival and dominance within the capitalist system. Social justice—the relief of old-age dependency—appears to have been singularly unimportant in motivating the corporation and only one of several goals for the union. The unemployed middle-aged worker, technologically but not physically superannuated, was an embarrassment to all concerned. Neither group could countenance the expense of allowing the pension or the home to become unemployment relief.

The primary historical importance of private pensions and old-age homes lies in the participation of each mechanism in the process of redefining social ties and obligations. Both the corporation and the union intended the pension as a mechanism of depersonalization, a tool for sloughing off traditional obligations to older workers. The corporation wanted to rationalize its firing process; the union, its relief function. The old-age home threatened to separate the worker from family and geographical community, and to leave him isolated, dependent for fraternity on occupational ties. For most workers, even for those whose jobs were meaningful and central to their lives, the prospect of retiring to comradeship with one's fellows was not all that appealing. To the extent they had an option, they chose geography and family ties over those of occupation. It was a choice made both possible and necessary by the new concept of retirement and its primary agent, the pension.

100. *Typographical Journal* 35 (July 1909): 27–28; ibid. 22 (March 1903): 283.
101. Ibid. 22 (June 1903): 584; W. H. Bentley, "A Veteran," *Railway Conductor* 46 (March 1929): 137, 139; *Railroad Trainmen's Journal* 16 (October 1899): 950.

PART THREE THE STATE AND THE
CONSOLIDATION OF
RETIREMENT

6 Railroad Workers and the New Deal

On June 23, 1934, Senator Robert F. Wagner wrote to Franklin Delano Roosevelt, urging him to sign the Wagner-Hatfield bill for retirement of railroad employees. He gave the president three reasons. By retiring some fifty thousand workers immediately, the legislation would reduce unemployment. It would provide a testing ground for a general program of social security, then under serious consideration. Finally, Wagner turned to what he called the most important reason why the bill should become law—overwhelming public interest. "The great masses of working people," he wrote, "feel that this measure more than any enacted at the recent session of Congress rounds out the first cycle of recovery by assuring them that they, as well as the home owner, the farmer, the banker and the municipality are receiving consideration under the New Deal."[1]

The letter is most revealing of the function of retirement and its relationship to social security in the Depression. Wagner did not emphasize how the bill would provide security for retired railroad workers, for this was not the intent of the legislation. In 1934, retirement had not yet become strongly identified with security; its central function of unemployment relief was economic rather than social, part of the process of relief rather than reform. Wagner's third reason was not hyperbole but an extrapolation based on his own detailed knowledge of pension politics in the railroad industry. The bill he asked Roosevelt to sign had genuine grass-roots origins among thousands of middle-aged and old railroad workers—employed, furloughed, and retired. By 1934, as part of a nationwide organization, the Railroad Employees National Pension Association (RENPA), the aged had for the first time in the nation's history organized a powerful mass movement that compelled the attention of the standard railway unions, the railroads, and the senator from New York. Considering how often and how critically the retirement issue divided railroad workers along age, occupation, and union lines, RENPA's accomplishment was all the more impressive.

1. Robert F. Wagner Papers, Georgetown University Library, Georgetown University, Washington, D.C., box 327, file 19.

THE INDUSTRY

The difficulties that beset the railroad industry in the 1930s were not entirely of Depression origin. Since 1910 there had been little new construction in the industry, and the number of railroad jobs had leveled off in 1920. In the decade before 1928, some 250,000 railroad employees had been displaced, largely by labor-saving machinery and techniques. Faced with declining growth rates and with age regulations that militated against their securing other jobs, older employees turned to seniority systems for job protection.[2]

After 1929, industry unemployment grew dramatically. Between November 1930 and November 1931, for example, 16 percent of all railroad employees were laid off. Because most of the layoffs were accomplished under seniority provisions in union contracts, the effect was to age an industry that, because of hiring age limits and because the industry was itself almost a century old, already harbored a working population older than most. In 1920 the average age of a railroad employee was thirty-two and the average seniority, seven years. By 1925 the corresponding figures were thirty-eight and thirteen; by 1930, forty-two and eighteen; by 1935, forty-six and twenty-three; and by 1939, fifty and twenty-six.[3] In 1933, more than three-fourths of all railroad employees had at least ten years' continuous service on their present road, and half had seniority of at least fifteen years. An estimated 64 percent were at least forty years old, and 12 percent were over fifty-five.[4] Aging also occurred as a result of economies pursuant to consolidation. Work-force consolidation at a West Albany, New York shop in 1930 increased the average age of the employees from thirty-five to forty-two years.[5]

Among the most dangerous of industries and one of the first to achieve great size, railroading also pioneered in the development of pension plans for

2. John Clifford, "Ready for Unemployment Caused by Labor Saving Machinery," *Brotherhood of Locomotive Firemen and Enginemen's Magazine* 85 (August 1928): 138–39; Archibald M. McIsaac, *The Order of Railroad Telegraphers: A Study in Trade Unionism and Collective Bargaining* (Princeton, N.J., 1933), pp. 96–97, 259; *Railway Age Gazette* 48 (20 May 1910): 1272; *Railroad Trainman* 27 (May 1910): 410.

3. *New York Times*, 15 January 1932, p. 2; Dan H. Mater, "Effects of Seniority Upon the Welfare of the Employee, the Employer and Society," *Journal of Business* 14 (October 1941): 388; J. H. Ambruster, "The Pros and Cons of the Age Limit," *Railroad Trainman* 45 (May 1928): 347–48.

4. Data are drawn from a Department of Labor survey carried out between May and October 1933 and involving 980 railroad families. Although I have been unable to locate this study in the National Archives, some of the findings are available in *Railway Conductor* 51 (June 1934): 185–86.

5. See boilermaker questionnaire, in American Federation of Labor, Railway Employees Department (AF of L-RED) Papers, Labor-Management Documentation Center, Labor and Industrial Relations Institute, Cornell University, Ithaca, New York, box 49–A, file 7. These questionnaires were part of an effort by the United States Department of Justice to generate data for a defense of the constitutionality of the Railroad Retirement Act.

superannuated and disabled employees. By 1922, an estimated 84 percent of railroad personnel were covered. The typical plan was noncontributory and allowed for retirement at age seventy provided that the employee had twenty years' continuous service if applying for superannuation benefits and twenty or twenty-five years if applying for disability. Companies cut benefits drastically or eliminated plans altogether with the Depression. The Brotherhood of Locomotive Engineers (BLE) also discontinued its pension system.[6]

A large percentage of railroad workers were organized, under an array of competing jurisdictions. As of 1939, the American Federation of Labor contained the Brotherhood of Railway and Steamship Clerks, Freight Handlers, Express and Station Employees, with 100,000 members, mostly on the lower end of the salary scale; the Order of Railroad Telegraphers, with 50,000 members; the International Longshoremen's Association, with 40,000; and the Railway Employees Department (RED), which included the 10,000 members of the Switchmen's Union of North America and the seven shop crafts. Although only part of its membership worked on the railroads, the RED had about 350,000 members. Among the organizations not affiliated with the AF of L, the largest was the Brotherhood of Railway Trainmen (BRT), numbering over 116,000, followed by the Brotherhood of Locomotive Firemen and Enginemen (BLFE) at 61,000; the Brotherhood of Locomotive Engineers (BLE) at 59,000; the Order of Railway Conductors (ORC) at 35,000; the American Federation of Railroad Workers, at 20,000; the Brotherhood of Railway Signalmen, at 12,000; and eleven unions with smaller memberships, the most important of which was the American Train Dispatchers' Association (ATDA). Although these organizations often competed for members, for labor-management purposes they were united in the Railway Labor Executives Association (RLEA).[7]

Working relationships confounded the pension issue. The powerful BRT had two main groups of workers—those who worked on the trains (roadmen) and those who worked in the yards (yardmen). The former were conductors and brakemen, the latter switchmen. Under prevailing seniority regulations, one began as a brakeman, moved up to switchman, and concluded one's career as a conductor. During layoffs, a displaced conductor generally had the right to "bump" a switchman within the same district of the same line, and a switchman had similar rights to the jobs of brakemen. The other major seniority network

6. Murray Webb Latimer, *Industrial Pension Systems in the United States and Canada*, 2 vols. (New York, 1932), 1: 20, 24, 27, 30, 99; *Railway Age* 92 (26 March 1932): 545; ibid. (9 January 1932): 96; Franklin B. Althouse to Robert F. Wagner, November 1932, Wagner Papers, legislative files, folder "Railroads—Retirement Insurance."

7. Adapted from P. Harvey Middleton, *Railways and Organized Labor* (Chicago, 1941), appendix, p. 126.

was entirely separate, incorporating only engineers and firemen. Although engineers belonged to the BLE and firemen to the BLFE, their working conditions were virtually identical and their duties overlapping. The engineer had the first position in the cab, the fireman the second. Promotion from fireman to engineer was by seniority and examination, assuming availability of positions at the higher level. During retrenchment or in periods of light traffic, engineers could bump junior firemen.[8]

THE FIRST RAILROAD RETIREMENT ACT

Until well into the early 1930s, federal retirement legislation for railroad employees seemed a marginal possibility at best. Negotiations between the railroads, represented in the Association of Railway Executives, and the twenty-one standard railway unions of the RLEA had focused on work sharing through the six-hour day and on the railroad demand for a 10 percent wage cut. Not until January 1932 did the unions propose that the roads join them in advocating federal retirement insurance, and then the measure had to undergo the purgatory of an employer subcommittee. In the meantime, the roads had won their 10 percent cut, and the unions had received in return only promises to provide new jobs and preserve old ones. The agreement, ratified January 31, 1932, included federal retirement legislation as a subject for future consideration by a joint labor-management committee.[9]

During 1932, several important events took place. Senator Wagner introduced a retirement bill, written by the railway unions, providing for voluntary retirement at age sixty-five or upon the completion of thirty years' service. Under the plan, workers would receive an annuity equal to 2 percent of average annual wages multiplied by years of service and would contribute from 2 to 5 percent of wages to the retirement fund each year. At the Interstate Commerce Commission (ICC), hearings began on the six-hour day, with the railroads insisting that a decrease in the working day without a corresponding decrease in wages would increase maintenance costs. In a related incident, Walter C. Teagle, president of Standard Oil of New Jersey, denied the charge of BRT president Alexander F. Whitney that Teagle's "share-the-work" movement represented "communism in

8. Joel Seidman, *The Brotherhood of Railroad Trainmen: The Internal Political Life of a National Union* (New York, 1962), pp. 6, 8, 10–11, 36; *Railway Conductor* 51 (July 1934): 219; George R. Horton and H. Ellsworth Steele, "The Unity Issue Among Railroad Engineers and Firemen," *Industrial and Labor Relations Review* 10 (October 1956): 48–49.

9. *New York Times*, 16 January 1932, p. 23; ibid., 18 January 1932, p. 3; ibid., 31 January 1932, p. 1; ibid., 1 February 1932, pp. 1, 10.

its worst form." In November, Whitney said railroad management had failed to live up to the January 31 agreement, claiming 110,000 layoffs in the past eight months. The railroads pointed to an unexpected decrease in traffic and asked the unions to extend the 10 percent wage cut for another six months.[10]

In January 1933 the Senate Committee on Interstate Commerce opened hearings on a railroad pension system, and the next month the RLEA announced that it had met with Columbia University Professor A. A. Berle, acting as Roosevelt's representative, and had decided to obtain through legislation what had been denied in collective bargaining, including the six-hour day, a twelve-hour maximum, payroll reserves for unemployment insurance, full-crew and train-length laws, and federal retirement.[11] Organized labor soon found itself in opposition to the administration's railroad legislation, which created the office of federal coordinator of transportation and charged its occupant (Joseph B. Eastman, from the ICC) with promoting efficiency while maintaining employment at May 1933 levels. A provision for the six-hour day had been removed in the Senate after Roosevelt announced, through the chairman of the Interstate Commerce Committee, that it was "unworkable in this emergency and that it would ruin the bill."[12] No sooner had Eastman taken office than he construed the section of the Emergency Railroad Transportation Act which prohibited dismissals of employees in effecting retrenchments as applying only to actions taken by his office; voluntary economies, with consequent furloughs and dismissals, could be pursued by individual roads.[13]

Late in 1933 there were signs of change in labor-management relations. Eastern railroad presidents announced in December that they were seriously considering working with labor on a joint legislative program, of which pensions and federal regulation of competitive modes of transportation—buses and trucks particularly—would be major elements. Before one thousand union delegates in Chicago, Secretary of Labor Frances Perkins told of some of the findings of a sociological investigation carried out by her department in conjunction with the rail unions. Field workers were impressed with the rank reductions among railroad workers still employed: engineers who had been reduced to firemen, conductors with many years service doing the work of brakemen, senior clerks functioning as janitors. Among the unemployed, they found families without

10. Ibid., 3 March 1932, p. 2; ibid., 12 May 1932, p. 30; ibid., 1 November 1932, p. 3; ibid., 18 November 1932, p. 2; ibid., 21 December 1932, p. 14.
11. Ibid., 12 January 1933, p. 25; ibid., 24 February 1933, p. 10.
12. Quoted in *New York Times*, 28 May 1933, p. 8; ibid., 29 April 1933, p. 1; ibid., 23 July 1933, sec. 2, p. 5.
13. Eastman to Senator Fred H. Brown, Wagner Papers, box 327, folder 19.

homes and without savings, forced to borrow on life insurance and eventually to cancel it. Some had not served milk for four years.[14]

Based on the report, which was released to the public in April of the following year, Perkins recommended several forms of state legislation, including provision for aged workers. Three days later, F. H. Fljozdal, president of the Brotherhood of Maintenance of Way Employees (BMWE), made use of Christmas Eve day and the Labor Department study to emphasize unemployment and actual starvation among railroad workers, despite the fact that the roads were far behind in maintenance. "If, under private ownership and management," he told convention delegates, "such intolerable and inhuman conditions are to prevail, then social justice and economic welfare necessitate the government's taking over the industry."[15] During the first three months of the new year, however, the major issue between labor and management continued to be whether the 10 percent wage cut should be extended (the course eventually taken) or enlarged to 15 or even 20 percent.

Retirement fared well at the hands of Congress. In June 1934, the Senate unanimously passed the union-promoted Wagner-Hatfield railroad retirement bill, which at this point was a compulsory retirement measure. The House added its approval within a few days. The president, however, had not made up his mind. During the last ten days of June he consulted with Eastman and Perkins, the two federal officials closest to the problem.[16] Eastman's position was a matter of public record. In hearings before House and Senate committees, he had demonstrated how a retirement system, in contrast to unemployment insurance, favored older rather than younger employees. He had objected to the compulsory retirement provision of the bill and argued for a system of flexible retirement based on physical condition. Eastman also introduced a variant of class analysis into the debate. A provision in the bill allowing the employee to select months of highest payment as a basis for annuity benefits would, he said, be of particular benefit to the higher-paid conductors and engineers. Employees in these groups, moreover, tended to be in the upper age brackets and would benefit disproportionately from prior service credits and low initial rates of contribution. A large body of railroad labor, lower paid and with high turnover rates, would receive little and pay a great deal. On the crucial issue of unemployment, Eastman argued that the railroads could blunt the impact of anticipated retirements by simply not replacing older employees. Should the railroads require additional

14. *New York Times*, 27 April 1934, p. 17.
15. Ibid., 24 December 1933, p. 16; ibid., 15 December 1933, p. 35; ibid., 21 December 1933, p. 1.
16. Ibid., 15 June 1934, p. 21.

labor, they would be likely to discriminate against former employees and instead hire younger men who had not accumulated the suddenly expensive service credits.[17]

In the end, however, Roosevelt's thinking was most influenced by Perkins, whose evenhandedness and political sagacity he admired.[18] On the negative side, Perkins counseled, was the possibility that retirement legislation would retard a more well-developed program of social insurance which would go beyond the hazards of old age. The pay-as-you-go aspect of the plan presented future dangers. On the positive side, the bill dealt with superannuation and would have some impact on railroad unemployment. A veto, Perkins said, would probably be laid to Eastman's influence and jeopardize his future relationship with organized labor. She recommended approval. Although he disliked the legislation for being crudely drawn and for making no sound provision for funding increasing pension burdens, Roosevelt was impressed with the bill's job-creation potential and hopeful it would improve the morale of the entire railroad work force, and he signed it.[19]

IN THE COURTS: FROM RETIREMENT TO SOCIAL SECURITY

The carriers took legal action immediately. One hundred and thirty-seven roads filed suit in the District of Columbia Supreme Court, asking the court to enjoin the Railroad Retirement Board, an agency created by the legislation, from enforcing the pension law. The petition held that the legislation violated the Constitution's interstate commerce clause by affecting a number of employees not engaged in interstate commerce, including clerks, attorneys, physicians, the heads of the railway labor unions, and employees of the retirement board itself, and it claimed that the carriers had been deprived of property without due process. The suit declared that although the legislation had been theoretically justified on the grounds of efficiency and safety and the relationship of each to interstate commerce, the real purpose of the retirement act was to provide for "satisfactory retirement of aged employes" and to "make possible greater employment opportunity and more rapid advancement of employees in the service

17. U.S., Congress, Senate, Committee on Interstate Commerce, Subcommittee, *Retirement Pension System for Railroad Employees: Hearings on S. 3231*, A Bill to Provide A Retirement System for Railroad Employees, to Provide Unemployment Relief, and for Other Purposes, 73d Cong., 2d sess., 23–26 April 1934 (Washington, D.C., 1934), pp. 154–55, 159–62; *New York Times*, 21 June 1934, p. 35; *Railway Age* 96 (23 June 1934): 907 (editorial).

18. George Martin, *Madam Secretary: Frances Perkins* (Boston, 1976), chaps. 21, 26.

19. Perkins to President, 22 June 1934, Record Group 174, "Records of the Department of Labor," Office of the Secretary, General Subject Files, 1933–40, box 11, file "Bills Before Congress, 1934, Miscellaneous"; *New York Times*, 1 July 1934, p. 1.

of carriers."[20] The roads also claimed that the law's compulsory retirement provisions deprived them of experienced men who were still valuable.[21]

The District of Columbia tribunal denied the petition for injunction, pending a test of constitutionality. In October, on the basis of the memorandum prepared by Alfred A. Wheat, chief justice of the court, the act was declared unconstitutional. Wheat argued that the legislation was confiscatory; that Congress had illegally assumed authority to pass legislation affecting employees not engaged directly in interstate commerce. The decision was the first in the District of Columbia overturning legislation emanating from the Roosevelt administration. Rail stocks rose dramatically. The *New York Times* agreed with Wheat and advised labor not to waste time with an appeal bound to be fruitless.[22]

By March of the following year, however, the principals were before the Supreme Court of the United States. Arguments ranged over the entire case, but the relationship between age, efficiency, and interstate commerce was critical to both parties. Representing the railroads, attorney Jacob Aronson claimed, against all evidence, that railroad employees were not any older than those in other industries. Then, turning to the court, he asked, "Is it right to use a deadline of sixty-five years in speaking of all classes of endeavor?" For the government, Assistant Attorney General Harold M. Stephens replied, "It is a commonplace fact that physical ability, mental alertness and cooperativeness tend to fail after a man is sixty-five." The *New York Times* captured the irony of the moment: "Justice Roberts is 60. Justice Brandeis is 79. Ages of other members of the high tribunal fall between those years."[23]

Announcing the May decision, the headline of the *New York Times'* front page read, "Rail Pensions Act Voided by Supreme Court, 5 to 4; Social Program in Peril."[24] The *Times* was not alone in recognizing the critical nature of the decision. While historians of the New Deal have treated *R.R. Retirement Board v. Alton R.R.* as just another in a series of early conservative decisions,[25] it was more than that, for the Court took the opportunity to strike deeply at the legal underpinnings of social legislation. Ignoring the basis of Wheat's lower-court opinion, the majority began from the assumption that two of the stated aims of the legislation—retirement of aged employees and relief from unemployment—were not in themselves proper objects. While efficiency and safety in interstate

20. *New York Times*, 14 August 1934, pp. 1, 6.
21. Ibid.; and ibid., 11 August 1934, p. 8.
22. Ibid., 16 August 1934, p. 27; ibid., 25 October 1934, pp. 1, 41, 22.
23. Ibid., 15 March 1935, p. 6.
24. Ibid., 7 May 1935, p. 1.
25. William E. Leuchtenburg, *Franklin D. Roosevelt and the New Deal: 1932–1940*, New American Nation Series (New York, 1963), p. 144.

transportation were appropriate goals under the Constitution, the Court contended that neither was accomplished by the Railroad Retirement Act. It accepted the railroad claim that the work force was younger than that in heavy industries and, in an argument that reversed the historic positions of capital and labor, used data provided by the ICC to demonstrate that an older work force was not necessarily accident prone. Then it went a step further and asserted that even if a statistical relationship existed between superannuation and safety, the retirement act, by indiscriminately retiring older workers whether superannuated or not, "irrespective of their fitness to labor," was not a reasonable vehicle for promoting safety. If safety and economy required the elimination of certain aged employees, they should be immediately released; the pension was incidental, if not irrelevant, to these purposes.

Only one of the petitioners' arguments remained intact at this point—the assertion that efficiency was dependent upon morale, itself a product of anticipated security in old age. The Court had to counter this viewpoint, which was fast becoming an article of faith among businessmen attuned to industrial psychology, or concede some tie between the pension and interstate commerce. The justices took up the matter in two separate ways. On the one hand, they found the proposition to be an absurd extension of what was in itself a reasonable principle. Relief from fear of old-age dependency and increased efficiency might well be related, but to acknowledge such a relationship would eliminate all limits on "so-called regulation," since a wide variety of social services and goods, including medical attention, nursing, housing, clothing, and food, would then be justifiable. Pivotal Justice Owen J. Roberts, on the other hand, admitted that the retirement legislation resulted in security but insisted that economy and this particular variant of efficiency were inversely linked:

> Assurance of security, it truly gives, but, quite as truly, if "morale" is intended to connote efficiency, loyalty and continuity of service, the surest way to destroy it in any privately owned business is to substitute legislative largess for private bounty and thus transfer the drive for pensions to the Halls of Congress and transmute loyalty to employer into gratitude to the Legislature.[26]

Less than four months later, Roosevelt signed into law a restructured retirement measure, passed almost unanimously by House and Senate.[27] In May, however, this seemed unlikely. Labor leaders were particularly distressed. George

26. 295 U.S. 330. Quotations are from the full text of the decision, *New York Times*, 7 May 1935, p. 16. See also ibid., p. 1. The minority opinion can be found in ibid., 7 May 1935, p. 17.
27. *New York Times*, 20 August 1935, p. 12; ibid., 23 August 1935, p. 25.

M. Harrison, president of the Brotherhood of Railway Clerks (BRC) and chairman of the RLEA, called the decision "one of the most reactionary . . . handed down by the court" and claimed that that body's attitude toward employers' contributions made the decision "a serious obstacle to the consummation of the whole New Deal program." Whitney emphasized the necessity of dealing with unemployment and superannuation if recovery was to proceed. The editor of the journal of the Brotherhood of Railway Mail Clerks scored the Court for "a modern Dred Scott decision on the whole progressive and New Deal movement. It is a tragedy that five aged gentlemen can block the will of the people."[28] In the business world, the decision was welcomed for the protection it seemed to offer against legislation as different as the National Industrial Recovery Act, the Wagner labor-relations bill, the thirty-hour week, and train-length regulation. *Traffic World* lauded what it interpreted as a sweeping indictment of government intervention in internal business affairs. "It is pretty sound in principle," wrote its editor, "to say that no employer may be compelled to pay an employe after his working days are over—though many employers do just that and are to be commended for it. When we try to compel by law things that can only be enforced by sentiment and charitable thinking, we always get in trouble."[29]

The Roosevelt administration was concerned about the possible consequences of the decision without sharing the sense of impending doom. Those preparing the general social security package could take some comfort in the knowledge that a future test of its constitutionality would hinge on the taxing power rather than on the interstate commerce clause.[30] More important, what had begun as a constitutional matter rapidly became a turning point in social history. The overriding purpose of the original legislation—the relief of unemployment through retirement—had been entirely submerged in the arguments surrounding the first railroad retirement act, and it would continue to remain so, for it hardly seemed suited to the conservative constitutional environment established by the Supreme Court. Efficiency, a secondary but important purpose, had taken its place as the dominant argument, but it too had been destroyed by the Court. Now, to achieve the original purpose, the administration turned to the taxing power and the general welfare clause of the Constitution.

In the process, the ideology of social security was given formal sanction. After May 1935, proponents of retirement legislation talked less about effi-

28. Ibid., 7 May 1935, p. 18. See also Arthur M. Schlesinger, Jr., *The Age of Roosevelt*, vol. 3, *The Politics of Upheaval* (Cambridge, Mass., 1960), pp. 274–75.

29. *Traffic World* 55 (15 June 1935): 1132; *Railway Age* 98 (18 May 1935): 761; *Business Week*, 11 May 1935, p. 7.

30. Arthur J. Altmeyer, *The Formative Years of Social Security* (Madison, Wis., 1966), pp. 39–40.

ciency, economy, and unemployment relief than about social security and the needs of older workers, which were now a central policy goal rather than ancillary to some larger purpose. This change was visible almost immediately. On May 15, when the RLEA announced its determination to shepherd a revised retirement bill through Congress, the new tone was in evidence. Workers were entitled to pensions "after a long and useful life in industry." Conditions in the 1930s necessitated a retirement plan "to insure workers of security in their declining years." Timothy Shea, assistant president of the BLFE, announced that the Court's decision would not deter his union's quest for the pension. "Railroad workers," he declared, "feel they are entitled to a pension in their old age, and if there is no other way to get it, will support government ownership."[31]

The *Alton Railroad* case gave formal sanction to a process—the transformation of retirement into social security—which had been taking place for at least three decades. This transformation was most obvious in the states, where during the Progressive period commissions regularly took up the questions of retirement for state and municipal employees and general old-age pensions for all citizens of advanced age. Until the mid-1920s, these commissions responded more favorably to public-employee retirement than to the old-age pension (and more readily to arguments premised on problems of efficiency than on old-age dependency), but the questions could never be, and never were, entirely separate. Public-employee retirement plans were deemed necessary in part because the elimination of older workers was difficult to accomplish under conditions of potential dependency. The old-age pension was of value in part for its role in freeing workers to retire by decreasing dependency. From encouraging public-employee retirement, to applying similar inducements to all older persons living in the state, was not an inconsequential step, but neither did it involve an entirely new way of conceptualizing the status of the elderly. Some leaders in the old-age insurance and old-age pension movements—including Lee Welling Squier and Abraham Epstein—found quite compatible the older notion of retirement as an instrument of efficiency and order and the newer one of social justice for the dependent aged. In striking down the Railroad Retirement Act, the High Court had deprived pension advocates of arguments that for years had sustained the pension movement, and it had forced a strategic retreat to the explanation and ideology of social justice. Retirement was close to being subsumed into social security.[32]

31. *New York Times*, 16 May 1935, p. 33; ibid., 18 May 1935, p. 23.

32. State of New York, Commission on Pensions, *Report of the Commission on Pensions*, Legislative Document No. 92, 30 March 1920 (Albany, 1920), p. 59; Massachusetts, General Court, Joint Special Committee on Pensions, *Report*, House Document No. 1203, January 1921 (Boston, 1921), pp. 9–10, 17–19, 21–22, 48–49; Lee Welling Squier, *Old Age Dependency in the United*

THE RAILROAD VIEWPOINT

At no time during this process did the railroads become thoroughly convinced that a federal pension system would serve their interests. They were reluctant to surrender control of a mechanism that was cost-flexible and had done much to make the work force more stable and quiescent. A federal pension would sever the carefully nurtured ties binding a worker to a particular line. The roads had no special interest in reducing unemployment, and they argued that unemployment and old-age security were separate problems and functions and ought not to be confounded in the same legislation. The Association of Railway Executives was concerned lest the Railroad Retirement Board use pension fund accumulations to provide unemployment relief.[33] The most consistent ground of opposition to federal retirement, however, was cost. Before every congressional committee, railroad representatives, especially those from the smaller lines, argued the injustice of burdening the railroads with an expensive pension system while allowing truckers and the shippers on inland waterways, who had provided nothing in the way of superannuation benefits, to escape unregulated.[34] This attempt to define transportation, rather than just railroading, as the industry to which legislation should be applied, was not concocted in order to frustrate retirement advocates, nor was it, in light of what we know of the history of transportation regulation, unreasonable. The federal coordinator of transportation had consistently called for across-the-board regulation of public carriers.[35]

States: A Complete Survey of the Pension Movement (New York, 1912). Michel Dahlin argues that Epstein used efficiency arguments "out of a desire to persuade his audience" (Ph.D. dissertation in progress, chapter entitled "The Pension Debate: Search for a Public Solution"). She firmly separates the old-age pension movement of the 1920s, which she claims was designed "solely to cure the problem of dependency in old age," from previous pension and retirement movements, which clearly were not so designed. I find her argument unconvincing—especially in light of the history of the Social Security Act of 1935—but not much more so than my own. We need further research on this question.

33. U.S., Congress, Senate, Committee on Interstate Commerce, *Retirement Pension System: Hearings on S. 3231*, pp. 104–06; U.S., Congress, Senate, Committee on Interstate Commerce, Subcommittee, *Hearings on S. 59*, To Provide Full Crews on Trains in Interstate Commerce, 74th Cong., 1st sess., 19–27 June 1935 (Washington, D.C., 1935), pp. 183, 245; U.S., Congress, Senate, Committee on Interstate Commerce, Subcommittee, *Pensions and Retirement for Employees of Interstate Railways: Hearings before a Subcommittee of the Committee on Interstate Commerce on S. 3892 and S. 4646*, 72d Cong., 2d sess., 11–19 January 1933 (Washington, D.C., 1933), p. 23.

34. U.S., Congress, Senate, Committee on Interstate Commerce, Subcommittee, *Retirement System for Employees of Carriers: Hearings on S. 3151*, 74th Cong., 1st sess., 11, 15, and 22 July 1935 (Washington, D.C., 1935), p. 183; Senate, Committee on Interstate Commerce, *Pensions and Retirement: Hearings on S. 3892 and S. 4646*, p. 390. See also *Manufacturers Record* 101 (14 January 1932): 20–21, for a statement of opposition to compulsory retirement premised on the need for flexibility to maintain "cordiality" in labor-management relations.

35. Senate, Committee on Interstate Commerce, *Pensions and Retirement: Hearings on S. 3892 and S. 4646*, pp. 390–91, 172, 163; *Railway Age* 94 (11 February 1933): 203 (editorial); ibid. 95

Although these arguments never fully disappeared, railroad tolerance of the federal pension grew during the 1930s to the point where negotiations and legislation became possible. As the Depression forced layoffs and reduced or eliminated the existing private benefit systems, the roads proved reluctant to release older employees who had no annuity protection and to interfere with seniority. Instead, they fired and furloughed younger employees. Legislative retirement became increasingly attractive as an efficiency measure.[36] It might also have remained a limited vehicle for relieving the pressure of labor costs had not the Emergency Transportation Act of 1933 shut off the normal cost-cutting avenues and limited the roads to maximum staff reductions of 5 percent each year for deaths and retirements.[37] The relatively conciliatory attitude of the railroads in late 1933 and early 1934 was also a product of a decision by organized labor to move with management for the regulation of competitive transportation facilities and to organize the bus and truck drivers. And by late 1934 and early 1935, retirement also seemed increasingly viable as an alternative to repeated calls for government ownership.[38]

CONFLICTS WITHIN THE WORKING CLASS

The above narrative treats labor as if it were one unit. The reality was more complex. In fact, one function of the history of retirement is to clarify and characterize how this relatively new issue transformed union and working-class politics, as workers and union leaders sought to define their often disparate interests in an unfamiliar arena. In the 1930s, this definitional process was complicated by massive unemployment among railroad workers, for which retirement was only one of several solutions of widely varying appeal for different groups of employees. Led by Whitney, the trainmen steadfastly pursued what was

---

(30 December 1933): 899–900; ibid. 96 (23 June 1934): 907 (editorial); *New York Times*, 13 January 1935, p. 27; U.S., Congress, House, Committee on Interstate and Foreign Commerce, *Railroad Employees Retirement System: Hearing on H.R. 9596*, To Provide a Retirement System for Railroad Employees, and Thereby to Provide Unemployment Relief, and for other Purposes, 73d Cong., 2d sess., 8 June 1934 (Washington, D.C., 1934), pp. 47, 48, 52.

36. Samuel H. Cady, "Railroad Pensions—A Suggested Plan," *Railway Age* 89 (15 November 1930): 1039–41; Henry E. Jackson, "The Railroad Pension Problem," *Railway Age* 89 (6 December 1930): 1227–32; Charles L. Dearing, *Industrial Pensions* (Washington, D.C., 1954), p. 24; Senate, Committee on Interstate Commerce, *Pensions and Retirement: Hearings on S. 3892 and S. 4646*, p. 23.

37. Statement by Henry A. Palmer, editor of *Traffic World*, in *New York Times*, 19 November 1935, p. 33.

38. *Railway Age* 96 (13 January 1934): 31; *New York Times*, 20 September 1934, p. 40; ibid., 13 May 1935, p. 2; ibid., 8 May 1935, p. 23.

known as full-crew legislation, a political approach to unemployment which benefited BRT members at the expense of other railroad workers—if one accepts the assumption that total employment was fixed.[39] In spite of his criticism of Teagle's work-sharing programs, Whitney also spearheaded the movement for the six-hour day among railroad employees. With Alabama's senator Hugo Black, the primary advocate of the thirty-hour week, and brain-truster Rexford G. Tugwell, Whitney shared an analysis of unemployment that emphasized the role of technology in the creation of a leisured society and the need for work sharing to distribute income and balance production and consumption. The plan naturally appealed less to those who had work than to those who did not, and Whitney found himself attacking union members with seniority rights for contributing to unemployment by working long hours. His suggestion that yardmen be limited to twenty-six working days per month was soundly criticized by these lower-paid employees, who felt they had borne an excessive share of the unemployment burden.[40]

It was also possible to share work by limiting the number of miles an employee could run in a given month. Mileage limits had particular appeal for furloughed employees and for those lower down on seniority lists, like brakemen and firemen, who could achieve added security and perhaps even promotion to a higher rank through the limits. Opposition came from the engineers and conductors, who in the absence of limits generally could run as many miles as they wished. Whitney's advocacy of mileage limits also embittered an inherently difficult relationship with his organizational competitor, the ORC. Although the conductors' president, J. A. Phillips, presented the issue as one of principle, arguing that older workers with seniority were entitled to a reasonable standard of living unattainable at the proposed mileage limits, and that the process of work spreading would "simply bring about the pauperization of all workers," the BRT-ORC conflict was clearly drawn on seniority lines. By the late 1930s, when federal mileage limits seemed a real possibility, the issue had generated intense controversy within a number of rail unions.[41]

39. *Railway Age* 103 (31 July 1937): 127 (editorial); Walter F. McCaleb, *Brotherhood of Railroad Trainmen: With Special Reference to the Life of Alexander F. Whitney* (New York, 1936), p. 125.

40. McCaleb, *Brotherhood*, pp. 210–11, 135; Brotherhood of Railroad Trainmen, *Shorter Workday: A Plea in the Public Interest* (Cleveland, 1937), pp. 7, 21, 27–28, 46–48, 53; *BLFE Magazine* 98 (May 1935): 264 (editorial); Eliot Harris, "Black of Alabama in Dramatic Drive for 30-Hour Week," *Railway Conductor* 50 (March 1933): 67–68; Clifford, "Remedy for Unemployment," pp. 138–39; F. L. Carroll to William Green, 17 October 1933, AF of L-RED Papers, box 49, file 4; *Railway Conductor* 52 (March 1935): 87–88.

41. J. A. Phillips, "14,615 Full-Time Road and Yard Jobs," *Railway Conductor* 52 (February 1939): 39 (quotation); Horton and Steele, "Unity Issue," pp. 63–64; *BLFE Magazine* 106 (April 1939): 288–91; *Railway Conductor* 51 (January 1934): 13.

Retirement, although hardly universally popular among union leaders or railroad workers, succeeded where work-sharing programs did not, largely because it seemed to offer a relatively inexpensive method of reducing unemployment. While the thirty-hour week and mileage limits took from one group of workers and gave to another while maintaining the number of potential workers, retirement reduced the employables absolutely, and it did so—at least so proponents argued—through a completely benign reward for past service. Estimates on the immediate impact of proposed retirement legislation varied from 25,000 retirements to over 100,000, the larger number contingent upon passage of a bill providing for compulsory retirement at age sixty-five or below. The BLE claimed to have discovered in retirement a virtual panacea for railroad unemployment. Pension policy, it had resolved in convention, "may easily be arranged by the adjustment of the retirement age to take up the slack of unemployment, affording a retirement pension to the older worker and a job and wage to the younger worker, thereby doing away with the necessity of unemployment insurance."[42] Although federal retirement was a more popular unemployment remedy within unions such as the ORC, with a high concentration of older members, after mid-1933 every rail union advocated some version of it.[43]

Federal retirement legislation also offered organized labor a way out of existing private pension systems. The private correspondence of the officials of organized labor indicates that charges of coercion and manipulation were more than propaganda. As early as 1928, the trainmen recognized federal pensions as a way of escaping the "gratuities handed out by the railroads and used to tie the employes to their jobs and hamper them in fighting for their rights."[44] Memories of the 1922 national strike of the Federated Crafts remained fresh for the AF of L's B. M. Jewell, who in 1930 recalled railroad threats to discontinue pensions if recipients refused to scab. Jewell also charged that some railroads continued to take employees out of service as they reached retirement age, neglecting to pay the pension on the fabricated excuse that employees had refused to return to work following a legitimate strike settlement.[45]

---

42. House, Committee on Interstate and Foreign Commerce, *Railroad Retirement: Hearing on H.R. 9596*, p. 33; Senate, Committee on Interstate Commerce, *Retirement Pension System: Hearings on S. 3231*, pp. 15–17; Senate, Committee on Interstate Commerce, *Pensions and Retirement: Hearings on S. 3892 and S. 4646*, pp. 37–38.

43. Edmund E. Pugsley, "Unemployment or Age Insurance—Which?" *Railway Conductor* 52 (February 1935): 43; McCaleb, *Brotherhood*, p. 207; *Signalman's Journal* 15 (June 1934): 124, 127.

44. *Railroad Trainman* 45 (July 1928): 539; ibid. 52 (November 1935): 645.

45. Jewell to Frank Morrison, 1 August 1930, AF of L-RED Papers, box 48, folder 3. See also J. B. Ruck to Jewell, 31 May 1930; Henry R. Corbett to J. G. Luhrsen, 10 September 1931, ibid.; "Railroad Retirement Pension Act of 1934," *Yale Law Journal* 44 (December 1934): 301–03 (the best contemporary analysis of the legislation).

Organized labor, nonetheless, came slowly and reluctantly to support federal retirement legislation. There were a number of reasons for this hesitancy. The effort required a shift in orientation away from collective bargaining and toward politics. Benefits to union members deriving from political negotiations were one step removed from union influence; member loyalty would in some degree be reduced and transferred to the national government. Edwin A. Krauthoff, counsel for the RLEA in the Senate hearings in 1935, feared that payment of benefits to previously separated employees with prior service would result in their return to the labor market to establish pension eligibility, glutting the market with older workers and contributing to the problem the pension was intended to solve.[46] Donald R. Richberg, serving in the same capacity two years earlier, spoke of the "question of social policy" involved in a program that transferred employment rights from fifty-five-year-old operatives earning high salaries to cheaper, younger workers. Behind the transfer lay an aggregate wage reduction.[47]

More important, organized railroad labor never felt completely comfortable with a program that emphasized potential workers (the unemployed) and would deprive the union of its committed senior members. During the early 1930s, union policies reflected the desire of employed railroad workers to maintain wages rather than finance a pension plan, although by January 1932 the RLEA was apparently willing to trade a 10 percent wage reduction for various employment stabilization measures.[48] Nor were union leaders solicitous of the needs of thousands of railroad workers who had retired before pension legislation took effect in 1937. Some were covered under railroad plans, but nothing in the federal law required the roads to make or continue payments.[49]

Labor's retirement legislation also bypassed a growing group of middle-aged unemployed whose prospects of finding railroad work had been dimmed to insignificance by hiring age limits. One sixty-one-year-old former telegrapher, unemployed through force reduction after forty years' service and about to lose pension and seniority benefits after a year without work, pleaded with Senator

46. Senate, Committee on Interstate Commerce, *Retirement System: Hearings on S. 3151*, p. 120; cf. p. 182 (Parmelee testimony).

47. Senate, Committee on Interstate Commerce, *Pensions and Retirement: Hearings on S. 3892 and S. 4646*, pp. 28–29.

48. H. H. Stead to Bert M. Jewell, 30 May 1932, AF of L-RED Papers, box 49, part 3; *Railway Age* 96 (9 June 1934): 830 (editorial); *New York Times*, 16 January 1932, p. 23.

49. F. H. Fljozdal to C. A. Render, 21 July 1932, AF of L-RED Papers, box 49, part 3; E. F. Medeiros to Franklin Delano Roosevelt, 29 August 1935, Franklin Delano Roosevelt Papers, Roosevelt Library, Hyde Park, New York, Official Files 1095, "Railroad Retirement Board"; Robert Shaffer to T. C. Cashen, no date, AF of L-RED Papers, box 50, file 1.

Wagner not to forget (echoing Roosevelt's phrase) "us forgotten men."[50] Another wrote to an AF of L official from the Panama Canal Zone, where he had obtained employment on the Panama Railway by falsifying his age by five years. Since the pension laws provided for retirement at sixty-five, and railroads had age limits of thirty-five to forty, "just what are we to do from 45 till we reach 65?" He added, "They wonder why there are so many communists."[51]

As these comments from the middle-aged would indicate, retirement proved a disruptive issue within organized labor, and usually some age-related problem lay at the heart of the controversy. As an unemployment mechanism, retirement appealed to a relatively small share of the unemployed railroad workers: those close to jobs who had a reasonably good chance of obtaining work as their seniors left the labor market. For every unemployed railroad worker who stood to gain, however, there were five and perhaps ten for whom retirement offered nothing. For these, retirement was a poor alternative to unemployment benefits.[52]

Retirement functioned as an adjunct to the seniority system. With one exception—a lopping off of the last years of the work life in favor of transferring work to younger people—it reinforced seniority and left intact the distribution of income within the work force. As the Depression deepened, junior employees liked seniority less and were tempted by the work-sharing solutions, including the six-hour day, the thirty-hour week, and mileage limits. They also favored compulsory over voluntary retirement for the assurance of promotion it provided.[53] The original 1934 railroad legislation had a compulsory provision, but by 1937, when court action forced the issue into the collective bargaining arena for final settlement, this clause had been removed in favor of completely voluntary retirement. The old had triumphed over the young. As a result, retirement did not serve as well as it could have the function for which it was originally intended, having become instead a social program for the aged.[54] Younger workers turned on the senior employees in their unions, accusing them of selfishly refusing to allow a new generation an opportunity to participate in the material rewards that should naturally accrue to middle-aged workers.[55] When hostility

50. J. G. Otis to Robert F. Wagner, 14 December 1933, Wagner Papers, legislative files, "Railroads-Retirement Insurance."

51. W. H. Hetherington to T. C. Cashen, 17 February 1938, AF of L-RED Papers, box 50, file 1.

52. Senate, Committee on Interstate Commerce, *Retirement Pension System: Hearings on S. 3231*, p. 154.

53. Seidman, *Brotherhood of Railroad Trainmen*, p. 36.

54. *New York Times*, 27 February 1937, p. 27; ibid., 17 March 1937, p. 1.

55. *BLFE Magazine* 107 (August 1939): 133; ibid. 106 (June 1939): 467; *Railroad Trainman* 56 (February 1939): 66.

began to focus on the seniority system itself, retirement was ripping away at union solidarity. "I would much prefer," wrote a disgruntled fireman, "to climb the ladder of success by standing on ability and integrity rather than standing on seniority and some other brother's neck."[56]

The situation was complicated for the railroad chiefs by the knowledge that although most railroad employees nearing pension age were more than willing to exchange their job rights for future security, a vocal minority wanted both. They offered a remarkable array of explanations for opposing their own retirement. A number of railroad employees had, or sensed they would have, difficulty adjusting to the reduced living standard afforded by the pension. A yard service employee, retired at age seventy-two after failing to pass a physical examination, found his income reduced from $250 to $63 per month. He blamed the retirement system for forcing out the older workers who had built the unions and fought the hard battles for better salaries and working conditions. A sixty-six-year-old former telegrapher, "pensioned" by the Maine Central Railroad as a caretaker at $10.36 per week, was upset at the prospect of seeing his income halved under retirement legislation. Other telegraphers, he claimed, were in the "same box." An engineer for the Pennsylvania Railroad described compulsory retirement as confiscatory of property, equivalent to the impact of Prohibition on cafe owners.[57]

Others eloquently defended the right to pursue commitments to property and family. Seventy-year-old E. K. Bryan wrote Roosevelt in the critical days of June 1934 describing real estate investments he had made over a period of twelve to fifteen years in order to provide for his family after he died. In excellent health, full of "the vigor and determination to do my work," Bryan protested that the pending retirement legislation would destroy his ability to make necessary mortgage payments. Bitter and worried, he asked, "Is a man who devotes his whole life to one line of work to be side-tracked in order that some younger

56. *BLFE Magazine* 106 (April 1939): 287. Ronald Schatz and David Montgomery present seniority as an attempt to reduce job insecurity and to control the power of the foreman by replacing his arbitrary authority with a "clear, objective standard on layoffs." It was this, and its ability to prevent conflict within the work force should not be minimized. Nonetheless, it was also a subjective institution serving one age group at the expense of another—one of the costs of solidarity, it would seem. See Schatz and Montgomery, "Facing Layoffs," *Radical America* 10 (March–April 1976): 15–27. Cf. Arthur R. Porter, Jr., *Job Property Rights: A Study of the Job Controls of the International Typographical Union* (New York, 1954); Frederick H. Harbison, *Seniority Policies and Procedures as Developed Through Collective Bargaining*, Princeton University, Department of Economics and Social Institutions, Industrial Relations Section (Princeton, N.J., 1941), pp. 52–54; Mater, "Effects of Seniority," pp. 409, 413; McIsaac, *Railroad Telegraphers*, pp. 96–97, 259.

57. H. W. [Onliveau?] to W. J. Frost, no date, AF of L-RED Papers, box 50, file 1; Thomas H. Mullen to E. J. Manion, 29 November 1932, Wagner Papers, legislative files, "Railroad Pension Hearings"; *Railway Age* 105 (29 October 1938): 636.

man, with less experience, less judgment and fewer responsibilities, may secure a slight increase in his compensation?"[58] A Butte, Montana worker raised the possibility that a significant number of sixty-five-year-old railroad workers, having married late in life, had obligations to young dependents of grade-school and high-school age. Compulsory retirement would force their children prematurely into the working world.[59] One may question whether such complaints had the universal character their authors usually claimed for them. Nonetheless, the principals in railroad retirement—senators, union officials, the president—received hundreds of such letters, each a testimony to the powerful individual impact of a broadly conceived social policy.

AT THE GRASS ROOTS: THE RAILWAY EMPLOYEES NATIONAL PENSION ASSOCIATION

In the final analysis, however, the standard railway unions were driven to support retirement by a massive campaign with roots close to one element of the rank and file.[60] From its beginnings in 1929, the movement was led by W. W. Royster, who for almost two decades had served as state legislative chairman of the Minnesota branch of the BLE and as a member of the union's state joint legislative board, composed of representatives of engineers, firemen, trainmen, and conductors. Until 1929, the legislative efforts of the Minnesota board to deal with unemployment had centered on work sharing, but early that year, it asked Royster to devise a pension plan, which it quickly endorsed. The following year, representatives of eleven unions of Washington State railroad employees, organized as the Association of Railway Employees and, under the leadership of J. B. Reed, modified and expanded the Royster document into what became known as the Washington Plan.[61] The movement grew rapidly, taking its

58. E. K. Bryan to President, 25 June 1934, FDR Papers, Official Files 1095, "Railroad Retirement Board."

59. W. W. Bordner to Robert F. Wagner, 10 June 1934, Wagner Papers, legislative files, 1639, "Railroad Retirement Pension."

60. One explanation of the aggressiveness of railroad workers in seeking retirement legislation may be inferred from a study by Lewis Lipsitz relating the nature of work to political attitudes. Lipsitz found that workers who were conscious of having some degree of control in their work—a category that would include most railroad employees—were more likely to believe the political world manipulatable. See "Work Life and Political Attitudes: A Study of Manual Workers," *American Political Science Review* 58 (December 1964): 951–62.

61. Joseph A. Wise, "Keen Support Comes to Bill," from *Federation News*, 14 January 1933, in AF of L-RED Papers, box 49, file 3; transcript of speech given by W. W. Royster at Odd Fellows Hall, Oakland, California, 17 November 1935, in Brotherhood of Locomotive Firemen and Engineers Papers, Labor-Management Documentation Center, Labor and Industrial Relations Institute, Cornell University, Ithaca, New York, box 20, file "Railroad Retirement Act"; Latimer, *Industrial Pension Systems*, 1: 34.

strength from almost two dozen new state pension associations. In late June 1930, Roosevelt, then governor of New York, commented positively on the Washington Plan. An interassociation meeting in Chicago on Labor Day brought Reed into contact with Illinois railroad pension advocates and resulted in an agreement that the Washington Plan was the appropriate model for national legislation. J. A. Filbert, president of the Association of Railway Employees of the state of Illinois, agreed with this decision while emphasizing that the Washington Plan did nothing for the unemployed middle-aged. But that was the last that was heard of that issue.[62]

When delegates gathered for the second convention of the Railway Employees National Pension Association (RENPA) in Chicago in mid-November 1931, the organization had on its books 330 local clubs, and there were 90 more awaiting certification by the national office. According to one projection, there would be 700 more within three months. The Los Angeles club claimed 1,200 members, the Boston club 1,000, the Decatur, Illinois club 800. The press run for the organization's *National Pension Review* was some 320,000 copies. RENPA's paid organizers had been very effective.[63]

In the years to come, Royster and other officials of RENPA would regularly claim that their pension bill had the support of 95 percent of rank-and-file railroad workers.[64] This figure, which one would expect to be much larger than the corresponding figure for support of the pension association, may be too high. The organization's strength lay in skilled and older workers. At the November 1931 convention, a majority of the delegates were engineers, and a number were conductors, clerks, and shopmen. Women were well represented, the train dispatchers notable by their absence. According to one report, the delegates generally had at least thirty years' seniority: "It is what we might term an old man's convention." At the 1934 convention, about 95 percent of the delegates were trainmen, conductors, or engineers, ranging from forty to seventy-six years of age and averaging fifty-nine years. At that time the organization claimed a membership of more than one million, but there is evidence that dues-paying membership was closer to twenty thousand. In June 1932, when the association distributed postcards to be filled out and mailed by members in support of the

---

62. "Minutes of Meeting Held in Chicago, Illinois, on Labor Day, September 1, 1930: Discussions as to the Possibility of Providing a Pension for Old and Disabled Railroad Workers of America," sponsored by the Chicago and Eastern Illinois Volunteer Relief Association, in AF of L-RED Papers, box 48, file 3.

63. Report to J. G. L[uhrsen] on the November convention of RENPA, 19 November 1931, and listing of delegates in attendance at the convention, AF of L-RED Papers, box 49, file 2.

64. See, for instance, National Chairman, RENPA to Wagner, no date, Wagner Papers, box 327, file 19.

association pension plan, one of the objects of the campaign, the RLEA, received almost 9,500 cards, including some 1,500 from trainmen, 900 from engineers, 800 from conductors, 700 from firemen, and 700 from telegraphers. Although the organization was generally not successful in recruiting lower-paid workers, 500 maintenance-of-way employees, the sort that usually performed menial tasks, participated in the mailing.[65] An occupational analysis of a petition in support of RENPA retirement legislation in Congress reveals that of 323 identifiable signatures in support of the bill, about 30 percent came from brakemen, hardly an elite among railroad workers; 17 percent from conductors and 22 percent from engineers, occupational groups likely to be older and more middle-class; 5 percent from firemen; 7 percent from yardmen; 2.5 percent from telegraphers; and 17 percent from a wide variety of occupations, including clerks, icemen, salesmen, watchmen, ticket agents, cashiers, linemen, and switchmen.[66] In short, while active participation in the affairs of the organization was restricted to middle-class and older railroad workers, support for RENPA was broad-based.

The pension association's populist tone was evident in a meeting held in Chicago in early October 1932.[67] It was a Friday evening, and some two hundred persons, mostly older, with a smattering of blacks and women, gathered at the Metropolitan Masonic Temple on the city's West Side. Royster, who chaired the session, must have been disappointed with the turnout, for there were three hundred empty seats in the hall. Introducing the main speaker, Royster compared the position of the pension association with that of the Chicago Cubs, struggling against the Yankees in the World Series. They had fought the gallant fight but needed a "pinch hitter." Royster asked, "Who will be our pinch hitter?" Someone in the crowd responded, "Senator Glenn."

The Illinois politician was a curious ally. A Republican with strong ties to federal judge James Herbert Wilkerson, who was known to organized labor for his injunction-issuing proclivity, the senator was opposed for renomination by

65. Report to J. G. L[uhrsen], 19 November 1931, in AF of L-RED Papers, box 49, file 2; President, BMWE to Members, RLEA, 5 May 1932, transmitting report from a field man on the RENPA meeting in Centralia, Illinois, in AF of L-RED Papers, box 49, file 3; "Report of Proceedings of the Convention of Railroad Employees' National Pension Association, Incorporated, at the Hotel Sherman, Chicago, September 10 to 13, 1934," AF of L-RED Papers, box 49-A, file 5. The cards received by the RLEA are tabulated in D. B. Robertson to Members, RLEA, 21 June 1932, AF of L-RED Papers, box 49, file 3.

66. The petition, from the Tucson area, is in Wagner Papers, legislative files, folder "Railroads-Retirement Insurance." Signatures of maintenance-of-way personnel were absent from this petition, but these employees may simply have been unavailable.

67. The following account is from a report of the meeting of the American Train Dispatchers Association, 10 October 1932, addressed to All Chief Executives, in AF of L-RED Papers, box 49, file 3.

the AF of L and the twenty-one standard railroad organizations.[68] In speech made thick by a severe cold and sore throat, he told of his birth in Mattoon, Illinois, a railroad town, and of his lifelong sympathy with the plight of the railroad worker. He talked at some length of the economic problems of the railroad industry, stressing the unfair competition of buses and trucks. The dangerously large buses should be regulated off the highways. He arrived at the pension issue late in his address, contrasting the sound Royster measure with the bill sponsored by the labor executives. The union chiefs came in for particular attention. They were "'sleek fellows,' riding around in luxury spending the money of the hard working men." Far better, he said, to stand with those who did the actual railroad work instead of the "men who are somewhere else." Several times, when referring to union leaders, he came back to that phrase.

Otis F. Glenn's political alliance with the Royster pension movement was more one of convenience than shared values. While his analysis of the problem of railroad decline was a favorite of railroad management rather than workers, he at least recognized the problem. Although those listening to his Masonic Temple address would not have agreed with his general view of organized labor, they shared some of his sense of distance from the union bureaucrats and must have relished his populist rhetoric. Most of those present could recall something of William Jennings Bryan, perhaps even his famous "Cross of Gold" address to the 1896 Democratic convention. Like the Populist and Democratic parties in the 1890s, RENPA was strongest in the South, West, and Midwest, and some of its appeal was antiestablishment, as Royster made clear at an early organizational meeting in Chicago. "The problem is ours," he said, "There is nobody, no Donald Richburg [*sic*], no Clarence Darrow, or no United States Senator that can come in here and tell us what we ought to have. We are all capable of doing our own thinking and we know what we want."[69]

The railway pension movement shared with the later Townsend pension movement several key elements of economic analysis. Royster, Francis Townsend and, interestingly, Whitney, who was a Townsendite, believed that technology, the product of American genius and creativity, had ushered in a new era of abundance, defined as the ability of the few to produce goods for the many. They agreed that consumption and production had somehow to be balanced or rebalanced if the potential of the new economy was to be realized, and that

68. C. J. McGlogan to Fred Miller, 24 October 1932, AF of L–RED Papers, box 49, file 3.

69. "Minutes of the Meeting of Associated Railway Employees, Held at Great Northern Hotel, Chicago, Illinois, December 15, 16, 17, 1930," typescript, AF of L–RED Papers, box 48, file 3, p. 4.

retirement was, in part, a mechanism for shifting income and work in order to achieve this adjustment and reduce unemployment.[70] Like Townsend, Royster was accused of being little more than a con artist, interested in lining his pockets with the dollars of railroad workers and using RENPA to extort political office from the BLE. Townsend's organization was investigated for possible fraudulent uses of the mails; Royster's was not, although the idea was in the air.

For a social analysis of the railroad pension movement, the factual basis of the accusations may be of less importance than the language in which they were couched. The strongest indictment was presented to Royster and other members of the board of directors of RENPA by Irene Behring, for twenty months an employee of the association, the last eight as office manager. Having discovered that Royster had claimed as business expenses several personal items (amounting to less than $150), Behring believed that Royster was being protected from removal by a handpicked, corrupt board of directors and by officers, like Secretary-Treasurer E. J. Ellingson, who was himself "casting longing eyes at a berth in the Order of Railway Conductors." Behring informed Royster that she had overheard an April conversation in which Ellingson had lamented a recent board cut in personal expenses. "What can we do?" Royster had replied. "You know, Ed, as well as I do that this is going to be a big thing. It may take two or three years, and then we can tell them all to go to H- -l." What, she asked, had happened to the high ideals? What had gone wrong? How had Ellingson and Royster become "cheap go-getters?" Her answer was biblical in derivation. Brought "too near the flesh-pots," they had been led astray, away from the ideals of service to the rank and file. Their indiscretion was the more serious for its victim, the railroad worker sorely in need of the pension. "GOD only knows," she wrote, "how much the little fellows, buoyed up in their belief of honest leadership, have contributed in real 'blood-money' to the Association, *and any one spending a dime of this money carelessly is a derelict from decency, integrity and honor, and should be called to a strict accounting."*[71]

The pension association appealed to others with religious scruples. At some of the meetings officers and delegates forcefully and freely expressed their religion and its relationship to the proceedings. At the 1931 convention, a Montana organizer spoke directly to the issue of fraud. "I have put the principle forth that

70. McCaleb, *Brotherhood*, p. 207; Resolution, undersigned W. W. Royster, in Wagner Papers, legislative files, "Railroad Pension Hearings." Numerous letters in favor of the Townsend plan are printed in *BLFE Magazine*. See, for instance, 98 (February 1935): 86–87.

71. This account is from Irene Behring to W. W. Royster, 29 June 1933; Irene Behring to A. F. Whitney, 24 October 1933, AF of L–RED Papers, box 49, file 4; Memorandum, George M. Cucich, 25 January 1933, AF of L–RED Papers, box 48, file 3.

everybody connected with this movement was a Christian at heart," he said. This principle "has taken the fear out of the people that they are [go]ing to be gypped." At this particular meeting religious feelings were especially in evidence, and by the time F. B. Althouse rose to speak, the atmosphere resembled a revival. The Iowa delegate asked those assembled to build the organization on Christian values: "If each and every delegate will take the life of Christ, into your life, have Christ by your side every day in your daily living, it will be right as long as Christ will sanction what you are doing."[72] This was an exceptional moment at an exceptional convention. The usual course of things was more sedate. But meetings were generally spirited affairs, and it was not uncommon for delegates to describe with anguish the plight of the aged or to express with emotion their commitment to the "gospel" of the pension.[73]

It would be a mistake to conclude from the tone of the organization that the association's appeal was primarily social, even in the broadest sense of the word. RENPA had a well-developed, often-articulated, and essentially reasonable economic philosophy and political program that appealed to thousands of railroad workers because it suited their needs better than anything else offered. Association conceptions of technology, unemployment, consumption, and the pension— as well as of the interrelationships between these elements—were within the economic orthodoxy of the day. The plight of older workers was commonly acknowledged in 1929, as was the social necessity of transferring work from the elderly to younger men with families to feed. Royster's emphasis on protecting the widows of railroad workers and his complete rejection of the shorter workday and shorter work week in favor of the "shorter work life" were not so universally accepted, but the concern for widows, though it accounts for some of RENPA's attraction, was not central to its program, and the disdain for the more common forms of work sharing was hardly radical. When RENPA counsel Herman L. Ekern testified before the Senate that the association's Hatfield bill would result in increased efficiency and create new jobs, the only questions were "How much?" and "How many?"[74]

72. RENPA, *Minutes of the Second Annual Convention of the Railroad Employes' National Pension Association*, Congress Hotel, Chicago, 16–19 November 1931 (n.p., n.d.), in AF of L–RED Papers, box 49, part 2, p. 29.

73. "Minutes of Meeting of Associated Railway Employees, Great Northern Hotel," pp. 44, 42.

74. See Senate, Committee on Interstate Commerce, *Pensions and Retirement: Hearings on S. 3892 and S. 4646*, pp. 47, 49, 50, 56–57, 62, 81–82, 402; Senate, Interstate Commerce Committee, *Retirement Pension System: Hearings on S. 3231*, p. 26; RENPA, *Minutes of Second Convention, 1931*, p. 24; Report to J. G. L[uhrsen]; "Minutes of Meeting of Associated Railway Employees, Great Northern Hotel," pp. 47, 52; J. A. Filbert to B. M. Jewell, 20 September 1930, AF of L–RED Papers, box 48, file 3.

ORGANIZED LABOR RESPONDS TO THE RANK AND FILE

When Congress passed the Hatfield-Keller bill in the spring of 1934, its action reflected at once RENPA's substantial political clout and the essential rationality of its program. Though amended to make the accumulation of service credits more difficult, the bill included provisions for compulsory retirement at sixty-five and voluntary retirement with thirty years' service which were acceptable to organized labor.[75] This substantial feat, which the Court was soon to negate, was accomplished in the face of a concerted effort by the standard railroad unions to isolate the pension association as an extremist organization. This tactic was pursued despite evidence that belied labor's claims.

The rail unions might have undercut the pension association and captured some of its enthusiasm for their own cause had they been more responsive to the pension issue in the late 1920s. Having remained out of the pension arena until older workers felt compelled to establish their own organization (while remaining within the unions), the rail unions proceeded to deny the nascent group even minimal cooperation. RENPA was refused access to union publications (with the exception of the ORC journal) and had difficulty even obtaining names of union officers. At the conventions of the major brotherhoods, the growing sentiment for pensions was treated as a passing, if somewhat dangerous, fancy.[76]

The sources of concern were several. Union officials were reluctant to support a movement that seemed destined to fail because it covered only one industry and because the courts would define the result as "class" legislation. Others felt that the very existence of a separate association devoted to pensions could serve only to distort labor's balanced political program by overemphasizing retirement at the expense of related problems, such as wages and the shorter workday. Train dispatchers' president J. G. Luhrsen was apprehensive lest RENPA be the first of several such issue-oriented organizations, tearing away at union solidarity.[77]

At the heart of the union complaint was the charge of dual unionism. In a sense this was the converse of the other criticisms, for it implied that RENPA was threatening not so much as a narrow misguided interest group that violated labor's evenhanded approach to labor issues as for the breadth of its program

---

75. Royster speech, 17 November 1935.

76. Ibid.; "Minutes of Meeting of Associated Railway Employees, Great Northern Hotel," p. 9.

77. B. M. Jewell to W. R. Ratley, 11 June 1931, AF of L–RED Papers, box 48, file 3; Donald R. Richberg, "Report of Old Age Pensions to the Railway Labor Executives Association," July 1931, AF of L–RED Papers, box 48, file 3, pp. 6, 11; J. G. Luhrsen, "In Re: Adequate Pensions for Railroad Employes," 31 January 1934, AF of L–RED Papers, box 49, file 4.

and the depth of its vision. Those who took this view—and they included Luhr-sen, Jewell of the AF of L's RED, D. B. Robertson of the BLFE, and Whitney of the BRT—cited Royster's rejection of the shorter workday and shorter work week as evidence that he had gone beyond the pension question to take positions "contrary to the established principles of the standard railroad labor unions." They noted the growing interest among railroad officials and otherwise conservative politicians like Glenn in RENPA's pension clubs.[78] More important was evidence that the pension association was recruiting in company unions and informing potential members that they were a bona fide union organization. This, complained union officials, had the effect of legitimizing the company unions as well as confirming the dual character of the pension association. The persistence of the pension association after the standard railway unions had formulated their own retirement bill in mid-1931 was also seen as proof that RENPA was a "dual outlaw movement."[79]

Actually, it was a good deal less than that. At RENPA's early meetings over pensions, the question of the propriety of establishing an independent association was actively debated and studied, always to a negative conclusion. Although the December 1930 convention voted to establish a national organization, it intended that it function to promote railway pensions through the existing national labor bodies. There was some discussion of the dual union question at the November 1931 meeting, at which one delegate suggested the possibility that the standard labor groups had outlived their usefulness and that RENPA should serve workers in a variety of nonpension capacities. These remarks were not favorably received by the delegates, and Chairman Filbert dispensed with the issue by simply affirming the organization's single-minded devotion to the pension. While delegates to the 1934 convention were clearly opposed to cooperation with the railroads on legislative matters, pension association officials had wanted to cooperate with organized labor.[80] Rebuffed, they grew independent while consistently denying aggressive intent. "We are not an insurgent bunch of men," wrote an officer of a Chicago relief association. "Neither are we attempting to disrupt that which the several brotherhoods and railway companies have, in the form of a pension."[81]

78. Report to J. G. L[uhrsen] (quotation); C. J. McGlogan to Fred Miller, 24 October 1932, AF of L–RED Papers, box 49, file 3; Wise, "Keen Support," in ibid.
79. B. M. Jewell to J. C. McGlon, 3 December 1934, AF of L–RED Papers, box 49–A, file 5; Fred Ross to James Burns, 8 September 1931 and other letters in ibid., box 49, file 3; D. B. Robertson to ?, 7 May 1931, ibid., box 48, file 3.
80. "Minutes of Meeting of Associated Railway Employees, Great Northern Hotel," pp. 18–19, 54–56, 58, 64; RENPA, *Minutes of Second Convention, 1931*, p. 13; "Report of Convention of RENPA, 1934."
81. T. A. Oakes to Jewell, 1 November 1930, AF of L–RED Papers, box 48, file 3.

As pension agitation mounted. labor leaders began to reconsider their policy of stony opposition. One of the first was Fljozdal of the BMWE, who in November 1930 informed his fellow members of the RLEA that the "clamor for old age pensions" was having an adverse impact on his union. "I sometimes think we are," he added, "as leaders of railroad labor, a little passive in this connection."[82] Machinist president R. W. Wharton prodded the RLEA to consider retirement legislation to help eliminate "sporadic movements by more or less irresponsible individuals."[83] Pushed by the rank and file, the union bureaucracy moved slowly into gear. By late September the RLEA was committed to federal pensions for railroad workers. Its subcommittee on pensions rationalized this conversion in the rhetoric of business unionism:

> Almost every business has a problem of disposal of waste of some kind; and it is often a serious element of expense. In mining, the disposal of waste material is a major item of cost; in restaurants and hotels it takes the form of the disposal of garbage; in power plants, there is the disposal of ashes and cinders; in iron mills, there is also disposal of slag, etc.
>
> The old age retirement problem arises from the embarrassment the management encounters in removing from the payroll those who are no longer efficient, on account of old age. The removal of human waste is more costly than the removal of material waste, because it must be done humanely.[84]

That fall the *Railroad Pension Review*, a Royster publication, criticized the railway labor organizations for delaying their retirement insurance program. A worried Whitney wrote, "I certainly dislike to see our membership turning bolshevik while our Association plays the part of Nero, who fiddled while Rome burned."[85]

In the early months of 1932, Washington became the center of the rail pension debate as both parties sought simultaneously to find sponsors for their bills and move their legislation through Congress. Under pressure from organized labor, Senator Smith Brookhart and Representative Robert Crosser refused to handle Royster's bill. It eventually was introduced by West Virginia's Henry Hatfield in the Senate and Kent Keller, a freshman representative from Illinois, who Robertson speculated must have done so through "lack of acquaintance with the activities of the Brotherhoods."[86] The standard unions had no such dif-

---

82. Fljozdal to All Members, Railway Chief Executives' Association, 3 November 1930, AF of L–RED Papers, box 48, file 3.
83. R. W. Wharton to Chief Executives, RLEA, 1 April 1931, in ibid.
84. Memorandum, RLEA Subcommittee on Pensions, 26 September 1931, ibid.
85. Whitney to A. O. Wharton, 30 December 1931, AF of L–RED Papers, box 49, file 2.
86. D. B. Robertson to J. G. Luhrsen, 4 March 1932, ibid.; Royster speech, 17 November 1935.

ficulties. RLEA counsel Richberg found willing allies in Crosser and Robert Wagner.[87]

Organized labor had entered the fray too late, after too much opposition, and with a bill that, if actuarially superior to the pension association measure, was not popular with rank-and-file workers. When telegrapher president E. J. Manion tried to convince his membership that Royster was only taking advantage of them, he received an indignant response. "Don't be alarmed, Mr. Manion!" wrote a veteran of fifty-two years' service. "We are of age, and we extend honor to whom honor is due. We are well aware Mr. Royster's path has been a thorny one, but he has blazed the way. We appreciate his worth and work, and permit me to add, that we are affectionately proud of him."[88]

The power and influence of RENPA and the ability of that organization to publicize the plight of the aged railroad employee provides a perspective from which to evaluate the New Deal. In June 1934, when Roosevelt gathered the opinions of Joseph Eastman, Frances Perkins, and Robert Wagner and prepared to make a decision on the merits of the first retirement measure, he would find no reference to social justice and none to social security except in the sense that railroad retirement was considered a stalking horse for the larger program. For New Deal liberals, retirement remained a mechanism for achieving certain economic and social goals, rather than a time in a person's life when work would cease in favor of some state of security. There was a good deal of cold-blooded calculation in the process. The benefits of retirement were expected to redound to the larger society and the young through unemployment relief and job creation, rather than to the aged. Older railroad workers, organized in a powerful national association, might force the society to act; but it was action in the form of retirement, not social security. If this was the welfare state, it was built along lines descended from the limited vision of retirement generated in the Progressive Era.

87. The RENPA measure was ready earlier than its union counterpart. Organized labor held up hearings. See Royster to Wagner, 15 September 1932, Wagner Papers, legislative files, "Railroad Pension Hearings."

88. Thomas H. Mullen to Manion, 29 November 1932, ibid. See also John Kobi to B. M. Jewell, 10 April 1932, AF of L-RED Papers, box 49, file 2. The authority of such responses convinced Manion and others of the necessity of compromise. See Manion to D. B. Robertson, 7 March 1932, AF of L-RED Papers, box 49, file 2, and Herman L. Ekern and Charles E. Brooks, "Memorandum on Proposed Consolidation S. 817 and S. 1529 . . .," Wagner Papers, box 327, folder 20; *Railway Age* 92 (12 March 1932):439.

7 Social Security and the Older Worker

⚔ The Social Security Act of 1935 has been enormously influential in defining the American self-image. Nearly every historian whose work has touched this legislation has felt compelled to acknowledge its critical place and function in twentieth-century United States history. Arthur M. Schlesinger, Jr. states that the act "meant a tremendous break with the inhibitions of the past. The federal government was at last charged with the obligation to provide its citizens a measure of protection from the hazards and vicissitudes of life. . . . With the Social Security Act, the constitutional dedication of federal power to the general welfare began a new phase of national history." Like Schlesinger, William E. Leuchtenberg acknowledges the weaknesses of the legislation yet calls it "a new landmark in American history," which "reversed historic assumptions about the nature of social responsibility, and . . . established the proposition that the individual has clear-cut social rights." The Social Security Act was part of a process by which "nineteenth-century individualism gave ground to a new emphasis on social security and collective action," and the state changed from a "neutral arbiter" to a "'powerful promoter of society's welfare.'" James MacGregor Burns ascribes much of Roosevelt's political dominance in the 1936 election to the social security program. "The towering fact," writes Burns, "was that at last the national government had acted to underpin the future security of Americans." Social security was only the most obvious example of a variety of programs that "had brought a new condition in the relations among men," a genuine "pioneering in the readjustment of human relationships." Dexter Perkins's survey of the New Deal era terms the Social Security Act "more fundamental and more far-reaching than the relief program," a much-needed effort through which the United States finally took on functions that European nation-states had carried out for decades. J. Joseph Huthmacher's treatment of Senator Robert F. Wagner contains no general appraisal of the legislation, yet the author's acceptance of Wagner's traditional liberal rhetoric betrays a similar conviction. Wagner sought nothing less than the fulfillment of a social bill of rights, which he defined as including "a steadily increasing measure of security, a steadily rising standard of living, a steadily lengthening period of leisure well spent, a never ending increase in the value and nobility of life."[1]

Several historians have challenged the right of the Social Security Act to this lofty position. Paul Conkin sees it as a sorry compromise that excluded significant groups of people and produced generally minimal benefits. Because it was essentially compulsory insurance and thus failed to distribute wealth, the Social Security Act "at most . . . set some enduring precedents and established a new area of social responsibility." Barton Bernstein also finds the legislation "more important as a landmark than for its substance," yet he concludes that in making workers pay for their own old-age insurance, the government "denied its financial responsibility for the elderly." For Roy Lubove, social security marked a "turning point in American history" in its transfer of welfare functions to public institutions; but he is much more impressed by the system's failure to distribute income and by its reliance on the mechanism of labor-force participation.[2]

There is in much of the literature a tendency to assume an identity between the historical function of old-age security legislation and the reasons for its passage. The process is simple and seductive. Because the Social Security Act called for state aid to old people, and because it has functioned to provide such aid, those behind the legislation—from Franklin D. Roosevelt to Frances Perkins and Wagner—have generally been described as humanitarians, seeking to bring security to a group that lacked it. This is so completely assumed, such an article of faith, that the question of motivation is seldom addressed and evidence hardly systematically presented. Burns says nothing at all about motive. Huthmacher allows Wagner to speak for himself and assumes that he is consistent.

1. Arthur M. Schlesinger, Jr., *The Age of Roosevelt*, vol. 2: *The Coming of the New Deal* (Cambridge, Mass., 1958), p. 315; Leuchtenburg, *Franklin D. Roosevelt and the New Deal: 1932–1940*, New American Nation Series (New York, 1963), pp. 132–33, 331, 340; Burns, *Roosevelt: The Lion and the Fox* (New York, 1956), pp. 267, 268; Perkins, *The New Age of Franklin Roosevelt: 1932–1945*, Chicago History of American Civilization (Chicago, 1957), pp. 32–33; Huthmacher, *Senator Robert F. Wagner and the Rise of Urban Liberalism* (New York, 1971), p. 344, also p. 180, which concludes the section on New Deal social security programs. See also Clarke A. Chambers, *Seedtime of Reform: American Social Service and Social Action, 1918–1933* (Minneapolis, 1963), pp. 181–82, 257, 267, and W. Andrew Achenbaum, *Old Age in the New Land: The American Experience Since 1790* (Baltimore, 1978), pp. 137, 141.

2. Conkin, *The New Deal*, Crowell American History Series (New York, 1967), p. 60, also pp. 61, 64; Bernstein, "The New Deal: The Conservative Achievements of Liberal Reform," *Towards a New Past: Dissenting Essays in American History*, Barton Bernstein, ed. (New York, 1969), p. 274; Lubove, *The Struggle for Social Security: 1900–1935* (Cambridge, Mass., 1968), pp. 179–80. See also Gaston V. Rimlinger, "Welfare Policy and Economic Development: A Comparative Historical Perspective," *Journal of Economic History* 26 (December 1966): 556–71, especially 569.

George Whitney Martin's recent study of Secretary of Labor Perkins largely treats the problem of motivation as a given, implying that both Perkins and Roosevelt had nothing in mind but security for the aged. This is Schlesinger's approach as well.[3] Only Leuchtenberg seems to believe there is something to be discussed. "Roosevelt and his aides," he writes, "fashioned a government which consciously sought to make the industrial system more humane and to protect workers and their families from exploitation." In approaching reform, on the other hand, "the New Dealers reflected the tough-minded, hard-boiled attitude that permeated much of America in the thirties." Leuchtenberg resolves this apparent conflict by arguing that New Deal reformers, like the screen characters of the period played by James Cagney and Humphrey Bogart, were fundamentally sentimental, their cool exteriors only a hard shell:

> Unlike the earlier Progressive, the New Dealer shied away from being thought of as sentimental. Instead of justifying relief as a humanitarian measure, the New Dealers often insisted it was necessary to stimulate purchasing power or to stabilize the economy or to "conserve manpower." The justification for a better distribution of income was neither "social justice" nor a "healthier national life," wrote Adolf Berle. "It remained for the hard-boiled student to work out the simple equation that unless the national income was pretty widely diffused there were not enough customers to keep the plants going."[4]

Having broached a difficult problem, Leuchtenberg dismisses all but idealistic impulses as somehow foreign to the spirit of the times.

An alternative interpretation of the old-age provisions of the Social Security Act of 1935 can be constructed by reexamining what participants in the process of reform said about what they were doing or about what they had done. The New Dealer who emerges was a rational, calculating type. While hardly unaffected by the human realities of old-age dependency in the Great Depression, he or she operated within a framework of ideas about the economy and the role of

3. *Madam Secretary: Frances Perkins* (Boston, 1976), chap. 26; Schlesinger, Jr., *Coming of the New Deal*, p. 304. Michael Taussig claims that the Social Security Act, while designed as an income-maintenance program, had the unintended effect of influencing older workers "with weak desires to continue unattractive work" to retire from the labor market. Although Taussig is unaware of the extent to which retirement was intended by the authors of the legislation, his reasoning explains why older workers might have retired in response to what appear to be minimal incentives. Taussig also persuasively characterizes the 1935 legislation as a "mechanism for financing the growing separation of the aged and the larger societies," though there were mechanisms such as the old age home which would have accomplished that separation more completely. See Michael K. Taussig, "Long-Run Consequences of Income Maintenance Reform," in Kenneth E. Boulding and Martin Pfaff, eds., *Redistribution to the Rich and the Poor: The Grants Economics of Income Distribution* (Belmont, Calif., 1972), pp. 393, 381.

4. *Roosevelt and the New Deal*, pp. 332–33, 337–38, 338.

consumption, technology and leisure, and unemployment. This conception of an appropriate way of treating the aged was also a product of parallel ideas about the social demands and needs of youth. Although New Dealers had a sense that they were doing something entirely new in creating the social security system, the important truth in this perception should not obscure the precedents, including the Civil Service Retirement Act of 1920 and the Railroad Retirement Act of 1934, which illuminate and explain the activity. The Social Security Act was, therefore, a piece of retirement legislation, which promised to accomplish what other retirement legislation had accomplished—the removal of people from the work force. Finally, the New Deal's commitment to social justice for its aged population deserves attention. The record shows that the Roosevelt bureaucracy could pursue policies detrimental to the interests of older workers. In their struggles against age discrimination, the middle-aged received minimal succor, and that not until late in the decade. Many of those over sixty-five found that social security was insufficient and that at some point even Eleanor Roosevelt had ceased to respond to their needs.[5]

SOCIAL SECURITY AND RETIREMENT

In considering the bills that eventually became the Social Security Act, Congress spent much of its time debating the adequacy of benefit payments and the administrative relationships between state and national governments. Yet the *Congressional Record* and the hearings held before the House Committee on Ways and Means and the Senate Finance Committee also reveal interest in old-age security as a retirement mechanism with a potential impact on unemployment. There was a good deal of activity in the House toward reducing eligibility in the bill from age sixty-five to sixty; ultimately, a motion to recommit the bill for this, among other purposes, received over 160 votes. This agitation came in some measure from those who wished to make the legislation relevant to the needs of unemployed workers between sixty and sixty-five years of age by including this group in the legislative definition of old age. It also appealed to those who wanted the legislation to absorb larger numbers of unemployed. Charles Truax of Ohio said the age limit of sixty-five fixed in the (Robert) Doughton bill (H.R. 7260) was "undesirable and not entitled to favorable con-

5. The increasingly hostile response to Eleanor Roosevelt as the representative of the administration's position on social security can be traced in the Eleanor Roosevelt Papers, Franklin D. Roosevelt Library, Hyde Park, New York, boxes 969, 970.

sideration by the real friends and supporters of equitable old-age pension legislation." William Sirovich of New York, a former physician, surgeon, and social worker, described the years between twenty and sixty as "the great productive period of human existence" and *advocated* the Doughton bill as a method of reducing unemployment.[6]

The measure's sponsor in the Senate was Robert Wagner, still enmeshed in the politics of railroad retirement and convinced that a general old-age measure could help to solve unemployment as surely as the analogous railroad legislation. Opening Senate debate on June 14, 1935, he offered a number of suggestions that he thought would appeal to business. "The incentive to the retirement of superannuated workers," he argued, "will improve efficiency standards, will make new places for the strong and eager, and will increase the productivity of the young by removing from their shoulders the uneven burden of caring for the old."[7] In his public addresses he made clear his belief that even in normal times technology would create a group of 4 to 6 million ablebodied unemployed. Retirement compensation could be used to secure "the withdrawal of those who are older and less efficient, and who deserve and want a few years of rest."[8]

The old-age insurance portions of the Social Security Act were created by and drafted in the Committee on Economic Security (CES), appointed by the president in mid-1934 to develop programs in old-age security and unemployment insurance. Within the CES, four persons took more than a cursory interest in the specific provisions of possible old-age insurance legislation: Barbara Armstrong, professor of law at the University of California at Berkeley, brought to Washington to draft the legislation dealing with old age; Murray Latimer, a member of the Railroad Retirement Board and recent author of an impressive study of industrial pension systems; J. Douglas Brown, a young economist from the Industrial Relations Section at Princeton University; and Otto Richter, an

---

6. U.S., Congress, House, *Congressional Record*, 74th Cong., 1st sess., 1935, 79, pt. 5, pp. 5689 (Truax), 5787, 5788–89 (Sirovich), pt. 6, pp. 6068–69 (vote to recommit). See also pt. 5, pp. 5537 (Wood), 5544 (Knutson); pt. 6, p. 5910 (Zioncheck).

7. U.S., Congress, Senate, *Congressional Record*, 74th Cong., 1st sess., 1935, 79, pt. 9, p. 9286.

8. Quoted in Huthmacher, *Robert F. Wagner*, p. 177. Roosevelt's position on the idea of the government pension as a form of unemployment relief is obscure. But see the typewritten memorandum of a discussion on old-age pensions, featuring Roosevelt (then governor of New York), William M. Leiserson, Lieutenant Governor Herbert Lehman, a congressman from Pennsylvania, the governor of Massachusetts, and Leo Wolman, in Frances Perkins Papers, Rare Book and Manuscript Library, Columbia University, New York, N.Y., box 61. Roosevelt opened the discussion with this statement: "This year there will probably be an attempt to reduce the age from seventy to sixty-five—in other words, we will be approaching the obsolescent worker. In your judgment how does old age insurance tie in with the old age dole?"

actuary. According to Armstrong, CES's executive director, Edwin Witte, played a minor role in old-age insurance; in fact, for a time he, Secretary of Labor Frances Perkins, and Harry Hopkins all opposed it.[9]

Armstrong's oral history memoir, compiled for Columbia University's Oral History Collection in 1965, is a remarkable document. Armstrong leaves no doubt that old-age insurance was conceived with retirement in mind. Roosevelt, she argues, had to choose between keeping older workers in jobs and creating opportunities and hope for youth: "The interest of Mr. Roosevelt was with the younger man. And to that extent, I went along." The limit of $15 per month on earned income (the maximum one could earn without losing social security benefits) was an outgrowth of Depression conditions. "That's why that little ridiculous amount of $15 was put in," Armstrong recalled. "Let him earn some pin money, but it had to be on *retirement*. And retirement means that you've stopped working for pay." Although those who drafted the act were concerned with providing economic security to retired persons, there was never any doubt that these persons had to be retired to receive benefits. "He would not get *retirement* benefits unless he retired," said Armstrong. "*We never* called these benefits anything but *retirement* benefits." Asked by the interviewer if the existence of labor-force objectives did not make the act "political," Armstrong replied: "I don't call that political. For heaven's sake, I call that most definitely *economic* and social."[10]

CES leaders were understandably anxious that a strongly negative reaction to old-age insurance on the part of big business might place that particular aspect of the committee's work in jeopardy. For Armstrong, this problem boiled down to the CES Advisory Council, an aggregation of businessmen including Marion Folsom of Eastman Kodak, Walter Teagle of Standard Oil, and Gerard Swope of General Electric. If a positive reaction from these public figures did not make

9. Barbara Armstrong Memoir, Columbia University Oral History Collection, Butler Library, Columbia University, New York, N.Y., vol. 1, pp. 31, 36, 46–47, 74–75, 78, 105–06, 188–89, 194.

10. Ibid., vol. 2, pp. 255, 257, 259. Other accounts confirm Armstrong's analysis. See Wilbur Cohen, in *Problems of Aging: Transactions of the Fourteenth Conference*, 7–8 September 1951, St. Louis, Mo., Nathan Shock, ed. (Caldwell, N.J., 1952), pp. 86–87; Solomon Barkin, "Economic Difficulties of Older Persons," *Personnel Journal* 11 (April 1933): 400; Abraham Epstein, "The Older Workers," in *Annals of the American Academy of Political and Social Science* 154 (March 1931): 31; Arthur J. Altmeyer, *The Formative Years of Social Security* (Madison, Wis., 1966), pp. 40, 42; Edwin E. Witte, *The Development of the Social Security Act: A Memorandum on the History of the Committee on Economic Security and Drafting and Legislative History of the Social Security Act* (Madison, Wis., 1962), pp. 100–102, 160. An economist, Barkin had been with the New York State Commission on Old Age Security since 1929. Epstein had been executive secretary of the American Association for Old Age Security since he founded the organization in 1927.

passage of old-age insurance likely, it was at least essential. When it became clear that the Advisory Council was behind the program, Armstrong was elated.[11]

The process through which Folsom arrived at this position began in the mid-1920s. George Eastman of Eastman Kodak, Folsom recalled, was a "rugged individualist." As a result, the company had no pension plan, and some inefficient older workers, personally acquainted with Eastman and lacking resources to support themselves in retirement, had to be kept on the company's payroll. Although Kodak developed a retirement program later in the decade, the experience made Folsom realize that state old-age insurance could function as a surrogate, providing employees with adequate retirement incomes and thus making separation possible.

As a member of the CES Advisory Council, Folsom stressed the contribution old-age insurance could make to corporate efficiency. By encouraging employees to plan for retirement and to retire, social security would increase productivity. (In his memoir, Folsom implies that the stimulation to retirement caused by social security allowed Kodak to eliminate its program for mandatory retirement at age sixty-five.) Folsom also sought to convince his corporate colleagues that old-age insurance, like unemployment insurance, would function to stabilize the economy by promoting countercyclical spending. The Advisory Council's approval of old-age insurance indicates that Folsom's fellow businessmen were sympathetic to these arguments.[12]

Armstrong was well aware that her acerbic qualities were not likely to sit well with Congress. CES testimony before House and Senate Committees therefore fell largely to the congenial Brown and to Latimer. Much of this testimony confirms and enlarges upon the oral history sources. Before the Senate Finance Committee, Brown claimed that the CES had insisted on worker contributions to the system not only to establish the contractual right of a worker to his annuity, but also to insure that the annuity would be large enough to induce the retirement of superannuated workers and the displacement of women and children who would otherwise be supporting dependent old people. For maximum labor market impact, Brown and others working with the CES favored compulsory retirement at age sixty-five. Of particular concern was the need to find some

11. Armstrong Memoir, vol. 1, pp. 80–81.

12. Marion B. Folsom Memoir, Columbia University Oral History Collection, vol. 1, pp. 78, 130, 46, 47, 63. Wilbur Cohen, Witte's reserach assistant in 1934, argues that Folsom, Brown, Witte, and Arthur Altmeyer came to social insurance as a "form of remedial legislation to deal with the problems of labor unrest and industrial society which grew out of labor-management problem[s]" (Wilbur Cohen Memoir, Columbia University Oral History Collection, pp. 34–35).

mechanism to increase the employment opportunity of those over forty-five years of age.[13]

Murray Latimer was one of few persons with historical perspective to appear before the Congress. As a member of the Railroad Retirement Board, he was intimately familiar with the purposes of the legislation creating the board and with related conditions in the railroad industry. He headed the CES Technical Committee on Old Age Security. Latimer's prepared statement for the Senate committee surveyed the disruptive impact of older workers, employed and seeking employment, on wage rates, efficiency, and work prospects of younger elements in the labor market. He was distressed at the legislation then being considered because the level of pensions provided, "even if raised considerably above existing standards, would not be high enough to induce any considerable voluntary withdrawals from the labor market; nor would employers be able to retire superannuated employees without friction."[14] Larger benefits were especially vital under a contributory system, Latimer argued, because collections would necessarily begin when employees were young and dependency a remote possibility. These younger employees would expect their contributions to purchase not only future annuities, but the removal of older workers and an increase in the rate of promotion.[15]

Latimer took the committee through the Railroad Retirement Act and the Civil Service Retirement Act, explaining the mechanisms by which each induced or compelled retirement. Then he returned to the relationship between benefits and employment impact under the pending legislation. His concluding statement on the matter was ambivalent:

> Whether the relation between the two initially is reasonable I do not know, it is a matter of judgment; but nevertheless in my own judgment the annuities set in this act are to be regarded as minima amounts rather than maxima for the purpose which the system is supposed to accomplish, namely, the protection of the aged group, their removal from employment, and the quick supplanting of what we think is a system which would be unsatisfactory in the long run.[16]

In short, Latimer believed that, as constructed, the system would not have much employment impact. He did, however, see the old-age provisions of the Social

13. U.S., Congress, Senate, Committee on Finance, *Economic Security Act: Hearings on S. 1130, A Bill to Alleviate the Hazards of Old Age Unemployment, Illness, and Dependency, to Establish a Social Insurance Board in the Department of Labor, to Raise Revenue, and for Other Purposes*, 74th Cong., 1st sess. (Washington, D.C., 1935), pp. 282–83. See also pp. 1106–07.

14. Ibid., p. 755, also p. 754.

15. Ibid., pp. 744–45.

16. Ibid., pp. 749, 746–48.

Security Act as part of the history of retirement with all its labor-market implications and—if it is not reading too much into a brief statement—he expected the system to take its place within that retirement history at some point in the future when benefits were increased.

Other provisions of old-age insurance were also designed within a labor market context. For reasons of cost, the CES rejected suggestions that the retirement age be lowered below sixty-five; it resisted a higher age of sixty-eight or seventy—the latter was then common in state old-age pension programs—because of anticipated congressional and public opposition to late retirement in a period of high unemployment.[17] The act also operated to discourage over-sixty-five employment by subjecting earnings for such workers to taxation for social security purposes (under Title VIII) but not counting earnings after that age in determining benefits.[18]

During the 1950s, when the retirement test was being reconsidered in light of changing employment conditions, it was common to interpret the original old-age provisions within a labor-market context. Secretary of Labor Maurice J. Tobin did so in a 1949 appearance before a subcommittee investigating low-income families. Julius Hochman, criticizing the development of retirement from his position as vice-president of the International Ladies Garment Workers' Union, claimed the labor-market impact of social security was "no secret" at the time of passage and "was in line with the general practice prevailing in industry and business enterprise at the time."[19] From the perspective of 1954, the National Association of Manufacturers (NAM) placed the original legislation in the context of prevailing ideas of a mature economy, for which the withdrawal of the aged from the labor market was envisioned as a permanent, if partial, solution. This, as well as cost reduction, was the purpose of the retirement test.[20] Al-

17. Wilbur J. Cohen, *Retirement Policies Under Social Security: A Legislative History of Retirement Ages, the Retirement Test and Disability Benefits* (Berkeley, 1957), pp. 3, 18, 19. See also Robert J. Myers letter, "Bismarck and the Retirement Age," *The Actuary* (April 1978), p. 7.

18. *Congressional Record*, 74th Cong., 1st sess., 1935, 79, pt. 9, p. 9536 (King).

19. Hochman, "The Retirement Myth," in William Haber and Wilbur J. Cohen, eds., *Social Security: Programs, Problems, and Policies* (Homewood, Ill., 1960), p. 106; Tobin, "Problems of Low Income Families: Progress and Programs," typescript statement, delivered before the Subcommittee on Low Income Families of the Joint Committee on the Economic Report, 13 December 1949, in Record Group 174, "Records of the Department of Labor," National Archives, Washington, D.C., Office of the Secretary, General Subject File, 1950, box 239, file "1950—Pensions, Miscellaneous," p. 24. Hereafter referred to as RG 174, DL-OS-GSF. In late 1940, a conference exploring the reemployment of labor and capital took up the question of whether deterrents to employment under social security ought to be removed or modified. See Otto Beyer Papers, Manuscript Division, Library of Congress, Washington, D.C., box 31, file "Round Table . . . ," agenda for forthcoming conference. On social security in the context of anticipated unemployment following World War II, see *Business Week*, 1 September 1945, pp. 107–08.

20. NAM, Industrial Relations Department, Policy Committee Division, *Retirement Security in*

though this after-the-fact evidence is not very revealing of events in the Senate Finance Committee or the House-Senate conference, it does indicate that for important elements in labor, business, and government, the history of old-age security went far beyond the welfare state.[21]

SOCIAL SECURITY AND THE CONSUMER ECONOMY

The Social Security Act, in its old-age as well as its unemployment provisions, was also intended to stimulate consumption. The Depression only clarified what was essentially a long-term problem of demographics. By the late 1920s some observers of the business scene were concerned about the market impact of age discrimination, especially among the important bread-winning workers over forty-five.[22] In 1932, *Advertising and Selling* published an article entitled "The American Market Faces Middle Age." "What is it going to mean to American business," asked the author, "when its market stops growing? When sales quotas strike the reality of there being no more people this year than there were last? When there is a constantly increasing proportion of old people to children?"[23]

The following year, University of Geneva professor L. Hersch argued in the *International Labour Review* that a fall in the birth rate and consequent relative growth in the proportion of old people was restricting consumption and contributing to an ongoing imbalance between consumption and production. All of Hersch's suggested remedies—reduced hours of work, limitations on working ages for older and younger workers, and higher wages (to increase consumption)—found their way into New Deal programs.[24] Alexander Whitney, president of the Brotherhood of Railroad Trainmen, who took his cue from the Townsend movement, envisioned the replacement of 16 million unemployed older workers with no income by 8 million employed older workers with effective

a Free Society (New York, 1954), pp. 19, 16, 12. See also Stephen Raushenbush, *Pensions in Our Economy* (Washington, D.C., 1955), pp. 17–18; and Lewis Meriam, *Relief and Social Security* (Washington, D.C., 1946), p. 74.

21. Records of the Senate Committee on Finance in the National Archives are sparse and unrevealing on this subject, and there are none for the House Committee on Ways and Means.

22. "Employment Age Limitations," Abstract of Discussions at a Meeting of Eastern Section of the Taylor Society, Boston, 5 April 1929, in *Bulletin of the Taylor Society* 14 (October 1929): 224–25.

23. Robert R. Updegraff, "The American Market Faces Middle Age," *Advertising and Selling* 19 (18 August 1932): 13.

24. L. Hersch, "The Fall of the Birth Rate and Its Effects on Social Policy," *International Labour Review* 28 (August 1933): 157–61.

purchasing power. Like John Brophy of the Committee for Industrial Organization (CIO), who in 1937 was calling for an extension of social security benefits
to uncovered groups as a means of developing purchasing power, he must have
been disappointed at the comparatively meager stimulus provided by the original
measure.[25]

Yet the liberal advocates of the legislation, including Wagner and Perkins,
expected payments under the old-age assistance portion of the act to aid the
troubled consumer economy. Wagner made this point on the Senate floor, and
before the Senate Finance Committee, he claimed old-age payments would
spread purchasing power "to an enormous extent."[26] More than anyone else,
Frances Perkins spoke for the administration. In appointing Perkins chairperson
of the CES, Roosevelt had told her, "You care about this thing. You believe in
it. Therefore I know you will put your back to it more than anyone else, and you
will drive it through."[27] For the Senate Finance Committee she carefully developed production-consumption ideas that were central to Hersch's concept of
"organic" unemployment. She believed in old-age security as a recovery program. The creation of purchasing power through the transfer of income to those
who would not otherwise have it, she said, was "a part of the essential assumption upon which this whole idea rests." Challenged by Senator Daniel Hastings
to assess the merit of this increase in purchasing power relative to the provision
of goods and services essential to security, Perkins held firm. "I think the two
things are inseparably related to each other," she explained. "A part of the whole
civilization of the United States of America rests upon the fact that we have
been able to achieve a high standard of living. We have it not only because each
individual has relatively a somewhat higher income, but also because our joint
incomes create a larger purchasing power which makes it possible to make a
demand upon manufacturers so that they have large mass production, which in
turn lowers the price. It is a system which is really within a circle, and I think it
is impossible to separate one from the other." But if, asked Hastings, purchasing
power was so important, why set the federal contribution at $15? That decision,
answered Perkins, was a product of current fiscal limitations. "If we find that we
have got a larger national income than we think we have, we can act differently

25. *Railroad Trainman* 52 (February 1935): 67; "Report of Director John Brophy to the Meeting
of the Committee for Industrial Organization in Atlantic City, October 11, 1937," Katherine Pollack
Ellickson Papers, Labor-Management Documentation Center, Labor and Industrial Relations Institute, Cornell University, Ithaca, New York, microfilm reel 2.
26. Senate, Committee on Finance, *Economic Security Act: Hearings*, p. 6; *Congressional
Record*, 74th Cong., 1st sess., 1935, 79, pt. 9, p. 9286.
27. Martin, *Madam Secretary*, pp. 342–43.

later."[28] This idea was prominently displayed in the CES report to the president and found its way into Roosevelt's message on signing the Social Security Act, when he made clear his belief that the legislation would have countercyclical as well as welfare functions.[29]

THE ALTERNATIVE PENSION MOVEMENT

Some measure of the relationship between retirement and social security may also be gleaned from a comparison of the administration's liberal stance with that of two popular and more radical alternatives to social security. One was "The Workers' Unemployment, Old Age, and Social Insurance Act," known as the "Workers' bill" and introduced by Minnesota representative Ernest Lundeen; the other was the Townsend movement. Each of these alternatives had substantial public support. Hearings on the Lundeen measure produced some eighty advocates, including socialists, dissident union chiefs within the AF of L, college professors, and members of Congress. The Townsendites claimed over three million adherents.[30]

Perhaps the most important facet of the Lundeen and Townsend movements was the extent to which their economic assumptions were shared by congressional leaders and the Roosevelt administration. Radical in the amount of money they proposed to allocate for old-age and unemployment relief and in the method by which that relief was to be distributed, advocates of the Lundeen Workers' bill were deeply concerned with the extent and severity of unemployment among the middle-aged, workers over fifty or fifty-five. Unlike Darwin Meserole and the National Unemployment League, Lundeen did not begin with the assump-

28. Senate, Committee on Finance, *Economic Security Act: Hearings*, pp. 104–05. On Perkins, see also *Washington Times*, 7 November 1933, Civil Service Clipping Collection, U.S. Civil Service Commission Library, Washington, D.C., file "Age Limits." Epstein found the purchasing power idea overemphasized (Senate, Committee on Finance, *Economic Security Act: Hearings*, p. 509). As fiscal problems eased in the 1950s, this did in fact become a more important facet of social security operations. See Walter Galenson, "Social Security and Economic Development: A Quantitative Approach," *Industrial and Labor Relations Review* 21 (July 1968): 559, and J. Douglas Brown, "The American Philosophy of Social Insurance," reprinted in Haber and Cohen, eds., *Social Security*, p. 46.

29. U.S., Committee on Economic Security, *Report to the President of the Committee on Economic Security* (Washington, D.C., 1935); William Haber and Wilber J. Cohen, eds., *Readings in Social Security* (New York, 1948), p. 101.

30. U.S., Congress, House, Committee on Labor, Subcommittee, *Unemployment, Old Age and Social Insurance: Hearings on H.R. 2827*, A Bill to Provide for the Establishment of Unemployment, Old Age and Social Insurance and for Other Purposes, and *H.R. 2859, H.R. 185, and H.R. 10*, 74th Cong., 1st sess., 4–8, 11–15 February 1935 (Washington, D.C., 1935); David Hackett Fischer, *Growing Old in America* (New York, 1977), pp. 181–82.

tion that full employment was possible.[31] Perkins presented the Senate Finance Committee with a similar viewpoint. "All of us," she said, "are concerned with the fact, for instance, that old age in many instances today begins at fifty. . . . We could gradually be asked to extend our old-age coverage to cover a man of that age; but no industrial system which any of us sets up today could possibly afford to maintain all the people over fifty years of age who happened to be without work." Operating from this fiscal logic, Perkins and the Roosevelt administration proposed to treat middle-aged unemployment as a problem of unemployment, rather than of old age.[32] As Perkins must have realized, this was not quite fair. If the fifty-five-year-old worker could not find a job for a period of years, it was not because he was unemployed (a temporary problem) but because, in the world of the machine, he was superannuated—that is, old (a permanent condition). The Roosevelt administration's efforts on behalf of these middle-aged unemployables were exceedingly limited throughout the 1930s, but this is not germane to its analysis of the economic malaise. Had more generous relief emerged as a fiscal possibility, the administration would have welcomed the retirement of 2,250,000 workers over sixty-five which the Lundeen people anticipated should their bill become law.[33]

The Townsend movement was, properly defined, the Townsend Old Age Revolving Pension Plan, a California-based operation headed by Francis Townsend. As a generic term, it also included a wide variety of lesser organizations. The most significant legislative expression of the movement on the national scene was a measure introduced in the House by California representative John McGroarty, calling for pensions of $200 per month to retired persons over sixty years of age. The disparate elements of the generic Townsend movement were linked through a series of economic and social assumptions and beliefs. The enormous productive power of mechanized industry had wrought major and essentially permanent changes in the modern economy. By making possible the production of more goods with fewer workers, mechanization had, on the one

31. See testimony by Smith College economist Dorothy Douglas, in House, Committee on Labor, Subcommittee, *Unemployment, Old Age and Social Insurance: Hearings on H.R. 2827*, pp. 653, 671; Darwin Meserole to Ernest Lundeen, 3 March 1938, Ernest Lundeen Papers, Hoover Institution Archives, Stanford, California, box 321, outcard 284.

32. Senate, Committee on Finance, *Economic Security Act: Hearings on S. 1130*, p. 103 (Perkins) and p. 283 (Brown).

33. The Lundeen measure, H.R. 2827, is in Robert F. Wagner Papers, Georgetown University Library, Georgetown University, Washington, D.C., box 329, folder 23. The retirement estimate for the bill was prepared by the Research Section of Interprofessional Association for Social Insurance; it is printed in Senate, Committee on Finance, *Economic Security Act: Hearings on S. 1130*, pp. 1170–71. In early 1935, Lundeen saw his bill not as hopelessly radical but as a possible "golden mean" between "the President's meager allotment" and the "fantastic Townsend plan." See Ernest Lundeen to Mary Van Kleeck, 22 January 1935, Lundeen Papers, box 322, outcard 181.

hand, created an economy of abundance and, on the other, made obsolete a large group of the least efficient workers—the oldest—and deprived that group of much of its purchasing power. The Townsend and Townsend-like plans promised to restore some of this lost purchasing power, bringing recovery from the Depression as well as relief to recipients, and to retire from the labor market from 4 to 10 million people over age sixty. On the latter point, Townsend supporters were especially vehement. Speaking in favor of the McGroarty measure, Representative Albert Carter said: "In this bill . . . we have the proposal that the older persons shall be taken out of gainful employment. I say to you that just as sure as we are here this afternoon we are going to establish that principle in this country."[34]

The slogan on a Townsend pamphlet, "Youth for Work / Age for Leisure," is indicative of another idea that permeated the movement: the old would move aside not simply to balance the labor market, but to provide work for the young. "The plan," wrote a Long Beach, California resident to the president, "is to '*make*' all American citizens *stop work* when sixty years of age—Put youth in their places, and *The Big Problem is solved. . . .* Last year you spent much to keep the old at work & the youth idle—No one was happy.—Now try the other please."[35] Such pleas were made from motives of fear and self-sacrifice. Deprived of opportunity by the new mechanized economy and the Depression, a restless youth would turn to crime and radicalism. Parents—many of whom could not even spell Townsend's name correctly—pleaded with Roosevelt to support a program to release their children from conditions conducive to criminality. The "Townson [*sic*] Revolving Bill," wrote one woman, "would kill this depression which is making criminals of the young by compelling them to either go hungry or steal."[36] A New York man advocating a plan much less expensive than Townsend's wrote that the aged should be retired for their own benefit, but

34. *Congressional Record*, 74th Cong., 1st sess., 1935, 79, pt. 6, p. 5884; L. H. Mingins, "Citizens National Insurance," typescript, received 29 August 1934, in Record Group 47, "Records of the Committee on Economic Security," National Archives, Washington, D.C., Subject File, box 38, file "Old Age Pensions"; U.S., Congress, House, Subcommittee on Labor, *Investigation of Unemployment Caused by Labor-Saving Devices in Industry: Hearings on H.R. 49*, 13, 14, 17, 20 February and 2 March 1936, 74th Cong., 2d sess. (Washington, D.C., 1936), p. 69 (Gildea); C. Stewart McCord, "Retirement Insurance: The Sales-Tax-Form-of-Saving-Money-for-Old-Age," unpublished paper (1931), Franklin Delano Roosevelt Papers, Franklin Delano Roosevelt Library, Hyde Park, New York, Official Files 494, "Pensions, 1933–1945," box 1; California State Plan, *Ham and Eggs for Californians* (Hollywood, 1938), pp. 22–25, copy in FDR Papers, Official File 3385, "California State Retirement Life Plan."

35. Mrs. Mary T. Elliott to Roosevelt, 21 May 1934, FDR Papers, Official File 494A, "Old Age Pensions, 1933–45," box 2. The slogan is from Old Age Revolving Pensions, Inc., *Old Age Revolving Pensions* (Long Beach, Calif., 1934), in ibid.

36. Emma R. Abbott to Mrs. Franklin D. Rosefelt [*sic*], 25 March 1935, Eleanor Roosevelt Papers, box 963.

added, "I really have more interest in youth obtaining its rightful opportunity. . . . Remember it is youth or the so-called students who generally start revolutions."[37] A California woman wrote Roosevelt that the retirement of the old was the only salvation for the "Graduates" of today, and employment the "first permanent step to stop Crime." And she presented another problem, which may have been more common than the infrequency of its mention would indicate. "To get rid of such old men," she said, "is to have work for the boy or girl that they dont have to do just as the old employer says or loose there job. Our Country is going down on account of so littel work for the young girl she is at the mercy of these old men in the Office here in California."[38] More typical were those who simply felt their children had been deprived of a normal young adulthood, forced into idleness or into a caretaking role, unable to take full advantage of the possibilities that were supposed to be available: "We educate our boys and girls & there is no place for them."[39] Much of the Townsend variety of pension advocacy, whether immediately concerned with crime, revolution, or jobs, emerged from the desire to reestablish an opportunity that was believed to be a remedy for most of America's social ills.[40]

Historians of the New Deal are generally agreed that the "radical" pension movement of the early and mid-1930s forced Roosevelt's hand on the social security issue, and there is evidence that something of this sort took place.[41] However, it has been taken for granted that the Roosevelt group was "conservative," the Townsendites "radical," and that their differences were profound ones of ideology. We know that Roosevelt disliked the Townsend plan as a national system, financed through general taxation. He believed it would bankrupt the government and produce a catastrophic inflationary spiral. Early in February

Note!

37. L. H. Mingins, "Citizens National Insurance," typescript, received 29 August 1934, RG 47, CES, Subject File, box 38, file "Old Age Pensions," p. 3.
38. Zula Mae Crain Dunham to President, 5 December 1934, FDR Papers, Official File 494, "Pensions, 1933–1945," box 1.
39. P. W. Smith to Roosevelt, 21 October 1938, FDR Papers, Official File 3385, "California State Retirement Life Plan"; Clara B. Mears to Mr. and Mrs. FDR, 21 May 1937, Eleanor Roosevelt Papers, box 969.
40. See also Harry Elmer Barnes, *Battling the Crime Wave: Applying Sense and Science to the Repression of Crime* (Boston, 1931), pp. 5, 89–97, 40–47, which treats criminality in the same context of idleness, and the materials on crime and unemployment in American Association for Labor Legislation Papers, Labor and Industrial Relations Institute, Cornell University, Ithaca, New York, microfilm reel 66.
41. Fischer, *Growing Old*, pp. 182–83; Leuchtenberg, *Roosevelt and the New Deal*, p. 131; Frances Perkins, *The Roosevelt I Knew* (New York: Harper Colophon, 1964), p. 294; Schlesinger, *Coming of the New Deal*, p. 307. The clearest exceptions to this point of view are Schlesinger, *The Age of Roosevelt*, vol. 3: *The Politics of Upheaval* (Boston, 1966), pp. 40–41, and Burns, *Lion and Fox*, pp. 224–26. Roosevelt's approach, according to Burns, "was to outmaneuver the leaders and to give way a bit to the blast, not to steal the ideological thunder of the left. He did not exploit the potentialities of encouraging and allying himself with the new millions of labor."

1935 he explained as much to a dozen members of Congress who had come to the White House to find out whether he would support pensions of from $50 to $200 per month. In a letter to his friend Felix Frankfurter, Roosevelt described his reaction:

> I explained the financial limitations, and that a sum greater than my recommendation might spell either failure to borrow or starting the presses. One of the spokesmen said—"Mr. President, is it not our sole duty to pass an ideal Old Age Pension bill and after this is done you can tell the Ways and Means Committee and the Treasury to find some way of raising the necessary money." I thought (silently) of one of our mutual friends from the Hill who came in the other day, slumped into his chair and said to me— "What the Hell is the use of education anyway? Let's reserve it for a select committee of one thousand and teach everybody else to speak but not to read, write, or think."[42]

These legislators, at least, got further than Townsend, who was unable to secure an appointment with the president.

Others in the administration generally agreed with this assessment of the alternative pension movement. As chairperson of the CES, Perkins announced in the fall of 1934 that the "impossible" pension schemes then being promoted constituted a major obstacle to the success of more reasonable legislation. Executive Director Witte developed an elaborate economic critique of the Townsend Plan which characterized its taxing provisions as hopelessly inadequate given present levels of national income and strongly suggested that the income-generating revolving feature of the plan might do more harm to the economy than good. Witte tried to enlist the U.S. Post Office in his campaign against the pension associations. Both J. E. Pope's Old Age Pension Association and the Townsend group were formally investigated and, in the Townsend case at least, exonerated.[43]

It is equally important to note what was *not* a part of the administration's evaluation of the alternative pension movement. Neither Roosevelt nor his lieutenants were willing to suggest that Townsend had misunderstood what had hap-

42. Roosevelt to Frankfurter, 9 February 1935, FDR Papers, President's Personal File (PPF) 140, "Frankfurter," box 1; Roosevelt to J. E. Pope, 19 August 1935; summary of Roosevelt to James Davis (the president's nephew), 9 March 1935, PPF 683, "Old Age Pensions"; Roosevelt to Pope, 27 July 1933, Official File 494, "Pensions, 1933–45," box 1, all in FDR Papers.

43. Speech, initiated by E. E. W[itte] and sent to Perkins, 25 October [1934?], RG 47, CES, Speeches and Press Releases, President's Messages, Executive Orders, box 3, file "Speeches (C)"; CES, "Why the Townsend Old Age Revolving Pension Plan is Impossible," Special Staff Report, January 1935, in RG 47, CES, Special Staff Reports, box 24, file, "Why the Townsend Plan is Impossible." On the investigations, see materials in RG 47, CES, Townsend Plan, box 43, file "Townsend Plan"; memorandum, Perkins to President, 19 August 1935, FDR Papers, PPF 683, "Old Age Pensions"; and memorandum, "Re: Old Age Pensions," no date, prepared for Eleanor Roosevelt by George Allen, Eleanor Roosevelt Papers, box 3027.

pened to the American economy, or that his general approaches to recovery—through retirement and purchasing power--were conceptually flawed. When Latimer testified on the need for a more aggressive retirement measure than the administration's, he went no further than other critics of Townsend. "It is not necessary," he told the Finance Committee, "to go to the fantastic lengths of the Townsend plan to get the stimulus for that removal."[44] Permanent technological unemployment, the role of purchasing power in recovery, the need to serve the young—these were emphases that hardly deserve to be called radical. It was generally accepted, moreover, that the aged would have to (or be privileged to) take a larger role in absorbing the fruits of the new technology, or the "new leisure," as it was called.[45]

Leaders of the alternative pension movement believed that New Deal programs differed from their own only quantitatively. Pension leader Pope found the Social Security Act entirely inadequate in scope but reasonable in intent. In August 1935 he assured the president that his Old Age Pension Association would not oppose his reelection. The Townsend director of public relations, Frank Peterson, responding to Witte's accusations of pension racketeering, expressed the frustration he felt at being unable to convince others of the mainstream nature of his pension organization. "Big business," he wrote Witte, "is too stupid to see that the Townsend Plan will be the means of giving it a new lease on life—that capitalism can only be saved by retiring permanently ten million of our old people, and at the same time giving these old people the means by which to once more restore purchasing power in the United States."[46]

44. Senate, Committee on Finance, *Economic Security Act: Hearings*, p. 746.
45. Thomas H. Greer, *What Roosevelt Thought: The Social and Political Ideas of Franklin D. Roosevelt* (East Lansing, Mich., 1958), pp. 46–51. The new leisure can be traced through H. S. Person, "The Work-Week or the Work-Life?" *Bulletin of the Taylor Society* 13 (December 1928): 235–36 (comments by J. Douglas Brown in the discussion which follows); Louis I. Dublin, "Population Changes and Consumption: A Forecast for Our Industrial Future," *Bulletin of the Taylor Society* 17 (October 1932): 162–64; George Barton Cutten, *The Threat of Leisure* (Washington, D.C., 1926), pp. 4–6, 12; Louis C. Walker, *Distributed Leisure: An Approach to the Problem of Overproduction and Underemployment* (New York, 1931), pp. 3–11; L. P. Jacks, *Ethical Factors of the Present Crisis* (Baltimore, 1934), pp. 20, 24–25, 37–38; Paul T. Frankl, *Machine-Made Leisure* (New York, 1932), pp. 169–72; Eduard C. Lindeman, *Leisure—A National Issue: Planning for the Leisure of a Democratic People* (New York, 1939), pp. 12, 15; Roger Payne, *Why Work?: Or the Coming "Age of Leisure and Plenty"* (Boston, 1939), pp. 300, 288, 305.
46. Pope to Roosevelt, 9 August 1935, FDR Papers, PPF 683, "Old Age Pensions"; Peterson to Edwin C. [*sic*] Witte, 17 October 1934, RG 47, CES, Townsend Plan, box 43, file "Townsend Plan"; Joseph R. Monaghan to My dear colleague, 2 March 1935, Lundeen Papers, box 322, outcard 231. This does not explain why, given their similarities, the Townsendites were ostracized by the New Deal. The explanation lies in the often expressed notion that the Townsend movement aroused false hopes and expectations. Like the Railroad Employees National Pension Association (chapter 6), the Townsend movement threatened control over the political process. See Executive Director, CES to Isador Lubin, 7 September 1934, RG 47, CES, Townsend Plan, box 43, file "Townsend Plan." and Martin, *Madam Secretary*, p. 349.

Social Security in Context

By 1935, Americans could look back on more than a half century in which retirement of older persons had been consciously employed to encourage mobility, efficiency, and social control. The scope of such activities was originally restricted to limited jurisdictions and markets: the public schools in a particular township or state; college professors; police in a city; ministers in a denomination; workers in a particular union or industry. With the civil service retirement legislation of 1920, the national government entered a field that had, with the exception of veterans, been the province of the states, the municipalities, and the private sector. In that act, the nation applied retirement to its own employees; in 1934, with the Railroad Retirement Act, it extended its jurisdiction to employees in interstate commerce and, in effect, recognized that the retirement of private-sector employees was a matter of national concern.

The association of welfare and economic functions within the same retirement measure was standard practice before and during the 1930s, and recognition of this is central to an understanding of the old-age provisions of the Social Security Act. Certainly the legislation balanced these dual functions less evenly than did contemporary railroad or civil service retirement legislation. The small sums it made available indicate that at the time of its passage it was primarily an old-age relief measure; the Depression insured that for the time being its full potential as a retirement instrument would go unrealized. Yet Wagner, Armstrong, and Brown anticipated some employment impact from the bill as passed, and Latimer advocated amendment to bring the measure closer to the railroad law. The act emerged from the history of retirement, and it was fashioned as its instrument.

Social security was not as revolutionary conceptually as we once thought. The act had legislative precedents at the federal level, in civil service and railroad retirement. Social security was new not so much qualitatively as quantitatively. Moreover, the addition of the context of retirement allows an extension of the existing radical critique of the system. Social security did fail to distribute income; it provided too little for too few; and it should not have been based on labor-force participation. Perhaps most important, it was in part intended to achieve a result that was in itself undesirable—a high rate of joblessness among older people. There are two trade-offs here. First, older workers were asked to surrender job rights in return for financial security. This idea predates 1935, but social security meant a significant extension of it. Second, older workers were encouraged to surrender job rights to younger workers who presumably had higher social claims to work. This may have been socially beneficial; it may, for example, have helped to prevent various forms of disorder, including strikes and juvenile crime. These were goals that many older workers shared, but to achieve them they had to give up that increasingly rare commodity, work. Finally, what they received in return was not simply security (adequate or inadequate), but a new *form* of security. Old people now depended on the monthly check rather than employment and on frameworks of social support developed at home rather than in the office or factory. Social security, in short, should be recognized as a system that for all its benefits creates and perpetuates the inherent injustices of retirement.

SOCIAL SECURITY AND THE FAMILY

The concept of the "welfare state" as an organizing device has also helped obfuscate the relationship between social security, the family, and the state. At issue is the oft-repeated idea, reflected in the historical interpretations that open this chapter, that old-age security involved the assumption, by the state, of functions previously delegated to or carried out by other institutions. The theoretical basis for this view was well established by 1919, when Arthur W. Calhoun published his three-volume study, *A Social History of the American Family*. Calhoun described the increasing dissolution and disorganization of the family under the impact of population dispersion, commercial development, and, most important, "the movement of political democracy which made the individual the social unit. . . . The reduction of family functions," he claimed, "has been due in large measure to the transfer of prerogatives to more inclusive social institutions," including school, shop, church, and state.[47] Calhoun assumed that the family had given over its functions out of weakness.

Coincident with the development of state old-age security legislation in the 1920s, sociologists and social workers began to examine family structures and their relationship to old-age dependency. The classic expression of this effort was William F. Ogburn's "The Changing Family," printed in the *Publications* of the American Sociological Society in 1928. In this article and at greater length in an essay written with Clark Tibbitts in 1933, Ogburn explained the conditions under which the family had abandoned protective functions, including protection from economic insecurity and old age, to the state. The critical factors were a decrease in family size and an increase in geographical mobility.[48]

47. *A Social History of the American Family: From Colonial Times to the Present*, vol. 3, *Since the Civil War* (Cleveland, 1919), pp. 169, 173, also p. 178.
48. Ogburn, "The Changing Family," *Publications of the American Sociological Society* 23 (1928): 124–33; William F. Ogburn, assisted by Clark Tibbitts, "The Family and Its Function," in

Whatever the truth of this perception of family decline, it was the dominant view in 1930, and it influenced the movement for old-age security. Not without reason, historians have adopted the Ogburn notion of transfer of function and concluded that the Social Security Act of 1935 was part of this transferral. The decision to save for old age was now in some measure taken from the individual or the family and transferred to the state; what was once a right or responsibility had become a social requirement. To the extent that old-age insurance encouraged retirement, the state now also played a significant role in employment decisions previously made in the family and by the market economy. After 1935, the national government had much to say about the home lives and work lives of older Americans.

In another sense, however, old-age insurance reflected a historic reliance on the home and family as caretaking institutions. There was never any intention of meeting the crisis of the 1930s by replacing the family with some other welfare institution—an expanded system of old-age homes, for example. The poorhouse and the old-age home split up the husband and wife; social security would assure their continued comradeship. The need to strengthen the family unit was an important element in the ideology that made the Fraternal Order of Eagles an advocate of state pensions throughout the 1920s. By funneling money back into the American family, social security promised to restore the primacy of home and family.[49]

With her strong, nostalgic feeling for community, Eleanor Roosevelt spoke for many Americans. "The community," she told the U.S. Chamber of Commerce in January 1934, "owes to its old people their own home life as long as they possibly can live at home. Old people love their own things even more than young people do. It means so much to sit in the same chair you sat in for a great many years; to see the same picture that you always looked at. . . . And that is what an old age security bill will do."[50] In the decade or two after 1900, railroad and typographical workers had rejected the old-age home in favor of the pension

Recent Social Trends in the United States: Report of the President's Research Committee on Social Trends, 2 vols. (New York, 1933), 1: 672–73, 683–85; Edgar Schmiedeler, *The Industrial Revolution and the Home: A Comparative Study of Family Life in County, Town, and City* (Washington, D.C., 1927); "Study of Aged Dependents Being Cared for Outside of Institutions by Private Social Agencies in New York City," AALL Papers, reel 65, p. 15; Martha Martin, "A Study of the Chicago Bureau for Care of the Aged" (M.A. Diss., U. Chicago, 1931), in Chicago Welfare Council Papers, Chicago Historical Society, Chicago, box 23, folder "Aged, 1931–32," pp. 53–55.

49. U.S., Congress, House, Committee on Labor, *Old Age Pensions: Hearings Before the Committee on Labor,* 71st Cong., 2d sess., 20, 21, 28 February 1930 (Washington, D.C., 1930), pp. 142, and 5, 13, 15, 17; U.S., Congress, House, Committee on Labor, Subcommittee, *Unemployment, Old Age and Social Insurance: Hearings on H.R. 2827,* pp. 446–47.

50. Copy of Address, delivered Washington, D.C., 5 January 1934, Eleanor Roosevelt Papers, box 3027.

as a caretaking mechanism for the old; the Social Security Act of 1935 considerably broadened this rejection.[51]

THE NEW DEAL AND THE OLDER WORKER

For a society experiencing a high level of long-term unemployment, the middle-aged worker—as young as thirty, as old as sixty-five—presents a peculiarly difficult problem. Those over sixty-five are relatively few in number. Presumably they have done their work, accomplished whatever it is they set out to accomplish, lived their lives. If they are retired, even with minimal pensions, one can plausibly argue that their burden is slight, or even that they are fortunate recipients of a reward for past service. Because they are old they have fewer dependents and may even have saved some money. In the midst of his pension activities, Robert Wagner received two letters, each suggestive of the larger problems of dealing justly with the middle-aged worker. One, from a woman, described how difficult it was for those over forty-five to secure work and how rapidly this led to dependency relationships. "If, by law," she concluded in reference to pension legislation, "men are forced from their work; then, by law, they should be adequately cared for."[52] The second writer advocated the employment of the middle-aged and old workers—all those who could not compete on equal terms in American industry—in routine clerical work for police, fire, and highway departments, and for the courts, the prisons, and other government agencies where their presumed deficiencies would have minor impact.[53] The first solution involved either recognizing the middle-aged worker as old and therefore entitled to a pension or as unemployed and entitlted to what might become permanent unemployment relief; either option would have entailed levels of expenditure then considered untenable as well as an uncomfortably complete commitment to popular ideas of technological unemployment. The second meant a retreat to nineteenth-century conditions that twentieth-century advocates of efficiency, through retirement and the pension, had done their best to eliminate.

51. State laws written during the 1930s to require adult children to support parents in financial need confirm this view. See Donald P. Kent, "Social Services and Social Policy," in John C. McKinney and Frank T. de Vyver, eds., *Aging and Social Policy* (New York, 1966), p. 212.

The limited and conservative purposes of social security have been well-treated in Lubove, *Struggle*, chapter 8; Leuchtenburg, *Roosevelt and the New Deal*, p. 132; Edward S. Greenberg, *Serving the Few: Corporate Capitalism and the Bias of Government Policy* (New York, 1974), pp. 114–18, and other works. I have only attempted to add to that critique here.

52. Caroline E. Gutliph to Wagner, 20 February 1932, Wagner Papers, legislative files, box 209, file 1079B, "Old Age Relief."

53. Reynold J. Mahlau to Wagner, Wagner Papers, legislative files, box 239, file 2516, "Old Age Pension."

Any kind of employment solution, whether it involved partially superannuated or fully efficient middle-aged workers, also raised difficult questions of social policy. As there were only so many jobs to be had, who was to hold them? On what grounds might a society experiencing massive unemployment make such crucial decisions?

The problem of the middle-aged unemployed became a matter worthy of concerted national attention in the late 1920s, coincident with the rise of the "new leisure." A Senate committee investigating unemployment and relief systems in late 1928 and early 1929 gave the problem its first important congressional exposure. The more active state labor departments became involved in discouraging age discrimination at the same time. Pennsylvania's, for example, issued a booklet, apparently designed to aid middle-aged job-seekers, which listed firms that did not discriminate on the basis of age. The NAM sponsored a national conference on "The Older Employee in Industry" in October 1929, and another important discussion of middle-aged unemployment took place the following January in Cleveland under the auspices of the American Management Association.[54] Although businessmen generally either defended their discriminatory practices or denied they existed, both the Calvin Coolidge and Herbert Hoover administrations characterized the problem as a serious one that warranted scrutiny. A Committee on Technological Unemployment appointed by the secretary of labor in May 1931 briefly treated the employment problems of the older worker and found them analogous to those of other "handicapped workers." The committee advocated retraining displaced workers, perhaps the first time a prominent body had done so. The suggestion, however, was laced with caveats that workers would be trained for jobs that did not exist or for which there was already an adequately trained work force.[55]

54. U.S., Congress, Senate, Committee on Education and Labor, *Unemployment in the United States: Hearings Pursuant to S. Res. 219*, A Resolution Providing for an Analysis and Appraisal of Reports on Unemployment and Systems for Prevention and Relief Thereof, Together with Senate Report No. 2072, 70th Cong., 2d sess., 11–14, 17–19 December 1928, 9 and 14 January, 7, 8, and 9 February 1929 (Washington, D.C., 1929); Pennsylvania, Bureau of Labor and Industry, Bureau of Employment, *The Firms Listed Herein Do Not Ban Men from Employment on Account of Age* (Harrisburg, Pa., 1928), copy in American Association for Old Age Security Papers, Labor-Management Documentation Center, Labor and Industrial Relations Institute, Cornell University, Ithaca, New York, box 33, file "Old Age-Middle Age-Employment Handicaps, etc"; NAM, "The Older Employee in Industry," typescript, conference at Hotel Roosevelt, 15 October 1929, in AAOAS Papers, ibid.; *Iron Age*, 125 (6 February 1930): 453–54.

55. Senate, Committee on Education and Labor, *Unemployment Hearings Pursuant to S. Res. 219*, pp. 14, 72, 128; statement by Secretary of Labor James J. James in the *New York Times*, 29 January 1928, p. 20; *The Index*, September 1929, p. 136; "Report of the Subcommittee on the Conservation of the Displaced Worker," included in "Report of the Committee on Technological Employment to the Secretary of Labor," appended to U.S., Congress, Senate, Select Committee on

It was inevitable that the unemployment problems of middle-aged and old workers would be linked to current proposals for government old-age pensions. Many persons, including Townsend supporters, believed that a humane old-age pension measure would reach down to the middle-aged worker of sixty (and eventually fifty-five or fifty) who was not in any obvious physical sense super-annuated. For these workers, the pension was a form of unemployment relief, albeit permanent.[56] Others began from the assumption that discrimination against middle-aged workers was primarily caused by the economics of private pension plans, and that a properly designed national pension system would free the employer from the need to protect his pension plan by hiring younger workers. "By the mere stroke of providing a pension system by the Government," argued Abraham Epstein, "you would eliminate the greatest hazard of the last 10 years, the arbitrary discrimination against persons over 40 or 45 years of age."[57] CES staff members Barbara Armstrong and J. Douglas Brown anticipated that a national system with flat payments (the same for older and younger workers) might have some of this effect, yet both believed discrimination was primarily based on differences in "physical and nervous strength" and that the problem would have to be handled through work programs.[58] The standard Labor Department response to those who complained of age discrimination was to point out that the New Deal's subsistence farm programs and homesteads were designed for those among the unemployed who might not be reabsorbed into the regular economy.[59]

Although the Congress and the executive branch liked to think that the problem of age discrimination and the middle-aged worker was confined to private industry, its own intimate involvement in the process was brought home in

Unemployment Insurance, *Unemployment Insurance: Hearings Pursuant to S. Res. 483*, A Resolution Establishing a Select Committee to Investigate Unemployment Insurance Systems, 72d Cong., 1st sess., 2 April, 19, 22, October, 5, 6, 12, 13 November, 10 December 1931 (Washington, D.C., 1932), pp. 585–606 (report of the subcommittee). For business opposition to a governmental commission on old age in industry, see *Commercial and Financial Chronicle* 130 (1 February 1930): 685–86.

56. *Congressional Record*, 74th Cong., 1st sess., 1935, 79, pt. 5, pp. 5812 (Dirksen), 5788–90 (Sirovich).

57. U.S., Congress, Senate, Committee on Pensions, *Old Age Pensions: Hearing on S. 3037*, a Bill to Protect Labor in its Old Age, 72d Cong., 1st sess., 26 March 1932 (Washington, D.C., 1932), p. 6.

58. Memorandum, "Re Possibilities of Encouraging the Employment of Older Workers," Mrs. Barbara Armstrong to Mr. Witte, 13 October 1934, RG 47, CES, Special Staff Reports, box 23, file "Old Age Security Staff Report."

59. Memorandum, Boris Stern to Miss J, 25 August 1933, and attached form letter, in RG 174, DL-OS-GSF, 1933–40, box 26, file "Committee—To Study Legislation re. relations of Employees to Federal Gov't," and James F. Coughlin to Perkins, 18 July 1933, ibid.

1933 during a public controversy over hiring age limits in the federal civil ser-vice.[60] On October 30 the Civil Service Commission, then composed of Harry D. Mitchell, Lucille F. McMillin, and George R. Wales, announced that after consultation with the heads of executive departments and independent offices, and as an economy measure, men and women over forty would no longer be allowed to take civil service exams. At the time, the age limit was fifty years. The official announcement exempted veterans' preferences and technical, professional, and scientific positions. It claimed that appointing officers (person-nel managers) in the government service were motivated by the same considera-tions as their private-sector counterparts: "They believe that the younger person will more quickly learn the details of his or her particular job and be more efficient in execution." The announcement produced an immediate backlash, led by Representative John Cochran of Missouri, chairman of the House Committee on Expenditures in Government Departments, who claimed the decision would set a bad example for industry. Cochran brought the chief executive into the squabble when he expressed doubt that Roosevelt would approve the commis-sion's action. Within three days the decision had been denounced by the Ameri-can Federation of Labor and its affiliate, the American Federation of Govern-ment Employees, headed by former civil service commissioner E. Claude Babcock. Anita Pollitzer of the National Woman's party characterized it as a new form of discrimination against women. Wagner, chairman of the National Labor Board, called it "wrong and foolish."

> It is the height of absurdity for such a decision to be made at this time when we are trying to turn heaven and earth to remedy unemployment. The com-mission's contribution to that movement is to bar the doors so as to deprive competent men and women of the right to take even the first step toward getting jobs.

Support for the decision came only from the National Federation of Federal Employees' president, Luther C. Steward, who justified his approval on the

60. Unless otherwise noted, the following account is from these newspaper accounts in the Civil Service Clipping Collection, file "Age Limits": *Washington Herald*, 8 November 1933, 31 October 1933, 1 November 1933, 2 November 1933, 4 November 1933, 16 November 1933; *Philadelphia Public Ledger*, 1 November 1933; *Washington Star*, 31 October 1933, 9 November 1933, 6 Novem-ber 1933; *Washington News*, 31 October 1933; *Washington Times*, 3 November 1933, 7 November 1933; *Washington Post*, 3 November 1933, 14 November 1933. See also House, Committee on Labor, *Old Age Pensions: Hearings, 1930*, p. 125 (Woodruff); letters and telegrams in RG 174, DL-OS-GF, box 26, file "Committee . . . to study Legislation re relations of Employees to Federal Gov't"; memorandum, Gary Moffett to Louis McH. Howe, 14 March 1933, FDR Papers, Official File, box 2 (no. 9); P. E. Johannsen to Guy T. Helvering, Commissioner of Internal Revenue, 26 July 1933, Record Group 9, "Records of the National Recovery Administration," National Archives, Washington, D.C., Labor Advisory Board, Leo Wolman files, box 8175, file "Labor, Child," dealing with age discrimination in Helvering's office. Hereafter referred to as RG 9, NRA-LAB-LWF.

ground that the ruling applied only to minor positions "at the bottom of the ladder."

Perkins had made her position known from the beginning. She told the press she had often favored older employees for their maturity, judgment, and permanency. She called the commission ruling "a very short-sighted policy," but tried to explain it as an attempt to reduce the number of persons taking the examinations. She, too, was affronted by the inefficiency involved in examining five hundred persons in order to fill two positions. Following a November 1 cabinet meeting in which the forty-year age limit was discussed, Roosevelt publicly assigned Perkins to consult with the commission. In the meantime, the commissioners had both rationalized the ruling and denied their responsibility for it. Mitchell, chairman of the commission, stressed that the decision had been based on the virtually unanimous agreement of government personnel officers, who in turn reflected the preference within departments for hiring between the ages of twenty and twenty-five. Under pressure, Mitchell attempted to shift some of the responsibility from the commission to J. G. Yaden, head of the examining division of his office, who had, he said, developed the original proposal, and to Babcock, who as secretary of the commission had defended lower age limits for clerical positions because such skills were "not readily acquired by persons over 45 years of age." Commissioner McMillin refused to answer questions and would not publicly explain the ruling. She did, however, join Mitchell in a letter to Roosevelt that welcomed the Perkins inquiry and expressed a desire "to have you know that the Commission is not trying to do an absurd thing."[61]

Perkins met with Mitchell and McMillin on November 6 and made some inquiries into the process by which the decision had been made. The following day she reported to Roosevelt. In a memorandum remarkable for its restraint, Perkins carefully presented the commission's arguments: examinations were expensive; employment officers preferred younger workers; retirement regulations required fifteen years of service for eligibility. When jobs were plentiful, she wrote, age limits "might be harmless." Under present conditions of unemployment, however, it was "unfair to set up any arbitrary exclusion principle." She recommended that the commission remove the age limit entirely.[62]

Perkins's public statements were of a different nature. In a press conference on November 7 she had pointedly included middle-aged workers among those groups whose incomes were important to the development of purchasing power;

61. Harry Mitchell and Lucille McMillin to Roosevelt, 3 November 1933, FDR Papers, Official File, box 2 (no. 1), "U.S. Civil Service Commission, 1933–1934."
62. Memorandum, Perkins to President, 7 November 1933, FDR Papers, ibid.

on November 8 she announced that three cabinet officers—Cordell Hull, Harold Ickes, and herself—had not been consulted when the ruling was under consideration, and she implied that she had not yet completed her investigation of the over-forty problem.

Presented with the Perkins memorandum, the commission acted quickly to satisfy Roosevelt and save face. It reopened the stenographic and typing exam, the most important category affected by the original ruling, to persons aged forty to fifty-three, justifying the cutoff on the basis of the excessive cost of integrating older persons into existing retirement systems.[63] In a public statement, the commission also announced it would ask departments and independent offices not to refuse to appoint merely on the basis of age. Cochran was not satisfied. "I wasn't making this fight for stenographers and typists only. It was for all those classes in which the ages have been lowered." As an example, he cited the commission action in cutting the age maximum for teachers of home economics in Indian service schools from forty-five to forty. He could discover no reason for such a limit. "I'll take the biscuits of a woman of forty-five before one of twenty-five," he added. Five days later, the commission responded by raising the age limits on two additional examinations, including that for home economics teachers, from forty to fifty-three. Again, the commission saved face, this time by raising a third category—another class of Indian school teachers—from thirty to forty. Little more than two weeks after the first order, Perkins closed the episode with the announcement that she would suggest to cabinet officers and others that subordinates be issued instructions to desist in discrimination against middle-aged civil service eligibles.

Many middle-aged workers were also affected by the efforts of Republican and Democratic administrations to relieve congestion within the federal civil service. In 1932 this was accomplished by virtually eliminating extensions for employees who had reached the age for automatic separation, and in 1933 through economy legislation providing for an increase in the retirement rolls. Although the latter measure was constructed to promote voluntary retirement, E. Claude Babcock, president of the Federal Personnel Association, recalled that a large number of federal employees were pressured to leave the service.[64] When the Civil Service Commission recommended optional retirement after

---

63. Harry B. Mitchell to Colonel M. H. McIntyre, Secretary to President, 8 November 1933, FDR Papers, ibid.

64. Act of 30 June 1932, ch. 14 (47 Stat. 382), copy in RG 47, CES, Speeches and Press Releases, President's Messages, Executive Orders, box 3, file "Executive Orders"; U.S., Congress, Senate, Committee on Civil Service, *Extending Classified Civil Service: Hearings on H.R. 960*, An Act Extending the Classified Civil Service of the United States, 76th Cong., 3d sess., 10–30 April 1940 (Washington, D.C., 1940), p. 104.

thirty years' service for all civil service personnel as a method of increasing efficiency through the hiring of younger persons, some federal officials began to question whether the government could afford it.[65] These doubts, and the reluctance of federal employee unions to accede to a compulsory measure that would have immediately retired twenty-two thousand persons, led in April 1933 to a compromise in which the president was granted discretionary authority to compel the retirement of employees with thirty years of service. At a time when layoffs were common, and when the released fifty-five-year-old worker might have real difficulty securing further employment, retirement's primary function was the relief of unemployment and unemployment insecurity, not old-age dependency. This was also the purpose of the liberalization of civil service retirement under the 1939 Neely-Ramspeck legislation, which brought postmasters under the federal retirement system and provided for optional retirement at age sixty-two for those with fifteen years' experience.[66]

The National Industrial Recovery Act (NIRA) again brought the administration face to face with its own participation in age discrimination. The product of disparate needs and conditions, the legislation, it was agreed, would at least protect labor by eliminating the cutthroat competition responsible for sweatshop conditions and by establishing a minimum wage and maximum work week in industry codes. For the middle-aged and older worker, the result was a disaster, in part because the act was not effective enough and in part because it was too effective. The NIRA did not eliminate competition. Aggressive employers seeking a competitive advantage under the National Recovery Administration's codes of "fair competition" violated the spirit of the legislation by speeding up their machinery in order to get more out of each (now more expensive) worker. Firms fired older workers who could not meet the redefined standard of productivity or handle intensified physical demands, or kept them on as "handicapped" exceptions at a reduced wage rate, in effect bypassing the minimum wage. To the extent that minimum wages were the rule, employers tended to retain only

65. Memorandum, Frank T. Hines, 10 January 1934, in FDR Papers, Official File, box 2 (no. 1), "U.S. Civil Service Commission, 1933–1934."

66. This account is developed from U.S., Congress, Senate, Committee on Civil Service, Subcommittee, *Civil Service Retirement: Hearing on S. 369, S. 801, S. 803, S. 804, S. 1177, S. 1826, S. 1862, S. 2346, and S. 2483*, Bill to Amend the Civil Service Retirement Act, 74th Cong., 1st sess., 16 April 1935 (Washington, D.C., 1935); and the Civil Service Clipping Collection, file "Retirement Legislation, 1924, 1933–1939," clippings *Washington Herald*, 21 April 1933, 27 April 1933, 16 June 1933, 9 September 1937; William V. Nessly, "President Gets Plan to Lower Retirement Age," *Washington Post*, 8 April 1937; *Washington Star*, 21 April 1933, 26 April 1933, 18 July 1939; *Washington News*, 25 April 1933; *Washington Times-Herald*, 8 May 1939. The principals in Neely-Ramspeck were Matthew Neely, senator from West Virginia, and Robert C. Ramspeck, representative from Georgia.

their most efficient workers and to release those who had previously been economical because they earned lower wages.[67]

The results had been anticipated. Six months earlier the issue of NIRA's relationship to older workers had been raised at a meeting of the Advisory Group of Industrial Economists, where at least one participant had pointed out that older workers would suffer massive unemployment unless the codes made provision for wage differentials. A woman garment worker had written the president in July 1933, asking if the code for that industry would contain a clause protecting older workers who could not work as rapidly as the "young mexican which we have compare with." She was promptly informed that no provision ensuring steady employment for older workers existed in any of the codes and that none was contemplated for garments: "Matters pertaining to skill or efficiency of individual workers are left entirely to the discretion of employers."[68]

Problems arose before the NIRA went into effect. An employee of the Industrial Rayon Corporation of Cleveland reported that a number of men that had been hired "in readiness for the new ACT have quit their tasks—stating that the work was too heavy and fast." Women had left because they could not keep up. "Many workers faint at their posts."[69] The older workers seem to have suffered more than others, if only because the new conditions violated their expectations. Many were long-term employees and had expected to hold their jobs despite the Depression. At the Kingsport, Tennessee, silk mills, thirty-two experienced employees were laid off without the promise of future work. They were replaced by learners, boys and girls, and married women whose husbands had jobs.[70] A forty-nine-year-old Troy, New York woman, employed by the Hall Hartwell Collar Company for twenty-five years, wrote of her search in the town's retail stores following the closing of the factory. Employers informed her bluntly that they could not give her work because of her age. "That was the

67. House, Committee on Labor, Subcommittee, *Unemployment, Old Age and Social Insurance: Hearings on H.R. 2827*, pp. 180–81 (Benjamin); U.S., Congress, House, Committee on Labor, *Old Age Pensions: Hearings on H.R. 1623, H.R. 7050, H.R. 7144, H.R. 7207, H.R. 7556, H.R. 7749, H.R. 7762, H.R. 8350, H.R. 8641, H.R. 9228*, 73d Cong., 2d sess., 12, 16, 22, 27, and 28 February, 1, 2, 7, 8, and 9 March 1934 (Washington, D.C., 1934), pp. 2 (O'Malley), 21 (Epstein); L. H. Mingins, "Citizens National Insurance," typescript, received 29 August 1934, RG 47, CES, Subject File, box 38, file "Old Age Pensions"; *Business Week*, 21 April 1934, p. 18.
68. A. R. Forbush to Elizabeth Hazleton, 1 August 1933, RG 9, NRA, Consolidated Approved Code Industry File (CACIF), box 1778, file "Cotton Garment Employment—Handicapped Workers Complaint"; Charles F. Roos, *NRA Economic Planning*, Cowles Commission for Research in Economics, Monograph No. 2 (1937; reprint ed., New York: Da Capo Press, 1971), p. 98; P. E. Johannsen to Guy T. Helvering, 26 July 1933, RG 9, NRA-LAB-LWF, box 8175, file "Labor, Child"; Mrs. Elizabeth Hazleton to Our Beloved President, 10 July 1933, RG 9, NRA, CACIF, box 1778, file "Cotton Garment Employment—Handicapped Workers Complaint."
69. Granville Hill to Perkins, 3 August 1933, RG 9, NRA, CACIF, box 1813.
70. Olaf G. Wexler to Hugh S. Johnson, ibid.

code." "Would you please tell me," she wrote, "if the code says if women should not get any work at that age. . . . Before the NRA came in I would all ways find work. now when they see A women is forty or a little more they have no work for her."[71]

In the traditionally competitive textile industry, employers handled the codes by manipulating work-force categories. A woman in Shelby, North Carolina reported that the local mill had fired her husband, who had ten years' experience and was fifty-six years old, and had given his job to a younger man. Meanwhile, her son had been working at the mill for twelve weeks as a "learner" (exempted from minimum wage provisions) and had yet to draw a salary. Belton, Texas yard workers complained that the mechanical division of the local mill was dismissing all workers over fifty years of age, most of whom had held their jobs since the plant opened sixteen years ago, "because they cannot run the two jobs instead of their old one." More than twenty older workers were released at a Mount Airy, North Carolina facility because they were unable to produce enough on the piece-rate system to "make" the minimum wage. Union workers at a Huntsville, Alabama textile mill insisted that the operator was using the age factor to release older union workers and to replace them with younger nonunion personnel.[72]

The exemption mechanisms designed to prevent such abuses were inadequate to the task and were often themselves abused. In recognition that older workers might be at a disadvantage under the minimum wage, industry codes could define older workers as "handicapped" and provide for a scaled-down wage commensurate with productivity. About half of the code industries did so, and in these industries, older workers presumably kept their jobs, though they might not earn the minimum wage. The exemption for older workers was not, however, universally desired, and it was especially unpopular with organized labor, which correctly interpreted it as another form of wage cutting designed to break down the minimum wage.[73] Employers, moreover, could exploit the handicapped exemption by moving basically efficient older workers from job to job until the worker landed in a position unsuited to his abilities. At that point, the employer forced the worker to apply as a substandard employee and accept

71. Mrs. Cecil Schermerhorn to President, 27 August 1934, RG 9, NRA, CACIF, box 1779, "Cotton Garment Employment—Handicapped Workers Complaint."

72. Complaints 914-A, 890-A, 906-A, in RG 9, NRA, series 398, Excerpts of Complaints, Clothing (Men's), Cotton Textile (1447a), file "601-A-947-A."

73. Leon C. Marshall, *Hours and Wages Provisions in NRA Codes*, Brookings Institution Pamphlet Series No. 16 (Washington, D.C., 1935), pp. 19, 76; Roos, *NRA Planning*, p. 175; telegram, J. S. Potofsky to Leo Wolman, 16 November 1933, RG 9, NRA-LAB-LWF, box 8175, file "Textiles."

a lower rate of payment. In industries without code exemptions, employers who traditionally relied on an older work force found that the legislation dramatically altered their competitive relationship within the industry. Most responded by changing the age structure of the labor force. A New York State firm employing only older persons suspended operations in January 1934 and attracted a considerable amount of attention. Individual firms could apply to state authorities for exemptions from code regulations, but the process for doing so was neither carefully defined nor well understood.[74] Thousands of older workers experienced the NIRA as unemployment, the speedup, increased insecurity, or, at best, employment at something below the minimum wage in an industry in which the code provided for handicapped exemptions.

If the Roosevelt administration felt any inclination to remedy this situation, the need to do so was attenuated with the Supreme Court's decision in the *Schechter Poultry* case, which declared the NIRA unconstitutional. A stronger economy and the impetus given union organization by the National Labor Relations Act also eased the pressure on the older worker. Not until Labor Day 1937, when Perkins broached the subject as a trial balloon over CBS radio, did the New Deal consider the issue worthy of public policy treatment. The states had taken the initiative. Earlier in the year, the Massachusetts legislature had passed the first state law designed to counter age discrimination, empowering its Department of Labor and Industry to publish the names of employers discriminating on the basis of age. Similar legislation had failed in New York, Pennsylvania, Illinois, Minnesota, and Texas, but these states had established commissions to conduct hearings on the problem. New York had created a Joint Committee on Middle-Aged Employment Discrimination, soon to be known as the Wadsworth Committee after its chairman, Assemblyman James J. Wadsworth.[75]

Perkins had correctly evaluated the climate of opinion. In the recessed economy of late 1937, there were large numbers of unemployed middle-aged workers with an interest in improving their position in the job market. Her ad-

74. Affidavit J. Fundaburk, 8 May 1934; Frank E. Walsh to E. F. McGrady, 21 May 1934; Mrs. J. A. Hall to President, 4 June 1934; Mrs. C. Meyer, 4 February 1933, to Roosevelt; G. W. Maxon & Co., Berlin, New York to NRA, all in RG 9, NRA, CACIF, box 1778, file "Cotton Garment Employment—Handicapped Workers Complaint." Employers seeking exemption were presumably to apply to state authorities, who were governed by a code of instructions issued by the Secretary's Committee on Minimum Wage, U.S. Department of Labor, in accordance with Executive Order No. 6606F. Roos argues that a high minimum wage, by inducing neglect of apprenticeship provisions, constituted "a kind of vested interest for middle-aged workers" (p. 175).

75. Philadelphia Industrial Relations Association, Employment Problems Committee, "Report on Older Workers," *Personnel Journal* 17 (1938–39): 105–06; New York State, Legislature, Joint Committee on Discrimination in Employment of the Middle-Aged, *Final Report*, Transmitted to the Legislature 21 March 1940, Legislative Document No. 80 (1940) (Albany, 1940), pp. 3, 5, 15.

dress drew praise from organized labor, from the growing number of "Over 40" associations which attempted to find work for their middle-aged members, and from veterans' organizations, which had shown considerable interest in the issue for several years.[76] American Legion involvement dated from its 1935 national convention. The organization had established a committee on employment information and sought the cooperation of federal and state agencies. As the average veteran approached forty-five years of age in 1937, the September convention reaffirmed the central importance of age discrimination in the veteran employment picture.[77]

In late October, at a National Conference on Labor Legislation held under the auspices of the Department of Labor, Perkins explained the social basis for her newfound interest in the older worker. She described an industrial community in which employment had recently doubled. The work force, however, had changed. The plant now employed young workers and left unemployed "their fathers and uncles." This idea—that the problem of unemployment among older workers was the cutting edge of potential revolutionary changes in family and social organization—dominated her remarks. Middle-aged workers were critical elements in community and family life. They raised the teenage children, maintained the home, trained their offspring in work, morals, and citizenship—all critical functions for an "orderly" society. "I think most of us realize," she said, "that only within a home in which the head of the family has a job which his children can respect, only within that home can we expect to have carried on those patterns of morals and those patterns of citizenship which we all realize are the very essence of life in a democracy." The remedies she proposed were hardly adequate to the task as she had defined it. She urged delegates to return to their states and work to counter the erroneous impression that pension plans and insurance laws necessitated discrimination. New habits must be formed. Education, not legislation, was her solution.[78]

In the same cautious vein, Perkins moved to establish a Labor Department advisory committee on the older worker. In December 1937, letters went out to

76. *New York Times*, 7 September 1937, p. 2; Memorandum, V. A. Zimmer to Perkins, 3 October 1937, RG 174, DL-OS-GSF, box 26, file "Committee to Study Legislation re relations of Employees to Federal Gov't"; Philadelphia Industrial Relations Association, "Report on Older Workers," p. 106; House, Committee on Labor, Subcommittee, *Unemployment, Old Age and Social Insurance: Hearings on H.R. 2827*, pp. 520–21 (Crosbie); House, Committee on Labor, *Old-Age Pensions: Hearings on H.R. 1623*, p. 6.

77. Report of Forrest G. Cooper before the National Convention of the American Legion, New York City, 23 September 1937, in RG 174, DL-OS, box 153, file "Employment—Veterans' Affairs."

78. Minutes of Labor Department conference, not dated, attached to memorandum, V. A. Zimmer to Perkins, 3 October 1937, RG 174, DL-OS-GSF, 1933–40, box 26, file "Committee to Study Legislation re relations of Employees to Federal Gov't," pp. 99, 98, 105, 106; *New York Times*, 17 October 1937, p. 15.

some twenty industry, labor, and government leaders, each affirming "that the problem is difficult and perhaps impossible of solution through legislative action."[79] Chaired by Harry W. Chase, chancellor of New York University, the committee functioned as a research group. Its report, released March 19, 1939, replicated Perkins's analysis in several important respects. Hiring discrimination was largely a matter of employer "prejudice," based on erroneous information about the capacities and productivity of older workers and their financial impact on pension plans. Their problem was acute not so much in its own right, but because workers in the forty-to-forty-four age group had "the heaviest family responsibilities, and their lack of employment means both deprivation and added burdens for the young." By noting that unemployment was most serious among the twenty-to-twenty-four age group, the committee implied, however, that if the young needed help it should come directly rather than through aid to the middle-aged. Perhaps for this reason its major recommendations—elimination of civil service age limits, integration of social security with civil service retirement, more attention to the problem by employers, unions, and the Federal Employment Service—were not of the sort that might have significantly affected labor markets had they been implemented.[80]

The parallel efforts of New York's Wadsworth Committee provide additional insight into the context in which this reform activity took place. Its most publicized activity was the Rochester Plan, under which the members of the Industrial Management Council of Rochester, an employer group representing thirty-six companies and thirty-six thousand employees, agreed to maintain a balance between older and younger workers approximating that within the working age groups of the city's population. In December 1939 the Associated Industries of New York, representing 1,456 employers employing 600,000 workers, agreed to maintain a similar balance. The ease of what would seem to have been a substantial accomplishment demands some explanation. Why had New York employers so obligingly given up their right to discriminate? One possibility is the desire of employers to counter the ground swell for antidiscrimination legislation. Another is that the Rochester Plan was a meaningless gesture that accomplished little in the way of distributing work. Rochester, at least, with its relatively large population of skilled workers, had no major age problem. More important, especially outside Rochester, was the desire of employers to

79. See copies of letters in RG 174, DL-OS-GSF, 1933–40, box 26; *New York Times*, 20 February 1938, p. 22.

80. Copy, "Report to the Secretary of Labor by the Committee on Employment Problems of Older Workers," Perkins Papers, box 86, file "Committee on . . . Older Workers"; the report is described in *New York Times*, 19 March 1939, p. 16. See also Bureau of National Affairs, *Labor Relations Reference Manual* 2 (1939): 951.

find an age-related formula for industrial stability. The Wadsworth Committee had selected Rochester for its initial survey because "that city seemed to have more industrial peace than any other city of its size in the State. The Committee was curious to know the cause, and to determine, if possible, whether age of employees was one of the factors which contributed toward that peace." The cooperating Rochester Industrial Management Council was, significantly, a non-union group.[81]

On April 27, 1939, Roosevelt issued a proclamation from his home in Hyde Park, New York. Essentially a plea for equal opportunity for older workers, it was grounded in the Perkins frameworks of "social equilibrium" and "family responsibilities," and it singled out the veterans of the World War for special attention. Roosevelt made no mention of possible legislative remedies, nor did he recognize New York representative James M. Mead's recent call for a permanent work-giving agency, modeled after the Civilian Conservation Corps, for all workers over age forty-five. Instead, he asked employers to cooperate by reviewing their employment policies and concluded by declaring the week of April 30, 1939 "Employment Week," and Sunday, April 30, as "Employment Sunday."[82]

Full of social analysis yet lacking in substance, the proclamation was typical of New Deal efforts on behalf of the older worker. The Roosevelt administration had no program for older workers comparable to the National Youth Administration. It could deal quickly and honestly enough with a particular problem like civil service age limits, but this piecemeal response was no substitute for systematic activity. The limitations of ad hoc measures were particularly glaring under the NIRA, where the problem was geographically diffuse and incapable of attracting consistent attention from the press. The effort mounted following Perkins's Labor Day address in 1937 eschewed national and state legislation and only scratched the surface of what could have been done. Its focus, moreover, was on a particular category of older workers, those in their forties, who could exert substantial influence through veterans' organizations, who had

81. New York State, Joint Committee on Discrimination, *Final Report, 1940*, pp. 118 (quotation), 123, 131–34; *New York Times*, 15 October 1939, p. 5; *Business Week*, 7 October 1939, p. 38; 13 August, 1938, pp. 30–31; Henry Simler, "Does the Man Over 40 Deserve a Break?" *American Business* 8 (February 1938): 30, 49.

The conservative orientation of the Wadsworth Committee is apparent also in its conclusion that the most important cause of the employment problems of the older worker was "physical unfitness in the middle aged." Moreover, the resolution creating the committee warned that "undue, top heavy, or artificial pressure in behalf of the middle-aged would result in senseless discrimination against youth" (*Final Report*, pp. 35, 15).

82. The full proclamation is in *Commercial and Financial Chronicle*, 148 (29 April 1939): 2508. For Mead's suggestions, see *New York Times*, 4 October 1938, p. 27; 5 December 1938, p. 4.

demonstrated their commitment to action in the 1932 Bonus March, and who were generally thought important to social stability.

This concentration on the middle-aged worker also makes sense in relationship to the labor-market analyses developed during the discussions over the old-age provisions of the Social Security Act. Although the New Deal was limited by finances in its ability to retire older workers under that legislation, its authors recognized that technology was undermining the job market for older workers and creating long-term unemployment, and that in the future the worker over fifty-five or sixty would have to be progressively removed from the labor market rather than brought back into it. Because the Roosevelt administration was convinced that it could not afford to accomplish this object immediately, those between fifty-five and sixty-five were relegated to obscurity, too old to work and too young to retire. Administration officials showed no interest in the Lundeen bill, the only measure designed to reach this group. Forty-year-olds, on the other hand, were obviously too young to be treated as potential retirees and of too much political significance to be ignored. The result was the very limited effort launched by Perkins in 1937. But for Perkins, Roosevelt, and others to have advocated the reemployment of workers sixty or sixty-five years of age would have been patently inconsistent with the administration's interpretation of the labor market and with the history and future of retirement.

8 The Triumph of Retirement: The Postwar Years

Between 1940 and 1965, retirement triumphed over alternative methods of dealing with the aged. This was, in part, a mechanical process. Pension plans grew in number and coverage; social security was extended to additional elements of the work force, while benefits were increased and retirement ages lowered. As this process met with resistance, the leading advocates and beneficiaries of retirement—corporations, labor unions, and insurance companies— became increasingly aggressive in marketing retirement as a consumable commodity, ignoring its origins as a device for corporate and bureaucratic efficiency and control. They stressed both preparation for retirement and the beneficial effect of integrating the retired into the growing network of organizations designed to provide the aged with some meaningful substitute for the workplace. They were assisted by a group of sociologists whose concept of "disengagement" affirmed the existence of a natural process by which the aged separated themselves from the workplace and other primary institutions. By the mid-1950s even the organizations of the retired had internalized the new ideology of retirement and had accepted the sheltered workshops, retraining programs, and age discrimination legislation that were the stock-in-trade of liberal capitalism and could hardly solve the problems created by technology and ongoing labor surplus.

THE GROWTH OF PENSIONS

The most active agents of pension expansion during the 1930s were the insurance institutions, which benefited from federal legislation that discriminated against banks and corporations and in favor of insurance companies as pension plan trustees. Because the Social Security Act provided minimum support levels for lower-paid elements of the work force, these plans were generally designed to benefit employees earning over $3,000 per year. The Treasury Department, responsible for issuing pension regulations, might have overlooked the income bias in the plans submitted for its approval had not the excess profits tax of 1940 stimulated the writing of new plans by reducing their net costs to the corporation. Under this legislation, pension plans became a convenient mechanism for deferring corporate income from high-tax to low-tax years. The payment of social security benefits was linked to the private system in the Revenue Act of 1942 and accompanying Treasury Department regulations, which held that plans could provide greater proportionate payments to upper-income groups by offsetting private plan benefits with social security.[1] To some extent, the post-1942 expansion in numbers of persons covered by private pensions was a result of the desire to provide deferred compensation (taxable at lower rates) to highly salaried management personnel. Other wartime factors were of substantial importance. High surtax rates on individuals made pensions attractive as a method of employee compensation, since the tax was deferred until the income was actually received, usually when the recipient's income was substantially reduced by retirement and his or her marginal tax rate consequently lower. Pension payments also gave the corporation a way out of wartime wage controls, for the deferred compensation of the pension was exempt from the controls. The great savings available to the employer (according to one estimate, the government was bearing 85 percent of the cost of some plans) as well as the traditional benefits of a pension system in labor stabilization, security, and efficiency produced at least five thousand new plans and the amendment of many others before the end of the war. Private plans covered 4.1 million workers in 1940, 6.4 million in 1945, and 9.8 million in 1950. By 1946, employers were allocating 17 percent of payroll to pension payments, a record figure even in comparison with the 10 percent allocated from 1942 to 1944.[2]

The labor and tax questions were not entirely distinct. The critical tax problem concerned the extent to which payments made by an employer to an employees' trust were deductible as "ordinary and necessary" expenses for tax pur-

1. Laurence G. Hanmer, "Pension Trust Business for Banks," *Trusts and Estates* 75 (November 1942): 474–76; Edmund J. Donegan, "Social Security Legislation—Its Threat to Private Insurance," *Eastern Underwriter* 37 (24 April 1936): 8–9; Louise Wolters Ilse, *Group Insurance and Employee Retirement Plans* (New York, 1953), pp. 296–99; Robert F. Spindell, "Congress Creates New Opportunities for Insurance Producers," *Eastern Underwriter* 42 (31 October 1941): 6; Robert Tilove, "Social and Economic Implications of Private Pensions," *Industrial and Labor Relations Review* 14 (October 1960): 26.
2. *Magazine of Wall Street* 70 (8 August 1942): 452 (editorial); Alfred M. Skolnik and Joseph Zisman, "Growth in Employee-Benefit Plans: 1954–57," in William Haber and Wilbur J. Cohen, eds., *Social Security: Programs, Problems, and Policies* (Homewood, Ill., 1960), p. 177; Rainard B. Robbins, *Impact of Taxes on Industrial Pension Plans*, Industrial Relations Monograph No. 14 (New York, 1949), pp. 7–16, 24, 46–49, 52; Peter Guy Evans, "Employees' Trusts Under the New Tax Bill," *Trusts and Estates* 75 (August 1942): 152; *Personnel* 20 (May 1944): 322; ibid. 22 (September 1945): 77; Gustave Simons, "Promoting Labor Harmony in the War Effort," *Commercial and Financial Chronicle* 159 (2 March 1944): 891, 905.

poses, even though they might not be required by union contract. The 1942 legislation allowed such deductions "for all the ordinary and necessary expenses paid or incurred during the year in carrying on any trade or business, including a reasonable allowance for salaries or other compensation for personal services actually rendered." The tax court had ruled that expenses were not ordinary and necessary if they were uncertain, indefinite, or illusory—conditions often pertaining to pensions. In 1947, however, a federal court in Cincinnati found this reasoning inconsistent with the needs of the modern corporation. Allowing the tax deductions, the court classed the payments as "a means of offense against attack, their purpose being to inspire in the labor force a spirit of loyalty and cooperation that would avoid labor strife." The larger the industrial unit, the court said, the greater the potential injury from labor strife and the greater the extent to which tension-reducing measures like pensions had to be interpreted as ordinary expenditures within the meaning of the statute.[3]

Pensions also grew in number as a consequence of prevailing ideas of unemployment in the years before and after 1945. In January 1943, President Franklin D. Roosevelt anticipated the concerns of millions of Americans by including in his list of postwar objectives a "right to a useful and remunerative job in the industries or shops or farms or mines of the nation." Two months later the National Resources Planning Board presented a lengthy report, based on a "New Bill of Rights," which along with the right to security in old age and to recreation, affirmed the "right to work, usefully and creatively through the productive years." So strong was the interest in full employment that in 1944 the Republican presidential candidate, Thomas Dewey, moved beyond the cautious statements of his party's platform and discussed the need to provide work for all those who desired it.[4]

When Congress began work on postwar employment legislation, it immediately became clear that the very idea of maintaining a work force sufficiently large to absorb marginal workers was a matter of some controversy. Many economists and businessmen, taking a page from the wages-fund theorists of the nineteenth century, believed that employment was inherently limited.[5] This view

3. *Lincoln Electric Co. v. Commissioner of Internal Revenue* (dec. June 5, 1947), *Labor Relations Reference Manual* 17: 57–58.
4. Stephen Kemp Bailey, *Congress Makes a Law: The Story Behind the Employment Act of 1946* (New York, 1950), pp. 27, 41–42.
5. *Problems of Aging: Transactions of the Fourteenth Conference*, 7–8 September 1951, St. Louis, Mo., Nathan W. Shock, ed. (Caldwell, N.J., 1952), pp. 106–07; Garth L. Mangum, "Manpower Requirements and the Supply of Labor," in Juanita M. Kreps, ed., *Technology, Manpower, and Retirement Policy* (New York, 1966), p. 33; Sumner H. Slichter, "Retirement Age and Social Policy," in Industrial Relations Research Association, *The Aged and Society: A Symposium on the Problems of an Aging Population*, ed. Milton Derber, (Champaign, Ill., 1950), p. 111.

produced more cautious suggestions for employment policy, predicated on the assumption that the removal from the work force of marginal groups, including employees of pensionable age, was both necessary and beneficial. One postwar planning agency, the Committee for Economic Development, in 1944 suggested a five-step order of layoffs, beginning with married women with working husbands, part-time workers with second jobs, and pensionable employees.[6]

Congress eventually dropped all but the pretense to full employment, titling its legislation the Employment Act of 1946 and dropping job guarantees in favor of a general policy declaration so thoroughly hedged as to be meaningless:

> The Congress hereby declares that it is the continuing policy and responsibility of the Federal Government to use all practicable means consistent with its needs and obligations and other essential considerations of national policy with the assistance and cooperation of industry, agriculture, labor, and State and local governments, to coordinate and utilize all its plans, functions, and resources for the purpose of creating and maintaining, in a manner calculated to foster and promote free competitive enterprise and the general welfare, conditions under which there will be afforded useful employment, for those able, willing, and seeking to work, and to promote maximum employment, production, and purchasing power.[7]

A virtual midcentury capitalist manifesto, this statement offered little prospect of the eventual reintegration of the retired into the economic mainstream. In fact, it promised more of the same: the continued definition of older people, particularly those over sixty-five, as incapable of and unwilling to work—except, of course, in emergencies. Retirement would retain its historic relationship to employment.[8] The main goal of public policy was not full employment but the prevention of another major depression.

The most important pension development of the late 1940s was the emergence of the pension plan as a legitimate subject of collective bargaining under the terms of the Wagner Act of 1935 as amended by the Taft-Hartley Act of 1947. In December 1945, the Amalgamated Clothing Workers of America (CIO) reached agreement with the manufacturers and contractors of men's and boys' clothing over a plan covering some 150,000 workers. The United Mine Workers struck in April 1946, in large measure over the retirement fund issue. And in 1949, after four years of negotiations and a rank-and-file rejection, the United Auto Workers (CIO) worked out a plan for the auto industry. Not until 1949 did

6. *Personnel* 21 (May 1945): 321.
7. Bailey, *Congress Makes a Law*, p. 228.
8. See also Carl Parrini, "The Unemployment Crisis," *History at Northern* (Spring 1975): 5; Harvey Swados, "Less Work—Less Leisure," in Eric Larrabee and Rolf Meyersohn, eds., *Mass Leisure* (Glencoe, Ill., 1958), pp. 359–60.

the National Labor Relations Board and the federal courts finally and affirmatively resolve the question of whether the pension was a condition of employment under the law and, therefore, whether employers could be compelled to good faith bargaining over the issue.[9]

AF of L and CIO affiliates participated in the rush of collective bargaining, which by mid-1950 had brought more than five million workers under negotiated plans. It was the policy of both these organizations to favor government over private benefits; the AF of L worked for legislative increases in social security benefits, while the CIO, hoping to secure the support of business leaders for social security increases, sought to negotiate plans under which the company provided the difference between some stated amount and social security.[10] Union interest in pensions was especially strong during the recession of 1948–49, when the traditional demands for higher wages met with resistance. With the pension, union officials could present the membership with a concrete gain in a time of economic stringency, and the company could defer the cost into a presumably more prosperous, and surely inflationary, future. Railroad workers, faced with the double-barreled problem of recession and diesalization, again created an independent organization, the Railroad Pension Conference, to press for thirty-year retirement, regardless of age. Retired railroad workers seeking improved benefits created the National Association of Retired and Veteran Railway Employees, with headquarters in Lakeland, Florida.[11]

The new plans were bargained. Though they held out some benefits for unions, they were not forced on big business by the muscle of organized labor. Indeed, claims Peter Drucker in *The Unseen Revolution* (1976), it was General Motors president Charles Wilson who in April 1950 took the first step toward "pension fund socialism" when he suggested to UAW officials a pension plan

9. Ilse, *Group Insurance*, pp. 317, 319; William C. Greenough and Francis P. King, *Pension Plans and Public Policy* (New York, 1976), pp. 63–64.

10. Memorandum, "AFL Attitude on Pensions," Herbert Little to Stan Wollaston, 8 December 1949, Record Group 174, "Records of the Department of Labor," National Archives, Washington, D.C., Office of Secretary Maurice J. Tobin, General Subject File, 1950, box 239, file "1950— Pensions, Miscellaneous"; Charles L. Dearing, *Industrial Pensions* (Washington, D.C., 1954), pp. 46–47, 51.

11. *Pensions and Health and Welfare Plans in Collective Bargaining*, Second Annual Conference Presented by the Institute of Industrial Relations, U. of California, and the Conference of Junior Bar Members in Cooperation with the Committee on Continuing Education of the State Bar of California, Institute of Industrial Relations and University Extensions, 13, 15 April 1950, ed. Anne P. Cook (n.p., n.d.), p. 29; Charles A. Hamm to A. E. Lyon, 27 July 1950, Railroad Labor Executives Association Papers, Labor-Management Documentation Center, Labor and Industrial Relations Institute, Cornell University, Ithaca, New York, box L-1, file "Leg-Railroad Retirement Act-Amendment to Jan 1950–July 1951"; materials in Brotherhood of Locomotive Firemen and Enginemen Papers, Labor-Management Documentation Center, Labor and Industrial Relations Institute, Cornell University, box 25, file "R.R. Pension Conference."

controlled by investment managers, who would eschew the traditional strategy of investment in public debt issues in favor of seeking a high return in the equity market, by buying stock.[12]

A quarter of a century later, Wilson's historic offer had become fifty thousand pension plans, almost all of them investment funds like GM's. By 1978, pension funds held over $500 billion in assets and some 20 percent of the nation's financial securities, public and private, equity and debt.[13] This growth, believes Drucker, has resulted in a peculiarly American form of socialism: employee ownership of business through the mechanism of the pension fund.[14] Strangely, however, the very employees who own American business "do not know it, do not perceive it, do not experience it." More curious still, pension-fund socialism "has had very little impact on American institutions, American power structure, American politics, even on American political rhetoric."[15]

Why, then, has Drucker created a socialism that has no impact, a working class of owners who are unaware of their dominance? He has done so because the idea of pension-fund socialism is critical to his main purpose—the indictment of any form of real socialism. The argument is as follows: we have lived under a form of socialism (pension-fund socialism) for twenty-five years, yet there has been no significant change in industrial relations; therefore, relations between capital and labor must be fixed by some other quantity than the ownership of the means of production by the working class. In short, we have had Marxian socialism and it does not work.[16]

In fact, pension-fund socialism is a gloss for the real truth that Drucker has uncovered in Wilson's April 1950 offer. Aware of the enormous sums that were and would be generated in pension funds, Wilson sought to insure that this growing pool of capital would be responsibly invested—that is, as capitalists like him would invest it. Three years earlier, southern Democrats and northern Republicans had established a legal framework for Wilson's effort. Section 302 of the Taft-Hartley Act asserted the right of management to a fiduciary role in all collectively bargained pension plans, eliminated organized labor's influence in the governance of corporate plans, and initiated the process of circumscribing investment options so that pension capital would find appropriate outlets.[17] The

12. Peter Drucker, *The Unseen Revolution: How Pension Fund Socialism Came to America* (New York, 1976), pp. 5, 7, 10–11.

13. Jeremy Rifkin and Randy Barber, *The North Will Rise Again: Pensions, Politics and Power in the 1980s* (Boston, 1978), p. 84; Drucker, *Unseen Revolution*, p. 12.

14. Drucker, *Unseen Revolution*, pp. 2, 97–98, 102.

15. Ibid., pp. 97, 164.

16. Ibid., pp. 133–35, 138.

17. Rifkin and Barber, *North Will Rise Again*, pp. 101–02.

"prudent man" concept of fiduciary responsibility, written into the 1974 Employee Retirement Income Security Act (ERISA), only defined what had been the standard investment practice for decades; the banks and insurance companies that control most of the funds have used these pools of capital to support a sagging market in the equity of the largest American corporations.[18] As Drucker demonstrates, a "revolution" in the sense of a radical reshaping of the pension system did take place in the postwar years. Its consequence, however, was not pension-fund socialism but pension-fund capitalism; neither, as Charles Wilson's actions demonstrate, was it "unseen." Business had found still another use for retirement.

SOCIAL SECURITY

Between 1950 and 1961, Congress made substantial modifications in the social security system. The retirement age was lowered to sixty-two for women in 1956 and for men in 1961. Average real monthly benefits rose rapidly during the first eight years of the decade, more than making up for inflation.[19] These gains have been widely interpreted as symbolic of the victory of the welfare state over the forces of social conservatism. Stephen Raushenbush's 1955 pension study argues that social security extensions were evidence of a general recognition that rugged individualism had reached the limits of its effectiveness. The critical 1954 amendments were introduced by the Eisenhower administration, which "joined hands with its predecessors and with the union representatives of the workers in insisting, in effect, that adequate security in old age meant more freedom rather than less." Writing in 1960, historian Eric Goldman used the Eisenhower administration's advocacy of social security to support his conclusion that the Republican mainstream was committed to using the federal government to preserve and extend the social gains of the New Deal. More recently, Charles Alexander has written that Eisenhower disliked big government but "believed that Washington had obligations to insure some degree of economic opportunity and security"; his administration "accepted and perpetuated the basic reality of the welfare state." Sociologists Harold Orbach and Clark Tibbitts have described the 1950s as the "age of security."[20] It follows that how-

18. Ibid., pp. 102, 92–97.
19. Greenough and King, *Pension Plans*, p. 87 (chart); Wilbur J. Cohen, *Retirement Policies Under Social Security: A Legislative History of Retirement Ages, the Retirement Test and Disability Benefits* (Berkeley, 1957), pp. 9–11.
20. Stephen Raushenbush, *Pensions in Our Economy* (Washington, D.C., 1955), pp. 40, 52, 53 (quotation); Eric F. Goldman, *The Crucial Decade—And After: America, 1945–1960* (New York: Vintage Books, 1960), pp. 282–83; Charles C. Alexander, *Holding the Line: The Eisenhower Era,*

ever inadequate were the payments (within limits of course) and however unfair it might seem that workers finance their own retirement, the purpose of the system, as designed in the 1930s and improved in the 1950s, was to provide security for the old.

In fact, social security emerged from a complex economic and political environment in which issues other than old-age dependency played a major role. During the early 1950s, a number of corporations reversed their historic opposition to benefit increases. They did so because they had come to see social security as a way of reducing costs. Confronted with collective-bargaining agreements that required the employer to make up the difference between social security payments and some fixed amount, they suddenly discovered that social security payments were insufficient. Not long after the automobile workers negotiated their first pension plan, the Ford Motor Company announced it would work for increased social security benefits. As a result of the 1954 social security legislation, according to *Fortune*, for a short time the steel companies "were paying next to nothing for pensions."[21] In a 1939 article, Marion B. Folsom, later Eisenhower's secretary of health, education, and welfare but then treasurer of Eastman Kodak, argued the need to integrate social security and private pension plans; greater total benefits would allow employers to retire older workers and achieve the gains in efficiency for which pensions had been devised.[22] Integration also meant a greater tax subsidy for higher-paid personnel.

The reductions in retirement ages were, at least in part, an expression of the historic notion of retirement rather than the more recent ideology of security. The proposal to reduce the women's age first achieved popularity (or notoriety)

1952–1961 (Bloomington, Ind., 1975), pp. 38, 40; Harold L. Orbach and Clark Tibbitts, eds., *Aging and the Economy* (Ann Arbor, Mich., 1963), p. 9, also p. 2. See also Eugene A. Friedmann, "The Impact of Aging on the Social Structure," in Clark Tibbitts, ed., *Handbook of Social Gerontology: Societal Aspects of Aging* (Chicago, 1960), p. 138; Alvin M. David, "Old-Age, Survivors, and Disability Insurance: Twenty-Five Years of Progress," *Industrial and Labor Relations Review* 14 (October 1960): 10, 12, 13; and reports of the John Kennedy and Dwight Eisenhower addresses on social security and aging in *Modern Maturity* 3 (October–November 1960): 6; ibid. (December–January 1960–61): 7.

The one-dimensional quality of this conception of the welfare state also has served to inhibit the development of a legitimate radical critique, for if conservatives, liberals, and radicals can agree on the purposes of social security, their disagreements must be proportionately circumscribed, limited to benefit levels and the philosophy behind the chosen fund-raising technique. See Roy Lubove, *The Struggle for Social Security: 1900–1935* (Cambridge, Mass., 1968), p. 179; Barton J. Bernstein, "The New Deal: The Conservative Achievements of Liberal Reform," in Bernstein, ed., *Towards a New Past: Dissenting Essays in American History* (New York, 1969), p. 274.

21. "The Steady Push for Pensions," *Fortune* 59 (June 1959): 215, quoted in Haber and Cohen, eds., *Social Security*, p. 183; Cohen, *Retirement Policies*, pp. 6, 9; Raushenbush, *Pensions*, p. 59; C. E. Jarchow, "Cost Aspects of Employee Security Plans," *Personnel* 22 (May 1946): 416–17.

22. M. B. Folsom, "Coordination of Pension Plans with Social Security Provisions," *Personnel* 16 (1939–40): 41, 44, 46.

in the recession of the late 1940s. It was defended by South Carolina senator Olin Johnston as a way of dealing with unemployment and old-age inefficiency in the depressed southern textile industry. Among other advocates were Nelson Cruikshank, director of the Department of Social Security of the AF of L–CIO, and—at least until economic conditions improved in the mid-1950s—most of the representatives of management, the insurance industry, and the public on the Senate Finance Committee's Advisory Council on Social Security. Opposition developed rapidly, centering in women's organizations and clubs but including the U.S. Chamber of Commerce, the Catholic charities, and HEW Secretary Folsom. The measure became law in 1956. In lowering the male retirement age under social security to sixty-two, the federal government had acknowledged the limited job opportunities available to older workers and the relationship between retirement and unemployment. Economist Juanita Kreps suggested in 1966 that similar considerations continued to be relevant to the private sector. A recent tax cut, she said, had not eliminated unemployment, and business and labor had increasingly turned to mandatory retirement to spread available work.[23]

Advocates of social security increases were also convinced of the economic potential inherent in the system. The seemingly stable economic conditions of the mid-1950s had not eliminated fears of a new depression, and social security was one of several measures expected to control the economic imbalances that many believed were responsible for the severity of the 1930s decline. It would assure some fundamental level of demand, a level that would increase over time as the population aged and in times of depression as older people left employment. By providing a sense of confidence in the future, it would create a proper climate for consumption. National City Bank pointed out that the housing boom, of major importance to the economy in the early 1950s, had benefited greatly from the ability of older people to hold onto their homes, thus forcing the younger generation to build.[24]

23. Cohen, *Retirement Policies*, pp. 27–34; Kreps, ed., *Technology, Manpower*, p. ix. See Ernest L. Olrich, "Social Security Benefits and Deferred Retirement: A Plan for Improved Manpower Utilization," *Personnel* 29 (January 1953): 361–62, and *Lifetime Living* 1 (September 1952): 10 (editorial), for suggestions that conditions of job scarcity prevailing in the 1930s were no longer applicable to the full employment, defense-based economy of the early 1950s.

24. Ida C. Merriam, "Social Security Programs and Economic Stability," in Universities-National Bureau Committee for Economic Research, *Policies to Combat Depression: A Conference of the Universities-National Bureau Committee for Economic Research*, Princeton University, 30–31 October 1953 (New York, 1954); Raushenbush, *Pensions*, pp. 71–73; Roger F. Murray, *Economic Aspects of Pensions: A Summary Report* (New York, 1968), pp. 40, 66, 68, 116, 118–19; George B. Hurff, "Our Older People: New Markets for Industry?" *Journal of Business* 27 (April 1954): 131, 136; Alan Sweezy, "Social Security and National Prosperity," *Science and Society* 8 (Summer 1944): 198, 200; K. E. Boulding, "Structure and Stability: The Economics of the Next Adjustment," in

This sanguine viewpoint, however, had always to be balanced with liabilities. Even in 1953, transfer payments (shifts of money from one group to another) accomplished through social security were not very large, only 1.2 percent of disposable income. This percentage, as well as the absolute sum involved, was subject to erosion from inflation, a serious problem in the 1950s which had to be solved if the program was to have any major countercyclical impact. The older population, moreover, was not a major purchaser in the pivotal durable-goods sector of the economy. By the mid-1960s there was also concern that rising fringe benefits, including the social security contributions required of business, were causing employers to pay overtime to existing workers rather than to expand the work force. As growth replaced stability as the basic goal of national economic policy in the late 1950s, social security was seen less in the context of its positive impact on the business cycle and more for its possible negative impact on capital formation and investment.[25]

A New Consciousness of Mandatory Retirement

In much the same way that the nation considered national health insurance in the 1910s and the equal rights amendment in the 1920s, so was mandatory retirement an issue of the 1950s. The public examination took place in the popular press and at a series of conferences on aging and retirement attended by representatives of labor, management, and academia. There was an aura of unreality about it, for the discussion assumed that retirement was, with obvious exceptions, a private-sector affair, to be handled in board rooms, union halls, and at the bargaining table. The federal government could affect retirement in private industry only indirectly. It could encourage and facilitate the public dialogue; it could place pressure on mandatory retirement systems by working toward full employment. The former was of marginal value; the latter was all-important but unrealistic in the long term, given the makeup of the American political economy. The recommendations of the 1961 White House Conference on Aging reflect this duality, suggesting the need for an examination of manda-

Policies to Combat Depression, pp. 71, 73; Walter Galenson, "Social Security and Economic Development: A Quantitative Approach," *Industrial and Labor Relations Review* 21 (July 1968): 559; *Lifetime Living* 3 (January 1954): 16–17 (editorial).

25. Raushenbush, *Pensions*, p. 67; Merriam, "Social Security Programs," in *Policies to Combat Depression*, p. 233; Hurff, "Older People," p. 136; Joseph W. Garbarino, "Fringe Benefits and Overtime as Barriers to Expanding Employment," *Industrial and Labor Relations Review* 17 (April 1964): 426–42; Dearing, *Industrial Pensions*, pp. 170–76; Maurice F. Ronayne, "The Older Office Worker—Backbone of American Business," *Personnel Journal* 39 (October 1960): 181.

tory retirement policies while advocating the high levels of employment which could prevent the exit of older workers from the labor force.[26]

Although American society seemed uninterested in any real solution of the problem, the discussion produced a depth of knowledge about retirement denied to previous generations. It was now clear that mandatory retirement was most common in larger firms, in older industries that had passed through growth peaks, and in organizations with a work force of relatively advanced age. Mandatory programs were generally maintained to increase the efficiency of the work force, create promotional opportunities for younger employees, and facilitate administration. Corporate officials were especially concerned with the continued efficiency of upper and middle management.[27]

The case for mandatory retirement as an efficiency mechanism did not go unchallenged. As it was common practice to establish a fixed age for retirement, programs were vulnerable to the charge that their indiscriminate application was inherently inefficient. Mandatory retirement, said HEW Secretary Arthur Fleming in 1959, "is a lazy man's device for dealing with a difficult program."[28] From this perspective, the problem seemed amenable to technical and scientific solutions. Jobs had to be analyzed for their precise content and workers for their skills and abilities. If a reasonable match between worker and job proved difficult, either part of the equation could be reconstructed. The worker might be retrained or—a much less common suggestion—the job might be redesigned to suit distinctive or declining abilities. Workers proven to be superannuated might be retired. This was the approach of the National Committee on the Aging and the New York State Committee on Aging, both of which conducted extensive inquiries into mandatory retirement in the 1950s.[29]

From a technical point of view, however, performance and task analysis

26. U.S., Department of Health, Education and Welfare, Special Staff on Aging, *The Nation and Its Older People: Report of the White House Conference on Aging*, January 9–12, 1961 (Washington, D.C., 1961), pp. 126, 142–44.

27. Margaret S. Gordon, "Work and Patterns of Retirement," in Robert W. Kleemeier, ed., *Aging and Leisure: A Research Perspective into the Meaningful Use of Time* (New York, 1961), p. 39; Jarchow, "Cost Aspects," p. 415; Helen Baker, *Retirement Procedures Under Compulsory and Flexible Retirement Policies* (Princeton, N.J., 1952), pp. 12, 36, 46; Fred Slavnick, *Compulsory and Flexible Retirement in the American Economy* (New York, 1966), p. 36; James E. Vallilee, "The Problem of the Old Employee," *Pulp and Paper Magazine of Canada* 46 (March 1945): 314; Eileen Ahern, "The Older Worker," *Personnel Journal* 31 (July–August 1952): 105.

28. *Modern Maturity* 2 (April–May 1959): 8.

29. Geneva Mathiasen, ed., *Flexible Retirement: Evolving Policies and Programs for Industry and Labor* (New York, 1957), pp. 44–65, 71–72, 76–90; New York State, Legislature, Legislative Committee on the Problems of the Aging, *New Channels for the Golden Years*, Legislative Document No. 33, 1956 (n.p., n.d.), pp. 7–9; J. Howard Wyner, "Toward More Flexible Retirement Policies: A Progress Report," *Personnel* 30 (March 1954): 386–89; *Lifetime Living* 2 (February 1953): 11.

proved exceedingly difficult. In 1955, few companies had objective measures for performance, and most claimed no need to develop systematic job analysis. Decisions about capacity to perform were generally left to medically trained plant physicians, who were properly cautious about getting involved in matters for which they were not prepared.[30] Beyond this there were those, like Dr. Robert A. Kehoe, head of the Charles Kettering Laboratory, who believed that the economy could not afford the luxury of supporting a large group of unproductive people and who looked to performance and task analysis as a means of employing even inefficient workers. But the right to work in this sense was not generally acknowledged.[31] Objectivity would not eliminate mandatory retirement; it would simply make it a more precise tool.

The discussion of retirement also revealed the links between mandatory retirement and labor-market conditions. In periods of general recession or declining activity, corporations were more likely to institute mandatory retirement and more reluctant to allow employees to continue working beyond the normal retirement age than in periods of growth. Firms experiencing a labor shortage were usually amenable to alterations in retirement regulations. Pension plans adopted between 1948 and 1950, a period of rising unemployment and general weakness in the economy, were much more likely to contain a mandatory provision than plans adopted in the more prosperous years between 1950 and 1955. A study by the National Committee on the Aging concluded that the relatively low percentage (20.3) of surveyed plans with a fixed retirement age "may be related to the relatively full employment that has prevailed during the period of the growth of the pension plan."[32] Although generally opposed to mandatory retirement in principle, labor unions followed the lead of their younger members and accepted negotiated provisions for mandatory retirement in the recession periods of 1948–49 and 1957–58. Cautious about releasing older workers into the labor market, unions tended to oppose liberalization of the social security retirement test.[33]

30. Wyner, "Toward Flexible Retirement," pp. 387–88; Mathiasen, ed., *Flexible Retirement*, p. 60; A. G. Kammer, "Optional Retirement Plans: Their Implications for the Industrial Physician," *Industrial Medicine and Surgery* 21 (July 1952): 343–44.

31. National Industrial Conference Board, "Retirement and Its Problems," typescript, 339th Meeting, 19 March 1953, Cincinnati, Ohio, National Industrial Conference Board Papers, Eleutherian Mills Historical Library, Greenville, Wilmington, Delaware, pp. 50–84.

For the argument that compulsory retirement involved economic waste for the nation as a whole, see also Hermon K. Murphey, "Against Compulsory Retirement," *Personnel Journal* 35 (July–August 1956): 100, and Slichter, "Retirement Age and Social Policy," p. 106.

32. Mathiasen, ed., *Flexible Retirement*, p. 115; Wyner, "Flexible Retirement," p. 394; Baker, *Retirement Procedures*, p. 63; Gordon, "Work and Patterns," in Kleemeier, ed., *Aging and Leisure*. p. 39.

33. Gordon, "Work and Patterns," in Kleemeier, ed., *Aging and Leisure*, pp. 40, 46; Mathiasen, ed., *Flexible Retirement*, pp. 104, 106–09.

RETIREMENT AS A SOCIAL PHENOMENON

The 1950s witnessed the first attempt to describe and assess the social impact of retirement. The early studies found a great deal of dissatisfaction with forced retirement. One estimated that 50 to 60 percent of those reaching sixty-five would choose to work if retirement could be deferred. The Life Extension Foundation calculated that 30 percent of those who had retired under mandatory systems would have preferred to be back at their jobs, and early in the decade there was evidence that many workers were neither applying for social security benefits for which they were eligible nor taking advantage of retirement under auto industry pension systems.[34] The old, the poor, and those who liked their work had the most difficulty adjusting to retirement.[35] In 1956, when Eleanor Roosevelt wrote that she would "rather die in the atomic war in a few seconds than live in a world that was constantly becoming more Communistic, and making me live in a narrower and narrower area," her subject was mandatory retirement. "Instead of letting them go quickly," she added, "you make them die more slowly."[36]

For a time it seemed as if retirement might be permanently assigned this negative definition. In 1952, *Lifetime Living* could not find a corporation head, labor leader, or pension expert who would defend mandatory retirement in a public forum.[37] By 1960, however, a competing definition had surfaced. Among sociologists, "activity theory," in which retirement was a violation of the organism's constant need for a high level of interaction, was yielding to the paradigm of "disengagement." Disengagement theorists argued that aging was "an inevitable mutual withdrawal or disengagement, resulting in decreased interaction between the aging person and others in the social system he belongs to." Retirement, defined as "permission to disengage," allowed the old to preserve self-

34. Baker, *Retirement Procedures*, cited in Ahern, "Older Worker," p. 105; Gordon, "Work and Patterns," in Kleemeier, ed., *Aging and Leisure*, p. 34; Mathiasen, ed., *Flexible Retirement*, pp. 102–03; Robert K. Burns, "Economic Aspects of Aging and Retirement," *American Journal of Sociology* 59 (January 1954): 389.

35. Harrison Terrell, "Executives Have Their Retirement Problems, Too," *Personnel Journal* 32 (June 1953): 65; G. Hamilton Crook and Martin Heinstein, *The Older Worker in Industry: A Study of the Attitudes of Industrial Workers Toward Aging and Retirement* (Berkeley, Calif., 1958), p. 89; Murphey, "Against Compulsory Retirement," p. 100; Richard H. Uhlig, "Employment and Retirement of a Group of Older Males," *American Sociological Review* 17 (February 1952): 91–93; Jacob Tuckman and Irving Lorge, *Retirement and the Industrial Worker: Prospect and Reality* (New York, 1953); Edrita G. Fried, "Attitudes of the Older Population Groups Toward Activity and Inactivity," *Journal of Gerontology* 4 (April 1949): 141–50; Edward B. Allen, "Psychological Factors That Have a Bearing on the Aging Process," in *The Social and Biological Challenge of Our Aging Population*, Proceedings of the Eastern States Health Education Conference, 31 March–1 April 1949 (New York, 1950), p. 126.

36. New York State, Legislative Committee on Aging, *New Channels*, p. 46.

37. *Lifetime Living* 1 (June 1952): 28 (editorial).

esteem while lowering activity levels. Release from the world of work prevented embarrassment caused by "recognition of decreased abilities by others in the work group."[38]

Parallel developments were taking place in the closely related field of work and leisure. Participants in a Corning roundtable took up the relationship between leisure and retirement in 1951. Santha Rama Rau, author and student of Eastern and Western cultures, was astonished at the inability of Americans to enjoy doing nothing. It was this attitude, Rau argued at Corning, which made retirement so difficult. Businessman Henry B. Higgins, whose views were representative of participants from labor, management, and the community of professional humanists, defined the problem of retirement as one of an absence of ideas about what to do with oneself and proposed a major national effort, beginning at age fifty, to educate people into leisure. Session chairman Lynn White, Jr., president of Mills College, agreed that attitudes appropriate to retirement had to be developed during the work life. "Perhaps," he said, "we have to glamorize leisure as we have not."[39] In an essay published the next year, David Riesman constructed an interesting analogy:

> Whereas the explorers of the last century moved to the frontiers of production and opened fisheries, mines, and mills, the explorers of this century seem to me increasingly to be moving to the frontiers of consumption. They are opening up new forms of interpersonal understanding, new ways of using the home as a "plant" for leisure, new ways of using the school as a kind of community center, as the chapel of a secular religion perhaps. But frontier towns are not usually very attractive. And frontier behavior is awkward: people have not yet learned to behave comfortably in the new surroundings. There is formlessness, which takes the shape of lawlessness on the frontier of production and of aimlessness on the frontier of consumption.[40]

Had Riesman chosen to apply this analogy specifically to retirement, he could only have concluded that the retired, existing on the new frontier of leisure and consumption, would soon learn to "behave comfortably." The problem of lei-

38. Gordon F. Streib and Clement J. Schneider, *Retirement in American Society: Impact and Process* (Ithaca, N.Y., 1971), pp. 172–77; Robert N. Butler, "A Life-Cycle Perspective: Public Policies for Later Life," in Frances M. Carp, ed., *Retirement* (New York, 1972), p. 167; Robert Blauner, "Death and Social Structure," *Psychiatry* 29 (November 1966); Robert Dubin, "Industrial Workers' Worlds," in Larrabee and Meyersohn, *Mass Leisure*, p. 215.

39. Eugene Staley, ed., *Creating an Industrial Civilization: A Report on the Corning Conference*, Held Under the Auspices of the American Council of Learned Societies and the Corning Glass Works, 17–19 May 1951, Corning, N.Y. (New York, 1952), pp. 64 (quotation), 63, 65, 76.

40. David Riesman, ed., *Individualism Reconsidered: And Other Essays* (Glencoe, Ill., 1954), pp. 211–12.

sure, as Riesman defined it, lay not in leisure itself but in twentieth-century man's awkward responses to it.[41]

Others, emphasizing that the capacity for leisure could not be separated from work environment, were less optimistic about the possibility of adjustment to retirement. Fixed retirement, argued G. Warfield Hobbs, bank vice-president and chairman of the National Committee on the Aging, "negates the principle that work is a value in itself."[42] The editor of *Lifetime Living* claimed that leisure made sense only in a rhythm with work; complete retirement, by disrupting that rhythm, created leisure in an inherently unpleasant form.[43] This view received its most influential expression in 1954, with the publication of *The Meaning of Work and Retirement*, a collection of essays identified with the major contributors, Eugene A. Friedmann and Robert J. Havighurst. Assuming that retirement was a product of technological efficiency and thus, in some sense, inevitable and permanent, the authors sought to develop a framework to explain and predict experience under retirement. They isolated two variables, one historical or generational, the other work related. Friedmann's examination of steel-worker retirement in the late 1940s convinced him that part of the dissatisfaction lay in something akin to Riesman's frontier; workers had no reasonable conception either of what to expect in retirement or of their rights within the system. Retirement was an alienating phenomenon, in part because workers who had grown up in the pre-1920 work-centered society found themselves unable to adjust to the post-1920 economy of abundance, with its leisure and consumption emphases. Here the work of Friedmann and Havighurst squared with Riesman's; they had simply given definition to Riesman's frontier. Future generations of Americans, reared in the arts of leisure, would know how to play in their old age.[44]

The second variable had more ominous implications. Among coal miners and steel workers, retirement dissatisfaction was more likely to be high among those for whom work fulfilled important noneconomic needs for status, place, and social contact. Although the authors stressed the attractiveness of retirement to many groups of workers, pointed out that workers with noneconomic work interests could still be satisfied in retirement, and predicted further adjustments

41. Men were expected to suffer the most severe adjustment problems and women to help them survive the trauma. See Irene Donelson, "Help Your Husband to Retire Successfully," *Harvest Years* 1 (December 1961): 3–6.

42. Mathiasen, ed., *Flexible Retirement*, p. 5.

43. *Lifetime Living* 2 (March 1953): 14 (editorial). See also Otto Pollak, "The Older Worker in the Labor Market," in Industrial Relations Research Association, *Aged and Society*, p. 57.

44. Eugene A. Friedmann, Robert J. Havighurst, et al., *The Meaning of Work and Retirement* (Chicago, 1954), pp. 32, 37, 39, 187, 191–92, 194.

as work itself took less enjoyable forms, their conclusion from the case studies was pessimistic. "If we assume a growing tendency toward retirement," they wrote, "the problem becomes one of finding satisfactory substitutes for the work experience, bearing in mind the possibility that there may be in any occupational group . . . a hard core of workers for whom there can be no adequate substitute for the job."[45]

When Friedmann and Havighurst published their book, American society was still struggling with retirement. The leisure-work nexus was central to social adjustment. If happiness was a matter of learning to appreciate the new leisure, retirement would be amenable to standard educational processes. If, on the other hand, as Friedmann and Havighurst had also suggested, dissatisfaction in retirement was a product of the centrality of the work experience in American society, more fundamental measures might be needed to prevent the alienation of a growing segment of the population. Riesman, in fact, reached this conclusion in work published later in the decade, and he began to advocate changes in work itself as well as a redistribution of work rewards (along the lines of progressive taxation). Havighurst's conclusion was not so radical. He suggested the cultivation of role flexibility, including a reduction in the work role after age fifty.[46]

The work-centered hypothesis could lead, therefore, to a conclusion that ran counter to a century of labor-management relations. Management was unaccustomed to modifying the means of production to promote the well-being of employees. Robert Dubin pioneered an alternative approach in 1956. In an article in *Social Problems*, Dubin claimed that for three out of four industrial workers, "work and workplace *are not* central life interests." Management's efforts to make work a central life interest were misguided, at odds with "the main drift of social developments." The answer lay in the principles enunciated by the Corning conference. "Our great social inventions," wrote Dubin, "will probably not come in connection with work life; they will center in community life."[47] This analysis, common enough among sociologists in the 1960s and 1970s, could justify a laissez-faire attitude toward retirement. As work morality yielded to fun morality, as the Protestant ethic lost meaning in a society of consumption rather than production, so would retirement cease to be a wrenching, uprooting

45. Ibid., p. 186, also pp. 182, 184–86, 93, 96.
46. David Riesman, "Leisure and Work in Post-Industrial Society," in Larrabee and Meyersohn, eds., *Mass Leisure*, pp. 370–71; Robert J. Havighurst, "Flexibility and the Social Roles of the Retired," *American Journal of Sociology* 59 (January 1954): 309, 311; Clement Greenberg, "Work and Leisure Under Industrialism," in Larrabee and Meyersohn, eds., *Mass Leisure*, p. 41.
47. Dubin, "Industrial Workers' Worlds," in Larrabee and Meyersohn, eds., *Mass Leisure*, pp. 215, 226, 227.

experience requiring social treatment. In the postindustrial society, retirement was not only natural but welcome.[48]

THE SELLING OF RETIREMENT

While this academic discussion was taking place, the retired and those approaching retirement age were being exposed to a barrage of propaganda that belied the existence of options and conflicting points of view among scholars. The selling of retirement had begun. Life insurance companies, deeply involved in the pension business, were the leading purveyors of the message that retirement, far from being evidence of maladjustment, was a bounty bestowed by the society and by the pension. Like any other normal period in one's life, it required careful preparation on the part of the individual and his employer. This might involve only the development of a proper attitude. Speaking at a 1952 session of the National Industrial Conference Board, Mutual Life Insurance Company vice-president H. G. Kenagy suggested preparing employees for retirement beginning at age fifty. "Just recently," he said, "house organs that are coming to my desk have been doing a splendid job of selling the idea and pointed [*sic*] to the fact that old age can be beautiful, and that the best of life is yet to come. . . . That is done by constant stories of happily retired people telling what they do, but still more, of course, emphasizing what they did to get ready for the life they are now living."[49] Retirement, as the life insurance agents emphasized in advertisements published in over three hundred newspapers in the late 1940s, was the joy of being at the ball park on a weekday afternoon.[50]

Insurance companies were among the first institutions to create formal retirement preparation programs. At Prudential, where retirement was mandatory at sixty-five for men and at sixty for women, company officials in 1949 created such a program. At its core was a group counseling center. Although the company recognized the negative frame of mind with which great numbers of Prudential employees approached retirement and even acknowledged the fears of

48. Margaret Clark, "An Anthropological View of Retirement," in Carp, ed., *Retirement*, p. 155; *Retirement Planning News*, no. 4 (1956): 1; Marvin B. Sussman, "An Analytic Model for the Sociological Study of Retirement," in Carp, ed., *Retirement*, pp. 31, 35. Zena Smith Blau ties the institutionalization of retirement to the failure of American society to produce a revolutionary proletariat. See Blau, *Old Age in a Changing Society* (New York, 1973), p. 143.

49. National Industrial Conference Board, "Pensions in a Defense Economy," typescript, Proceedings of the 328th Meeting of the Conference Board, Thursday, 24 January 1952, New York, Waldorf-Astoria, NICB Papers, Eleutherian Mills Historical Library, box 39, p. 21.

50. Julius Hochman, "The Retirement Myth," in Haber and Cohen, eds., *Social Security*, pp. 101–02.

financial insecurity behind it, the counselors began with the assumption that "many of their fears were not realistic" and ought to be dispelled.[51] Esso Standard envisioned its preparation program as a means of convincing potentially socialistic aging persons that industry was "doing something concrete about their uncertain future." In practice, however, this meant little more than selling an Esso value structure in which retired employees were expected to see their retirement as "active, fruitful and constructive" (although the corporation, by definition, no longer considered them useful) and were supposed to understand that "retirement is something earned by faithful service, a form of 'graduation' into a new phase of life rather than a 'casting out' process" (even though they had been, in fact, cast out).[52] Ray Griest, a retirement specialist hired by Lockheed Aircraft Company to head its preparation program, concentrated almost entirely on getting retired persons involved in something with a profit-making potential, such as remodeling houses, running a part-time repair service, or invention.[53] Many other similar corporate programs were developed under the auspices of Retirement Council, Inc., an organization founded by the same Henry Schmidt who established *Lifetime Living*. As of the early 1950s, however, corporate retirement preparation seems to have been restricted to a relatively small number of larger institutions.[54]

The most extensive labor-union program was developed by the United Automobile Workers in the early 1950s. Grounded in the conviction that technology had so changed industrial processes that the future belonged to the younger worker, the UAW program anticipated that even automobile workers would suffer some sense of loss upon retirement and that compensating satisfactions were necessary if retirement was to be an enjoyable experience. The Upholstery Workers, Steelworkers, and Retail-Wholesale clerks also developed retirement preparation programs at an early date.[55] A number of educational institutions

51. Robert Travers, "They're Building a Bridge to Retirement," *Lifetime Living* 1 (October 1952): 37–40.

52. Esso Standard Oil Company, "Preparation for Retirement," *Personnel Journal* 30 (November 1951): 210–11.

53. Kay Campbell, "They Prepare Workers for Retirement," *Lifetime Living* 3 (June 1954): 25–26, 56–57.

54. Inside back cover of *Retirement Almanac, 1967* (Cos Cob, Conn., n.d.); William Exton, Jr., "Preparing Employees for Successful Retirement," *Personnel* 28 (November 1951): 271–73; Charles P. Boyle, "Helping Employees Adjust to Retirement," pt. 1: "A Survey of Pre-Retirement Practices in Industry," *Personnel* 29 (November 1952): 266–67, 269; John Kinloch, "Planned Retirement," *Shell News* 17 (June 1949): 10–11; Baker, *Retirement Procedures*, p. 49.

55. United Automobile Workers, Older and Retired Workers Department, *Work and Retirement in a Changing World*, Union Research and Education Projects, University College, University of Chicago, Discussion Guide No. 1 (Chicago, n.d.), pp. 4, 13, 17; Charles E. Odell, "Employing Older Workers in the Next Decade: Problems and Possibilities," in United Automobile Workers Papers, Labor-Management Documentation Center, Labor and Industrial Relations Institute, Cornell

had courses and programs in retirement planning by the middle of the decade.[56]

Rather than develop an alternative approach to old age, the journals serving present or prospective retirees generally subscribed to the dominant ideology, developing a popular version of the sociology of disengagement. Between 1945 and 1955, *Retirement Life*, the journal of the National Association of Retired Civil Employees, muted its concern with employment discrimination and politics (except for its efforts to increase annuities) and was increasingly filled with the poems on leisure, the photos of retirement ceremonies, and the stories on hobbies and crafts that made up the mythology of retirement. The editors of *Retirement Planning News* chose the first issue, published in 1956, to express their dissatisfaction with the word *retirement*, since it was "likely to mean retirement from life, a withdrawal from the active world." Why not the "fulfillment years," a time of "opportunity to fulfill lifelong desires to do things he never quite had time to do before"?[57] While the new term at least promised an active old age, it also implied acceptance of the limitations on working age established by capital and labor. *Modern Maturity* was more concerned for the employment problems of older workers but continued to see retirement not as an unfortunate institution but as something for which older Americans were psychologically unprepared.[58]

Senior Citizen, first published in January 1955, epitomized the extent to which the ideology of retirement could be internalized by those most affected. Its creator and editor, Joy Elmer Morgan, had for thirty-four years been editor of the journal of the National Education Association. Although he could have remained with the NEA following his sixty-fifth birthday in 1954, Morgan believed in mandatory retirement, with limits related to the character of the occupation. Flexible retirement was appropriate to positions requiring experience, judgment, and wisdom; mandatory retirement was well suited to most factory and day-labor employment. From Francis Townsend, whom Morgan respected for his sincerity and intelligence, Morgan had absorbed an explanatory system. In this system, technology had created both unemployment and, through a surfeit of goods and a growing concentration of wealth, the absence of demand on which to base additional employment. As Townsend had focused on youth, so did Morgan. Peculiarly vulnerable to the alienation of unemployment, potentially violent, and expensive to care for, the young had to have work. When

University, Ithaca, New York, box 91e, file "Older and Retired Workers Department," p. 9; UAW, Older and Retired Workers Department, *Handbook on Retired Workers* (Detroit, 1957), same file.

56. *Lifetime Living* 2 (January 1953): 10; Kathryn Close, *Getting Ready to Retire*, Public Affairs Committee, Inc., *Pamphlet* No. 182 (New York, 1952), p. 21.

57. *Retirement Planning News*, no. 1 (1956): 1 (editorial).

58. *Modern Maturity* 1 (December 1958–January 1959): 10.

Morgan left the NEA for his voluntary labors, he was acting within the Townsend framework; he believed he was exercising his option to create employment by withdrawing from the regular labor market.[59]

In more subtle form, Morgan's publication and his new organization, the Senior Citizens of America, brought this message to some ten thousand largely middle-class readers: teachers, school superintendents, preachers, legislators. Morgan had anticipated the stresses of his own retirement, and he expected his readers to do the same. The term *senior citizen*, he wrote, was intended to describe a mature, responsible, spiritually self-disciplined person who had taken control of his present and future existence. Forty was an age for taking stock, for planning life's remaining years, and for developing the intellectual habits and tastes that would sustain one before and after retirement. "Failure to face the later years and to plan for them," Morgan wrote, "is a sign of infantilism and immaturity."[60]

THE MYTHOLOGY OF INDIVIDUAL RESPONSIBILITY

At this critical juncture in the history of retirement, one might reasonably anticipate a comprehensive examination of the institution and its role in the economy, if not in American life. Nothing of the kind took place. Indeed, the response to the important questions raised by retirement was at its best ritualistic and symbolic; at its worst, a form of blaming the victim. The keynote, perhaps, was the attempt to redefine symbolically the place and function of the aged and, at the same time, to involve the retired in this process of redefinition. The central element in this redefinition was the notion of responsibility; its foremost advocate was the American Association of Retired Persons (AARP), founded by Dr. Ethel Percy Andrus in 1955. As Andrus later recalled, her attempts to secure the cooperation of private insurance companies in providing health insurance for older persons had consistently failed because of the industry's "false and immature fears of aging." Then and later in the decade, Andrus was selling a particular conception of the old: independent, vigorous, purposeful people who "considered themselves as persons seeking solutions to America's problems—not being themselves a problem and a hopeless one at that."[61] Under her leadership, AARP

59. Personal Interview with Joy Elmer Morgan, 8 November 1976, Washington, D.C. (transcripts in author's possession).

60. *Senior Citizen* 1 (September 1955): 3–4 (editorial); ibid. (January 1955): 3; ibid. (March 1955): 3–4 (editorial); ibid. (April 1955): 3–4 (editorial); ibid. (June 1955): 3–4 (editorial); ibid. 3 (February 1957): 3–4 (editorial); ibid. (June 1957): 11–12 (editorial).

61. *AARP News Bulletin* 3 (September 1962): 1.

accepted the prevailing analysis of the origins of retirement, including the re-placement of a work-centered society by a leisure-centered one. To prevent old people from becoming a major burden on "their children, the community, and the total economy," retirement had, however, to be recast as a "period of pro-ductive and useful activity."[62] As the AARP by-laws stressed, the retired were expected to be active agents and participants in this process. Competence in retirement was an earned privilege, not an inherent right. Although AARP was interested in work as an alternative to retirement, its concern was perfunctory. The organization was sufficiently nonthreatening that companies regularly fi-nanced AARP memberships for their older workers.[63]

The theme of individual responsibility continued to be strong into the early 1960s. *Harvest Years*, a new retirement journal whose editor had held public-relations positions with the California and Hawaiian Sugar Company and with Smith-Corona Marchant, offered its first issue to guest editor Louis Kuplan, president of the International Association of Gerontology. In "The Individual's Responsibility in Retirement," Kuplan idealized a retirement that approached the asocial. "We must not," he insisted, "become dependent spiritually, socially, physically or financially upon relatives, friends or government."[64] That same year, the White House Conference on Aging produced a lengthy list of "obliga-tions of the aging," which Kuplan must have found reassuring. The conference was firm in its conviction that "the individual will assume primary responsibility for self-reliance in old age," though it was unable to decide if this was a rec-ommendation or an assumption.[65] When programs for the aging were placed under the direction of the welfare division of the Department of Health, Educa-tion, and Welfare in 1963, AARP and other organizations protested, again from the perspective of responsibility. Charles Odell, director of the Older and Retired Workers Department of the UAW, said: "I know there are at least a few persons who share with me the feeling that we are moving backward to the 'county

---

62. *Modern Maturity* 1 (October–November 1958): 11.

63. The bylaws are in *AARP News Bulletin* 5 (September 1964): 3; *Modern Maturity* 2 (October–November 1959): 31; *AARP News Bulletin* 1 (September 1960): 11. AARP's conservative stance, resembling that of Morgan's Senior Citizens of America, likely was a function of its origins in and early involvement with the National Retired Teachers Association. Relative to other occupa-tions, teachers had participated in their retirement programs, and they were suited, by education, to the prevailing ideology of social responsibility. See *AARP News Bulletin* 1 (July 1959): 3; ibid. (January 1960): 2.

64. *Harvest Years* 1 (15 February 1961): 7, 49.

65. Ibid. 1 (June 1961): 18; Donald P. Kent, "Social Services and Social Policy," in John C. McKinney and Frank T. de Vyver, eds., *Aging and Social Policy* (New York, 1966), p. 212. The editorial director of *Harvest Years* participated on the advisory committee for the White House con-ference.

poorhouse approach' rather than forward to the 'rights and responsibilities' approach."[66]

THE OLDER WORKER AND EMPLOYMENT

The alternative to retirement is work. That truism suggests the possibility of evaluating a society's commitment to a reassessment of retirement in terms of its treatment of older workers, particularly those over sixty or sixty-five. How did the society analyze the problem of the older worker? To what extent did the proposed solutions promise some reasonable resolution? An answer to the first question must begin with the observation that by the 1950s, analysts of the American employment scene had all but given up on the oldest elements of the population; their concern, as usual, was with the middle-aged, the workers over forty-five who had always had difficulty securing new employment after a job interruption. This group was on the verge of an intense job competition with the products of the World War II baby boom in 1955, when Secretary of Labor James P. Mitchell and President Dwight Eisenhower raised the question to prominence for the first time since the Frances Perkins–Roosevelt efforts of 1939. As Mitchell's lieutenants informed him, the problem was already serious. Substantial numbers of older workers were withdrawing from the labor force, having given up the search for employment. Of those between sixty and sixty-four, the withdrawal rate was 15.2 percent; of those between fifty-five and fifty-nine, 7.2 percent.[67]

Mitchell's incoming correspondence contained a variety of suggestions. One woman proposed reducing the age of eligibility for social security to forty-five, changing the insurance laws, and establishing shops in which older men could ply unwanted trades. A man suggested that it might be a good idea to give women equality with men. Like men, they should be encouraged to retire at an early age. If this were done, and if plant managers did not discriminate unduly, "between the two perhaps a fellow over 40 could *get* a job." Others asked for the names and addresses of firms that Mitchell had mentioned as employing older persons. They were directed to their employment bureaus. Eisenhower's

66. *Harvest Years* 3 (October 1963): 41; *AARP News Bulletin* 5 (March 1964): 2. See also Clark Tibbitts, "Retirement Problems in American Society," *American Journal of Sociology* 59 (January 1954): 306–07; National Association of Manufacturers, Industrial Relations Department, Policy Committee Division, *Retirement in a Free Society* (New York, 1954), pp. 3–6.

67. Raushenbush, *Pensions*, i, 50, 85; RG 174, Department of Labor, Office of Secretary (DL, OS), 1954, Organization Subject Files, box 74, file "Report Submitted to the Bureau of the Budget F.Y. 1956," section on older worker, p. 9. See also Joseph J. Spengler, "The Aging of Individuals and Populations: Its Macroeconomic Aspects," in McKinney and de Vyver, eds., *Aging*, p. 54.

1955 Labor Day address prompted a letter from a woman who had failed to find a job. It concluded: "We are parents. We are voters. We are citizens. And, be it ever so little, we are influencial [*sic*]. There are those among us who are driven to destruction, who are driven to question our economic system, who are driven to unethical practices, and who are driven to desperation."[68]

In 1955, the labor department sought funds to create an interagency Committee on Employment of the Older Worker, which would seek to determine if employment opportunities could be extended to the forty-five-to-sixty-four group "while at the same time youth who seek jobs are also given the opportunity to enter business and industry."[69] Such realism was unusual. For the most part, the treatment of age discrimination came up against the same confining analytical frameworks then being applied to racial issues. Discrimination was a mental state, grounded in prejudices that, said Mitchell, "are entirely out of step with modern industrial reality."[70] Production executives and personnel managers stereotyped older workers as less efficient and more costly in terms of overhead. "Age barriers," said Newell Brown, assistant secretary of labor and the chairman of the Federal Council of Aging, "are largely created by what men think."[71]

This analysis of the employment problems of older workers was of limited value as a stimulus to policy formulation. It simplified the problem unduly and yet made it incredibly complex. When employers learned the facts about older workers, age discrimination would disappear. But this would require a long-term program of education, a "wholesale change in attitudes," a "revolution in thinking."[72] So overwhelming did the task appear that state lawmakers were reluctant to pass antidiscrimination legislation, which they assumed would be ineffective. As a result, as late as 1957 legislation prohibiting discrimination on the basis of age was in force in only a few states. Federal antidiscrimination legislation, finally passed in 1967, proved difficult to enforce and, by establishing sixty-five

68. Mrs. Geo. Barry to James P. Mitchell, no date, RG 174, DL, OS, 1955, Organization Subject Files, box 108, file "Advisory Committee on Older Workers, January–September"; Jos. W. Lucas, Jr. to Mitchell, 19 November 1955, ibid., file "1955—COMMITTEE—Advisory Committee on the Older Workers (December)"; Margarette C. Matthews to Eisenhower, 25 September 1955, same file as Barry letter, above.

69. From "Report Submitted to the Bureau of the Budget F.Y. 1956," section on older worker, p. 10, cited note 67 above; T. Lynn Smith, ed., *Problems of America's Aging Population*, Southern Conference on Gerontology, Institute of Gerontology Series, vol. 1 (Gainesville, Fla., 1951), p. 30; remarks by Assistant Secretary of HEW Wilbur Cohen, in *Harvest Years* 3 (October 1963): 42.

70. *Modern Maturity* 1 (December 1958–January 1959): 33.

71. Ibid. 2 (August–September 1959): 11; New York State, Legislature, Joint Legislative Committee on Problems of the Aging, *Brightening the Senior Years* (n.p., 1957), pp. 20, 87.

72. California, Governor, *Proceedings of the Governor's Conference on the Problems of the Aging*, Sacramento, 15 and 16 October 1951 (n.p., n.d.), p. 62; John L. Thurston, "First National Conference on Aging: A Preview of Maturity," *Industrial and Labor Relations Review* 4 (January 1951): 169; *Problems of Aging*, ed. Shock, p. 92.

as the maximum age of legal protection, served to justify and encourage mandatory retirement of workers over that age.[73]

Between 1955 and 1965, no single solution to the employment problems of older workers received the attention given to retraining. The same analysis and specific mechanism were also applied to racial job discrimination. A Senate committee investigating unemployment insurance in 1931 had made the first tentative suggestions along these lines, but the most important antecedent from the 1930s was the widely held view that remediable physical defects were preventing the employment of significant numbers of workers who had passed middle age.[74] By the mid-1950s, with the appearance of scholarly works emphasizing the changing job mix of a presumably postindustrial society, retraining seemed an obvious answer,[75] and within a decade it had become the federal government's basic approach to manpower problems. Although the retraining was usually associated with, and applied to, delinquent youth, older workers seemed on the verge of acquiring a larger share of available funds.[76] Few recognized that in the absence of full employment, retraining was not a mechanism for creating employment but rather a device for redistributing existing jobs. To the extent that older workers were its beneficiaries, others—youth, blacks, the handicapped, veterans, women—would find their own difficulties increased. The same applies to the strenuous efforts of federal, state, municipal, and private employment agencies to counsel and place older workers.[77]

73. New York State, *Brightening Senior Years*, pp. 25–26; California, *Governor's Conference, 1951*, p. 64; E. E. Liebhafsky, "Unemployment and Labor-Force Participation," in Kreps, ed., *Technology, Manpower*, p. 104; U.S., Congress, House, Select Committee on Aging, *Retirement Age Policies: Hearings*, 2 pts., 59th Cong., 1st sess., 16 and 17 March 1977 (Washington, D.C., 1977), 1: 7; 2: 5.

74. U.S., Congress, Senate, Select Committee on Unemployment Insurance, *Unemployment Insurance: Hearings Pursuant to S. Res. 483*, A Resolution Establishing a Select Committee to Investigate Unemployment Insurance Systems, 72d Cong., 1st sess., 2 April, 19, 22 October, 5, 6, 12, 13 November, 10 December 1931 (Washington, D.C., 1932), pp. 586–87; Eugene Lyman Fiske, "The Care of the Older Employee," *National Safety News* 24 (November 1931): 24–25; *New York Times*, 30 March 1939, p. 25.

75. On the postindustrial society and the transformation of work, see the articles in *Dissent* (Winter 1972). One might begin with Daniel Bell, "The Post-Industrial Society: The Evolution of an Idea," *Survey* (Spring 1971).

76. Eleanor Roosevelt, "Aging in the Modern World," *Modern Maturity* 1 (October–November 1958): 23; "Notes on Youth," 1938, typescript, Eleanor Roosevelt Papers, Franklin Delano Roosevelt Library, Hyde Park, New York, box 3030; Fred A. Auman, "Retraining—How Much of an Answer to Technological Unemployment?" *Personnel Journal* 41 (November 1962): 507; Seymour L. Wolfbeing, "Measures to Improve Employability and Increase Work Opportunities," in Orbach and Tibbitts, eds., *Aging and Economy*, p. 63; Gerald C. Somers, "Retraining the Unemployed Older Worker," in Kreps, ed., *Technology, Manpower*, pp. 110–13, 123.

77. *National Safety News* 39 (April 1939): 81; *Business Week*, 1 September 1945, pp. 104–08; *Harvest Years* 1 (March 1961): 12–13; *Retirement Planning News* 5 (March 1960): 2; Ralph Johnstone, "Experience Unlimited," *Harvest Years* 2 (October 1962): 36–39. On full employment, see Elliott Currie, "The Politics of Jobs: Humphrey-Hawkins and the Dilemmas of Full Employment,"

The older the worker, the more circumscribed the job possibilities. The curious array of employment programs open to workers over sixty is itself evidence of the difficulty of finding work to supplement incomes steadily eroded by inflation. Some were private, some public, others had characteristics of each. Of the purely private experiments, the best known was Sunset Industries, a nonprofit project developed in the early 1950s with capital from Boston-area businessmen and private foundations. Its founders were critical of current charitable practices, concerned about the economic cost of age discrimination in old-age assistance, taxes, and productivity declines, and they had come to believe that some of the problems then generally handled under geriatic medicine might be soluble through work. The company hired only workers over sixty years of age, paid wages comparable to local profit-making industries, and sold its textiles in competitive markets. Within fifteen months of the opening, Sunset had plants located in Haverhill and Stoneham, Massachusetts, and in Bangor, Maine.[78]

Less ambitious but more typical, American Geriatrics Enterprises of St. Paul, Minnesota employed fourteen older workers repairing "skids" (wooden platforms for storing and moving goods) and in the repairing, painting, and stenciling of beverage cases. It was organized as a stock company with working capital supplied by bankers, businessmen, and civic leaders. Employees earned minimal wages, averaging $12 per day.[79] Chicago's Senior Achievement, Inc. was established in 1956 when existing agencies failed to find employment for older workers. Employees—95 percent of whom were receiving social security—performed a variety of tasks subcontracted by area manufacturers and made such items as tie racks, handlooms, and picture frames for Marshall Field and The Fair Store. Its combination of municipal sponsorship and private funding also worked in Philadelphia, where employees of The Elder Craftsmen, averaging over seventy-six years of age, made dresses, handbags, neckties, ornaments, and ash trays for sale on a consignment basis.[80]

With the possible exception of Sunset Industries, all of these efforts would have qualified as "sheltered workshops," a term describing the growing number of nonprofit service enterprises sponsored by charitable or welfare organizations and producing goods for local consumption.[81] They are reminders of how easily

Socialist Revolution 7 (March–April 1977): 93–114; Bailey, *Congress Makes a Law*, pp. 50, 107, 113, 123, 128–29.

78. Robert Travers, "No One Under 60 Need Apply," *Lifetime Living* 3 (June 1954): 52–54, 58–59.

79. *Modern Maturity* 2 (August–September 1959): 17; ibid. 2 (July–September 1959): 28–29.

80. *Retirement Planning News* 3 (March 1958): 1–2; *Modern Maturity* 3 (April–May 1960): 32–34.

81. Ethel Stein, "Sheltered Workshops," *Harvest Years* 4 (December 1964): 14–15.

private social-reform efforts could assume forms potentially, if not actually, exploitative. A few cities also had private or public community agencies specializing in securing employment for retired workers. The first, established in New York in 1953, was affiliated with that city's Federation of Jewish Philanthropies. Cleveland had a program for using retired persons as volunteers in community service projects. It, too, was under Jewish auspices.[82]

RETIREMENT AND EMPLOYMENT: THE FLORIDA MYTHOLOGY

Few opportunities awaited those who expected to find employment in the retirement states of Florida and California. The opportunities were probably better in Arkansas and Mississippi; these states, at least, were aggressively recruiting the retired by advertising employment possibilities. Through 1955, however, Florida's literature also emphasized the "endless opportunities to start small services and business ventures." Those about to retire wanted to have such information, and many expected to stay active and supplement pensions and social security with a small business. Instead, some found part-time work in the retail trades or an outlet for their savings and energies in marginally profitable industries like motel management—the remnants of competitive, entrepreneurial capitalism. The most fortunate made good money and found themselves quickly up against the income limits of social security. Most found a flourishing economy, but one from which they were, as producers, excluded.[83]

SUMMARY

What they found was retirement, that now triumphant version of the American dream. In the Progressive Era, a methodology of economic and social efficiency; in the 1930s, a way of insuring social order under conditions of wide-

82. *Retirement Planning News* 2 (June 1957): 4; National Council of Jewish Women, Inc., "A Senior Service Corp," Proceedings of the Senior Service Corp Institute, January 1963, mimeographed, in Papers of the Cleveland Section of the National Council of Jewish Women, Western Reserve Historical Society Library, Cleveland, box 12, folder 5. *Modern Maturity* was aggressively entrepreneurial until 1961. After that date, although the journal continued to advocate a vigorous retirement, it did so outside the context of the marketplace. See the series by Harold P. Winchester, "Maturing Creatively," one part of which is in *Modern Maturity* 3 (December 1960–January 1961): 32–33.

83. Lawrence Westbrook, "Arkansas," *Lifetime Living* 3 (January 1954): 56; Hodding Carter, "Mississippi's Gulf Coast," ibid. 3 (February 1954): 79; William R. Clelland, "Florida," ibid. 2 (January 1953): 38, 42, 63 (quotation); William H. Harlan, "Community Adaptation to the Presence of Aged Persons: St. Petersburg, Florida," *American Journal of Sociology* 59 (January 1954): 332–39; George and Jane Dusenbury, *How to Retire in Florida* (New York, 1947), p. 200; Raymond Maxwell, "So You'd Like to Run a Motel!" *Lifetime Living* 1 (August 1952): 20–22, 63.

spread joblessness—retirement was now all this and more, a full-fledged ideology, embodying a way of life and a way of thinking about the experience of being old.

This transformation took place under the aegis of corporate capitalists, for whom retirement remained a mechanism of efficiency and took on added importance as insurance against another Great Depression; under labor unions, who traded the job rights of older workers for the security of the pension and who could usually negotiate a retirement benefit even in periods of recession; under academics, most of them sociologists and leisure theorists, whose new paradigms of aging emphasized withdrawal and disengagement from work and the workplace and served as a rationale for retirement; under social service workers, who increasingly defined the needs of older people in terms of social activity outside the job.

By 1960, the ideology of retirement had been assimilated by *Modern Maturity*, *Retirement Planning News*, and other journals at the cutting edge of the new industry of retirement. These journals, and organizations representing older people and the retired, stopped conceiving of work as a realistic alternative to retirement. They were reduced to articulating a philosophy of "individual responsibility" which was little more than a response to charges that the aged were fast becoming a dangerously dependent population. In large measure they responded this way because there were no alternatives; Eisenhower's policies toward the employment of older workers were typical in their lack of substance. More than anything else, it was this absence of options which defined the triumph of retirement.

9 The Reconsideration of Retirement: The 1970s

Retirement's triumph was short-lived. By the late 1970s, about two decades after the institution reached its peak of influence and acceptance, retirement was in retreat. At every level of government, legislatures and commissions reviewed the complex web of retirement institutions. Pension plans, mandatory retirement, early retirement, retirement on disability, even social security were all weighed and evaluated. Participants in this process of reconsideration liked to place this movement in the history of American reform; just as antidiscrimination legislation of the 1960s was designed to liberate blacks and women from unfair obstacles to employment, so the attack on retirement was, according to this liberal mythology, nothing less than liberation for older people from enforced unemployment.

Though not without some substance, this explanation is inadequate. Retirement is being reconsidered because, as an institution, it has become too costly to maintain and because, as a mechanism of efficiency, it has become counterproductive. For the history of retirement, these ideas are new, peculiar to the 1970s; for the history of older people, however, they are restatements of a central theme developed throughout this book: in the last century, older people have been used to service the needs of larger and more powerful elements of the population. Until recently, many of these needs were met by moving older persons out of factories, government offices, the professions, and other labor markets; in the 1970s and 1980s, a new range of goals will be achieved by reversing this process and dismantling the edifice of retirement.

STATES, CITIES, THE PRIVATE SECTOR

The mid-1970s review of state and municipal retirement programs was designed to head off potentially serious funding problems. The chairman of the Massachusetts Retirement Law Commission, Carmen W. Elio, has warned of eventual bankruptcy should municipal plans—demonstrably weaker than state plans—continue to be haphazardly funded.[1] A recent investigation of public plans by a House of Representatives task force has turned up a variety of problems: the inability of local jurisdictions to depend on taxing authority as a source of short-term, emergency funding; pay-as-you-go financing in some 20 percent of state and local plans; inadequate or nonexistent actuarial practices (a fourth of the local plans had not undergone an actuarial evaluation in the last ten years); the frequent use of outdated mortality assumptions; temporary pension plan insolvencies or similar difficulties in Hamtramck, Michigan, Toledo and Lakewood, Ohio, and other cities. The investigation also revealed, however, that public-employee retirement systems have suffered few plan terminations and insolvencies and that permanent benefit losses have been rare. Eighty percent of the plans utilize the safer system of reserve funding.[2]

If the severity of the problem is not yet clear, governments have already begun the process of evaluation and repair. Many states have created retirement commissions. In 1976 a number of cities, including New York, were close to terminating coverage under social security in order to save money. By the end of 1975, 322 local municipal jurisdictions, covering 44,700 employees, had exercised their legal right to terminate. The Metropolitan Washington Council of Governments withdrew in 1976.[3]

In 1977, Los Angeles residents turned in a 58 percent majority in a referendum abolishing compulsory retirement ages for public employees and allowing those who could pass an annual physical examination to continue working. In Seattle, Mayor Wes Uhlman accomplished the same result through an executive order.[4] Opponents of mandatory retirement in the legislature of the state of Maine mustered enough votes to override a veto of a bill prohibiting forced retirement of public employees solely on the basis of age and mandating a study to determine whether the retirement ban should be extended to the private sector. State, county, and municipal employees, including teachers, came under the Maine law. Officials in New York State's Office for the Aging were pressing for similar action.[5]

1. Neal R. Peirce, "Defusing the Public-Pension Time Bomb," *Washington Post*, 27 August 1977, sec. A, p. 15.

2. U.S., Congress, House, Pension Task Force, *Report*, prepublication draft.

3. U.S., Congress, House, Committee on Ways and Means, Subcommittee on Social Security, *Coverage and Termination of Coverage of Government and Nonprofit Organization Employees Under the Social Security System: Hearings*, 94th Cong., 2d sess., 26, 27, 28 April 1976 (Washington, D.C., 1976), pp. 57–58.

4. Donald H. May, "Retire at 65? Many Deplore It," *Chicago Tribune*, 5 June 1977, sec. 1, p. 41.

5. Bureau of National Affairs, *BNA Pension Reporter*, no. 149, p. A–5. Hereafter cited as *BPR*

Also under attack were the most obvious excesses of existing retirement systems. In the District of Columbia, for example, the public learned that police and fire fighters routinely accrued additional retirement income by retiring on disability. In the worst year, 1969, 98 percent of all retirements from these departments were disability retirements. When several high-ranking police and fire officials filed for disability retirements in quick succession in early 1978 (one for hypertension; another for a back injury suffered in a fall in 1943), the city's newspapers took up the campaign. By summer the House Appropriations Committee had significantly reduced the D.C. retirement budget.[6]

Disaffection with these practices arises, however, less from some newfound sense of moral outrage than from the importance of these abuses as symbols of the fragility and even the potential destructiveness of our income-security programs. What seems most egregious now was at one point built into the system. To attract persons to dangerous occupations (law enforcement, fire fighting, the military), we offered those willing to engage in such activities a reduced work life, substantial resources with which to enjoy their leisure, and, in the case of the military, the right to receive a pension and continue working (a practice called double-dipping). In a public letter in defense of his hypertension-induced retirement, D.C. assistant chief of police Tilmon O'Bryant explicitly invoked the contractual nature of the process. "I have lived up to my end of the agreement," he said, "and the police department has also kept its promise."[7] That we now define these benefits as excessive says less about some objective injustice that has taken place than it does about our increasing desire to bring the social insurance systems under control by making them cost-efficient.

Private plans, interestingly, are in better shape than their federal, state, and local counterparts, largely because of strict funding requirements under the 1974 Employee Retirement Income Security Act (ERISA), which takes projected demographic characteristics into account. Two difficulties remain in the private sector: liabilities accrued and not funded before ERISA went into effect; and multiemployer plan terminations in declining industries such as millinery and milk driving. Neither should prove especially troublesome in the decades to come. Some multiemployer plans are, and all will be, insured by the Pension

149: A–5. U.S., Congress, House, Select Committee on Aging, *Retirement Age Policies: Hearings before the Select Committee on Aging*, 95th Cong., 1st sess., 16 and 17 March 1977, 2 pts. (Washington, D.C., 1977), 2: 160–90.

6. Ron Shaffer, "No Challenge to Pension of Fire Chief," *Washington Post*, 25 February 1978, sec. B, p. 1; Jack Eisen, "Retirement Fund for City Disabled Slashed on Hill," *Washington Post*, 14 July 1978, sec. A, pp. 1, 6; Ron Shaffer, "D.C. Fire Chief Johnson Traces Disability to Injury in 1943," *Washington Post*, 23 February 1978, sec. C, pp. 1, 5; letter Tilmon B. O'Bryant, *Washington Post*, 4 March 1978, sec. A, p. 16.

7. Letter Tilmon B. O'Bryant, *Washington Post*, 4 March 1978, sec. A, p. 16.

Benefit Guaranty Corporation (PBGC), a public agency with its own actuarially based system of insurance. The pre-ERISA obligations will burden the younger workers who must pay them, but according to the PBGC, this process will have been completed before the second and third decades of the twenty-first century, when the population's changing demographic structure will place special burdens of support on its youth.[8]

⟡ THE NATIONAL GOVERNMENT AND MANDATORY RETIREMENT

Although congressional interest in mandatory retirement has been of several years duration, the arrival in Washington in January 1977 of a Democratic administration interested in matters of social welfare brought a heightened sense of reality and importance to the flurry of proposals for revamping the nation's retirement system. Seventy-seven-year-old Admiral Hyman Rickover was the first witness at House hearings on double-dipping. He suggested consolidating fifty-five current civilian and military retirement programs into a single pension system of interchangeable credits.[9] In June, a three-judge federal court held unconstitutional State Department regulations requiring retirement of Foreign Service officers at age sixty. The State Department claimed early mandatory retirement was necessary in order to provide opportunity for younger employees, and because the work of Foreign Service officers presented "unusual physical and psychological difficulties." The judges found the first argument discriminatory on the basis of age, the second fallacious in light of the duties of other overseas personnel.[10]

House and Senate committees actively studied retirement. Under its seventy-six-year-old chairman, Florida Democrat Claude Pepper, the House Select Committee on Aging held two days of hearings on retirement-age policies. National cochairman of Senior Citizens for Carter during the recent presidential campaign, Pepper saw the elimination of mandatory retirement in the federal government as a first step in a more comprehensive program. With some seventy House cosponsors, he introduced a bill to that effect.[11] The most discussed legislation, however, was H.R. 5383, which in late July received a favorable report

---

8. Pension Benefit Guaranty Corporation (PBGC), "Potential Multiemployer Plan Liabilities Under Title IV of ERISA," 29 September 1977 (n.p., n.d.); PBGC, "Analysis of Single Employer Defined Benefit Plan Terminations, 1976," Publication No. PBGC 505 (n.p., n.d.); author's conversations with PBGC employees.

9. Mike Causey, "Rickover's Pension Plan," *Washington Post*, 27 July 1977, pt. C, p. 2.

10. Timothy S. Robinson, "Foreign Service Early Retirement is Ruled Illegal," *Washington Post*, 29 June 1977, pp. 1, 8.

11. House, Select Committee on Aging, *Retirement Age Policies: Hearings*, 1: 1–3.

from the House Committee on Education and Labor. This bill incorporated Pepper's provisions for federal workers but also sought to restrict mandatory retirement among workers in state, local, and private employment by raising from sixty-five to seventy the current upper age limit in the Age Discrimination in Employment Act of 1967.[12]

Meeting with the members of the House Select Committee on Aging, Carter said he "wanted to take into consideration the extension of that age in which people can live normal productive lives." As an example of the possibilities of living an active and even "inspiring" life after sixty-five, Carter cited his mother, Lillian, a Peace Corp nurse in India a decade earlier at the age of sixty-eight.[13] In early 1978, House and Senate agreed on a measure that raised the permissible mandatory retirement age from sixty-five to seventy in public and private employment and uncapped the age-seventy mandatory provision for federal employees.[14] Jimmy Carter signed the bill in April 1978, encouraging similar legislation in other political jurisdictions.[15]

THE POLITICAL ECONOMY OF RETIREMENT

We are in the midst of a genuine movement for social change. But why now? Why, in what has all the earmarks of a classically conservative decade, should our politicians be so forcefully opposed to the perpetuation of age discrimination? One set of answers to this question, which I have labeled liberal, explains social reform as the inevitable triumph of a benign, informed world view over ignorance, myth, and immorality. This is essentially Congress's conception of its role. As an explanatory device it is not only ahistorical but contrary to the evidence. The attack on age discrimination can only be understood in the context of the new national and international economic order of the 1970s and as one of a series of undertakings, here termed the New Efficiency, for which Carter is the primary spokesman. Advocates of the New Efficiency perceive the elimination of mandatory retirement as part of a larger process of strengthening and reinvigorating an economy in decline. (The economic decline may or may not be taking place, and the elimination of mandatory retirement may prove to

12. U.S., Congress, House, Committee on Education and Labor, *Age Discrimination in Employment Act, Amendments of 1977: Report* to Accompany H.R. 5383, H.R. 527, 95th Cong., 1st sess., 25 July 1977 (Washington, D.C., 1977), p. 1.

13. Bureau of National Affairs, *Taxation and Finance Report*, no. 137, p. G–5. Hereafter cited as *DER* 137: G–5. House, Select Committee on Aging, *Retirement Age Policies: Hearings*, 1: 2.

14. *BPR* 163: A–11. The legislation exempts executives eligible for large pensions at age sixty-five, and—until July 1, 1982—tenured professors.

15. *BPR* 178: A–20: Edward Walsh, "New Law Sets 70 as Retirement Age; President Advocates an Expansion," *Washington Post*, 7 April 1978, sec. A, p. 2.

be inefficient. The *perception* of decline, and of the role that the elimination of mandatory retirement can play in ending that decline, is all-important.) To the extent that this effort affirms the existence of standards by which to measure efficiency, and the need to apply such standards to determine individual productivity, the movement also reflects powerful demands for order and stability within American society.

According to the liberal view, any form of age discrimination is bad, its elimination is good, and the journey from one to the other is only a matter of time and knowledge. New York senator Jacob Javits captured something of this ideology of progress when he expressed his wish that the old-age measure that had cleared his Human Resources Subcommittee would be "a new Magna Carta for older people."[16] Age discrimination is seen as analogous to other forms of discrimination—racial, religious, sexual, and ethnic. Like racial discrimination, it is morally wrong, contrary to the Constitution, and potentially destructive of the social fabric. Wrote Congressman William F. Walsh in a statement to the House Select Committee:

> The Nation has finally learned that Black men and women . . . are entitled to the same opportunities for life, liberty, and the pursuit of happiness as those of us who are light-skinned. You would think we had learned from the Black experience that discrimination is patently unjust and will be overcome by one means or another. Would it not be easier to make that process voluntary, or must our senior citizens stage demonstrations and sit-ins to convince us they, too, have every right to equal treatment under the law?[17]

This statement—this version of the liberal explanation for social change—only begs the question, for it fails to account for the historical timing of the reform movement. Why is the political system especially receptive, at this moment in history, to the claims of the aged? One liberal response is that there is new evidence—on the impact of retirement, on its incidence, on the meaning of old age. This new evidence is credited with dispelling long-accepted and deeply held mythic views of old age; as reality confronts myth, social change becomes possible. Discrimination is defined as a product of "agism," of "rigidity of thought," of "folklore," of the "notion . . . that once you hit sixty-five, you take

---

16. *BPR* 148: A–6.

17. House, Select Committee on Aging, *Retirement Age Policies: Hearings*, 1: 9 and 2: 88 (Harold Sheppard testimony). The term *senior citizen* reflects the society's wish that this group would act responsibly as well as the group's own self-definition. Joy Elmer Morgan, founder of Senior Citizens of America in the 1950s, claimed in his journal that the words were intended to describe a mature, responsible, spiritually self-disciplined person who had taken control of his present and future existence. "Failure to face the later years and to plan for them," Morgan wrote, "is a sign of infantilism and immaturity" (*Senior Citizen* 1 [September 1955]: 3–4 (editorial), and other issues).

a lockstep into old age."[18] Senator Harrison A. Williams, Jr., opening hearings on age discrimination before his Subcommittee on Labor of the Committee on Human Resources, described the problems affecting thousands of older workers denied employment or turned out of present jobs: "They are the victims of pervasive, ill-founded myths which have distorted our society's vision of the aged. The plain truth is that misconceptions regarding the older worker's own desires and abilities are the sole basis for relegating these valuable employees to private lives of stagnation and decline." The Labor Department's Donald E. Elisburg, the administration's primary witness before Williams's committee, agreed. "Denial of equal employment opportunity," he said, "flows from stereotypes and prejudices against one group or another."[19] This ideological bias lifts mandatory retirement out of the material and social conditions that produced it. Age discrimination, it would seem, functions on the basis of a massive misunderstanding. It must, therefore, be amenable to education, to the new evidence.

This explanation founders on the very absence of such new evidence. In the medical area, only Dr. Susan Haynes, a medical researcher at the National Heart, Lung, and Blood Institute in Bethesda, Maryland, presented Congress with significant new data, purporting to show a higher than normal incidence of mortality in the third and fourth years after mandatory retirement. There is no evidence, however, that Haynes's study was known *before* congressional committees became interested in the problem, nor are the policy implications of the Haynes data inherently obvious. Although studies emphasizing the abilities and talents of older workers continue to appear, similar studies, equally persuasive at the time they were carried out and arriving at similar conclusions, have been commonplace since the 1940s.[20] A Louis Harris survey on aging, conducted for the National Council on Aging in 1974 and much discussed during House and Senate hearings, produced no genuine revelations. Its primary conclusions—that mandatory retirement was generally unpopular among retirees and yet increasingly common—were not new.[21]

Proponents of reform also have a historical rationale that contrasts past

18. House, Select Committee on Aging, *Retirement Age Policies: Hearings*, 2: 2–4, 16. Three of these phrases are Pepper's. He has, of course, offered other explanations.

19. U.S., Congress, Senate, Committee on Human Resources, Subcommittee on Labor, *Age Discrimination in Employment Amendments of 1977: Hearings on S. 1784*, To Amend the Age Discrimination in Employment Act of 1967. . . 95th Cong., 1st sess., 26 and 27 July 1977 (Washington, D.C., 1977), pp. 1 (Williams), 66 (Elisburg).

20. House, Select Committee on Aging, *Retirement Age Policies: Hearings*, 2: 42. For a view from the 1950s, see New York State, Joint Legislative Committee on Problems of the Aging, *Brightening the Senior Years* (n.p., 1957), pp. 19–20. Precisely the same arguments were employed by government officials at that time. See *Modern Maturity* 1 (December 1958–January 1959): 33 and 2 (August–September 1959): 11.

21. House, Select Committee on Aging, *Retirement Age Policies: Hearings*, 1: 12.

ignorance with present enlightenment. According to this script, the entire American retirement system dates to German chancellor Otto von Bismarck, who "happened on the age of 65" while constructing an old-age pension plan in 1875. New Deal reformers, young men who perhaps "could not foresee the implications of increased life expectancy," simply "did not question age 65." Their "arbitrary" decision, once made, was thoughtlessly incorporated in private pension plans.[22]

An interesting facet of this description is its insistence that the retirement system was constructed haphazardly and arbitrarily at every stage. In the case of the Social Security Act of 1935, this is true in one sense, false in another. The Committee on Economic Security, charged with developing the legislation, did not use life-expectancy data to establish eligibility for retirement under social security. It did, however, consider the possibility of using other ages. And however arbitrary the selection, the concern in 1934 and 1935 was not with what people would do *after* retirement, but at what age they would *enter* that state. Retirement was still largely a social tool, designed to achieve specific gains, such as unemployment relief and efficiency. It was not yet conceptualized as a period of leisure, granted as a reward for a lifetime of work, and policy makers were not, therefore, much concerned with the total experience of the retired person. Had Frances Perkins and other members of the CES had access to the most sophisticated life-expectancy data, it would have been irrelevant to their approach to social security.[23]

There are, finally, two other elements of the liberal view: the demographic and the organizational. Each has a certain mechanistic quality. The first begins with the fact that the elderly are an increasingly large percentage of the population; the second, with the equally clear organizational gains of old people. The American Association of Retired Persons, the American Retired Teachers Association, the National Association of Retired Federal Employees, the Gray Panthers—these groups speak, if not with unanimity, at least for members united by age. Reform, presumably, takes place when groups achieve a size (relative to

22. Ibid., 1: 6, 13 and 2: 49.
23. U.S., Congress, Senate, Committee on Finance, *Economic Security Act: Hearings on S. 1130*, A Bill to Alleviate the Hazards of Old Age Unemployment, Illness, and Dependency, to Establish a Social Insurance Board in the Department of Labor, to Raise Revenue, and for Other Purposes, 74th Cong., 1st sess. (Washington, D.C., 1935), pp. 282–83, 749, 746–48, 744–45, 754–55; U.S., Congress, Senate, *Congressional Record*, 74th Cong., 1st sess., 1935, 79, pt. 9, p. 9286; Wilbur J. Cohen, *Retirement Policies Under Social Security: A Legislative History of Retirement Ages, the Retirement Test and Disability Benefits* (Berkeley, 1957), pp. 3, 18, 19; Edwin E. Witte, *Development of the Social Security Act: A Memorandum on the History of the Committee on Economic Security and Drafting and Legislative History of the Social Security Act* (Madison, Wis., 1962), pp. 100–02, 160.

the total population, for example) and an organizational efficiency sufficient to push the system into change.

Demographic change, however, occurs too slowly, at least in terms of the aging of the total population, to account in more than a general way for specific historical movements. It may be necessary, but it is hardly sufficient. Demographics, moreover, were translated into organizational ventures as early as the 1890s, and the aged can be considered organizationally sophisticated as of the 1930s, when radical pension organizations flourished under Francis Townsend and in the midst of the railroad brotherhoods. By 1960, little was left to be accomplished in an organizational sense. This progress toward collectivity has, moreover, contributed little to the militancy of the aged. The Gray Panthers, the most radical of the organizations of the aged, participate in the political process in traditional ways. They, too, testify before Congress.[24]

EFFICIENCY

For a more viable explanation of the current interest in age discrimination, we must turn to the economy, and to the particular national and international conditions that confront the American business system in the 1970s. Mandatory retirement was established over the course of the last century because it served real and perceived needs; it is now being dismantled because it is increasingly seen as economically counterproductive for the firm and the nation; because the proposed alternatives seem to offer substantial benefits; and because it is generally accepted that mandatory retirement can be eliminated without significant social dislocation.

Enthusiasm for efficiency, and for the development of rational standards by which to judge it, has been a dominant theme among opponents of mandatory retirement. Appearing before Williams's Senate subcommittee, a representative of the National Retired Teachers Association applauded the application of a legitimate standard of competency:

> It is . . . stated that if mandatory retirement is abolished, people are going to get fired because of a lack of competence. I think that is precisely right. I don't think older Americans want to be protected by a law that protects them if they are incompetent. They don't want that. What they do want, and what this law is designed to provide, is protection against an arbitrary act of discrimination.[25]

24. On the possibility that organizational sophistication is contrary to militancy, see Frances F. Piven and Richard A. Cloward, *Poor People's Movements: Why They Succeed, How They Fail* (New York, 1979).

25. Senate, Committee on Human Resources, *Age Discrimination in Employment: Hearings*, p. 186; see also House, Select Committee on Aging, *Retirement Age Policies: Hearings*, 2: 26 (Miller).

Other witnesses used similar language. "The Department of Labor," emphasized the Carter administration's Elisburg, "is very much concerned about conditions in employment which result in the denial to individuals of the right to be considered on the basis of their ability to do the job. To stifle individual ability and productivity is to establish nonproductive economic and employment policies. It obviously costs society less when individuals are working then [*sic*] when they are not." Michael D. Batten of Kirschner Associates, a Washington, D.C., consulting firm with experience in industrial gerontology, revealed that a number of firms with which he had professional contact were "realizing that in dealing with their human resources they have been neglecting one of the most important factors of all—age." Given the proclivity of the Carter administration for zero-based budgeting, Batten added, "I think we ought to 'zero base' age in the labor force and begin to examine functional criteria, functional ability as the means to 'zero base' age." Taken literally, Batten's statement implies that all persons, of all ages, should be regularly required to justify their very existence in whatever economic subsystem they happen to work. What some saw as an effort toward equal opportunity for *employees*, Batten apparently interpreted as leading to full *employer* rights to select and reject the factors of production.[26]

To read the hearings on mandatory retirement and age discrimination is to see the American business system under attack *not* as callous, unthinking, and emotionally unconcerned with its workers, but as excessively solicitous toward the inefficient and unwilling to make hard, rational decisions.[27] Charles E. Odell, formerly with the United Auto Workers and testifying for the American Personnel and Guidance Association, recommended the application in public and private institutions of a system designed by Dr. Leroy Koyl for measuring employment criteria. The Koyl system, Odell insisted, was operational, its application awaiting only the development of appropriate managerial attitudes. "We simply lack the will," he said, "to bring about the basic changes. We go on encouraging the lazy man's way of handling the problem—drop everyone at a fixed age and avoid having to explain why some, if they choose, can go on working." Paul Findley, one of the most vocal House proponents of antidiscrimination legislation, welcomed this new course of efficiency:

It will cause personnel management, whether in the school system, in the factories or elsewhere, to establish standards of performance, perhaps

26. Senate, Committee on Human Resources, *Age Discrimination in Employment: Hearings*, pp. 66 (Elisburg), 95–96 (Batten), 101.

27. David Riesman argues this point, and sees Arthur Miller's Howard Wagner (the man who fired Willy Loman) as an exceptional case, in *Individualism Reconsidered: And Other Essays* (Glencoe, Ill., 1954), p. 223.

at very early ages. But I really think that's a good trend and should be quickened. But I certainly recognize that this will have, in a sense, revolutionary effect certainly on the employment practices and standards for those in the advancing years.

Out of necessity, employers will have to establish ways of determining performance, so that's good, I think.[28]

Others who gave such testimony to Senate and House committees included Harold Sheppard, director of the Center on Work and Aging of the American Institutes for Research, and Edward E. Marcus, chairperson of the Gray Panthers' Mandatory Retirement Task Force.[29]

To comprehend the meaning of these complaints, we need to probe the function of mandatory retirement for the two major opponents of its elimination: big business and the unions. The latter, while amenable to proposed changes under most conditions, have insisted on the right to maintain and establish mandatory retirement under collectively bargained agreements. Their case, as presented by Ben Seidman of the AF of L–CIO, is simple enough: in an economy suffering from general unemployment, and particularly in declining industries such as coal mining and millinery, mandatory retirement is an essential mechanism for the allocation of income and work. In practice this means encouraging the retirement of older workers in favor of younger workers not entitled to the long-term protection of social security. The critical ingredient in the allocation is the ability of each age group to survive without work.[30]

This testimony was greeted with derision by Senators Javits and Williams. Williams questioned the very need to increase opportunity in declining industries: "I think we put the finger on the problem as we observe that it is just the opposite, trying to get younger people interested in coming into employment has been the problem, particularly in coal mining. . . . Certainly in millinery and tailoring and things like that, the younger people are just not interested. The older people are needed because there are very few people." Javits resurrected several arguments, including minority rights and the myth of the arbitrary age sixty-five. "All we are dealing with," he said, "is one of the shibboleths of our time. Somebody said sixty-five. They probably should never have said it. How

28. House, Select Committee on Aging, *Retirement Age Policies: Hearings*, 2: 49–50 (Odell), 48, 69 (Findley).
29. Ibid., 2: 87, 91, 96.
30. Senate, Committee on Human Resources, *Age Discrimination in Employment: Hearings*, pp. 122–32; also House, Select Committee on Aging, *Retirement Age Policies*, 1: 26 and 2: 75–76. Labor also made the point that decisions were the product of a democratic process.

long do you keep your job? What kind of a person are you? How can you perform?"[31]

The opposition of big business has not been limited to collectively bargained agreements. Corporations defend their mandatory retirement programs for their contributions to social order and for their ease of administration. For General Motors, George B. Morris, Jr., vice-president for industrial relations, argued the need for an integrated, inclusive program of employee relations. The problem of older employees "should continue to be viewed in the perspective of the total employment and employee benefit plan areas. Only by keeping our sights clearly on the total picture can we expect to work out solutions for older employees which will be consistent with our objectives for all employees."[32] Several firms, including IBM and Ford, were concerned about the potential impact of the measure on the distribution of unemployment. Ford argued that the proposed legislation "would have a serious disruptive impact on our society."[33] Like the unions, these companies believe they are pursuing socially constructive policies; that these policies depend on the ability of labor and business to control the "total picture"; and that government intervention in mandatory retirement threatens this control.

Morris joined spokesmen for CBS, Bendix, and Ford in emphasizing how difficult it would be to establish and apply criteria by which to judge the efficiency of older personnel. Asked to indicate what advantages accrued to GM as a result of the arbitrary retirement age of sixty-eight established in the union contract, Morris replied, "I think the first thing is it puts the management in a position where we no longer have to make a decision when an individual is no longer useful." Even the Bendix Corporation, known for its aggressive, competitive managerial philosophy, argued that to eliminate mandatory retirement would produce problems of "accurate assessment," create "administrative complexities," and provide "a possible source of disagreement with the employee and management."[34]

These protests of business and labor were interpreted by the Congress not as valid arguments to be sacrificed in the interest of some greater good, but as *the problem itself.* Congressional advocates of the new retirement legislation believe that the American economy is not the efficient engine of production that

31. Senate, Committee on Human Resources, *Age Discrimination in Employment: Hearings*, pp. 131 (Williams), 129 (Javits), also pp. 69–70, a Javits reference to the "new concept of mobility of workers."
32. House, Select Committee on Aging, *Retirement Age Policies: Hearings*, 1: 19.
33. Ibid., pp. 94 (Ford), 103 (IBM).
34. Ibid., pp. 36 (CBS), 86, 81 (Bendix), 94 (Ford), 29 (GM).

it once was. Although the causes of this decline are never made explicit, its symptoms are clear enough; business is no longer aggressive, no longer competitive, no longer capable of making the hard-nosed decisions on which ultimate survival depends. An adverse balance of payments reflects the increasing difficulties encountered in marketing American products abroad.

Among the remedies for this economic malaise is the elimination of mandatory retirement. With this proposal, the Congress and the executive branch are requiring business and labor to divest themselves of one presumably unproductive element in the network of insurance and welfare measures grafted onto an earlier, purer form of capitalism. Although the mechanism for this change is national legislation, it portends a turn toward decentralization and increased autonomy, as business is forced to employ decision-making powers that have become rusty through disuse. The intermediate goal is something akin to a free market for labor resources.

Business opposition to reform, although hardly unanimous,[35] raises a further question: Why have the president and the Congress shown so little inclination to accept business forecasts of social dislocation? An answer emerges from an analysis of national labor markets in the 1970s and how labor-market conditions are interpreted and projected into the future. The heart of the matter is that unemployment is not now seen as a major economic or social problem, nor is it expected to be one in the late 1970s and early 1980s. One reflection of this sanguine outlook is a recent Labor Department study projecting the impact of the elimination of mandatory retirement at some 200,000 jobs, less than 1 percent of total employment and an amount considered minimal by Labor Department officials. The numerical estimate was accepted, and its marginal impact affirmed, by other witnesses before the Senate Committee on Human Resources. Representing the retired teachers, Lauren Selden at first denied that mandatory retirement in *any* way opened up opportunities for younger workers before conceding the possibility of some minimal relationship.[36] The hearings contain a number of references to a conclusion in Peter Drucker's *Unseen Revolution*. According to Drucker, the end of the postwar baby boom will soon produce a general labor *shortage*.[37]

35. See the report of a survey of management personnel conducted by William M. Mercer, Inc., in *BPR* 149: A–7.

36. Senate, Committee on Human Resources, *Age Discrimination in Employment: Hearings*, pp. 70, 78, 185–86.

37. House, Select Committee on Aging, *Retirement Age Policies: Hearings*, 2: 94, 96, 108. Retirement, on the other hand, continues to be employed to handle immediate labor market problems. See Mike Causey, "'Early Out' Won't Come Early," *Washington Post*, 31 August 1977, sec. C, p. 2, and "Steel Firm Sweetens Its Early Retirement to Trim the Payroll," *Wall Street Journal*, 19 September 1977, p. 18.

There is enormous complacency in all of this. Policy makers are convinced, it would seem, that the elimination of mandatory retirement will not unemploy, or prevent the employment of, any socially significant number of those associated with disorder—largely juveniles and blacks. The work force is so large that one witness anticipated no difficulty in 200,000 workers being "absorbed and distributed."[38] The figure itself was not scrutinized in a labor-market context, not even for one questionable assumption on which it is premised—that retirement is so totally ingrained that few will change their behavior patterns when it ceases to be required.[39]

This lack of interest in issues of social disorder is unusual for the twentieth century, but it makes sense in the 1970s. Urban revolt is a decade in the past. Even rates of juvenile delinquency are down. Washington, D.C., in particular, seems the quietest of cities; its residents boast of the many sidewalk cafes, the sort of amenity considered impossible in the city not long ago. "Prior to the 1960s," wrote columnist Nicholas von Hoffman in August 1977, "the fear of the fire bell in the night . . . was the bad emotion in every white gut. Then we had burn, baby, burn, and the whites found out that the night dream of slave rebellion was worse than the actuality. . . . White America knows it can tough out any long, hot summer black adolescents may heat up."[40] Relieved of the need, traditional in American politics, to balance programs designed to achieve economic efficiency with measures to insure social order, Carter and the legislative branch have turned to efficiency as the central goal of public policy.

SOCIAL SECURITY

If the elimination of mandatory retirement seems cost-free in the social sense, it also, conveniently, holds out substantial potential benefit for the general economy. Retirement is currently being reevaluated in part because its restructuring promises aid—some think of a substantial nature—to the ailing social security trust fund and private pension systems.

38. Senate, Committee on Human Resources, *Age Discrimination in Employment: Hearings*, p. 79; Joseph A. Califano, Jr., "The Aging of America: Questions for the Four Generation Society," Remarks Before the American Academy of Political and Social Science, Philadelphia, 8 April 1978, Department of Health, Education and Welfare Press Release, 8 April 1978, p. 13. One wonders what "distributed" means. If unemployment is "distributed," say geographically or socially among different population groups, does it then become less significant?

39. The problem of conditioning is an important one. See the perceptive comments of Representative Mario Biaggi in House, Select Committee on Aging, *Retirement Age Policies: Hearings*, 1: pp. 27–28.

40. Nicholas von Hoffman, "Meaningful Work for Willing Americans," *Washington Post*, 16 August 1977, sec. B, p. 4.

Even the creators of the social security system were aware of potential funding problems. In 1935, Treasury Secretary Henry Morgenthau, Jr., and Harry Hopkins, head of the Federal Emergency Relief Administration, were members of the President's Committee on Economic Security, which had been assigned the task of developing an acceptable program of unemployment and old age insurance. One afternoon when Hopkins was at home ill, he received a phone call from Morgenthau, who had just seen figures projecting social security expenditures in 1980 at over one billion dollars. When Hopkins asked Morgenthau if he anticipated difficulties in securing congressional approval for a $25 to 30 million pension bill in the current year, the conversation took this turn:

Morgenthau: Not this year but it's the things that it runs into.

Hopkins: Well there are going to be twice as many old people thirty years from now Henry than there are now.

Morgenthau: Well I've gotten a very good analysis of this thing and I'm going to lay it in her [Frances Perkins, secretary of labor] lap this afternoon. I'm simply going to point out the danger spots and it's up to somebody else to say whether they want to do it. I'm not trying to say what they should do—I want to show them the bad curves.

Hopkins: I wish I was going to be there.

Morgenthau: I wish you were too.

Hopkins: That old age thing is a bad curve.[41]

Several Western nations, including the United States, West Germany, and France, are now living the "bad curve" that Hopkins and Morgenthau discovered more than forty years ago and which was also predicted by congressional sponsors of the original legislation. It is essentially a product of the declining ratio between the number of employed and the number of retired, between those who provide support and those who are supported. In developing nations, like Mexico, population resembles a pyramid, with small numbers of old people at the top, increasingly larger numbers of people at lower levels. The United States of 1970 retains some of this pyramidal quality, but not much. Since 1880, demographic trends have aged the American population and contributed to an increase in the relative number of dependents. The fertility rate of American women—the number of births for each one thousand women of childbearing age (fifteen to forty-four)—was at 66.7 in 1975, well below the previous low of

41. Morgenthau, Diaries, Henry Morgenthau, Jr. Papers, Franklin D. Roosevelt Library, Hyde Park, New York, vol. 3, pp. 58–60.

75.8 established during the Depression in 1936 and close to half the birth rate at the peak of the postwar baby boom in 1957. Improved health care has contributed to a lower death rate, enlarging the percentage of old people in the population mix.[42]

In 1975, Social Security Commissioner Robert Ball claimed that a reversal in the trend toward early retirement and "greater labor force participation among older people in the next century" could produce "a significant saving for social security over what is currently estimated." Several witnesses before congressional committees characterized mandatory retirement as a system that rewarded dependency and forced older workers into reliance on the young. The result, according to the National Association of Retired Federal Employees, were income security programs "already . . . swollen beyond their fiscal limits."[43] Representatives and senators were very interested in the relationship of retirement to social security but generally unsure about the sums of money involved. One estimate put the savings at $600 million annually after five years; another at $2.1 billion. A Labor Department study placed theoretical 1976 savings somewhere between these two figures and argued that "these sums do not really represent great savings to the economy." Despite this conclusion, extraordinary interest in the issue has not abated.[44]

Raising the eligibility age under social security would have a greater trust fund impact than eliminating mandatory retirement, which surely explains the attention this idea has received. Administration officials, according to Commerce Secretary Juanita Kreps, are considering withholding full security benefits until recipients reach age sixty-eight. Although Kreps has stressed the goal of extending the work life beyond age sixty-five, the *explicit* function of such a step would be to reduce the burden on the social security system. Others who

42. William E. Simon, "How to Rescue Social Security," *Wall Street Journal*, 3 November 1976, p. 20; David E. Rosenbaum, "Social Security's Troubles," *New York Times*, 11 May 1977, p. 18; Robert Reinhold, "New Population Trends Transforming U.S.," *New York Times*, 6 February 1977, pp. 4, 42.

43. Senate, Committee on Human Resources, *Age Discrimination in Employment: Hearings*, p. 21n (Ball); House, Select Committee on Aging, *Retirement Age Policies: Hearings*, 2: 39 (NARFE), 41.

44. Pepper to Kreps, 1 August 1977, in U.S., Congress, House, Select Committee on Aging, *Mandatory Retirement: The Social and Human Cost of Enforced Idleness: Report*, 95th Cong., 1st sess. (Washington, D.C., 1977), appendix, pp. 51–52; Senate, Committee on Human Resources, *Age Discrimination in Employment: Hearings*, pp. 59, 336–37, 337 (quotation). See also the attempt of the Congressional Budget Office to cost the proposed changes, in U.S., Congress, House, Committee on Education and Labor, *Age Discrimination in Employment Act Amendments of 1977*, 25 July 1977, H.R. 95–527, part 1, 95th Cong., 1st sess. (Washington, D.C., 1977), pp. 13–14; House, Select Committee on Aging, *Retirement Age Policies: Hearings*, 1: 8–10; ibid., 2: 15, 23, 25, 38, 41, 109, 59, 100; and Senate, Committee on Human Resources, *Age Discrimination in Employment: Hearings*, pp. 59, 72, 80, 96, 111–12, 123.

have made similar proposals include southern Democrat Russell Long, the chairman of the Senate Finance Committee, who raised the same possibility in 1976; William Simon, secretary of the treasury under Richard Nixon and Gerald Ford; social gerontologist Harold Sheppard; and John Palmer, a senior fellow at the Brookings Institution. House Republican leaders have formally proposed raising the social security retirement age from sixty-five to sixty-eight between 1990 and 2001.[45]

The growing magnitude of public and private social insurance systems vis-à-vis the total economy has also created new interest in the ties between retirement policy and economic growth. Of major concern is the impact of rising rates of early retirement on personal savings and capital formation.[46] Another problem is the possibility that funding social security through a large increase in payroll taxes could, according to the Senate Budget Committee, "act as a serious impediment to recovery and price stability in the next decade."[47] Javits has suggested that a "universe" approach to retirement income (coordination of public and private systems) would allow the nation to anticipate the effects of severe economic downturns that "could ultimately cause the termination of many private pension plans and result in claims of potentially staggering unfunded liabilities being addressed to the federal government." Argues Javits: "A national retirement income policy would be primarily concerned with assuring retirement income security, but would also facilitate such other important goals as increasing capital formation and expanding employee stock ownership."[48]

THE NEW EFFICIENCY

The view of the politics of aging developed here—that the attack on age discrimination is a function of the needs, real or perceived, of the American

45. *Washington Post*, 31 July 1977, sec. A, p. 3; Edward Cowan, "One Way or the Other, Social Security Will Need Help," *New York Times*, 7 March 1976, sec. E, p. 3; William E. Simon, "How to Rescue Social Security," *Wall Street Journal*, 3 November 1976, p. 20; Spencer Rich, "GOP Backs Rise in Social Security Age," *Washington Post*, 10 September 1977, sec. A, pp. 1, 7; *Wall Street Journal*, 13 September 1977, p. 24 (editorial); *DER* 146: G–5; *DER* 103: G–9; House, Select Committee on Aging, *Retirement Age Policies: Hearings*, 2: 92. The 1975 Advisory Council on Social Security recommended consideration of this alternative. See Senate, Committee on Human Resources, *Age Discrimination in Employment: Hearings*, p. 145. Following the negative public reaction to Kreps's statements, the White House released a statement acknowledging that raising the benefit age was a possibility for the next century but was not being considered under current legislation (*DER* 168: G–3).

46. Martin Feldstein, "Toward a Reform of Social Security," *The Public Interest* 40 (Summer 1975): 82–85.

47. *DER* 109: X–2.

48. Statement of Senator Jacob K. Javits at the Pensions & Investments Conference on "Corporate Obligations/Outlook," Chicago, 29 September 1977, mimeograph, pp. 1, 2.

economy in the 1970s—is only one facet of a much larger phenomenon that might be labeled the New Efficiency. The New Efficiency encompasses most of the administration's initiatives in its first year in office: restructuring the federal civil service to increase incentive at all work-force levels; government reorganization; zero-based budgeting; a competitive climate for commercial airlines; more rigid enforcement of the antitrust statutes; currency devaluation to make American products more competitive in foreign markets; a welfare system with work requirements. Even elements of the administration's tax-reform program (such as the reduced deduction for the three-martini lunch), which are ostensibly grounded in notions of fairness, in fact reflect the belief, central to Carter and his aides, that the bloated American business system must be streamlined for combat.[49] Carter's election was not the triumph of a populist, dedicated to removing inequities in the interest of individual rights. Emerging from the South, one of the nation's few remaining areas of industrial growth, Carter promised to impose the aggressive characteristics of his region on a nation troubled by a sense of stagnation.[50]

Carter's autobiography, first published as a campaign document in October 1975, reveals a boy impressed by his father's "aggressive and innovative" selling practices and capable of parlaying $1 per day in peanut sales into the landlordship of five houses by age eighteen. Carter defines his academic and naval experiences as intensely competitive, and more than once he boasts of his own desire and ability to master detail and information. Carter believes that excel-

49. On civil service reform, see Mike Causey, "Carter Plans Elite Corps," *Washington Post*, 2 March 1978, sec. C, p. 2; Kathy Sawyer and Stephen J. Lynton, "Carter Asks Sweeping Civil Service Changes," *Washington Post*, 3 March 1978, sec. A, pp. 1, 18. On executive reorganization, Mike Causey, "Painless Reorganization," *Washington Post*, 21 October 1977, sec. C, p. 2. Contrast the opening comments for the Bendix Corporation (the firm from which came W. Michael Blumenthal, Carter's secretary of the treasury), with those of other firms, in House, Select Committee on Aging, *Retirement Age Policies: Hearings*, 1: 72. On perquisites, see Address by Daniel Halperin, Tax Legislative Counsel, Department of the Treasury, before the National Lawyers Club, Washington, D.C., 11 January 1978; Urban C. Lehner, "Salaries and Benefits at World Bank Are Envy of Washington," *Wall Street Journal*, 28 November 1977, pp. 1, 21, quoting a Treasury official: "How much of a premium do you need to pay to motivate these people?"; and "Persistent Perks," *Wall Street Journal*, 19 October 1977, pp. 1, 24, which quotes J. Robert Schultz, new president of the Barwick Corporation in Atlanta: "Too many luxuries for a company's top executives is often a sign of deeper problems in a company—specifically, a poor attitude on the part of management toward the work that needs to be done. . . . We're thin and trim now—and healthier for it." The central role of the *Wall Street Journal* in the campaign against perks also lends credence to this interpretation of the reform movement. For the Carter administration's analysis of international markets, see Jeff Frieden, "The Trilateral Commission: Economics and Politics in the 1970s," *Monthly Review* 29 (December 1977): 1–18.

50. This trend began with Richard Nixon, if not earlier. See Kirkpatrick Sale's description of the southern rim origins of the Nixon administration in "The World Behind Watergate," *New York Review of Books* 20 (3 May 1973), 9–16. For that matter, John Kennedy is credited with initiating the attack on perks.

lence is possible to define and possible to achieve, and that we must do both. In the Georgia Senate, Carter sought to secure a state salary commission with "solid objective credentials" and was frustrated at the avoidable absence of "clear and comprehensive issues." Even then, he wanted to "fix responsibility," to "assess performance," and to "evolve standard policies," and he believed that it was only bureaucratic confusion which made these goals unachievable. Carter began his term as governor of Georgia by insisting on the need to make efficient use of people. "We cannot," he said in his inaugural address, "afford to waste the talents and abilities given by God to one single person." His actions in that office reveal a powerful need to establish priorities, operate on the basis of merit, and develop long-term goals and long-range plans. On the last page of this autobiography, Carter emphasizes the concern of the American people for the "lack of competence and integrity" in government. "There must," he adds, be "no acceptance of mediocrity in any aspect of our private or public lives." The volume's final words, set in italics, also serve as its title: *Why not the best?*[51]

The New Efficiency of Jimmy Carter and the U.S. Congress resembles nothing so much as the old efficiency of the Progressive Era. Carter's lust for efficiency has its antecedents in Frederick W. Taylor's scientific management; in the campaigns of urban reformers to replace corrupt and inefficient ward bosses with commissions and managers; in the efforts of educational reformers to bring business principles to bear on the public-school systems; and in the several presidential commissions that sought to reorganize the federal bureaucracy and increase productivity.[52] Just as the intense competitive environment of the turn of the century made these activities seem necessary, so has competition in the international sphere served to spur the advocates of the New Efficiency.[53] In each case, too, there has been some disagreement about what was really efficient and whose interests were being served. Centralization enabled the new business elites of the Progressive Era to wrest control from local immigrant groups; today, it allows advocates of the New Efficiency to force reluctant corporations and

51. Jimmy Carter, *Why Not The Best* (New York: Bantam, 1976; orig. edition, 1975), pp. 25, 21–22, 44, 46, 51, 53, 99, 105, 119, 127, 128, 130, 179.

52. Harry Braverman, "Labor and Monopoly Capital: The Degradation of Work in the Twentieth Century," *Monthly Review* 26 (Summer 1974): 1–134; James Weinstein, *The Corporate Ideal in the Liberal State: 1900–1918* (Boston, 1968), chap. 4; David B. Tyack, "City Schools: Centralization of Control at the Turn of the Century," in Jerry Israel, ed., *Building the Organizational Society: Essays on Associational Activities in Modern America* (New York, 1972), pp. 57–72; Oscar Kraines, "The President Versus Congress: The Keep Commission, 1905–1909: First Comprehensive Presidential Inquiry into Administration," *Western Political Quarterly* 23 (March 1970): 5–54.

53. Radford Boddy and James Crotty, "Class Conflict, Keynesian Policies, and the Business Cycle," *Monthly Review* 26 (October 1974): 1–17.

government agencies to adopt decision-making habits presumably conducive to increased efficiency but on which there is as yet no consensus.

A major difference between the Progressive years and the 1970s is the general absence, in our own time, of the kinds of social problems that plagued the earlier period—urban violence, racial conflict, a militant labor movement, and massive industrial accidents. The existence of such a climate made Progressives conscious of the need to control, to preserve order, to balance competing claims to economic and social benefits. This helps explain why the aged were treated so differently in each of these periods. Retirement was an issue in the Progressive period, but it was conceptualized in fundamentally different terms. Retirement was *itself* then a mechanism for efficiency and a tool of modernization. It was also expected to contribute to social stability by reducing turnover among industrial workers, by binding workers to the future of a particular company, by creating a stable, conservative, teaching profession, beholden to Andrew Carnegie's pension fund for college professors or to local school boards. These goals and actions may have been sound in conception and necessary to those with authority in that culture, but in retrospect (the proponents of the New Efficiency would argue) they have been counterproductive in a long-term economic sense. They have stabilized the system, but at the cost of the ability of the American economy to compete in world markets. They have not made it more efficient. It is the function of the New Efficiency, and of its anti-age-discrimination component, to redress the balance.

If anything, this explanation is too rational, too mechanistic, and takes too literally those who talk of efficiency, waste, and human resource use. What do we expect to achieve through the New Efficiency? Carter's rhetoric suggests that efficiency may be a complex metaphor, reflecting basic needs that transcend, or at least differ from, the competitive capabilities of our business system. Efficiency necessarily means the ability to judge who and what are efficient, to set standards of performance grounded in some presumably objective reality. The New Efficiency asserts the existence of such standards. Within it, the movement to abolish mandatory retirement asserts the existence of standards by which to judge the performance of individuals over age sixty-five. There is evidence, moreover, that an insistence on standards may be fundamental to the decade of the 1970s. In the field of education alone, one might cite the case brought by Allan Bakke, which asserts the lack of validity of group-evaluated performance; the competency-based teacher-education programs in the public schools; and the new demands, in the colleges and high schools, for a return to lower grading scales and to the content-oriented, traditional curriculums of the 1950s. Each of these is in some way a reform against what is now seen as a central characteristic of the turbulent era of the Vietnam War: the absence of criteria, standards, and accountability. The New Efficiency may be the latest stage of America's continuing search for social order.

10 The Meaning and Function of Retirement

Retirement has had <u>no single function</u> in American history. From its beginnings in the private and public bureaucracies of the late nineteenth century, formal retirement has been a product of its appeal to institutions and social groups with disparate goals and viewpoints. <u>Until 1930, economy, efficiency, modernization, and depersonalization</u> were the most important uses of retirement; since then, <u>personal security and social welfare</u> have so dominated our conception of the function of private and governmental retirement systems that we have forgotten retirement's origins in the economic and social milieu of the turn of the century. Having adopted this generic definition of social security—the ideology of the welfare state—we have become incapable of understanding the history of retirement and its place in our culture.

Retirement goals cut across the boundaries that presumably divided labor from management, the public from the private sector. Specific needs might vary, but leaders in education, government, business, and the trade unions found common ground in the <u>pension as an institution of control.</u> Henry Pritchett's intent to use the Carnegie Foundation for the Advancement of Teaching as a mechanism for restructuring and shaping higher education had its parallels not only in the public schools, where retirement was supposed to help maintain the teaching profession as a source of social stability, but in the trade unions and corporations, where pensions were expected to bind workers to one or the other of these institutions, and in the federal bureaucracy, where the potential for dominance inherent in the pension was of concern to labor leaders. Because the pension <u>could be used effectively to control dissidents,</u> many workers came to favor contributory systems. While the Social Security Act of 1935 has been criticized for its contributory feature, the semicontractual nature of the contribution has appealed to some employees for the freedom it implies. Moreover, the location of the system within the national government rather than within the private sector promised relief from the sporadic attempts of business—most common in railroading—to use pension systems to manipulate employees. Retirement was also expected to induce progress and prevent social retrogression. This viewpoint was shared by Pritchett, William Osler, and a generation of high-level government officials, of whom the Pension Bureau's Gaylord Saltzgaber was a prototype, who were among the first to confront the potentially debilitating effects of burgeoning bureaucracy.

Pensions also fulfilled a variety of microeconomic ends. Depending on the nature of the bureaucracy and its particular needs, retirement has made it possible for institutions to replace inefficient older workers with younger ones and expensive salaried personnel with cheaper ones (the public schools and the railroads did so in the 1930s); it has allowed institutions to defer wage increases and, in times of inflation, to lower salaries through deferral. Turnover reduction was a major goal of pension systems between 1910 and 1930, while recruitment of superior personnel was of lesser importance. Pensions have also met the need, common in all bureaucracies but of special significance in declining industries and in periods of high unemployment, to maintain and provide promotional opportunity, the illusion if not the reality of personal progress and achievement. Where retirement systems did not exist, as in the sales profession in the 1920s, age discrimination served many of the same functions. The post-1940 growth in pension plans was a product of changes in collective bargaining after 1949 and of the tax advantages available under World War II regulations and legislation. Unions found that pensions satisfied their members in difficult times and opened up jobs in crowded industries and during recessions. Business still expected retirement systems to improve efficiency by making employees more secure and by facilitating dismissal, but as industrial relations became more sophisticated after 1930, corporations turned to other mechanisms of efficiency, control, and adjustment and ceased to demand so many internal benefits from the pension.

Retirement also emerged from, and was a reaction to, the changing tone of employer-employee relationships. It was, first, an attack on the systems of permanence that employees had attempted to build into bureaucratic structures. These systems included tenure in teaching, seniority on the railroads, and the elimination of the spoils system in the civil service. As workers sought to establish a property right to the job, managers, often joined by workers, turned to retirement as one of several mechanisms for diminishing the impact of that right. When the property right was allowed to exist for a decade or more and to become a part of employee expectations, a challenge to it could produce the high level of emotionally charged conflict experienced in Chicago over the relationship between tenure and retirement and in Washington, D.C., over general job security. In some sense, these contests pitted one impersonal bureaucratic mechanism against another.

Second, retirement was a reaction against the continued influence of personal modes of behavior in institutions in which personal relationships were increasingly seen as dysfunctional relics of the past. To a certain extent, the application of personal qualities to business affairs is inherently dysfunctional by capitalist definitions. Employment practices should reflect economic rationality rather than priorities established by family and friendship, Yet in 1890, in spite of mechanization and the rise of national competition, employment practices had not been fully rationalized. The economic and technological forces that made age discrimination a significant phenomenon in the late nineteenth century had not resulted in the complete elimination of protective attitudes toward older workers. Corporations might seldom hire older workers, but they also seldom fired them; some notion of personal or social responsibility remained. One can see it manifested at Du Pont; within the aging railroad work force; and in the civil service and teaching bureaucracies, where the inability to discharge aged employees coexisted uneasily with the new codes of efficiency. Public and private bureacracies had become old-age institutions, providing the money, status, and physical activity that would be dispensed a half-century later through social security programs, nursing homes, and old-age clubs and centers.

Whether we choose to regard those workers who lived under this system as employed or retired (informally pensioned, as contemporaries said) depends only on how one uses the words. It is more important to understand that work-centered retirement was a natural phenomenon in cities as well as rural areas and in large and complex bureaucracies as well as small firms. Many of the dislocating effects of midcentury retirement are not so much caused by retirement itself as by the destruction of an earlier version of retirement more suited to human needs for structure, sociability, and place. The agent of this destruction was formal retirement itself. One of its tangible manifestations was the old-age home. Because it often separated the old from their families and geographical communities, the old-age home was an especially disruptive institution. Workers rejected it, even when it offered retirement with fellow craftsmen.

Depersonalization was neither easily nor completely accomplished. At least within the public sphere, the existence of a formal pension system did not guarantee a purely rational approach to employee relations. Pensions under the Civil Service Retirement Act of 1920 were not sufficient to overcome knowledge that employment officers continued to have of the personal details of employees' lives. Bureau chiefs preferred to give extensions rather than discharge a clerk whose pension would not cover mortgage payments or decently provide for his family. Chicago school administrators eventually supported mandatory retirement when a voluntary system failed to induce retirement among teachers over seventy, but even then several school board members felt uncomfortable with the notion of subjecting faithful employees to an arbitrary system. Private-sector data is more difficult to obtain, but if Du Pont's experience is typical, a formal corporate pension plan was no guarantee of impersonality. The relatively late development of mandatory retirement in the post-World War II period, following a half-century of experience with voluntary arrangements, suggests that mandatory systems were installed when voluntary ones failed to induce retirement at desired ages.

Third, retirement has historically been sanctioned as a form of unemployment relief; older workers have been retired to create places for younger ones. This has been done most blatantly and most publicly in railroading, an industry of declining employment since 1920, but the same solution has been applied to other occupations, like typesetting, which were experiencing techological unemployment or technologically induced superannuation, a specific variety of the same phenomenon. The shorter workday and the shorter work life shared this unemployment-relief function. Particular elements of the federal bureaucracy— Navy Yard and Post Office employees in the 1920s, for example—advocated additional inducements to retirement when disarmament and technology, respectively, threatened job security. With the additional stimulus of the Depression, retirement as work sharing became a popular solution to national unemployment. It was put into practice with administrative changes in the application of civil service retirement; through the Railroad Retirement Act; and, in a necessarily limited form, given the resources available to the national government, in the Social Security Act of 1935.

Retirement as a method of alleviating unemployment has been carried out with the support of the aged. One of the most impressive aspects of the Townsend movement is the self-sacrifice of the old in the interest of jobs for the young. But this should not obscure the discrimination implicit in the mechanism or the felt need for such discrimination as a device for social order. When jobs were scarce in the 1930s, the Roosevelts, Eleanor and Franklin, ministered, relatively at least, to the needs of youth; it was the young who threatened disorder and violence and whose political sympathies seemed most crucial. Sharing this perspective, the aged welcomed their own retirement and missed an opportunity to insist on the right to work, regardless of age.

With the exception of the military pension, nineteenth-century retirement was carried out by cities and states, trade unions and corporations. Following a dramatic and frightening expansion in the bureaucracy of the nation-state in the Progressive period, the national government again asserted its preferences for youth and efficiency by creating a retirement system for its own civil service employees. During the Depression, the magic of retirement was applied to the sick industry of railroading—using the mechanism of federal law—and in 1935, when Congress passed the Social Security Act, the national government affirmed the importance of retirement for much of the American population. Private pensions came under the direct supervision of the national government in legislation passed in 1947, 1958, and 1974. The Retirement Act of 1978 represents an attempt to roll back what was now seen as a very expensive, complex, and inefficient instrument of public policy.

The emergence of the national government as the foremost arbiter of retirement parallels the larger history of government intervention in the economy. It also reflects the tendency since 1920 to conceive of the economy in national terms and to view retirement as an important ingredient in the broader macroeconomic picture. Retirement could become an instrument of national economic policy in the 1930s only if millions of workers could be reached by federal law; pension plans could prove a useful source of capital for business only if their use could be nationally restricted under Taft-Hartley and ERISA; retirement could be utilized in the struggle to arrest the long-term decline in the American economy only if the rollback took place nationally.

Older workers have generally welcomed the pension plan, if not mandatory retirement or the idea of retirement itself. The active core of the Townsend movement was composed of persons over sixty, working and retired. The Railway Employees National Pension Association, the equivalent of the Townsend organization on an industry level, was also buoyed by the enthusiasm of older workers. Teachers' and civil service pensions went unopposed by any large segment of employees in either occupation. Organizations of the retired, from the National Association of Retired Federal Employees to the more broadly based organizations of the 1950s such as the American Association of Retired Persons, have adopted a restricted attitude toward retirement. Just as most American unions have concentrated on wages and generally avoided work-place issues, so have the retirement associations emphasized benefits and accepted the necessity of retirement, the absence of work.

Retirement proved only mildly divisive as an issue among teachers, more so among railroad workers. As a group, the young were seldom as committed to retirement—especially to voluntary programs that reduced job-creation potential—as were older workers. Employed workers tended to be wage-minded rather than retirement-minded, unless they were close enough to the end of their work lives to appreciate the prospect of a pension. If the railroad experience in the 1930s is typical, a substantial majority of older workers supported retirement amid the objections of a vocal minority who wished to continue working. Data from the 1950s indicates that once the extreme insecurity of the Depression decade disappeared, the desire to remain at work became more widespread. This revival of interest in work helped make the selling of retirement a necessity for corporations and labor unions.

In almost every industry and in every period after 1890, the middle-aged found retirement systems frustrating and ineffective. Too old to find work, too young to retire, the middle-aged worker of fifty-five, fifty, or even forty-five was a constant embarrassment to the American economic and political system. By 1900, a sixty-year-old typesetter was considered superannuated, too old to operate the new technology. Yet he was also too old to retrain and too young for the union to retire. Thousands of railroad workers experienced the same anomolous circumstances. The Social Security Act of 1935 offered no old-age benefits to the worker under sixty-five, no matter how long he or she had been unemployed. Congress ignored the determined efforts of Francis Townsend and Ernest Lundeen to serve this middle-aged constituency. In the 1950s the middle-aged were reduced to writing bitter letters to Dwight Eisenhower and his cabinet officials, who refused to recognize the obvious: retirement (permanent unemployment insurance), rather than unemployment insurance, was the only appropriate device for dealing with the social problems of the long-term-unemployed middle-aged worker.

Although retirement was essentially a political device, imposed by one group upon another, its imposition was seldom challenged. Why have American workers welcomed, or acquiesced in, retirement? Anxiety about social disorder, which the old associated with youth, provides part of an explanation, and one of particular relevance for the critical decade of the 1930s. On another level, it is possible to see the aged, indeed the majority of the population, as victims of a twentieth-century redefinition of retirement. To some extent, this redefinition was a product of a natural inclination to accept the pension as a bounty, gift, or necessary financial reward. Even in 1900, during the early struggles over teachers' and civil service pensions, the alternative to the pension was no pension; the alternative to leaving work with this protection was not remaining at work but rather leaving work unprotected. Retirement on pension also appeared reasonable to the machinists, printers, trainmen, and other workers for whom the alternative was the social isolation of institutionalization in an old-age home. Because employees needed the basic forms of security the pension could provide, and because this security component could not be isolated from the pension's efficiency and control aspects, retirement was never completely divorced from a notion of security, however defensive.

The view of retirement as a separate period of time in which one reaps the rewards of past service has always been a part of the conceptualization of the institution, but its salience among other definitions of retirement began in the 1920s with the arguments of leisure theorists that technological unemployment could be, and indeed had to be, converted into leisure. Retirement was the inevitable result of the need to shorten the work life to spread available work. Although forced withdrawal from the workplace might have been interpreted negatively, leisure theorists chose to emphasize technology's potential for freeing Americans for new forms of leisure. At the same time, business made retirement and security difficult to separate. Under the influence of Elton Mayo and other practitioners of industrial psychology, employee performance and security became closely linked, and the corporate world thus had a strong incentive to define retirement as a state of security.

The massive insecurity of the Great Depression further obscured the historical origins of retirement. The development of old-age security during a time of insecurity and dependency has made it difficult to see that some of the roots of social security were in retirement, rather than retirement having its origins in social security. A complex program serving a number of social and economic functions, social security took on a singleness of purpose and a simplicity that its authors never intended and that has never been descriptive of reality. Even the Railroad Retirement Act, so clearly drawn as a retirement measure, to achieve efficiency, economy, and unemployment relief, was not impervious to the ideology of security. In striking down the original legislation, the Supreme Court refused to accept the acknowledged purposes of the legislation as appropriate or operative, thus forcing retirement advocates into legal defenses based on security.

Acceptance and enjoyment of the new leisure and of retirement itself required a definition of old age that minimized the need for the high levels of activity provided by the workplace. Disengagement theory served that purpose. Disengagement became an important way of conceptualizing aging and retirement in the decades after 1950. Golden Age Clubs, developed in Cleveland in 1940 and widespread by 1950, provided a different kind of adjustment mechanism, one which combined disengagement with activity theory. The clubs were premised on disengagement theory in the sense that traditional work was not considered essential to a healthy existence; they relied on activity theory, however, to the extent that their sponsors believed that complete disengagement was socially and individually destructive. Whether complete or partial, however, disengagement theory justified withdrawal from work and contributed materially to the creation of the mythology of retirement. Another link in the selling of retirement was forged in the late 1940s when insurance companies joined industry and labor in making retirement into a commodity. By 1960, therefore, the meaning of retirement had been transformed. It was now a form of leisure, a way of spending time following the conclusion of one's work life; it was a stage of existence, inevitable but to be welcomed and even celebrated. Once largely a device for maximizing productivity in a bureaucratizing society, retirement had become a state of being, apparently benign, classless, and apolitical.

The almost universal adulation that has accompanied the reconsideration of retirement in the 1970s has further undermined our ability to understand it as an ingredient in the national political economy. Because the retirement legislation of 1978 was popular with liberal politicians, with the labor unions, and with virtually every organization representing the old and retired, we have all too easily interpreted the law as a just if belated victory for those who want to work over those who would prevent them from doing so on the artificial basis of age.

This view of the legislation is both incomplete and flawed. It is incomplete in that it fails to take into account the costs that attend the elimination of mandatory retirement. Employees who remain at work occupy jobs that would be filled by others. In effect, the burden of unemployment is shifted from the retired to some other segment of the work force. If the labor-market impact of the law is not expected to be very large (some 200,000 jobs), neither will the retirement impact be substantial. To the extent that the legislation works, it has negative effects; to the extent that it fails to keep potential retirees on the job, it has no such impact—but then, neither is it a law worth celebrating as the elderly's Magna Carta.

The liberal view of the reconsideration of retirement is flawed because it confuses result and purpose. Although the new retirement law might well result in older workers enjoying a longer work life, this was not its sole purpose, nor even its most important one. The act became a possibility only in the context of challenges to American economic hegemony and only when influential elements within American capitalism had concluded that retirement as then constituted was unduly costly as well as inefficient in allocating labor. Once these conditions and perceptions existed, liberal reformers could have their way. Given the American experience with retirement over the last century, one could hardly have expected anything else.

Bibliographical Essay

One of the pleasures of working in a new area is the ongoing sense of discovery that accompanies the research process. I experienced that feeling often when exploring both manuscript and printed sources and especially in coming across a body of data sufficiently compelling to invite extended treatment. The chapter on railroad workers began with my desire to locate a manuscript collection large enough to shed some light on the subtleties of age relations within a particular occupational group and union structure. Although somewhat cumbersome to use, the records of the Railway Employees Department of the American Federation of Labor, housed at the Labor and Industrial Relations Institute at Cornell University, served the purpose.

Even more explicit are the records of federal agencies in the Progressive period, a time when almost every bureau and department was concerned with superannuation. These collections contain materials from every stage of the process by which older workers were measured for efficiency, from evaluations of individual clerks to verbatim accounts of committee meetings at which the meaning of retirement was discussed. Most productive were Record Group (RG) 56 (Treasury Department), RG 48 (Interior Department), RG 51 (Bureau of Efficiency), and RG 94 (War Department), the last difficult to use. All are in the National Archives in Washington, D.C. Ample materials of every sort exist for a much-needed history of military retirement. Parallel research in a good set of municipal records, coupled with published reports of city police and fire departments, would tell us much about the relationship of retirement to the Progressive process known as urban reform.

The Civil Service Commission Library, also in Washington, D.C., holds a variety of items relevant to the history of retirement. These include the early reports of the United States Civil Service Retirement Association; the National Civil Service League Papers; and a well-organized collection of newspaper clippings which contains several useful files on retirement.

My views of public-school teacher retirement were shaped by the Chicago experience, which can be traced through the extensive collection of the Chicago

Teachers' Federation at the Chicago Historical Society. It includes some verbatim transcripts of school board and CTF meetings. The Andrew Carnegie Papers at the Library of Congress and the Henry S. Pritchett Papers at Columbia University shed light on the origins of the Carnegie Foundation for the Advancement of Teaching and its interest in a retirement system for college professors.

A corporate perspective on age discrimination and retirement can be gleaned from several Du Pont-related collections at the Eleutherian Mills Historical Library near Wilmington, Delaware. Although these manuscripts are not arranged to facilitate research on aging or retirement, the documents they yielded were sufficiently thorough and frank, especially from the viewpoint of corporate policy, to reward the process of retrieval. The records of the National Recovery Administration (RG 9) offer another perspective on business, for they contain hundreds, perhaps thousands, of letters from older workers injured in some way by corporate implementation of the National Industrial Recovery Act. I have only scratched the surface of this material. Department of Labor records (RG 174) for the period since 1933 also contain materials of significance for the history of corporate policy toward the aged, and an index in the office of the department's historian makes them easily accessible.

Printed sources, particularly House and Senate hearings, were sufficient to support my revisionist interpretation of the Social Security Act of 1935. What might have remained a tentative thesis, however, was more than confirmed in the Barbara Armstrong and Marion B. Folsom Memoirs in Columbia University's Oral History Collection. The Armstrong Memoir is an exceptionally strong and convincing document. RG 47 (Committee on Economic Security), the Frances Perkins Papers at Columbia, and the Franklin Delano Roosevelt Papers at Hyde Park, New York, were all disappointing. Each collection yielded important documents, but none offered a reasonably complete body of materials on any subject relating to aging. An account of the House-Senate conference committee on the Social Security Act exists in the files of the Senate Finance Committee, but it was not made available to me.

Much of the book was written from printed sources. Municipal, state, and federal reports on retirement, pensions, old-age homes, age discrimination in employment, and other subjects contain bewildering quantities of information. Reports and hearings of House and Senate committees were essential in constructing the history of age discrimination, of retirement in education and the civil service, of social security, and especially in understanding the politics of retirement in the 1970s. Business trade journals contain considerable information on corporate policy toward older workers and can be approached through the standard periodical indexes. *Personnel Journal* and *Personnel* are particularly valuable for the late 1930s and 1940s. *Sales Management* and two different journals with the title *Salesmanship*, both published in the Progressive period, reveal how the ideology of efficiency could permeate a trade.

I was impressed with the potential research value of some trade-union periodicals, among them the *Machinists' Monthly Journal*, the *Typographical Journal*, and the *Railroad Trainmen's Journal*. They contain letters from union members, reports from locals, poems and recipes, committee reports, and proceedings of the conventions. Students of the social history of aging would be well served by a careful reading of these and similar publications.

The first important journal for retired persons was the *Annuitant*, published for federal retirees in 1922 and superseded by *Retirement Life* in 1957. Many of the early numbers are difficult to find. At least seven retirement journals began publication in the decade after 1955: *Modern Maturity*, *Senior Citizen*, *Retirement Planning News*, *Harvest Years*, *Lifetime Living*, and the *Bulletin of the American Association of Retired Persons*. They cover hobbies, health, travel, part-time employment, diet, clubs, politics, and other aspects of retirement in its golden age.

Scholars interested in writing about how older people lived and what they thought will find significant data in several collections. Many older persons wrote to Robert Wagner about pension issues in the mid-1930s. Their letters, part of the Wagner Papers at Georgetown University Library in Washington, reveal a good deal about how ordinary people felt about retirement, discrimination in employment, and social security. Several presidential collections housed at the Library of Congress—the Woodrow Wilson Papers, the Warren Harding Papers, and especially the Calvin Coolidge Papers—contain similar correspondence bearing on the condition of the middle-aged and old-aged in the decade following World War I. Letters in the records of the National Recovery Administration describe workplace conditions, relations between young and old, and the powerlessness of older workers in a bureaucratic setting. Labor Department files for the 1950s hold angry letters from older people who refused to tolerate the quiescent attitude of the Eisenhower administration. Most important as a historical source are the Eleanor Roosevelt Papers at Hyde Park. Here, in files relating to the Townsend movement, are thousands of letters from older people, many of whom took time to explain attitudes toward juvenile delinquency and crime, to describe the difficulties a son had in finding employment or the family in paying the rent. To my knowledge these letters remain unexplored.

Index

Academic freedom, 113–19 passim
Accidents, 146; among older workers, 40; in Progressive Era, 35; on railroads, 154; reduced by pension, 128; retirement and prevention of, 161
Accounting: age discrimination in, 50
Achenbaum, Andrew, 11
Activity theory, 227. *See also* Disengagement
Actuarial practices, 133, 243
Adaptability: of older persons, discussed by Osler, 7; of older workers, 21, 33, 46; of younger workers, 33
Adolescence. *See* Youth
Anti-age-limit league, 8
Advisory Group of Industrial Economists, 208
AFL. *See* American Federation of Labor
AFL-CIO. *See* American Federation of Labor–Congress of Industrial Organizations
Age: at pensioning, 135; conflicts within work force, based on, 168–69; determines position on pension, 106–07; of federal employees, 58; mix in railroad unions, 166–67; of population, affects consumption, 190; of railroad workers, 154; of Supreme Court justices, 160; sixty-five, selected for social security, 249
Aged: advocate retirement, 266, 267, 268; compared to women, 11; ideas of, related to age discrimination, 20*n*; limitations of, 12–13; physical problems of, 238; responsibilities of, 241; role of, 19th century, 11, 12; value social order, 268. *See also* Middle aged; Older workers
Age discrimination: caused by prejudice, 237–38; competition intensifies, 8; defined, 18, 18*n*; in federal service, 204–07; federal legislation on, encourages mandatory retirement, 237–38; and ideology of retirement, 215; impact of, on consumption, 190; liberals analyze cause of, 246–48; on railroads, 142; and the salesman, 44–49; and scientific management, 8; and shorter working day, 8; state legislation against,

210; state legislation on, 237; and teachers' pensions, 95; and unemployment, 16
Age Discrimination in Employment Act, *1967*, 246
Age limits: in hiring, 52; in civil service, 213
Aging: of work force, during World War II, 124. *See also* Population, aging of
Agism. *See* Age discrimination
Airline industry, 259
Alcorn, Robert, 76, 78, 86; favors retirement based on service, 85; organizes retirement movement in Naval Gun Factory, 67
Alexander, Charles, 221
Almshouse, 90; an alternative to retirement, 59; contrasted with responsibilities of aged, 235–36; feared, 84, 143–44
Altgeld, John Peter, 93
Amalgamated Clothing Workers of America, 218
American Association for Labor Legislation, 79; advocates public pensions, 50
American Association for Old Age Security, 50
American Association of Retired Persons (AARP), 249; advocates retirement, 234–35, 267
American Association of State Universities, 111
American Association of University Professors (AAUP), 116–17
American Chemical Society, 124
American Dictionary (Noah Webster), 11
American Express Company, 133
American Federation of Government Employees, 204
American Federation of Labor, 169, 173–74; and railroad labor, 155; and *1922* strike, 167; and teachers, 102; and Workers' bill, 192; bargains for pensions, 219; opposes age discrimination in civil service, 204; opposes private benefit programs, 51; organizes government employees, 76; Railway Employees Department opposes RENPA, 178